D0284006

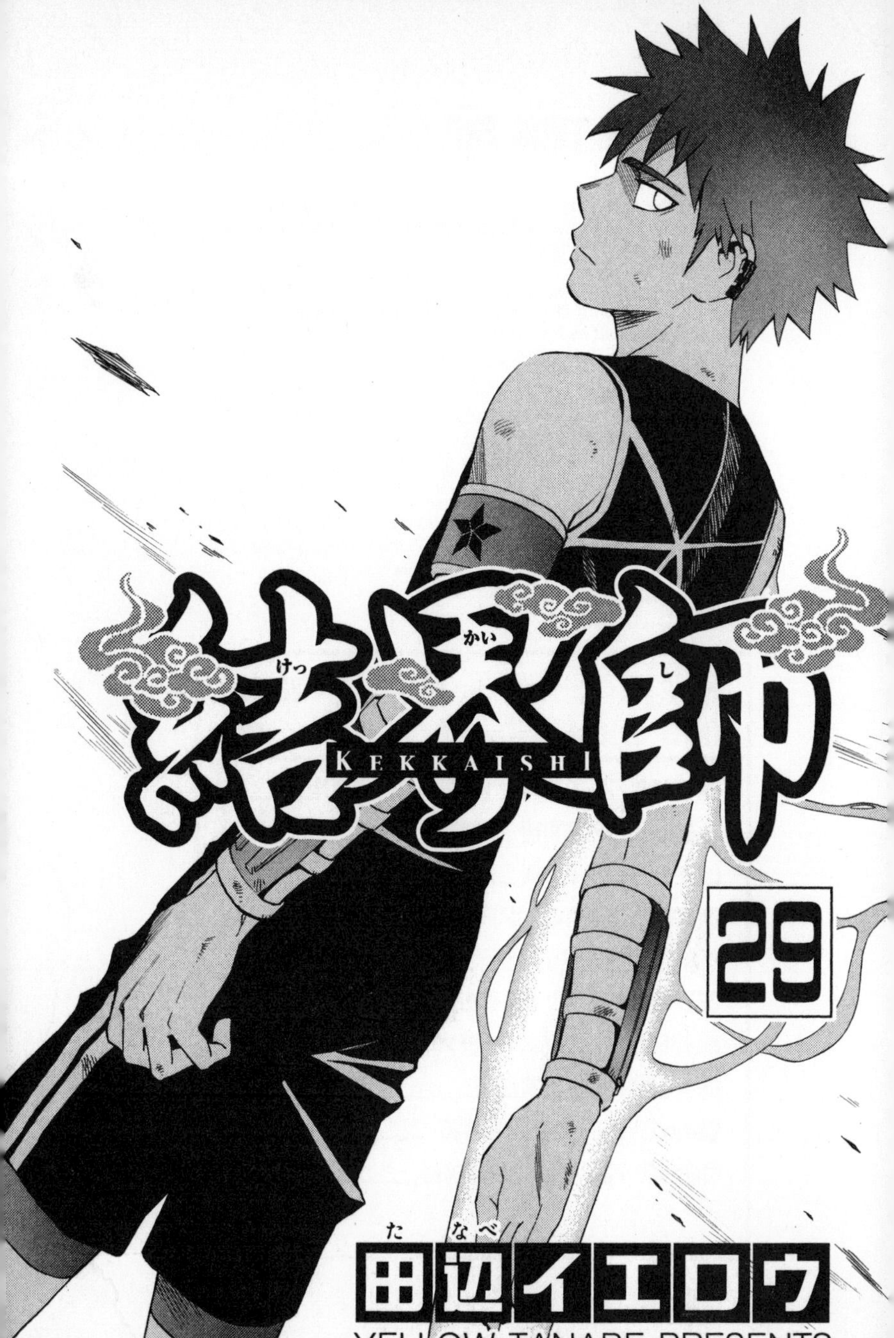

結界師
KEKKAISHI

29

田辺イエロウ

YELLOW TANABE PRESENTS

THE STORY THUS FAR

Yoshimori Sumimura and Tokine Yukimura have an ancestral duty to protect the Karasumori Forest from supernatural beings called ayakashi. People with their gift for terminating *ayakashi* are called *kekkaishi*, or "barrier masters."

Masamori is asking Yumeji, executive member of the Shadow Organization's Council of Twelve, some pointed questions when Zero, a hit man sent by the organization's Supreme Leader, arrives... Masamori unsuccessfully attempts to ward off Zero's attack, and Yumeji is killed.

Back at the Karasumori Site, Yoshimori finally masters the technique of emptying his mind. Using his new powers, he summarily defeats Michiru and Kakeru, the two witches who have been holding Karasumori in their thrall.

But then the heir to the Ogi Clan, Shichiro Ogi (a.k.a. Grim Reaper) shows up at the scene and proceeds to kill the witches and seriously wound Yoshimori's new friend and ally, Soji...!

KEKKAISHI VOL. 29
TABLE OF CONTENTS

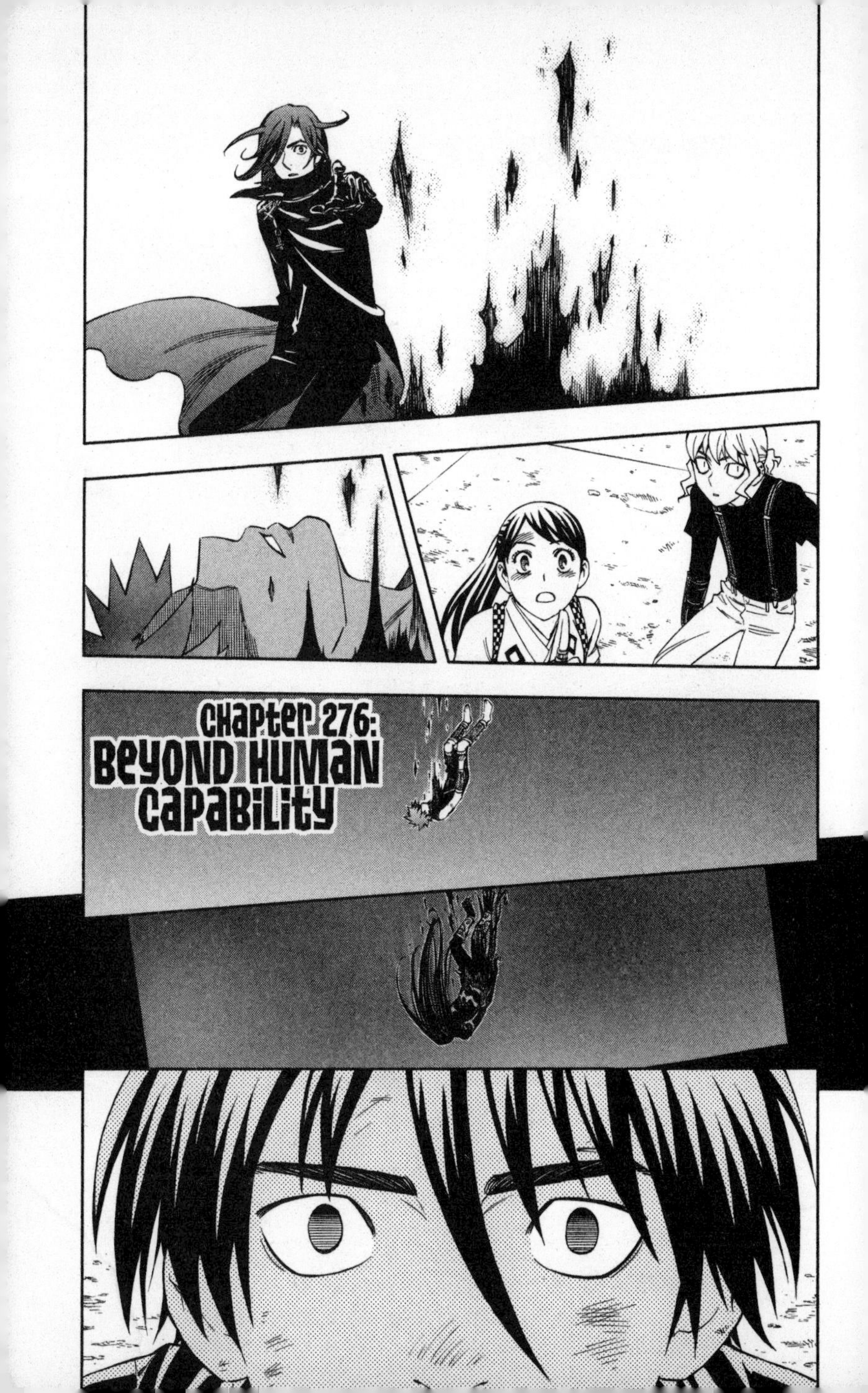
Chapter 276:
Beyond Human Capability

CHAPTER 276:
BEYOND HUMAN CAPABILITY

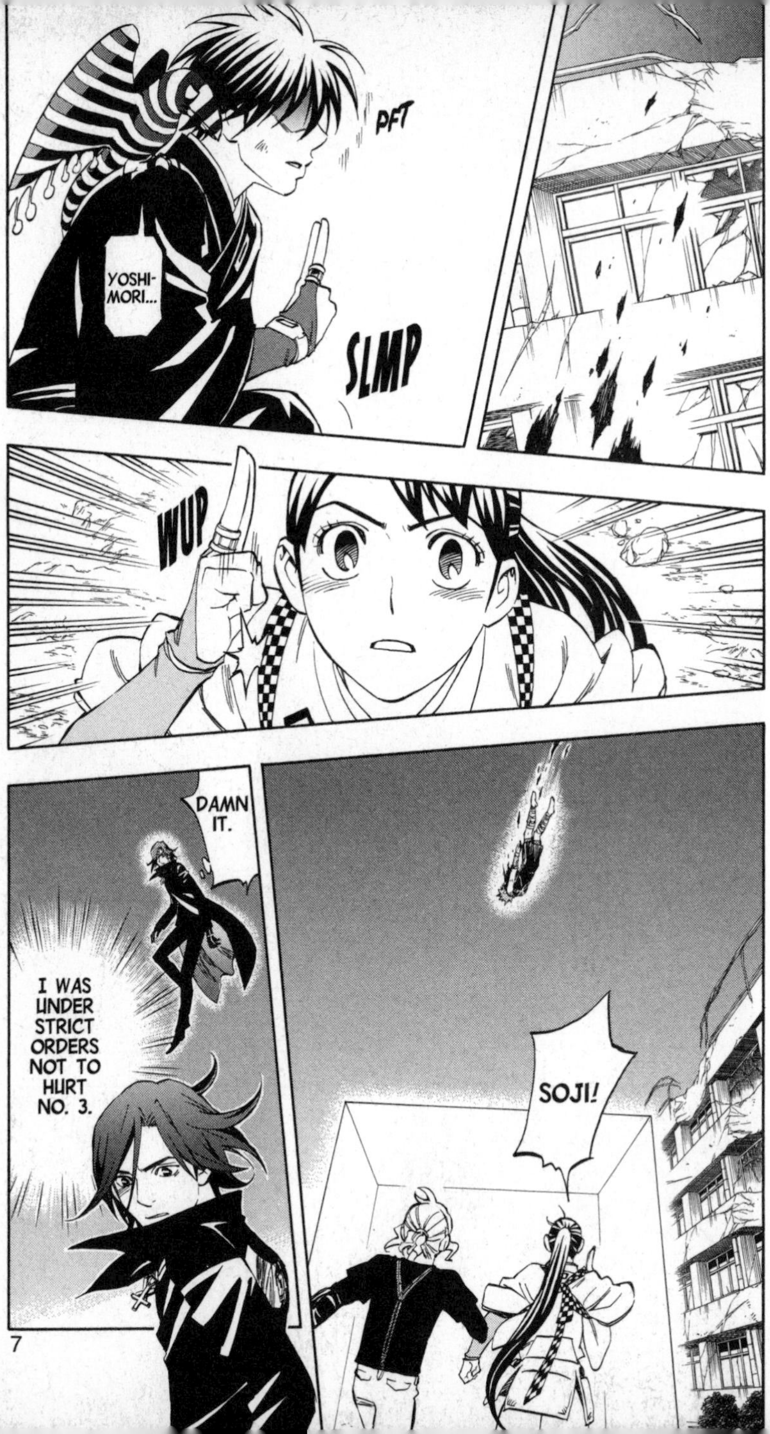
PFT
YOSHI-MORI...
SLMP
WUP
SOJI!
DAMN IT.
I WAS UNDER STRICT ORDERS NOT TO HURT NO. 3.

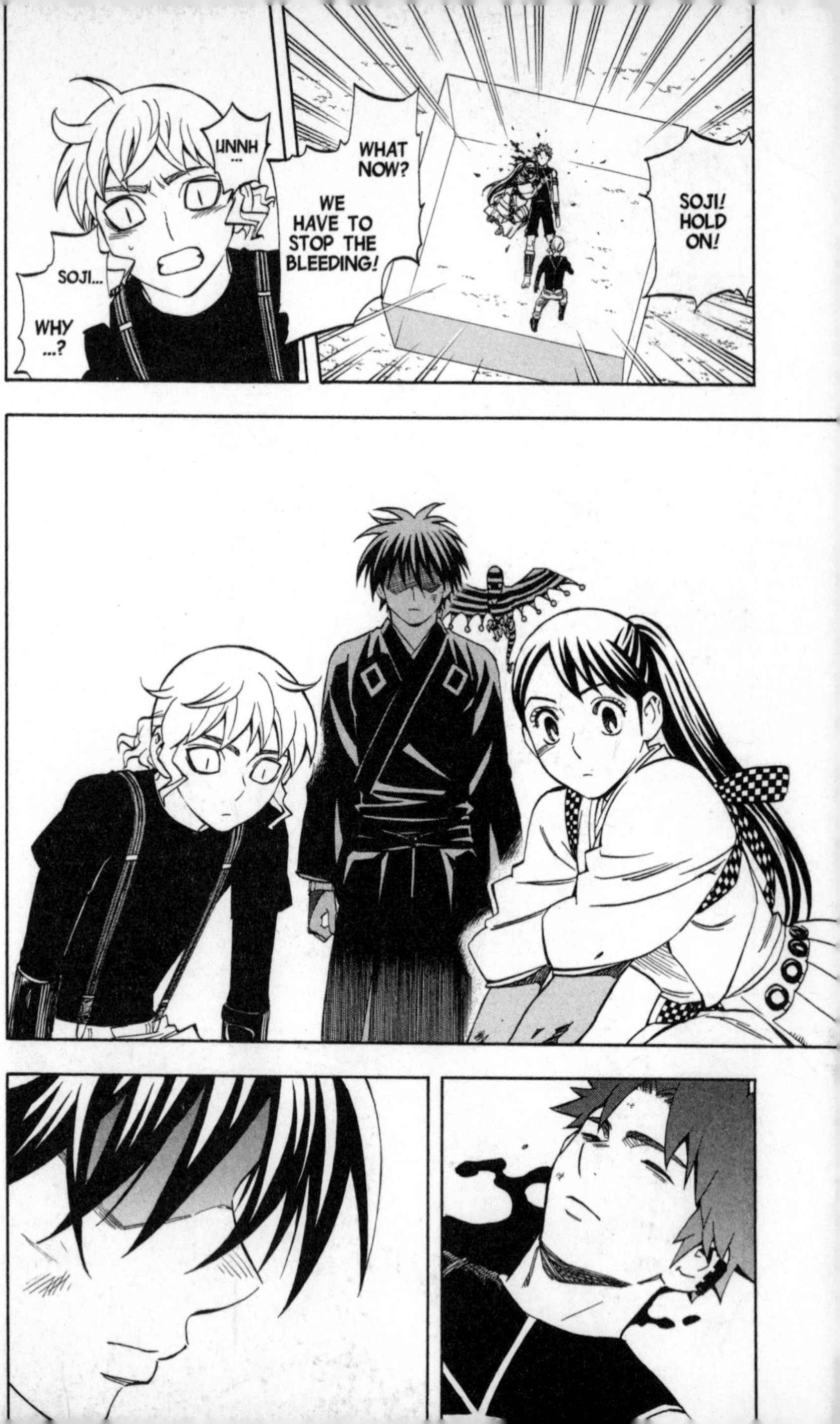
SOJI! HOLD ON!
WHAT NOW?
WE HAVE TO STOP THE BLEEDING!
UNNH ...
SOJI...
WHY ...?

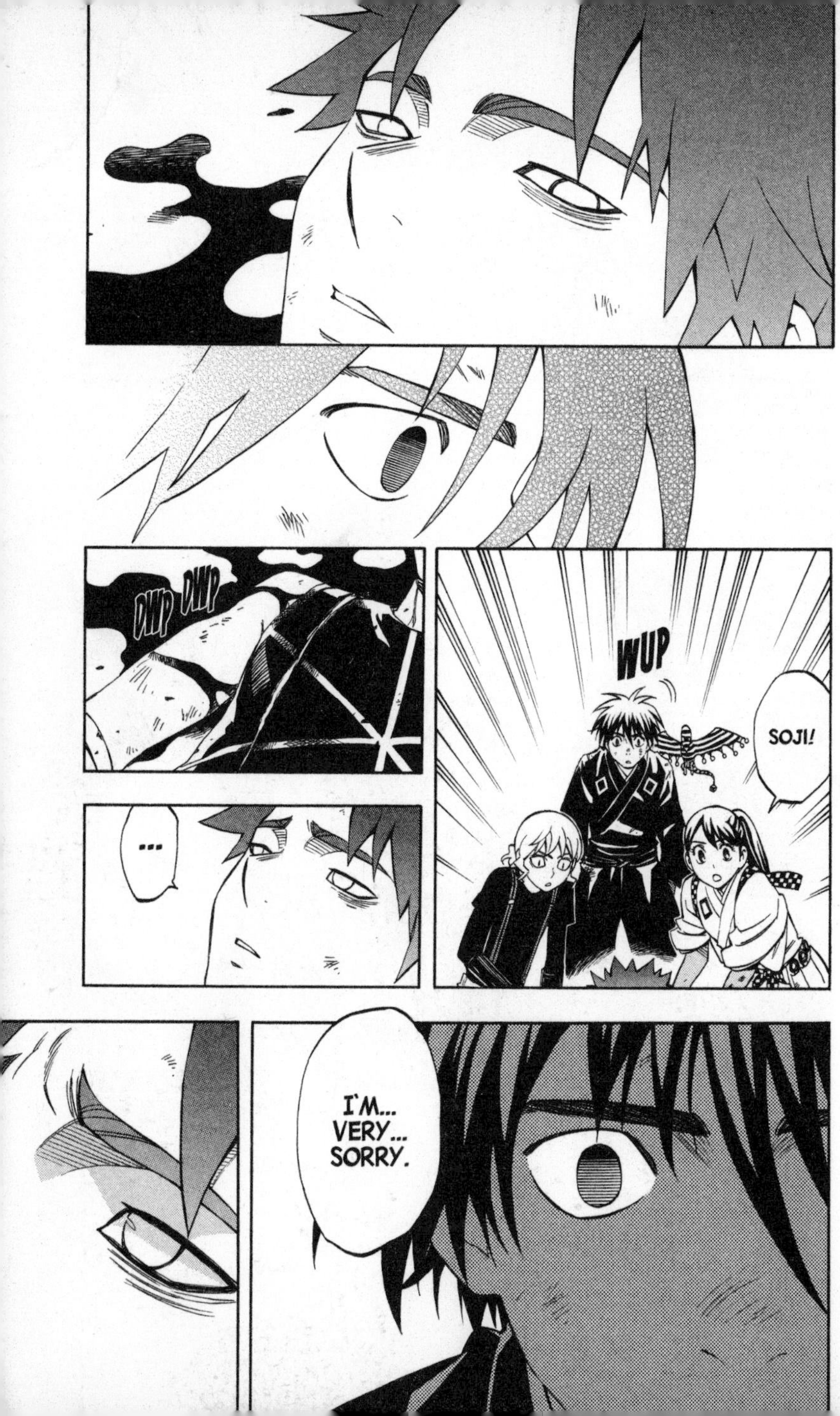
WUP
SOJI!
DWP DWP
...
I'M... VERY... SORRY.

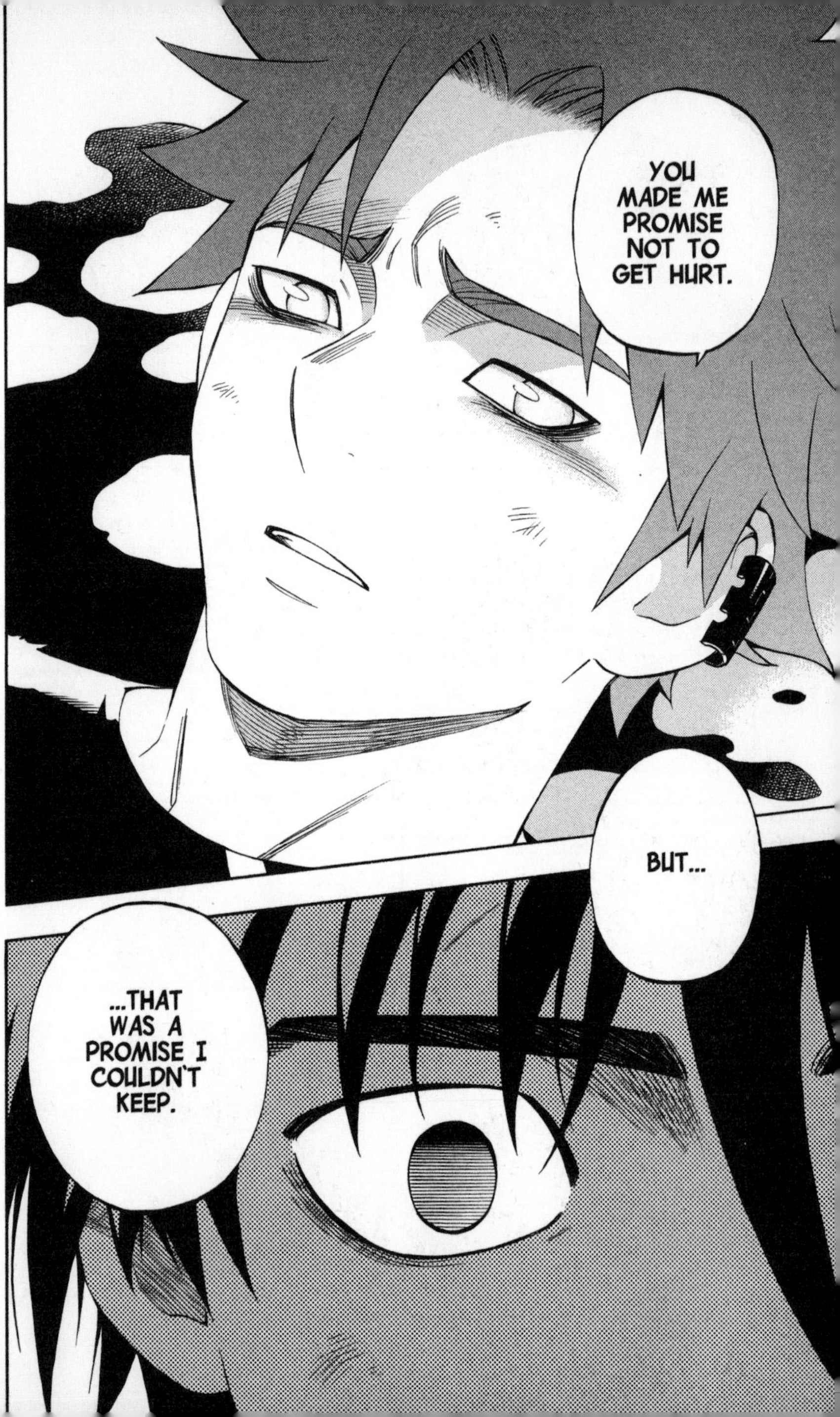
YOU MADE ME PROMISE NOT TO GET HURT.
BUT...
...THAT WAS A PROMISE I COULDN'T KEEP.

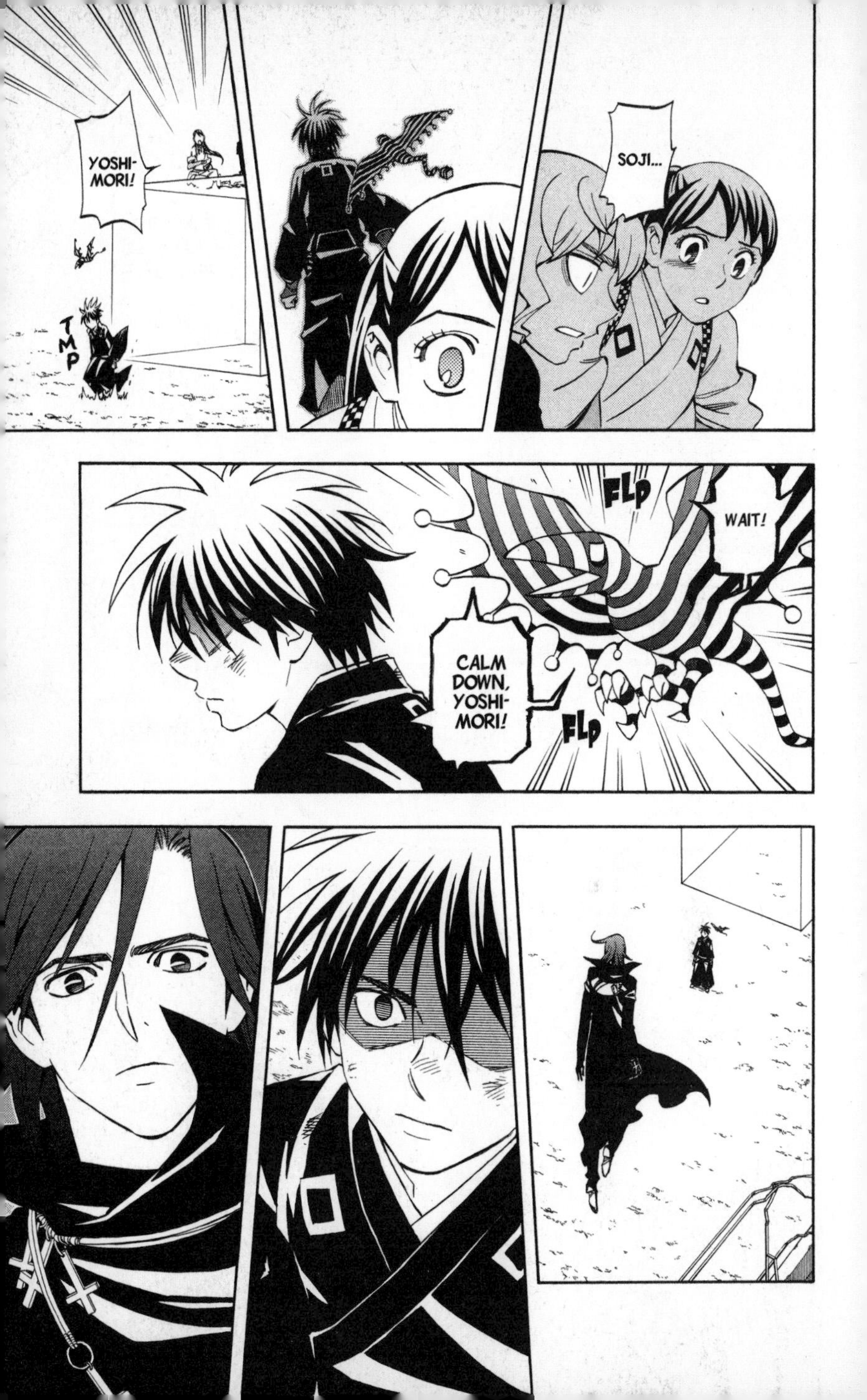
SOJI...
YOSHI-MORI!
TMP
WAIT!
FLP
CALM DOWN, YOSHI-MORI!
FLP

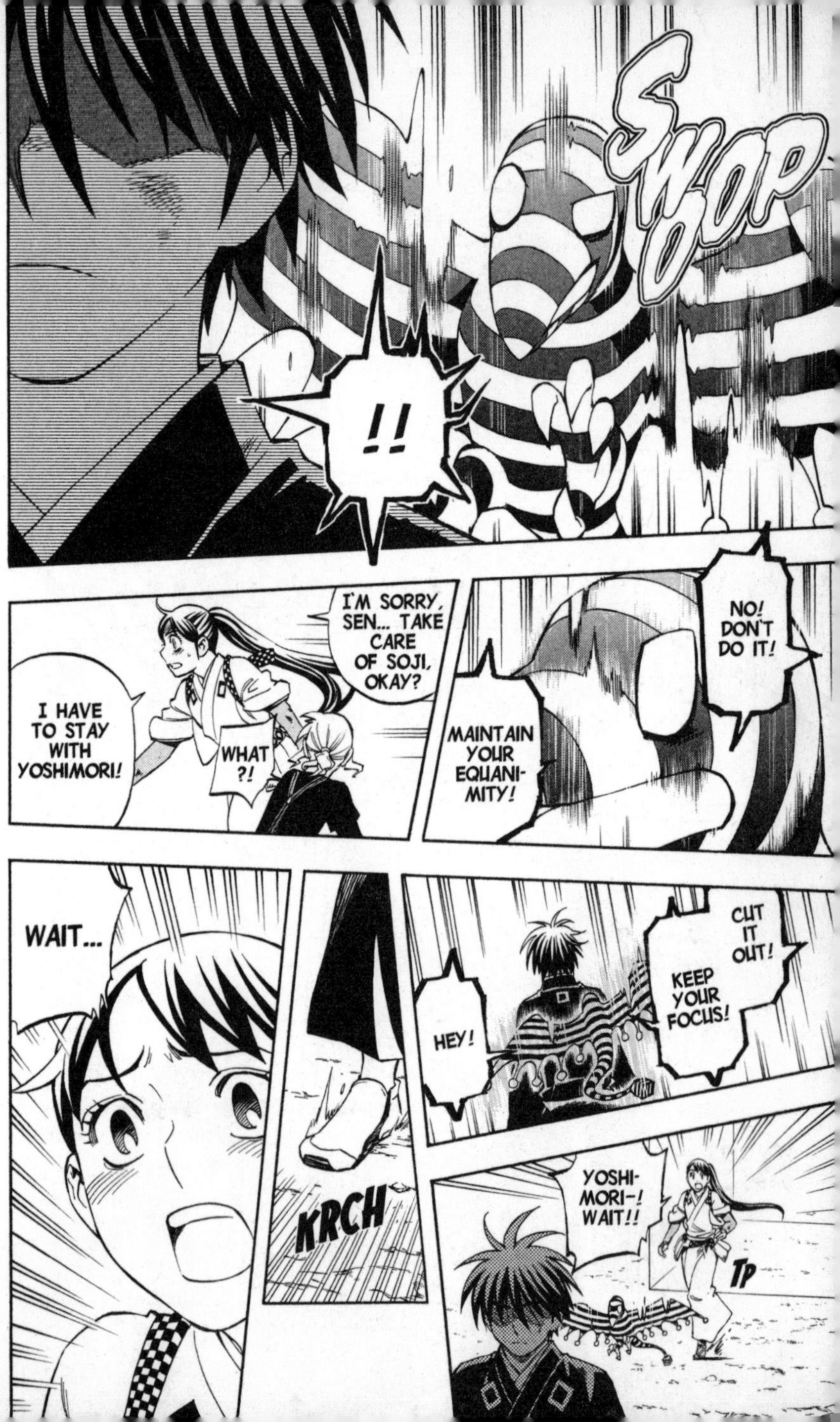
SWOP
!!
NO! DON'T DO IT!
MAINTAIN YOUR EQUANIMITY!
I'M SORRY, SEN... TAKE CARE OF SOJI, OKAY?
WHAT?!
I HAVE TO STAY WITH YOSHIMORI!
CUT IT OUT!
KEEP YOUR FOCUS!
HEY!
YOSHIMORI-! WAIT!!
TP
KRCH
WAIT...

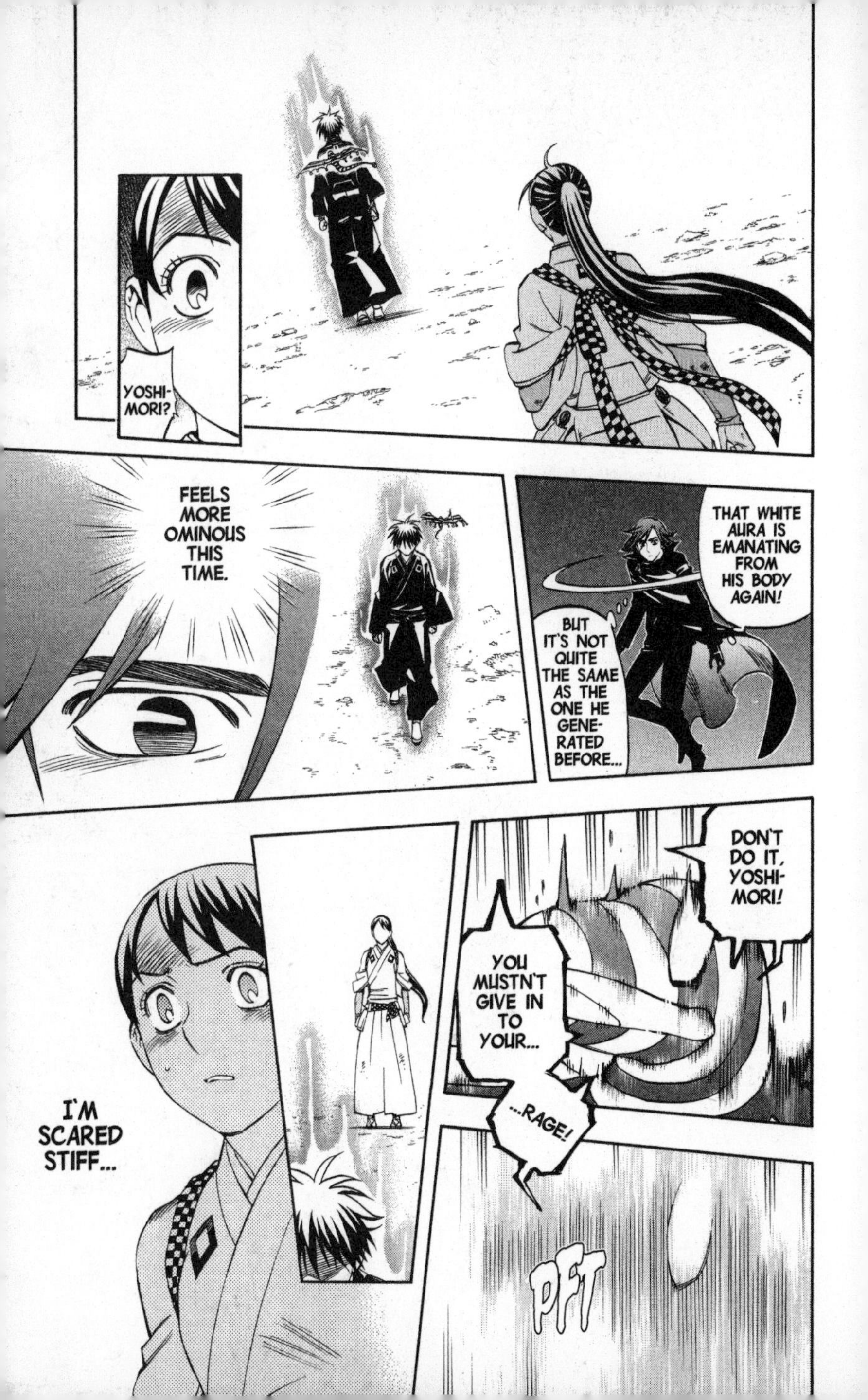
YOSHI-
MORI?
THAT WHITE AURA IS EMANATING FROM HIS BODY AGAIN!
BUT IT'S NOT QUITE THE SAME AS THE ONE HE GENE-
RATED BEFORE...
FEELS MORE OMINOUS THIS TIME.
DON'T DO IT, YOSHI-
MORI!
YOU MUSTN'T GIVE IN TO YOUR...
...RAGE!
PFT
I'M SCARED STIFF...

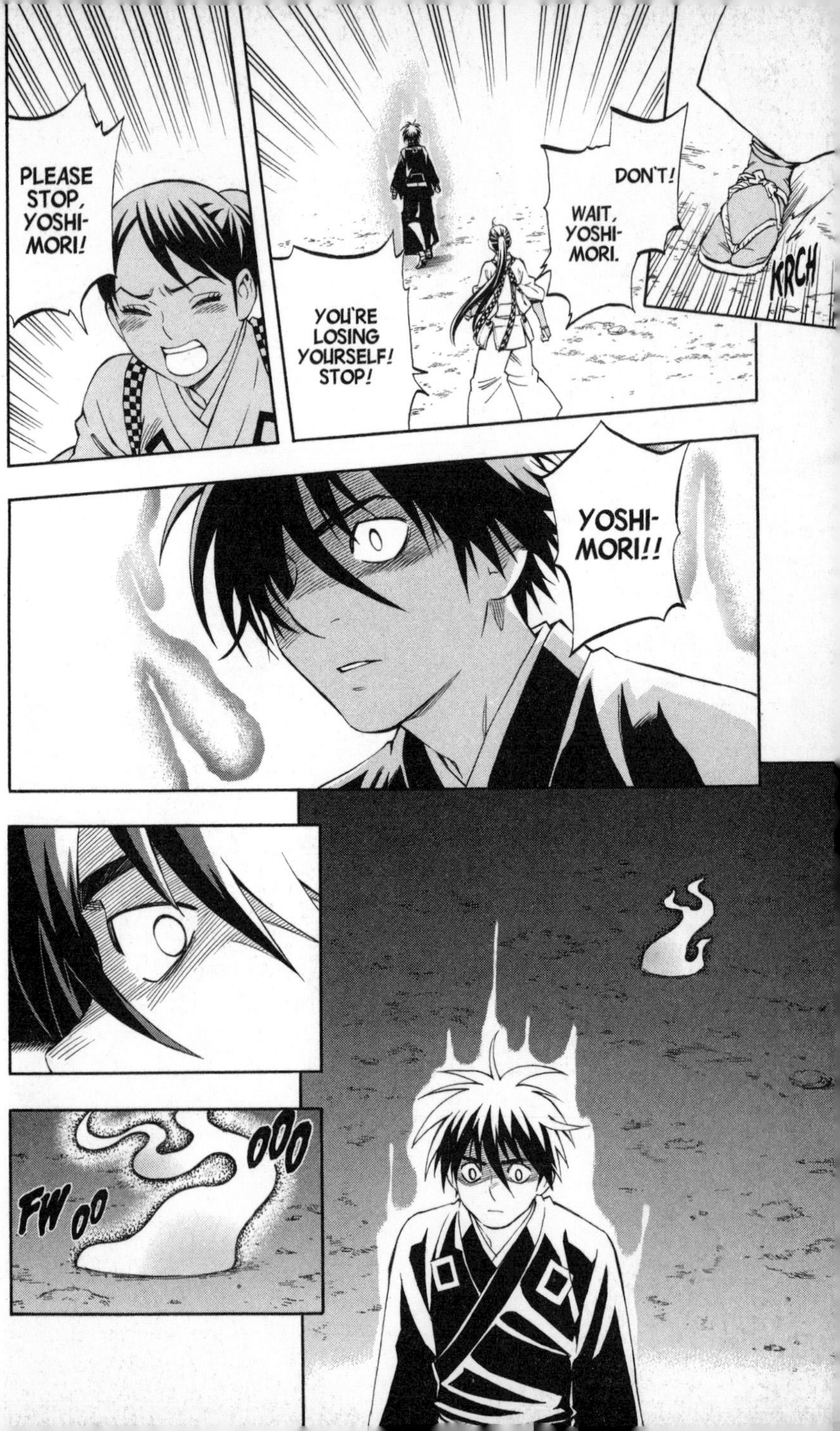
KRCH
DON'T!
WAIT, YOSHI-MORI.
YOU'RE LOSING YOURSELF! STOP!
PLEASE STOP, YOSHI-MORI!
YOSHI-MORI!!
FWOOOOO

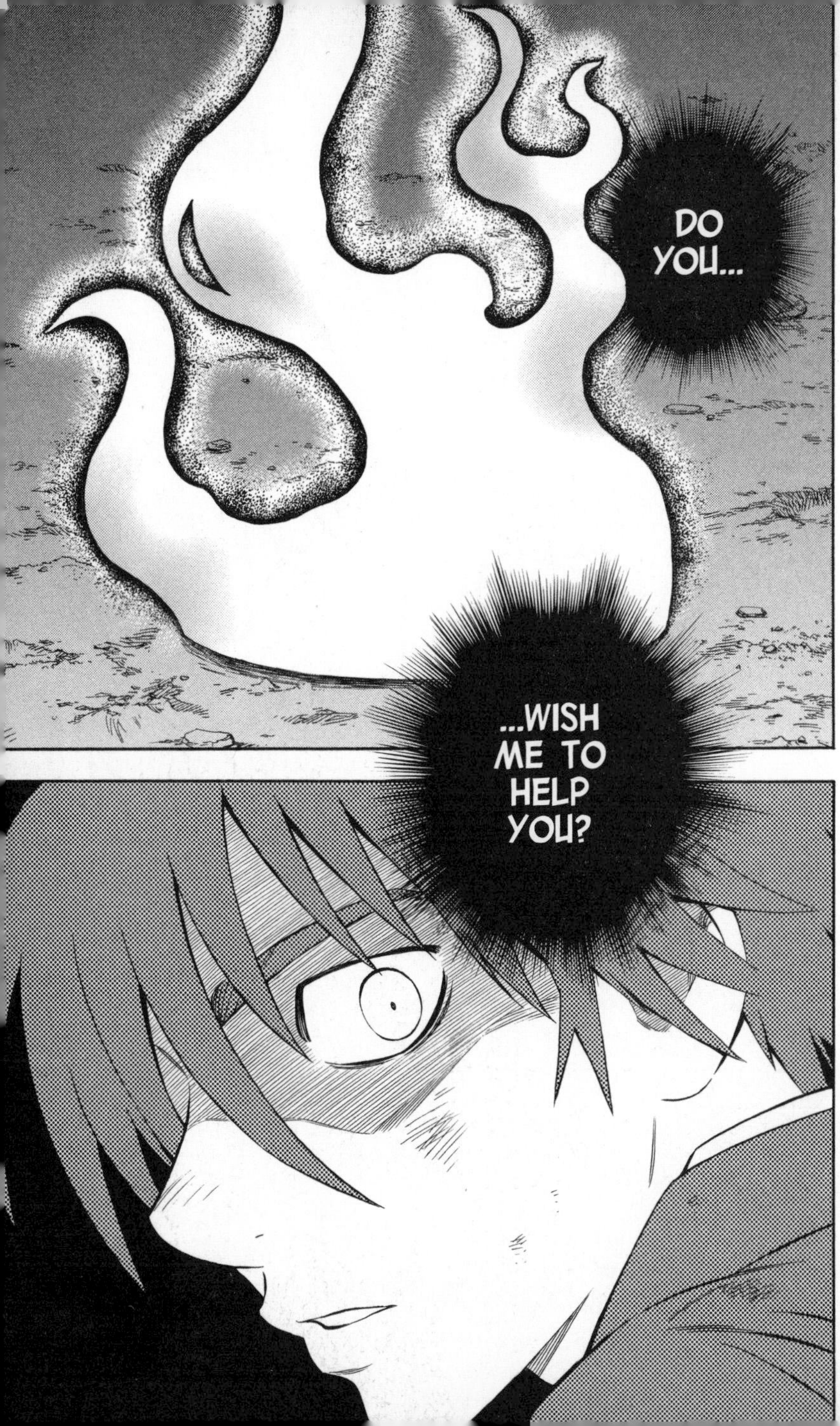
DO YOU...
...WISH ME TO HELP YOU?

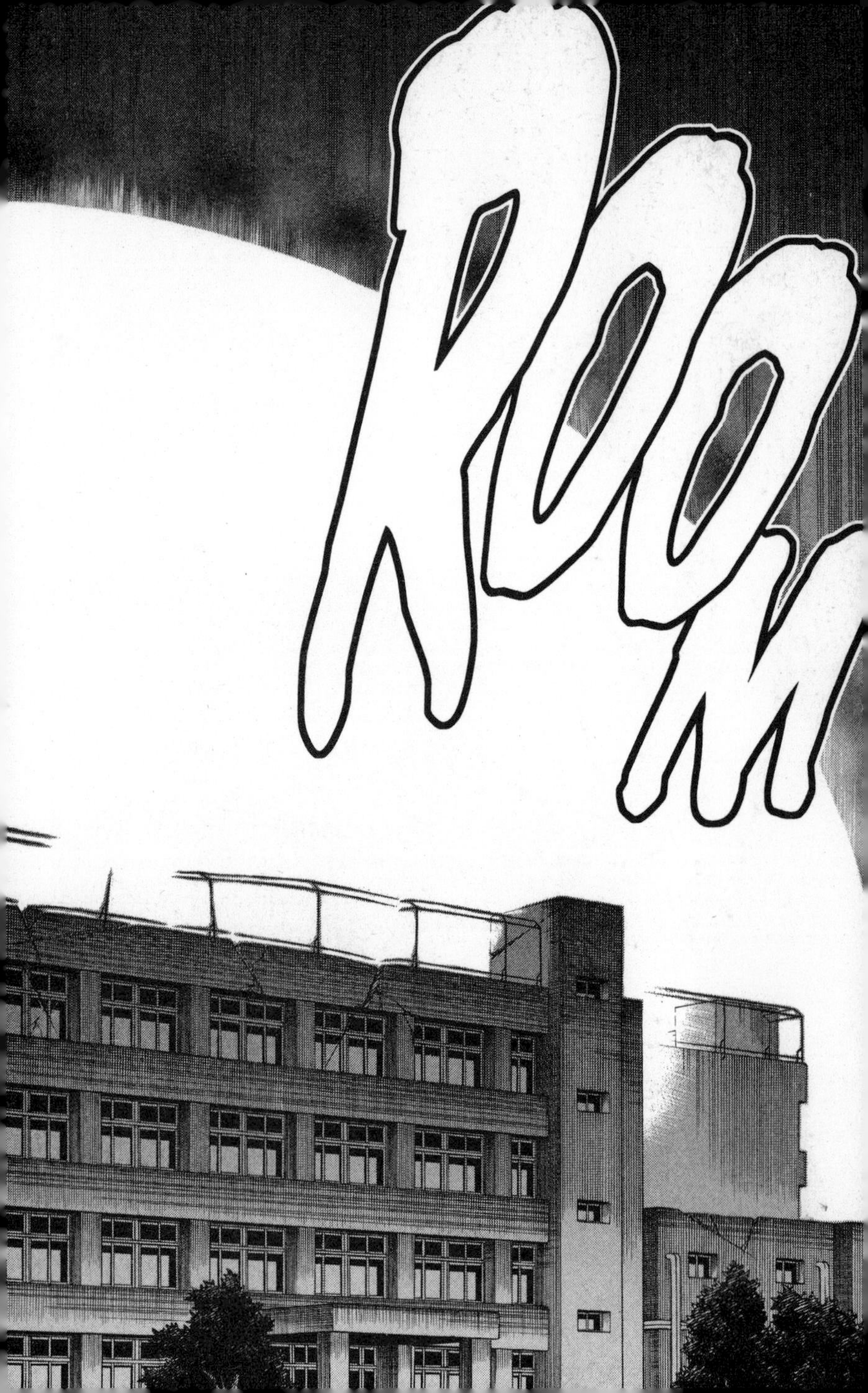

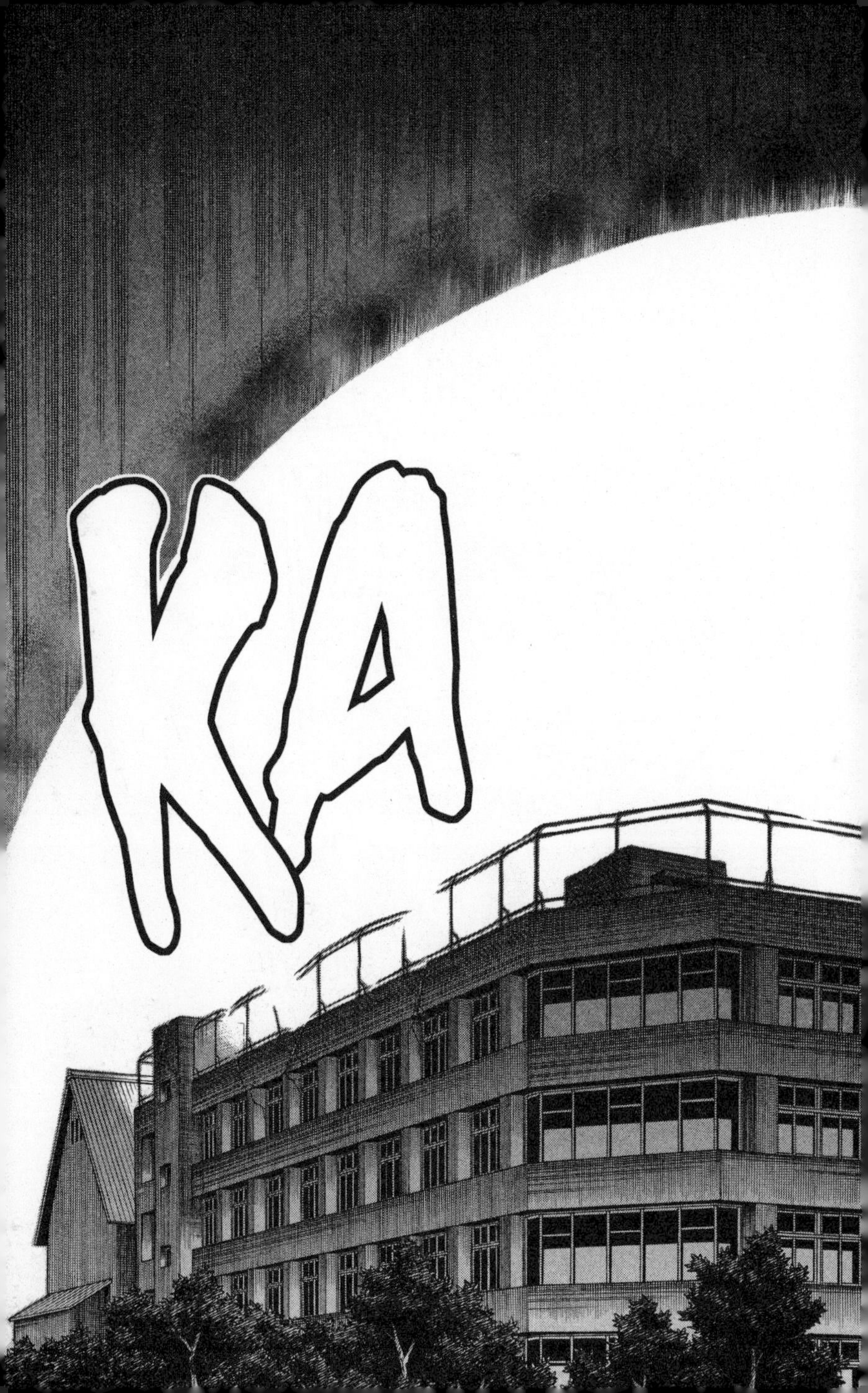
KA

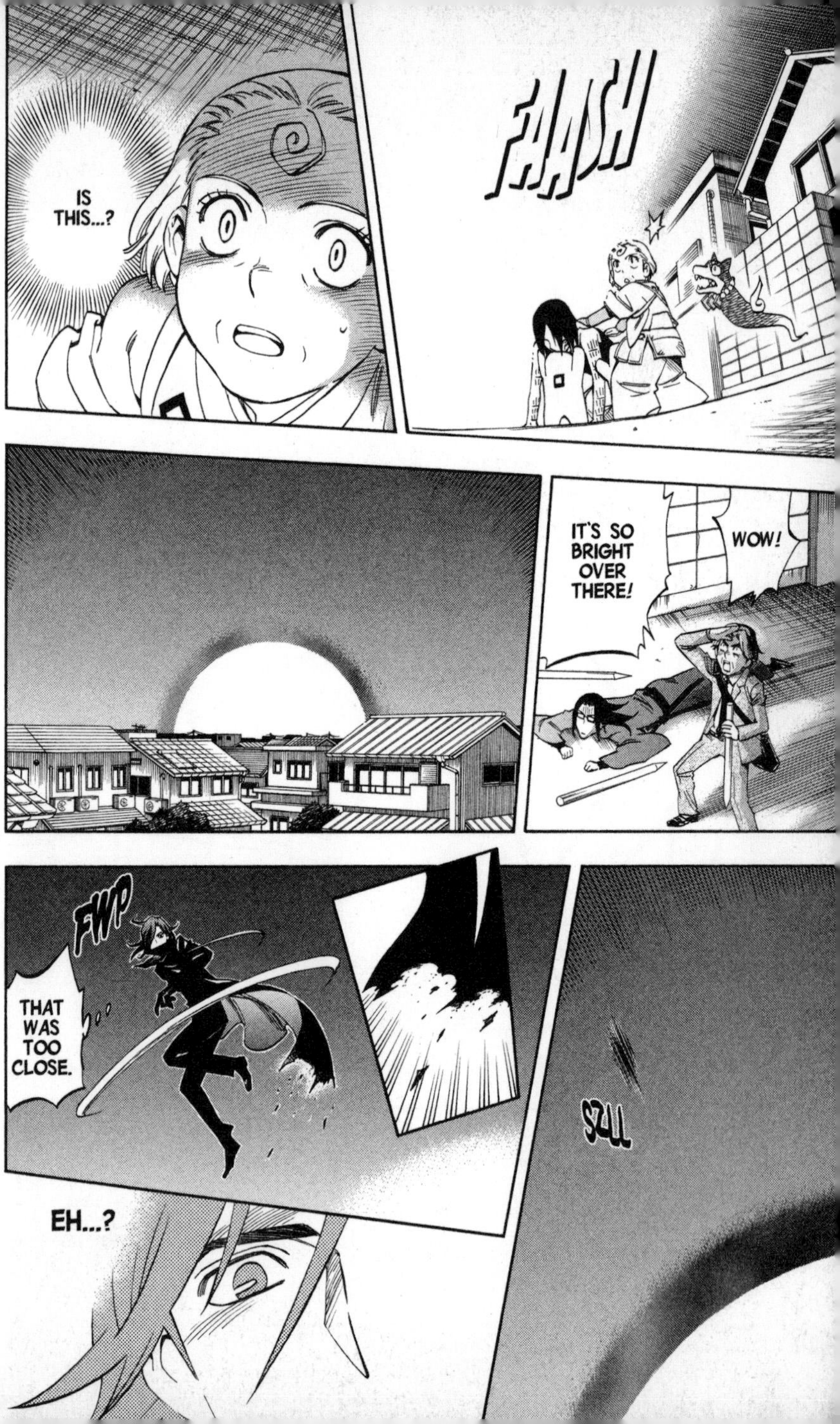
FAASH
IS THIS...?
WOW!
IT'S SO BRIGHT OVER THERE!
FWIP
THAT WAS TOO CLOSE.
EH...?

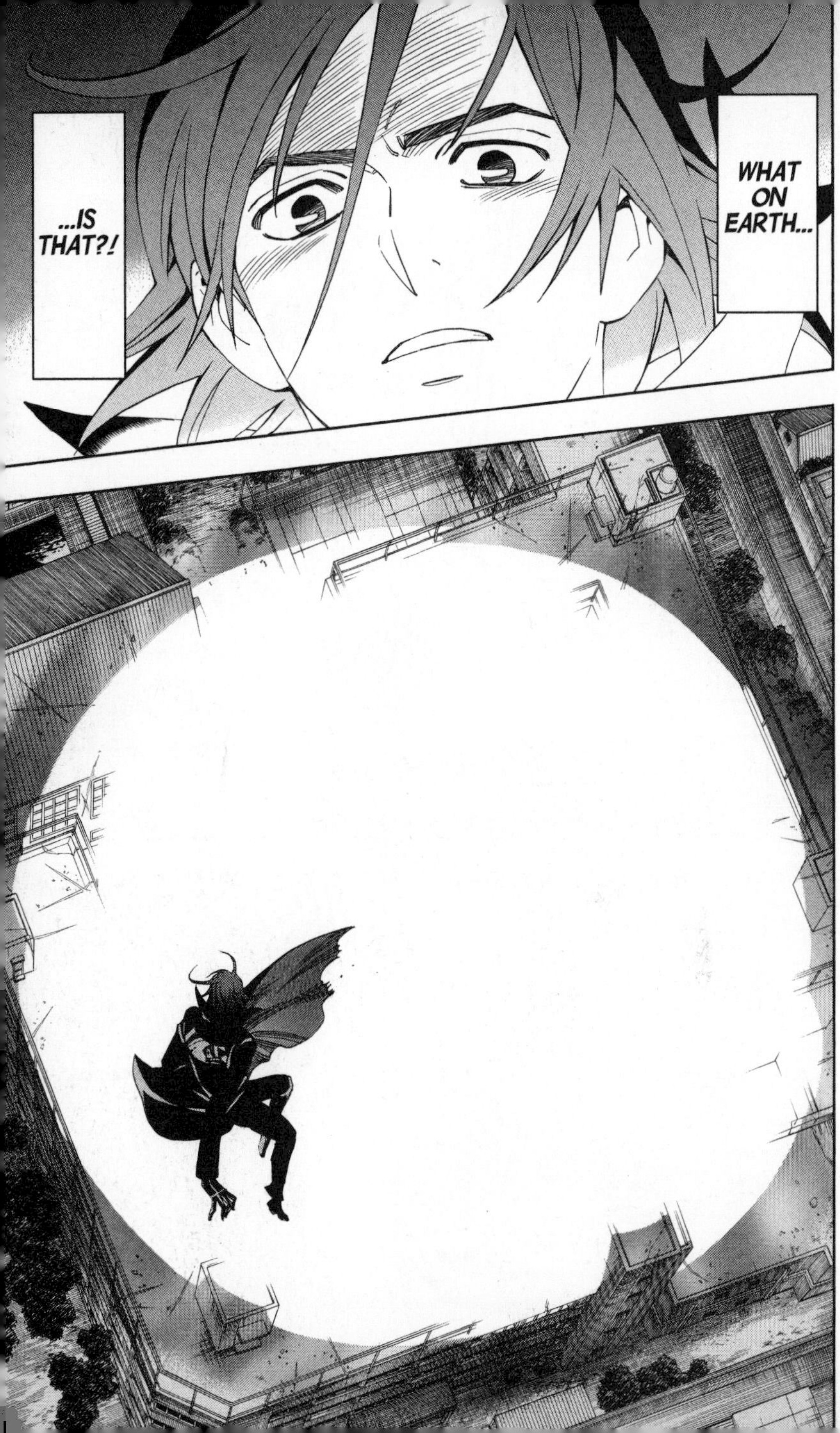
WHAT ON EARTH...
...IS THAT?!

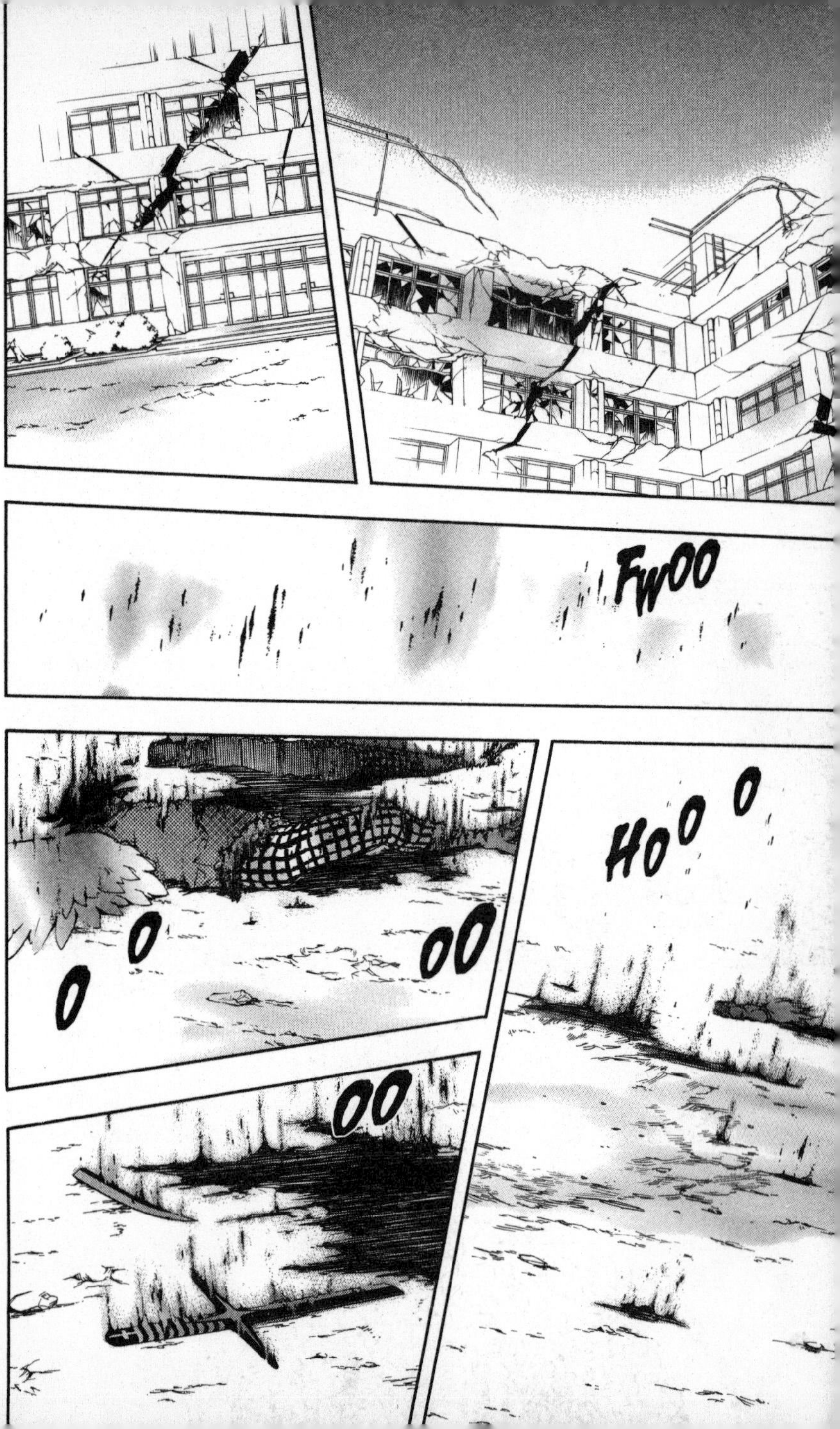
FWOO
HOOO
OO
OO
O O

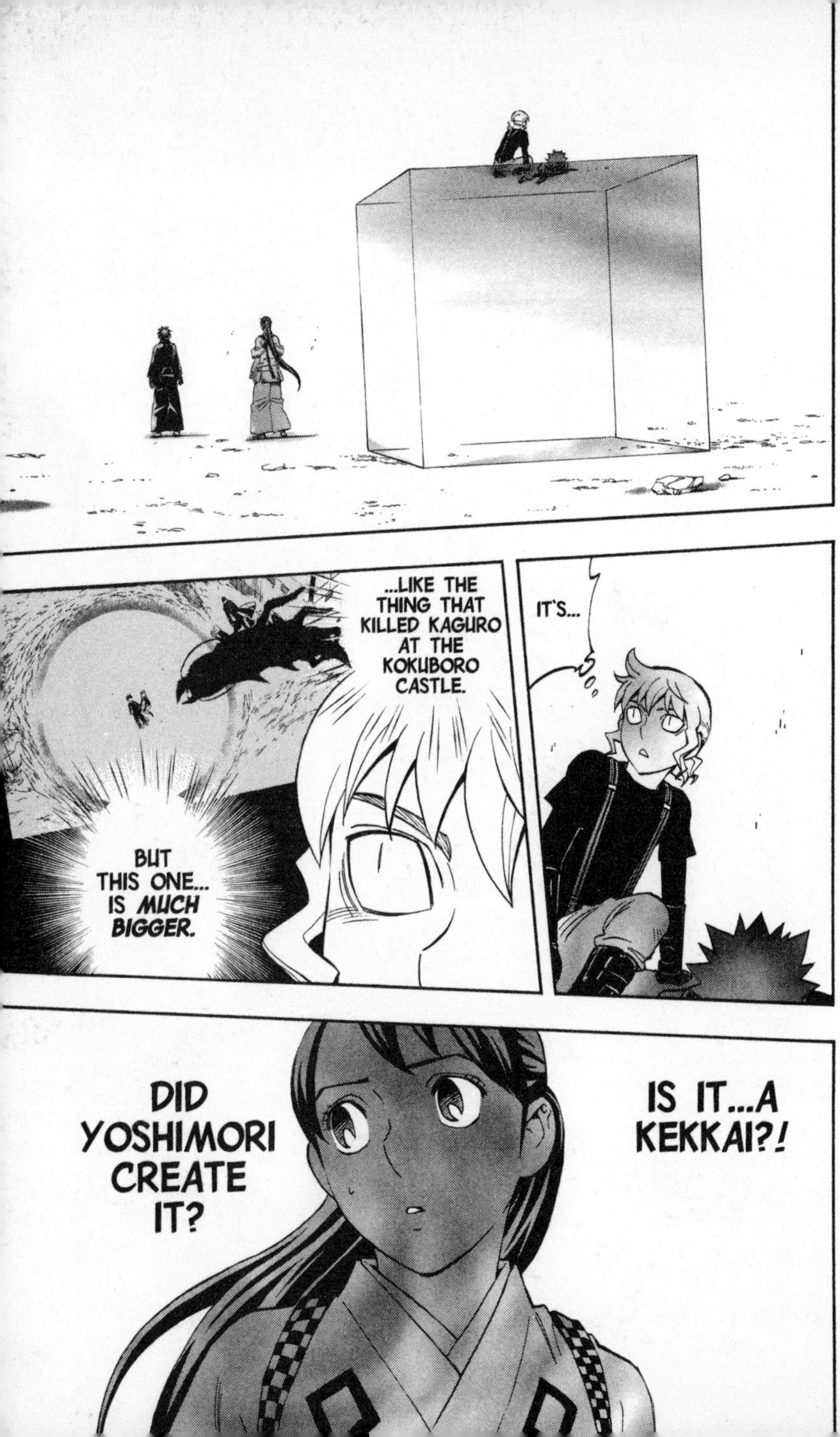
IT'S...
...LIKE THE THING THAT KILLED KAGURO AT THE KOKUBORO CASTLE.
BUT THIS ONE... IS *MUCH* BIGGER.
IS IT...A KEKKAI?!
DID YOSHIMORI CREATE IT?

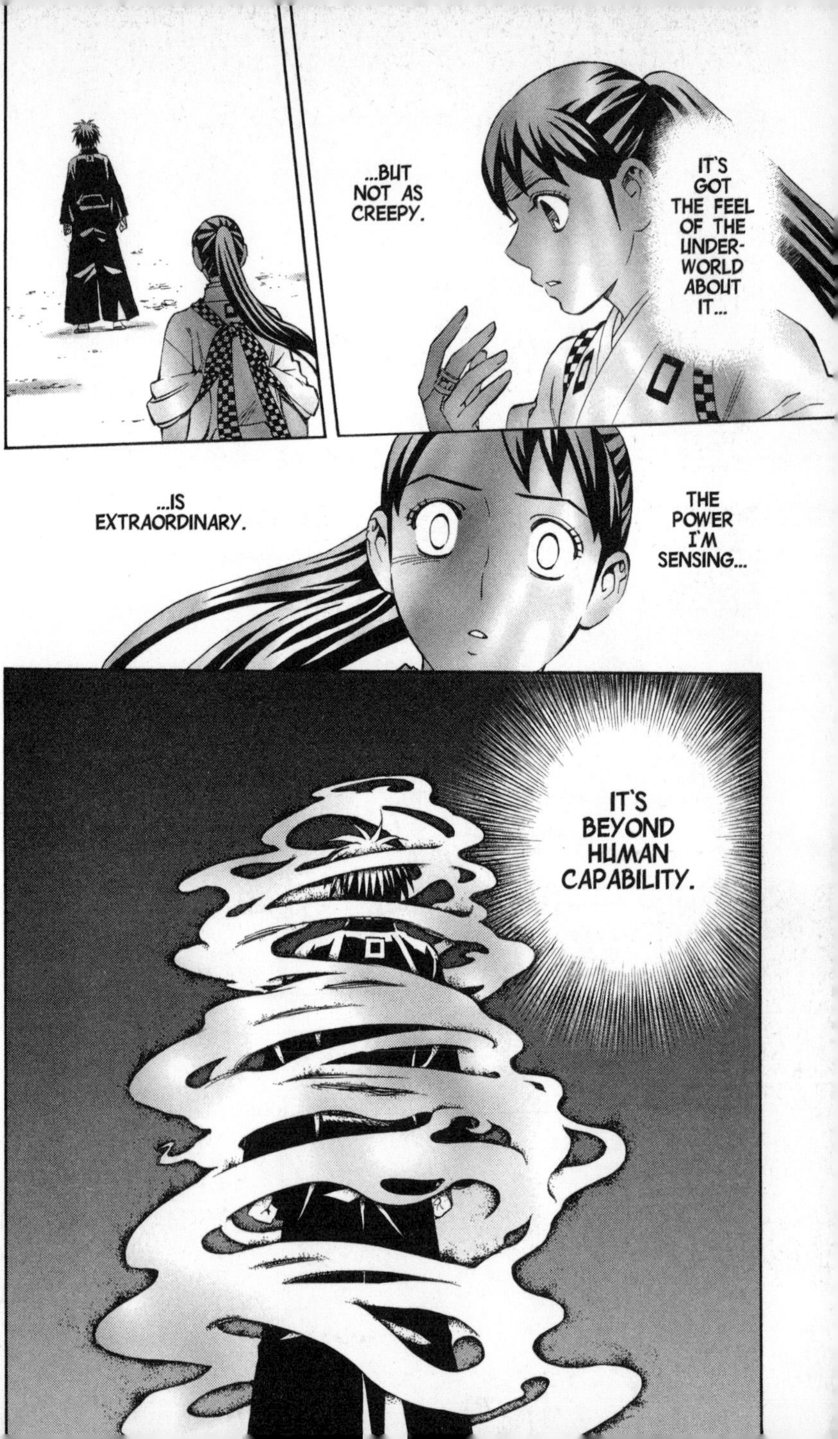
IT'S GOT THE FEEL OF THE UNDER-WORLD ABOUT IT...
...BUT NOT AS CREEPY.
THE POWER I'M SENSING...
...IS EXTRAORDINARY.
IT'S BEYOND HUMAN CAPABILITY.

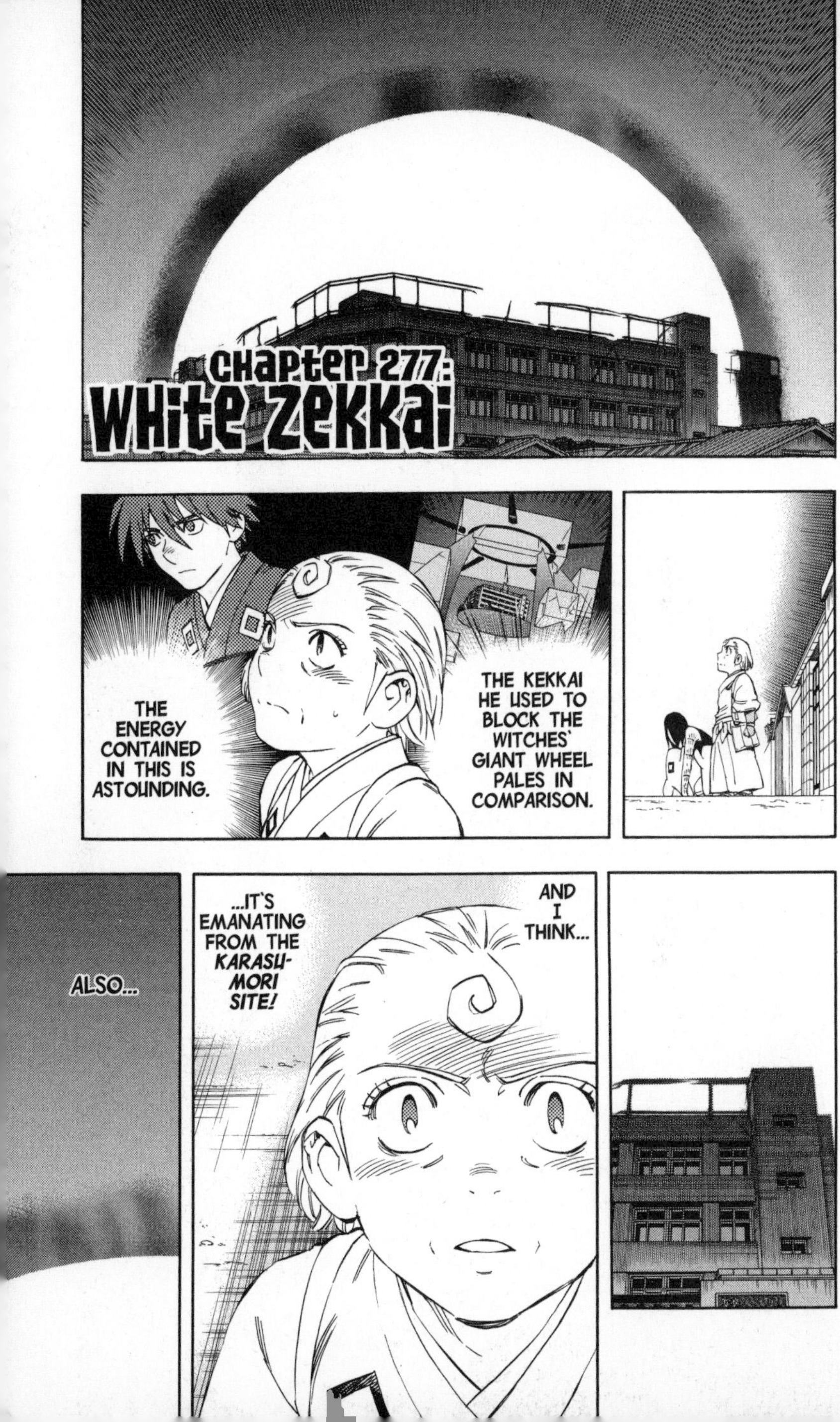
Chapter 277:
White Zekkai
THE KEKKAI HE USED TO BLOCK THE WITCHES' GIANT WHEEL PALES IN COMPARISON.
THE ENERGY CONTAINED IN THIS IS ASTOUNDING.
AND I THINK...
...IT'S EMANATING FROM THE KARASUMORI SITE!
ALSO...

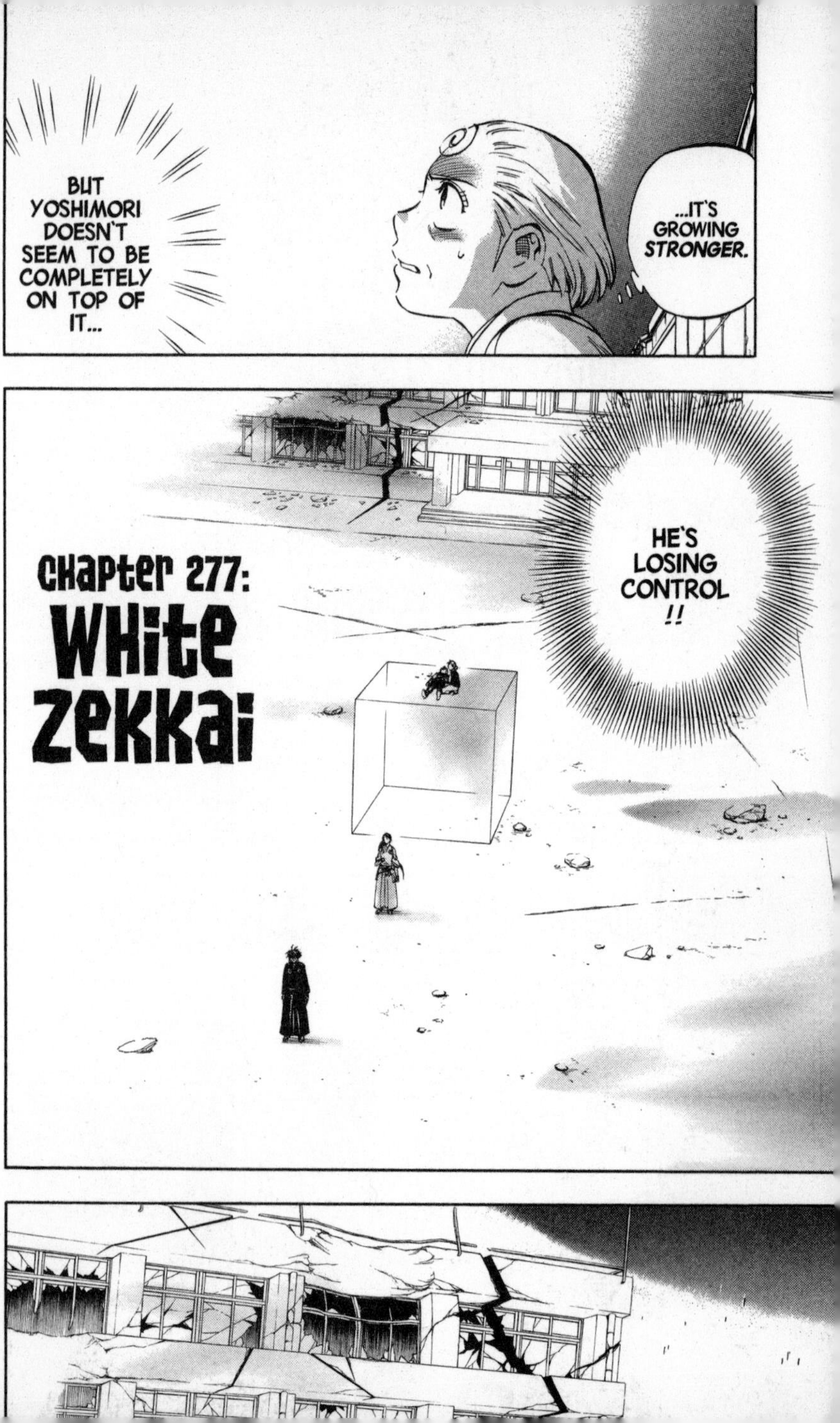
...IT'S GROWING STRONGER.
BUT YOSHIMORI DOESN'T SEEM TO BE COMPLETELY ON TOP OF IT...
HE'S LOSING CONTROL !!
Chapter 277: White Zekkai

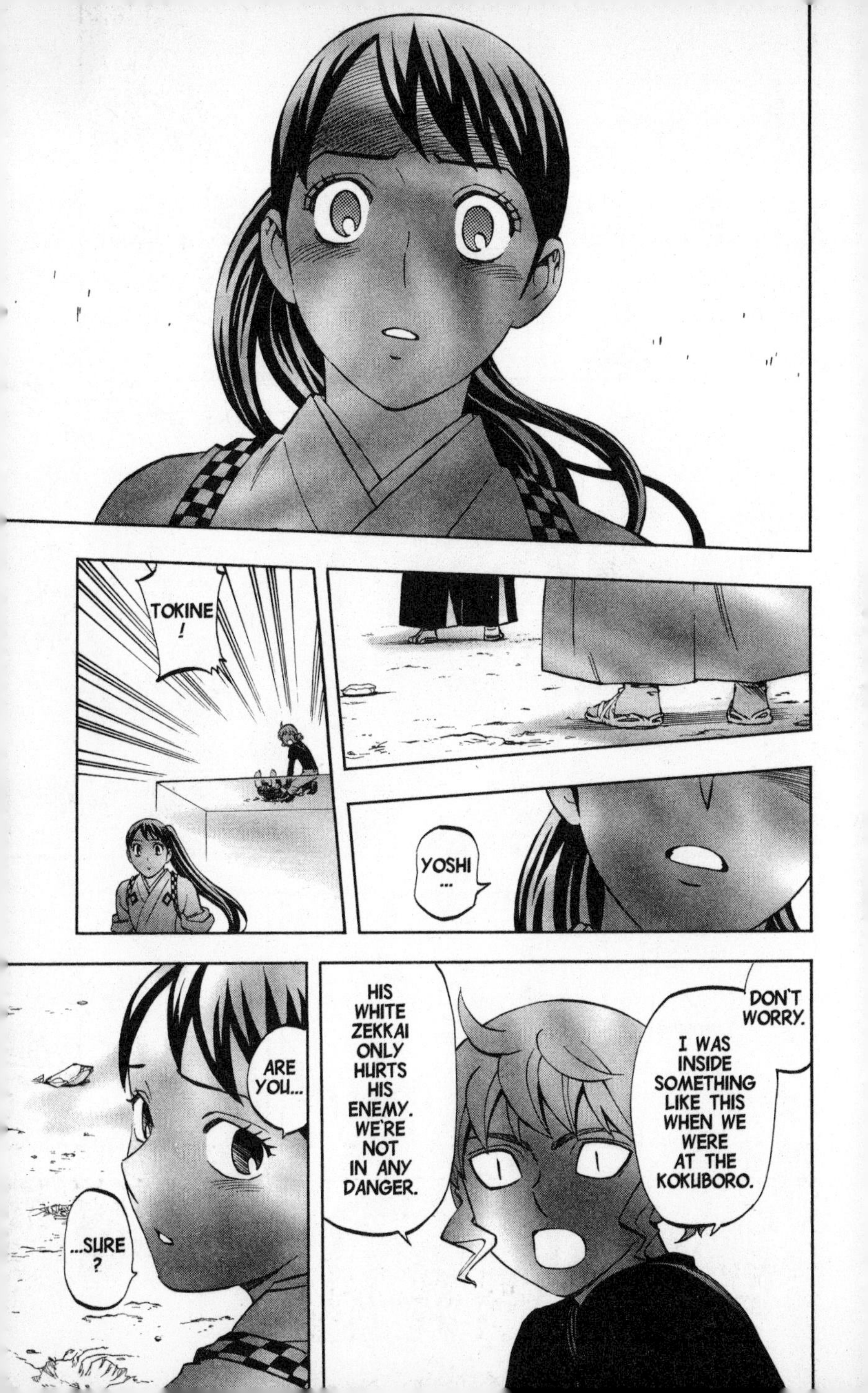
YOSHI ...
TOKINE!
DON'T WORRY.
I WAS INSIDE SOMETHING LIKE THIS WHEN WE WERE AT THE KOKUBORO.
HIS WHITE ZEKKAI ONLY HURTS HIS ENEMY. WE'RE NOT IN ANY DANGER.
ARE YOU...
...SURE?

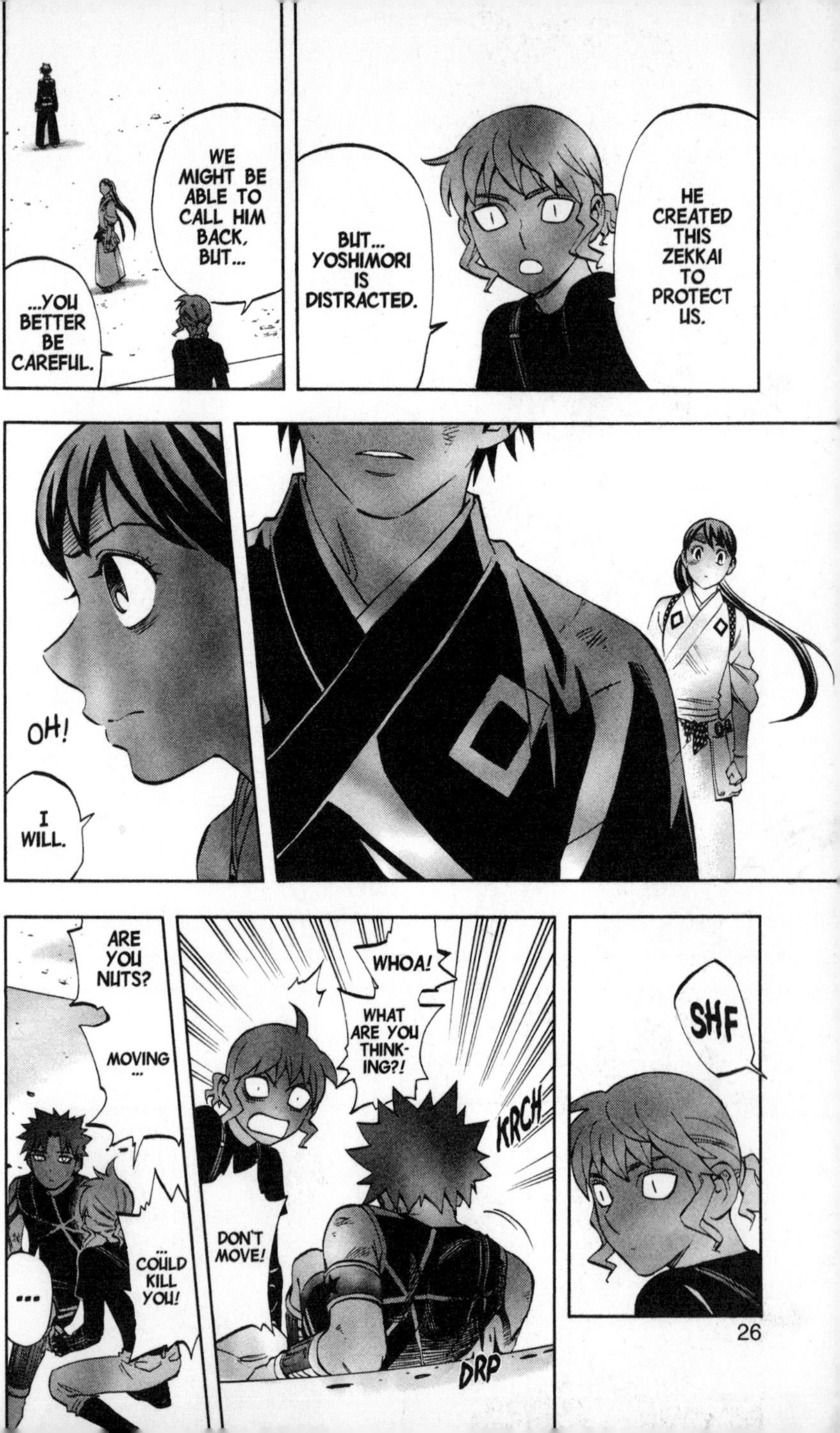
HE CREATED THIS ZEKKAI TO PROTECT US.
BUT... YOSHIMORI IS DISTRACTED.
WE MIGHT BE ABLE TO CALL HIM BACK, BUT...
...YOU BETTER BE CAREFUL.
OH!
I WILL.
SHF
WHOA!
WHAT ARE YOU THINK-ING?!
KRCH
DON'T MOVE!
DRP
ARE YOU NUTS?
MOVING...
...COULD KILL YOU!
...

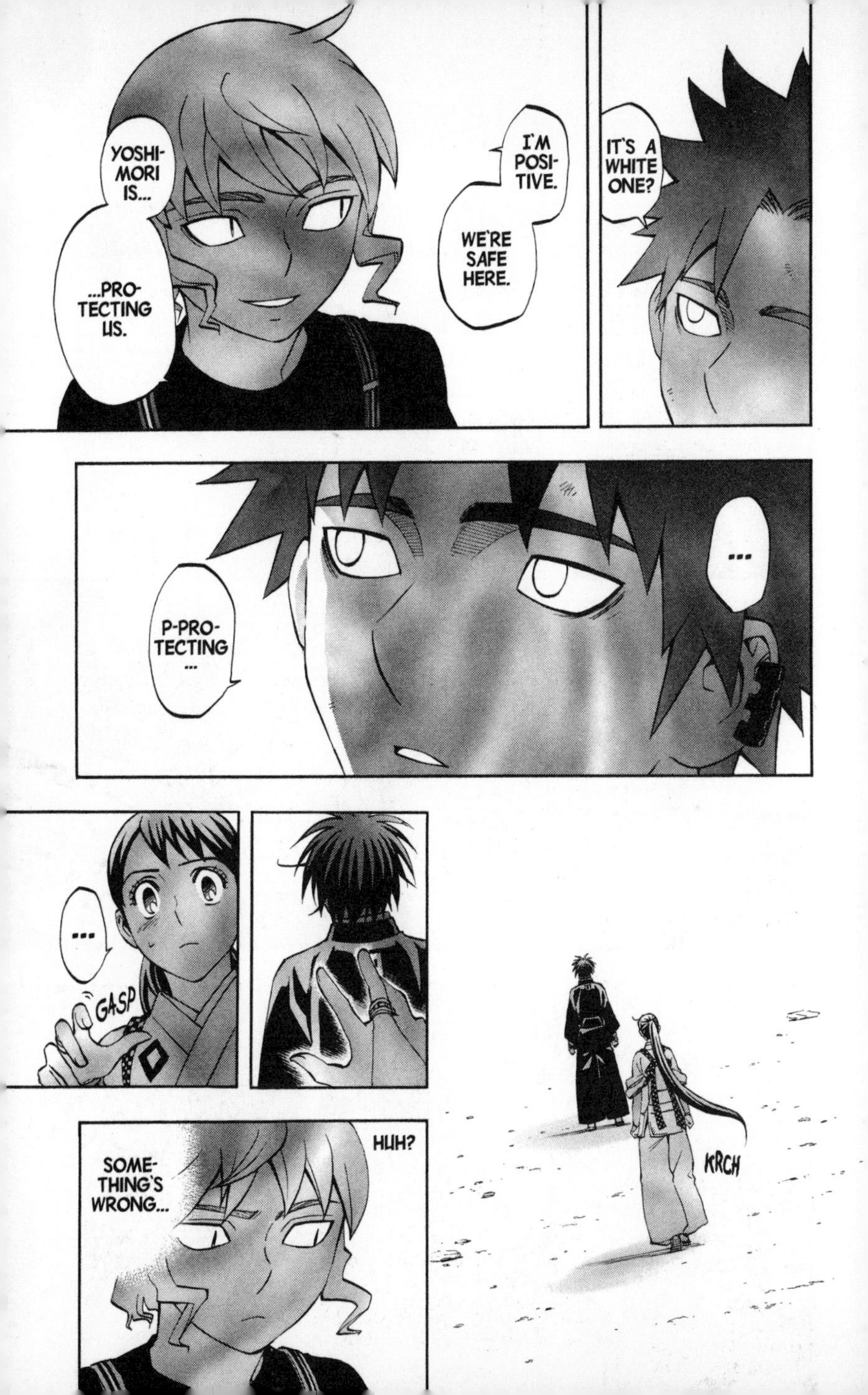
IT'S A WHITE ONE?
I'M POSITIVE.
WE'RE SAFE HERE.
YOSHIMORI IS...
...PROTECTING US.
...
P-PROTECTING ...
KRCH
...
GASP
HUH?
SOMETHING'S WRONG...

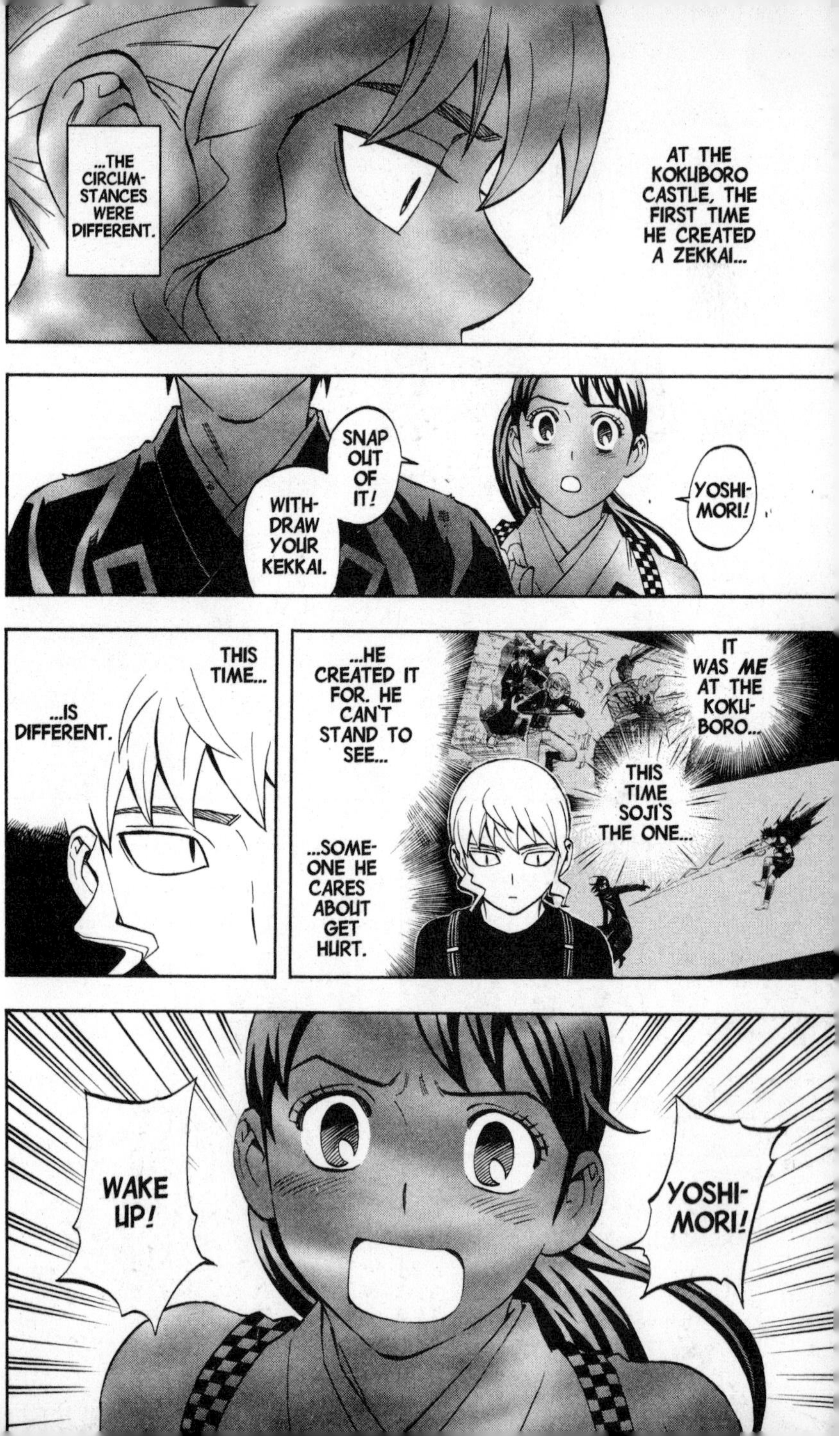
AT THE KOKUBORO CASTLE, THE FIRST TIME HE CREATED A ZEKKAI...
...THE CIRCUM-STANCES WERE DIFFERENT.
YOSHI-MORI!
SNAP OUT OF IT!
WITH-DRAW YOUR KEKKAI.
IT WAS *ME* AT THE KOKU-BORO...
THIS TIME SOJI'S THE ONE...
...HE CREATED IT FOR. HE CAN'T STAND TO SEE...
...SOME-ONE HE CARES ABOUT GET HURT.
THIS TIME...
...IS DIFFERENT.
YOSHI-MORI!
WAKE UP!

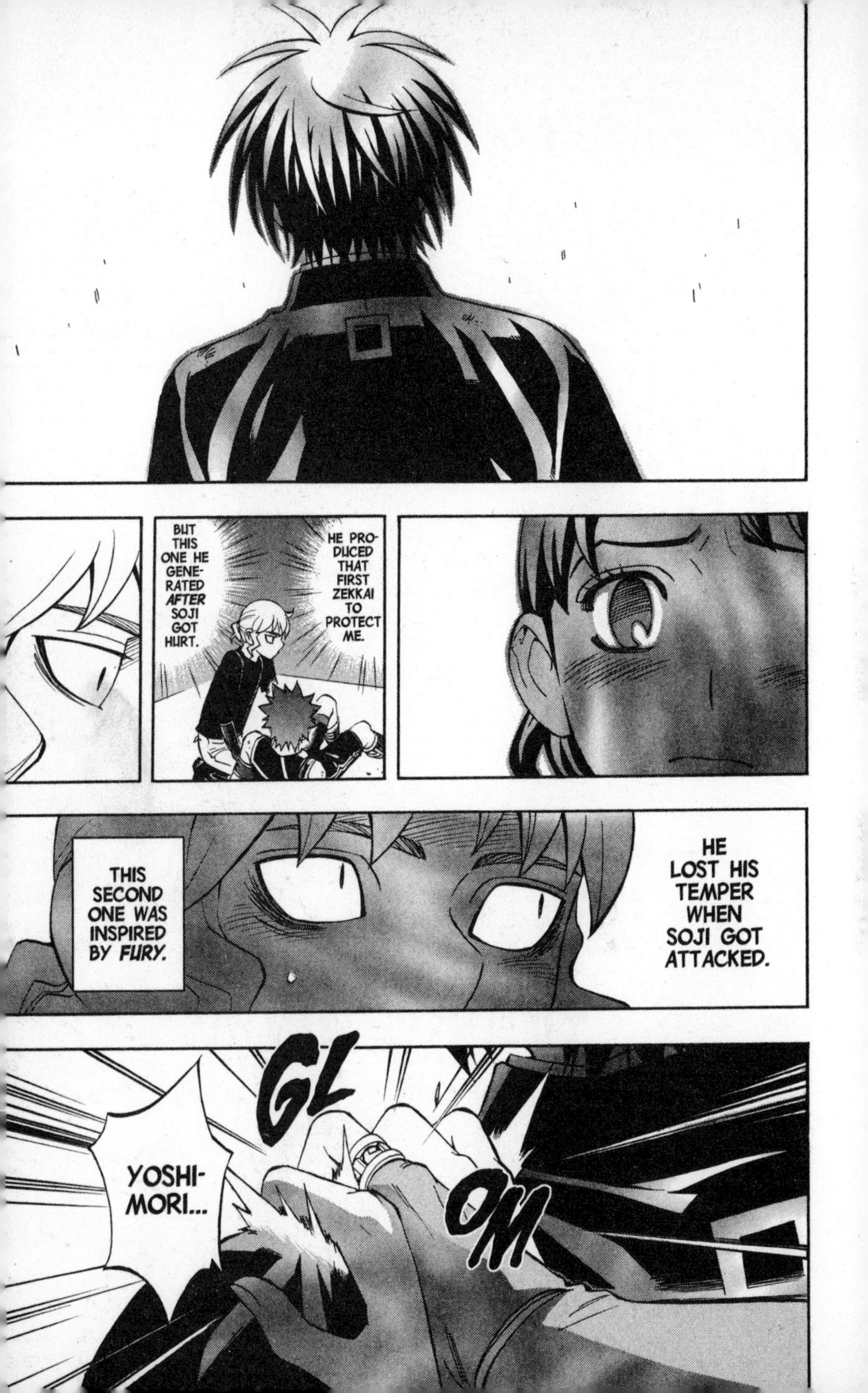
HE PRODUCED THAT FIRST ZEKKAI TO PROTECT ME.
BUT THIS ONE HE GENERATED *AFTER* SOJI GOT HURT.
HE LOST HIS TEMPER WHEN SOJI GOT ATTACKED.
THIS SECOND ONE WAS INSPIRED BY *FURY*.
GL
OM
YOSHIMORI...

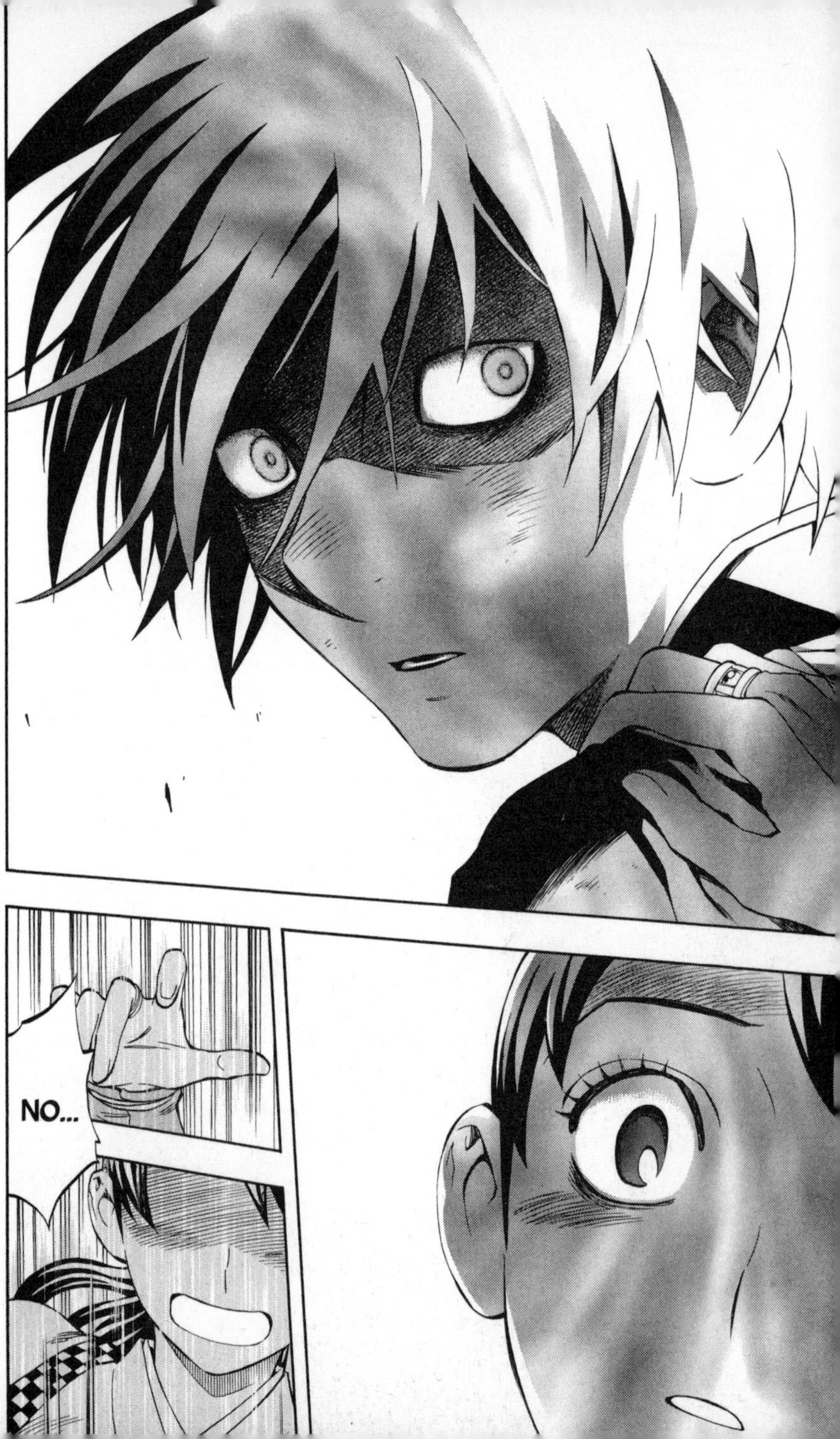
NO...

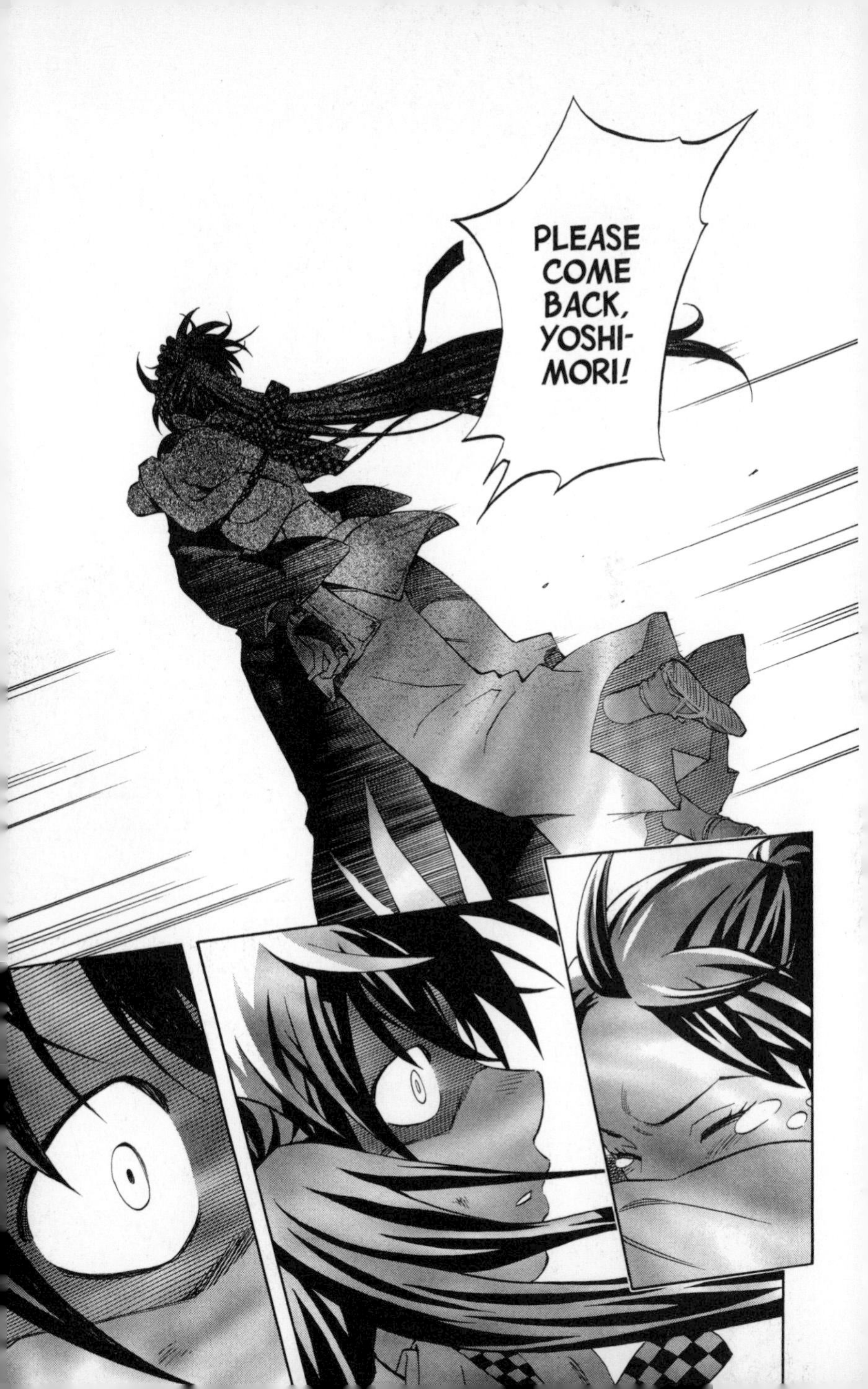
PLEASE COME BACK, YOSHI-MORI!

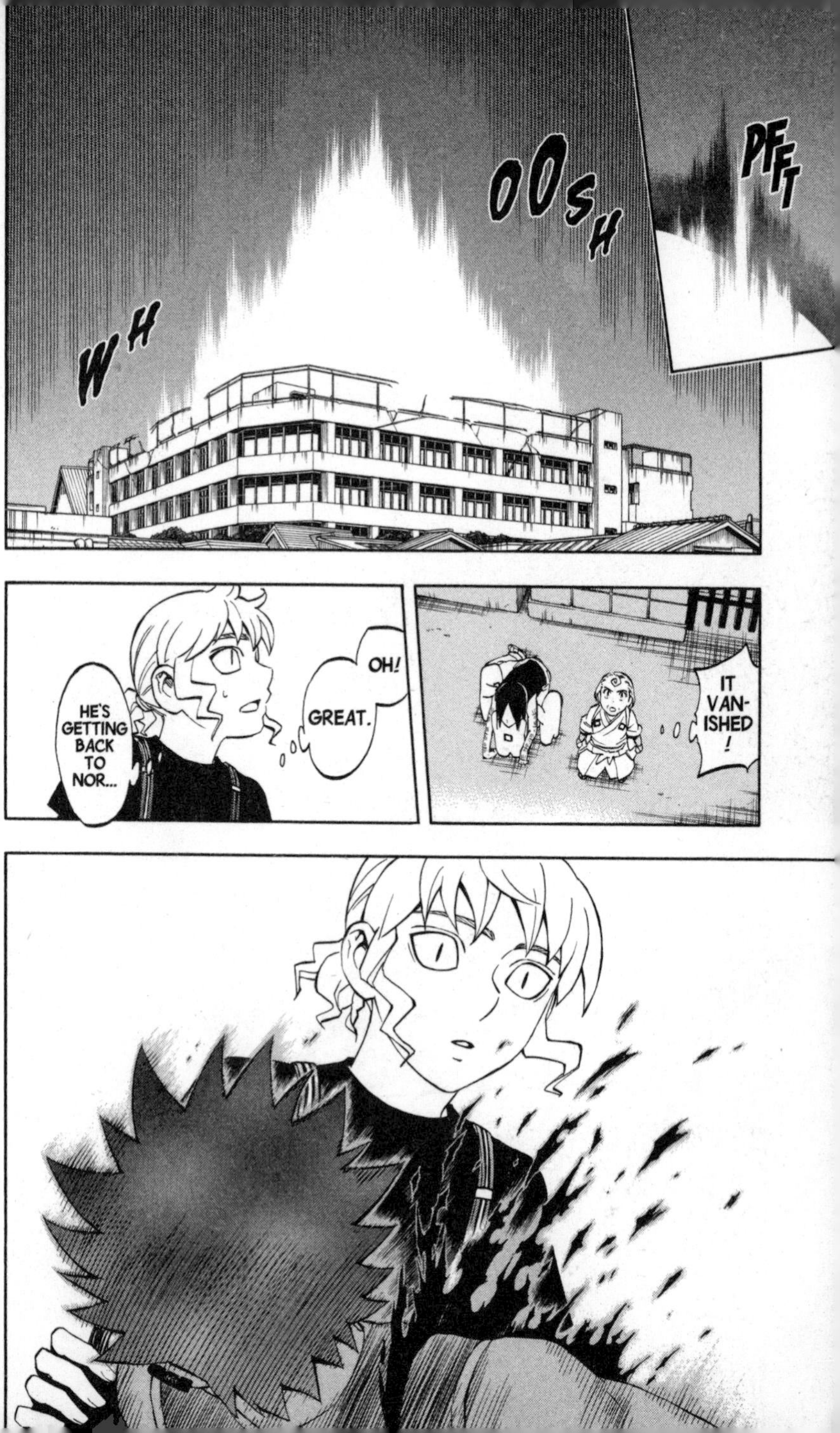
PFFT
WH OOSH
IT VANISHED!
OH!
GREAT.
HE'S GETTING BACK TO NOR...

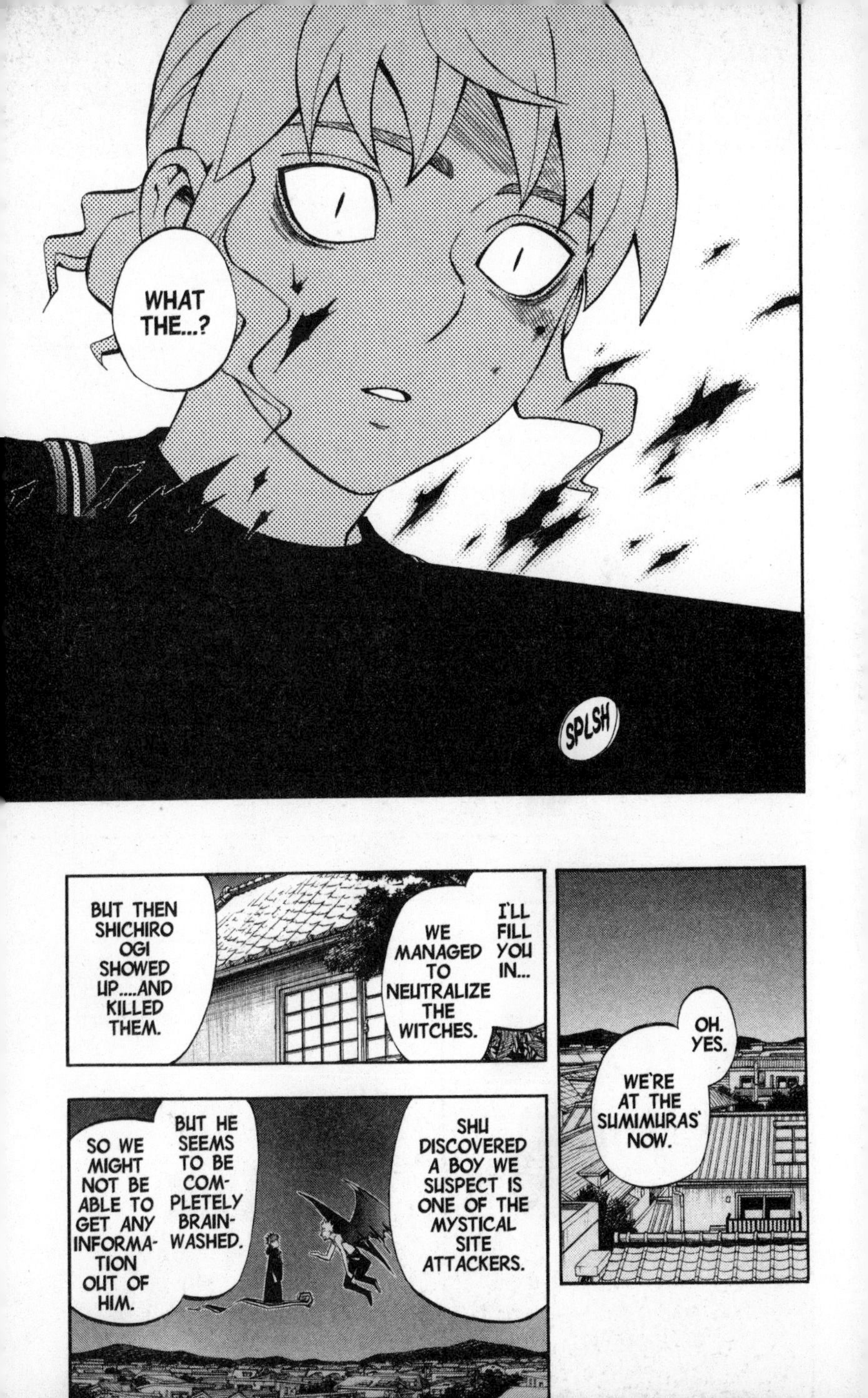
WHAT THE...?
SPLSH
OH. YES.
WE'RE AT THE SUMIMURAS' NOW.
I'LL FILL YOU IN...
WE MANAGED TO NEUTRALIZE THE WITCHES.
BUT THEN SHICHIRO OGI SHOWED UP....AND KILLED THEM.
SHU DISCOVERED A BOY WE SUSPECT IS ONE OF THE MYSTICAL SITE ATTACKERS.
BUT HE SEEMS TO BE COMPLETELY BRAINWASHED.
SO WE MIGHT NOT BE ABLE TO GET ANY INFORMATION OUT OF HIM.

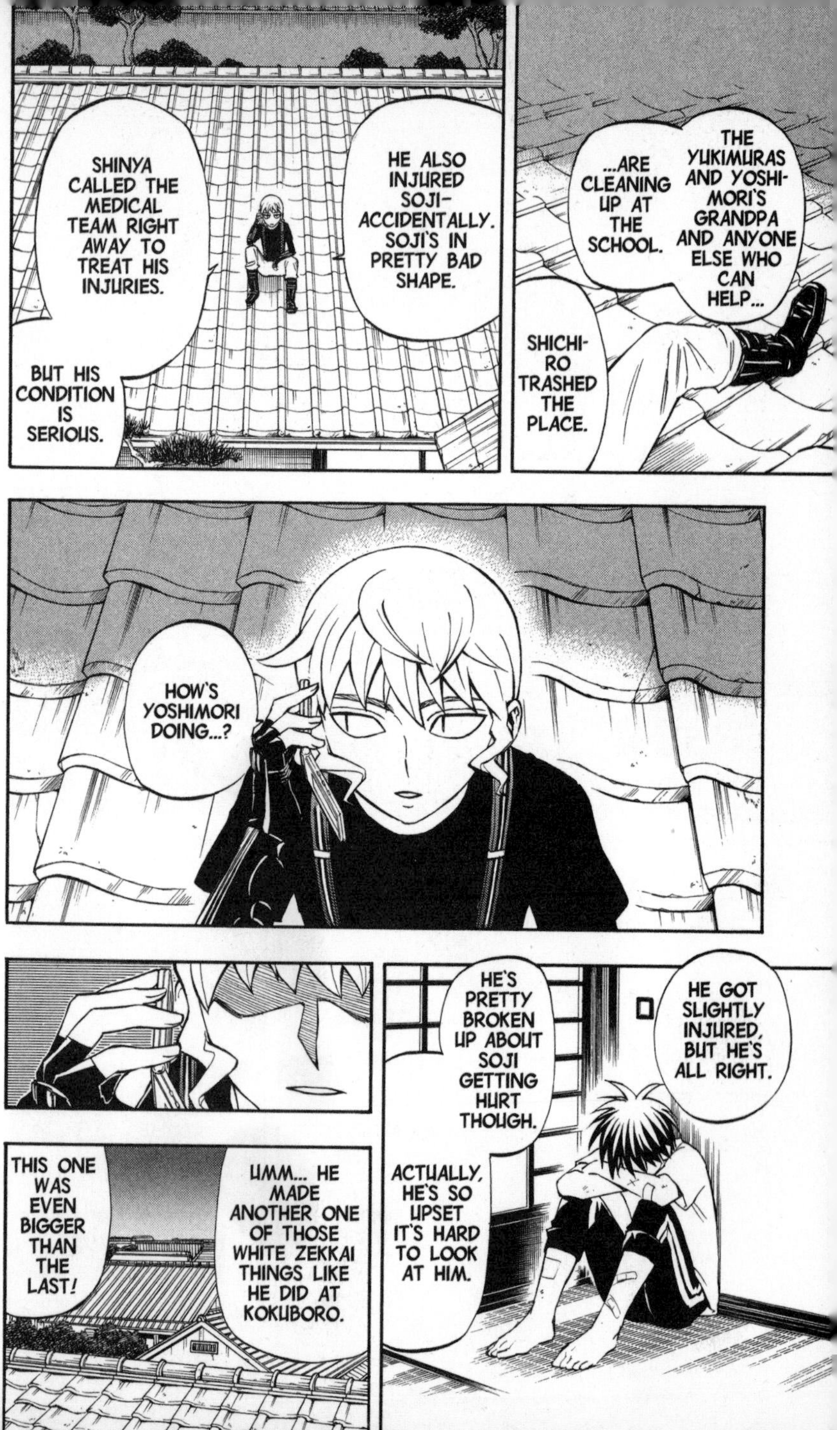
THE YUKIMURAS AND YOSHIMORI'S GRANDPA AND ANYONE ELSE WHO CAN HELP...
...ARE CLEANING UP AT THE SCHOOL.
SHICHIRO TRASHED THE PLACE.
HE ALSO INJURED SOJI-ACCIDENTALLY. SOJI'S IN PRETTY BAD SHAPE.
SHINYA CALLED THE MEDICAL TEAM RIGHT AWAY TO TREAT HIS INJURIES.
BUT HIS CONDITION IS SERIOUS.
HOW'S YOSHIMORI DOING...?
HE GOT SLIGHTLY INJURED, BUT HE'S ALL RIGHT.
HE'S PRETTY BROKEN UP ABOUT SOJI GETTING HURT THOUGH.
ACTUALLY, HE'S SO UPSET IT'S HARD TO LOOK AT HIM.
UMM... HE MADE ANOTHER ONE OF THOSE WHITE ZEKKAI THINGS LIKE HE DID AT KOKUBORO.
THIS ONE WAS EVEN BIGGER THAN THE LAST!

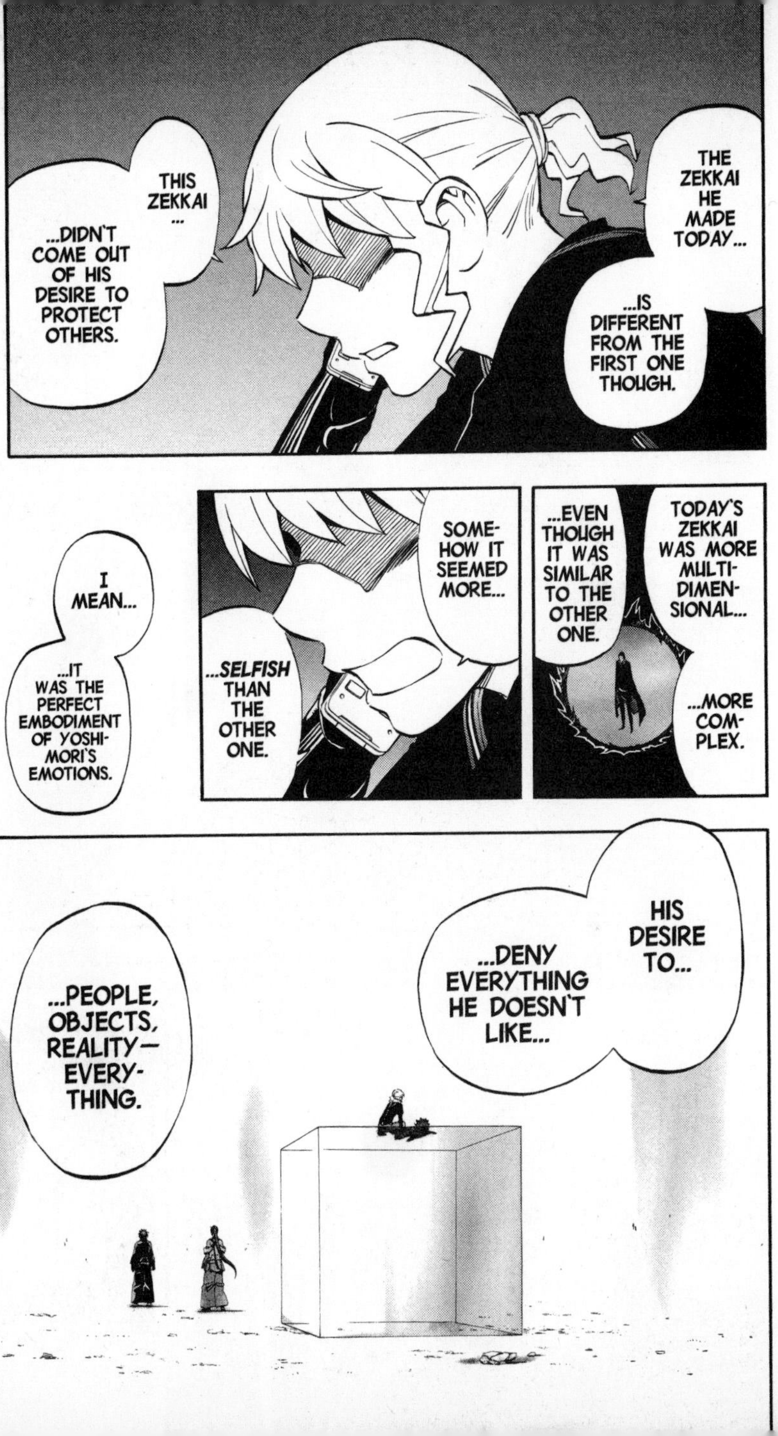
THE ZEKKAI HE MADE TODAY...
...IS DIFFERENT FROM THE FIRST ONE THOUGH.
THIS ZEKKAI ...
...DIDN'T COME OUT OF HIS DESIRE TO PROTECT OTHERS.
TODAY'S ZEKKAI WAS MORE MULTI-DIMENSIONAL...
...EVEN THOUGH IT WAS SIMILAR TO THE OTHER ONE.
...MORE COMPLEX.
SOME-HOW IT SEEMED MORE...
...*SELFISH* THAN THE OTHER ONE.
I MEAN...
...IT WAS THE PERFECT EMBODIMENT OF YOSHIMORI'S EMOTIONS.
HIS DESIRE TO...
...DENY EVERYTHING HE DOESN'T LIKE...
...PEOPLE, OBJECTS, REALITY—EVERYTHING.

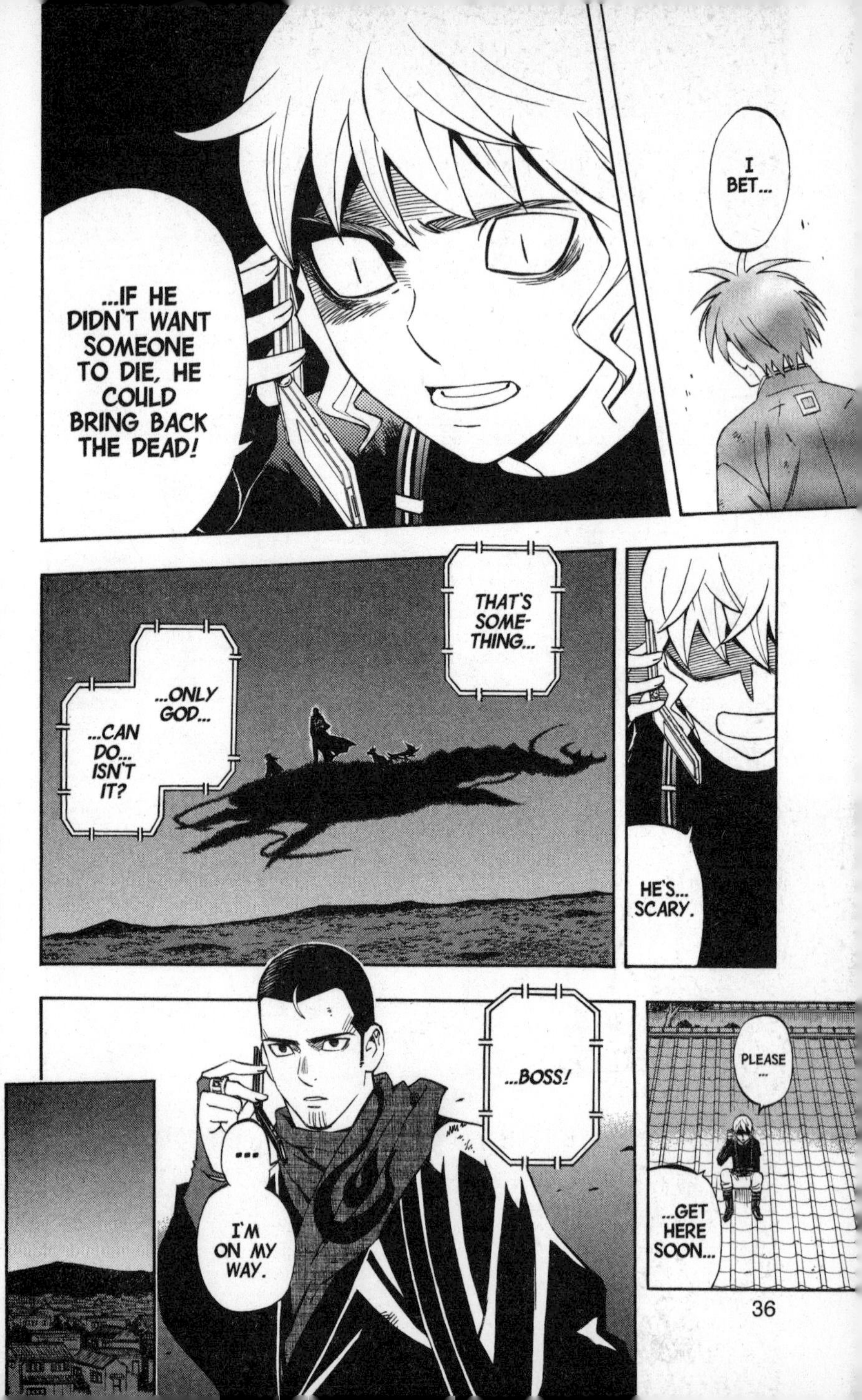
I BET...
...IF HE DIDN'T WANT SOMEONE TO DIE, HE COULD BRING BACK THE DEAD!
HE'S... SCARY.
THAT'S SOME-THING...
...ONLY GOD...
...CAN DO... ISN'T IT?
PLEASE...
...GET HERE SOON...
...BOSS!
...
I'M ON MY WAY.

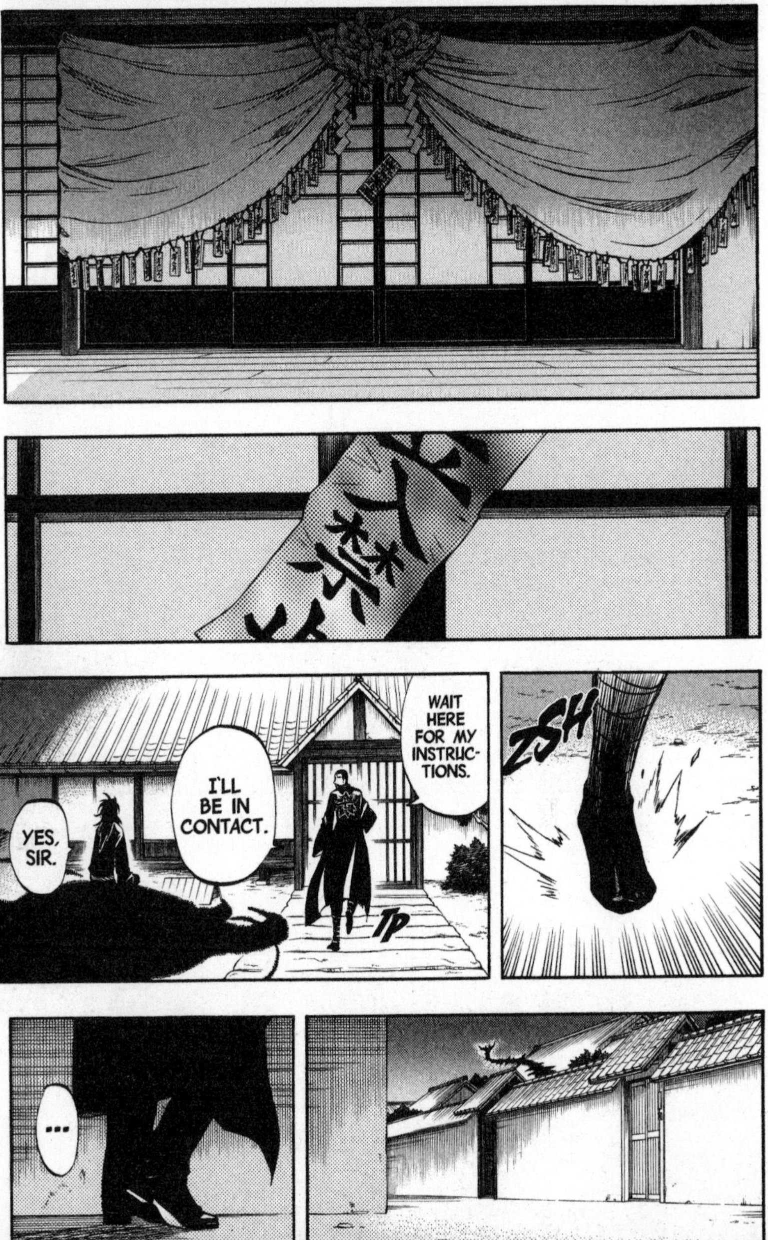
ZSH
WAIT HERE FOR MY INSTRUC-TIONS.
I'LL BE IN CONTACT.
TP
YES, SIR.
...

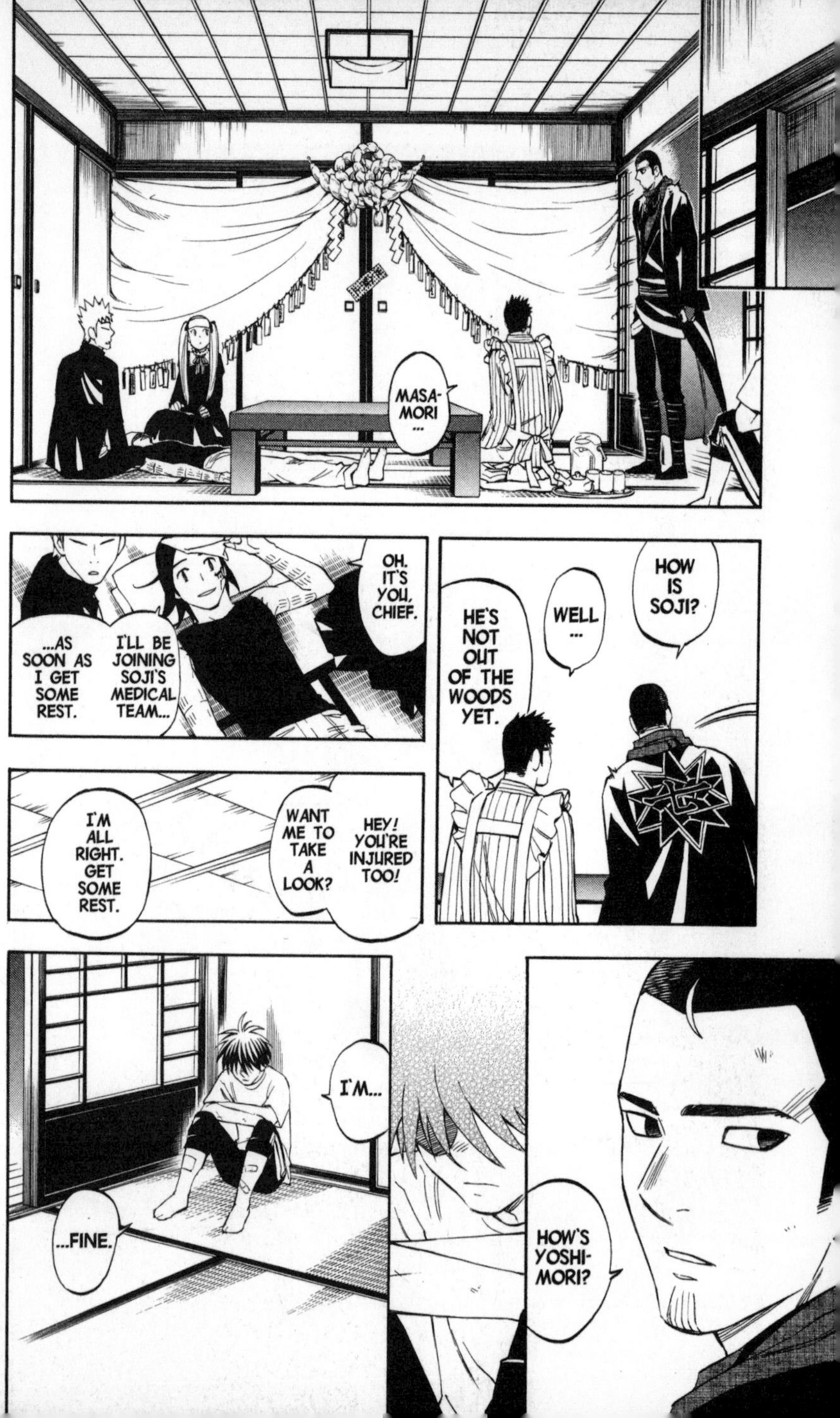
MASA-MORI ...
HOW IS SOJI?
WELL ...
HE'S NOT OUT OF THE WOODS YET.
OH. IT'S YOU, CHIEF.
I'LL BE JOINING SOJI'S MEDICAL TEAM...
...AS SOON AS I GET SOME REST.
HEY! YOU'RE INJURED TOO!
WANT ME TO TAKE A LOOK?
I'M ALL RIGHT. GET SOME REST.
HOW'S YOSHI-MORI?
I'M...
...FINE.

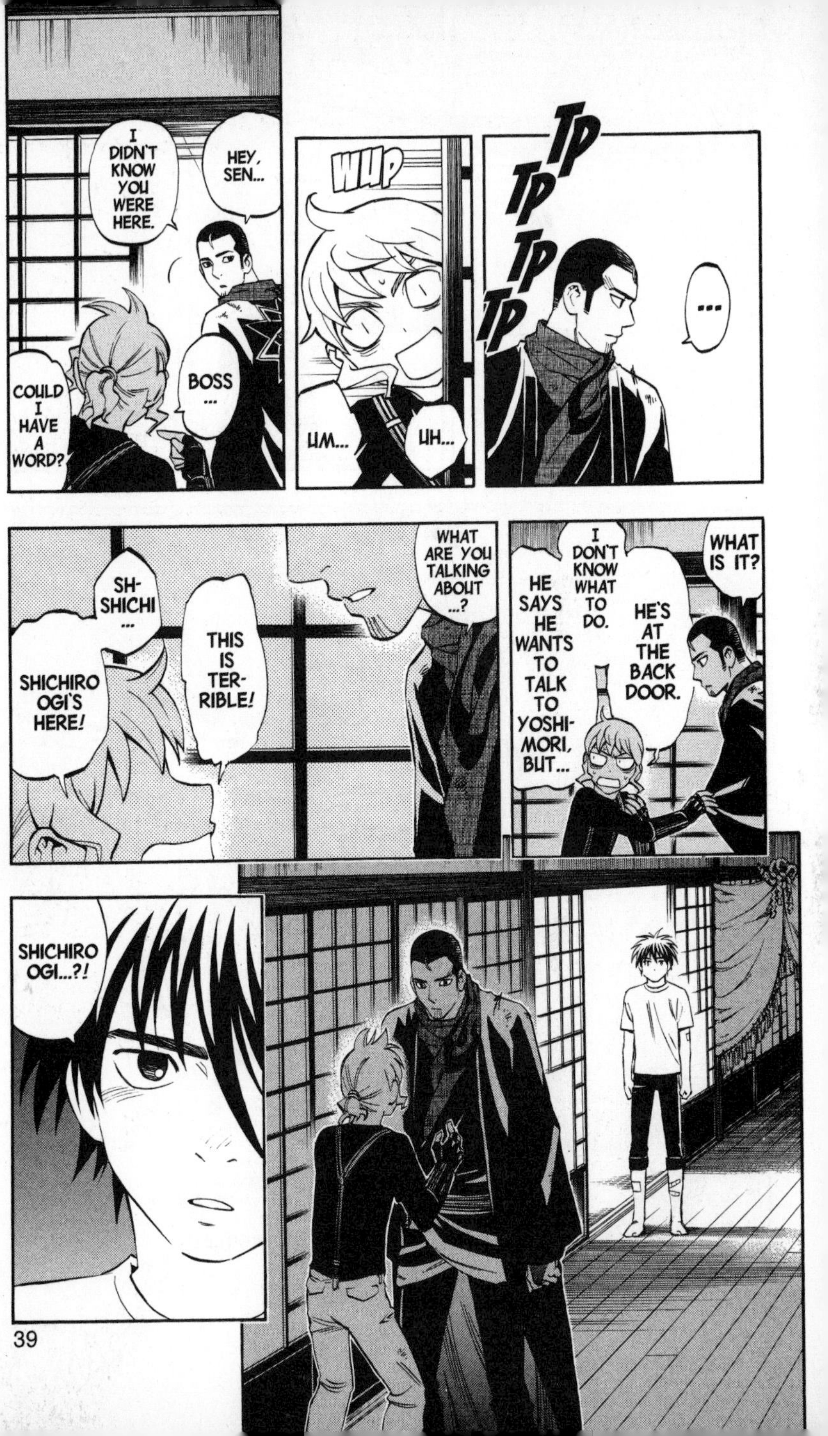
TP TP TP TP TP
...
WUP
UH...
UM...
HEY, SEN...
I DIDN'T KNOW YOU WERE HERE.
BOSS...
COULD I HAVE A WORD?
WHAT IS IT?
HE'S AT THE BACK DOOR.
I DON'T KNOW WHAT TO DO.
HE SAYS HE WANTS TO TALK TO YOSHIMORI, BUT...
WHAT ARE YOU TALKING ABOUT...?
THIS IS TERRIBLE!
SH-SHICHI...
SHICHIRO OGI'S HERE!
SHICHIRO OGI...?!

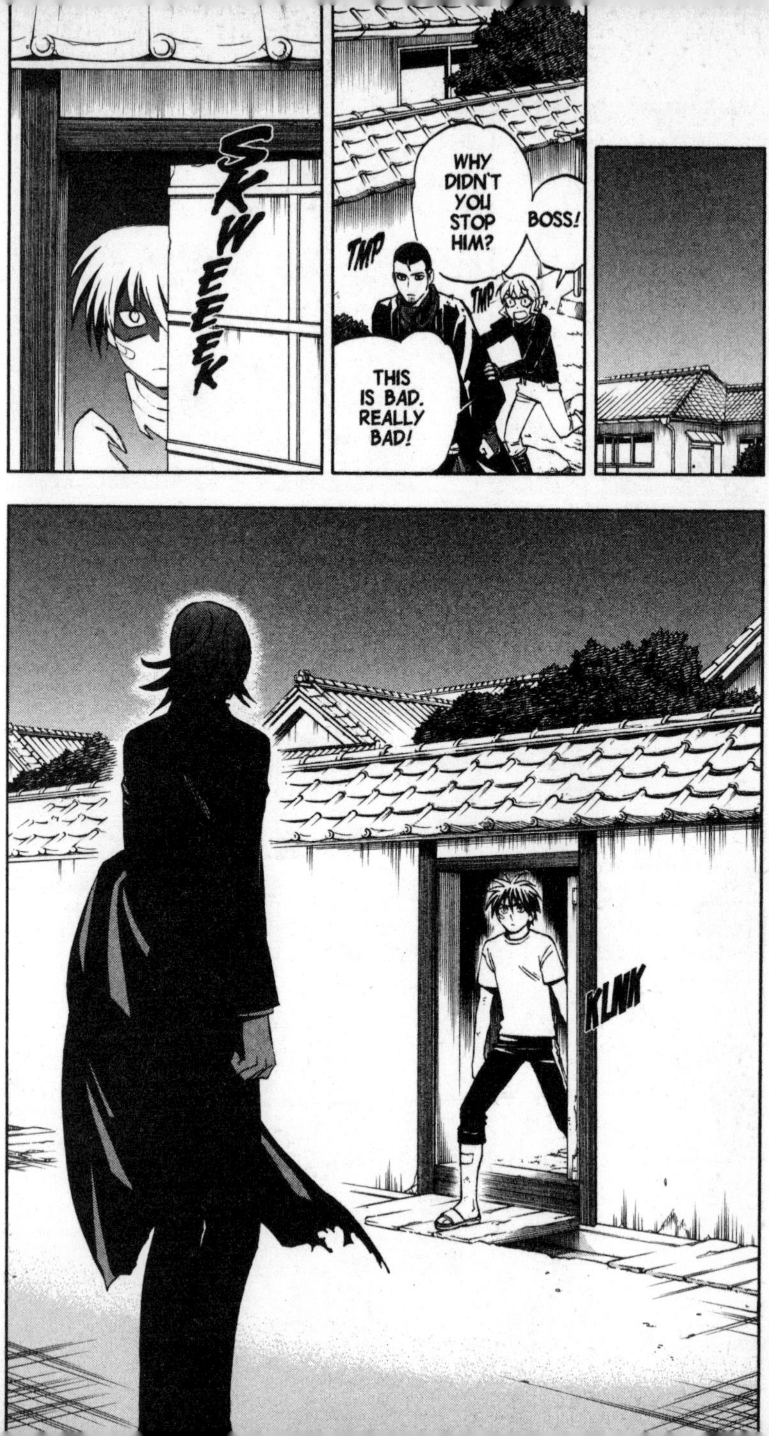
BOSS!
WHY DIDN'T YOU STOP HIM?
TMP
TMP
THIS IS BAD. REALLY BAD!
SKWEEEEK
KLNK

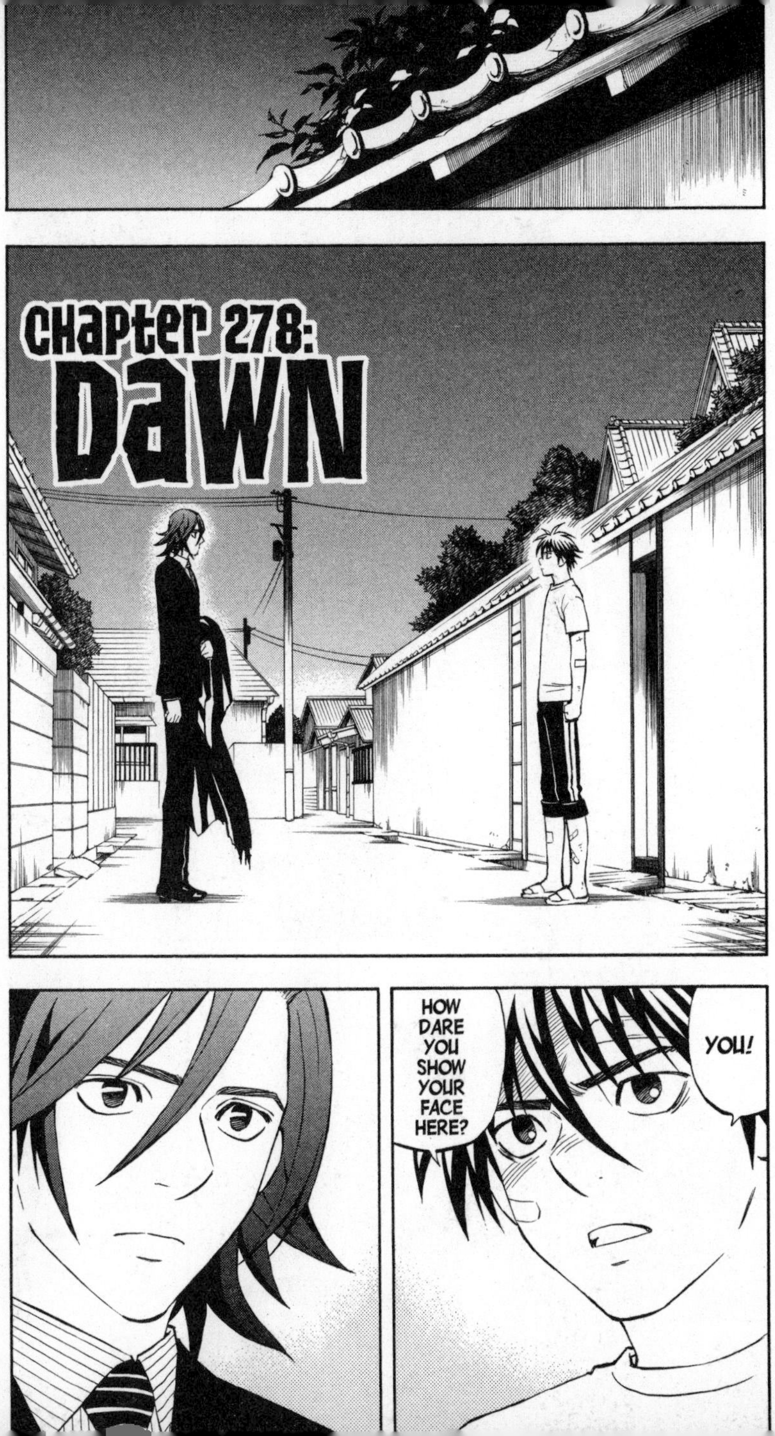
CHAPTER 278:
DAWN
YOU!
HOW DARE YOU SHOW YOUR FACE HERE?

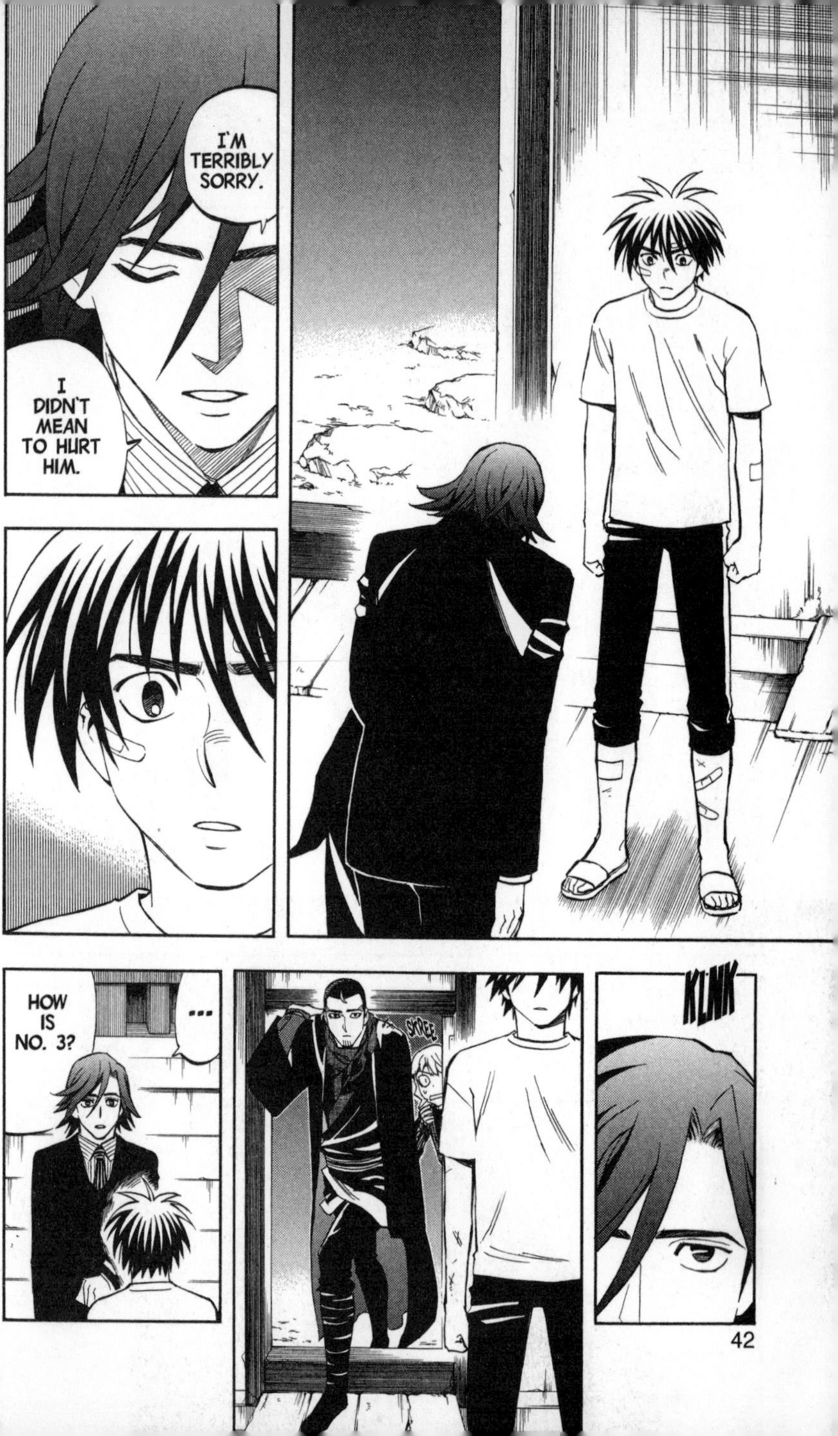
I'M TERRIBLY SORRY.
I DIDN'T MEAN TO HURT HIM.
KLNK
SKREE
...
HOW IS NO. 3?

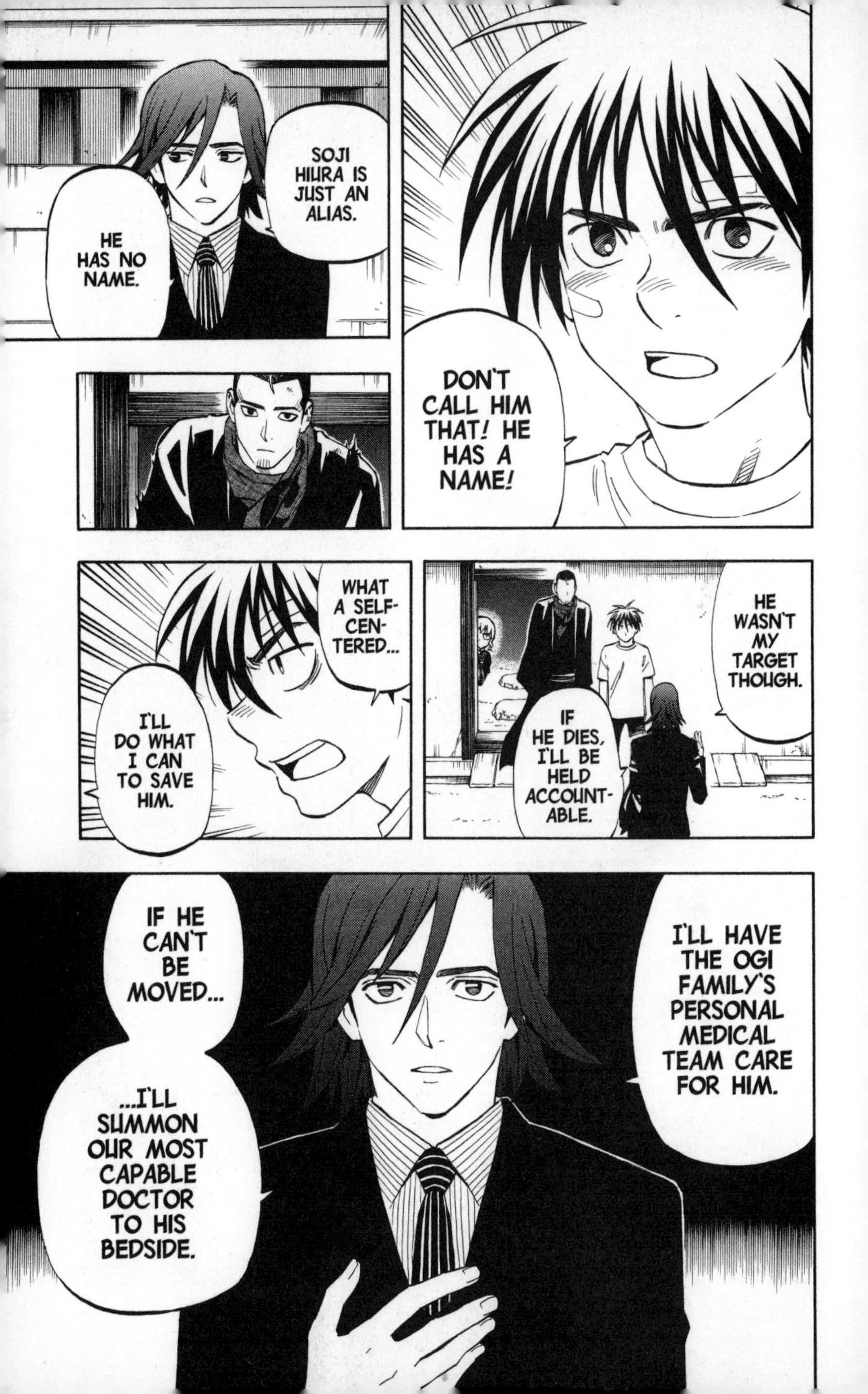
DON'T CALL HIM THAT! HE HAS A NAME!
SOJI HIURA IS JUST AN ALIAS.
HE HAS NO NAME.
HE WASN'T MY TARGET THOUGH.
IF HE DIES, I'LL BE HELD ACCOUNTABLE.
WHAT A SELF-CENTERED...
I'LL DO WHAT I CAN TO SAVE HIM.
I'LL HAVE THE OGI FAMILY'S PERSONAL MEDICAL TEAM CARE FOR HIM.
IF HE CAN'T BE MOVED...
...I'LL SUMMON OUR MOST CAPABLE DOCTOR TO HIS BEDSIDE.

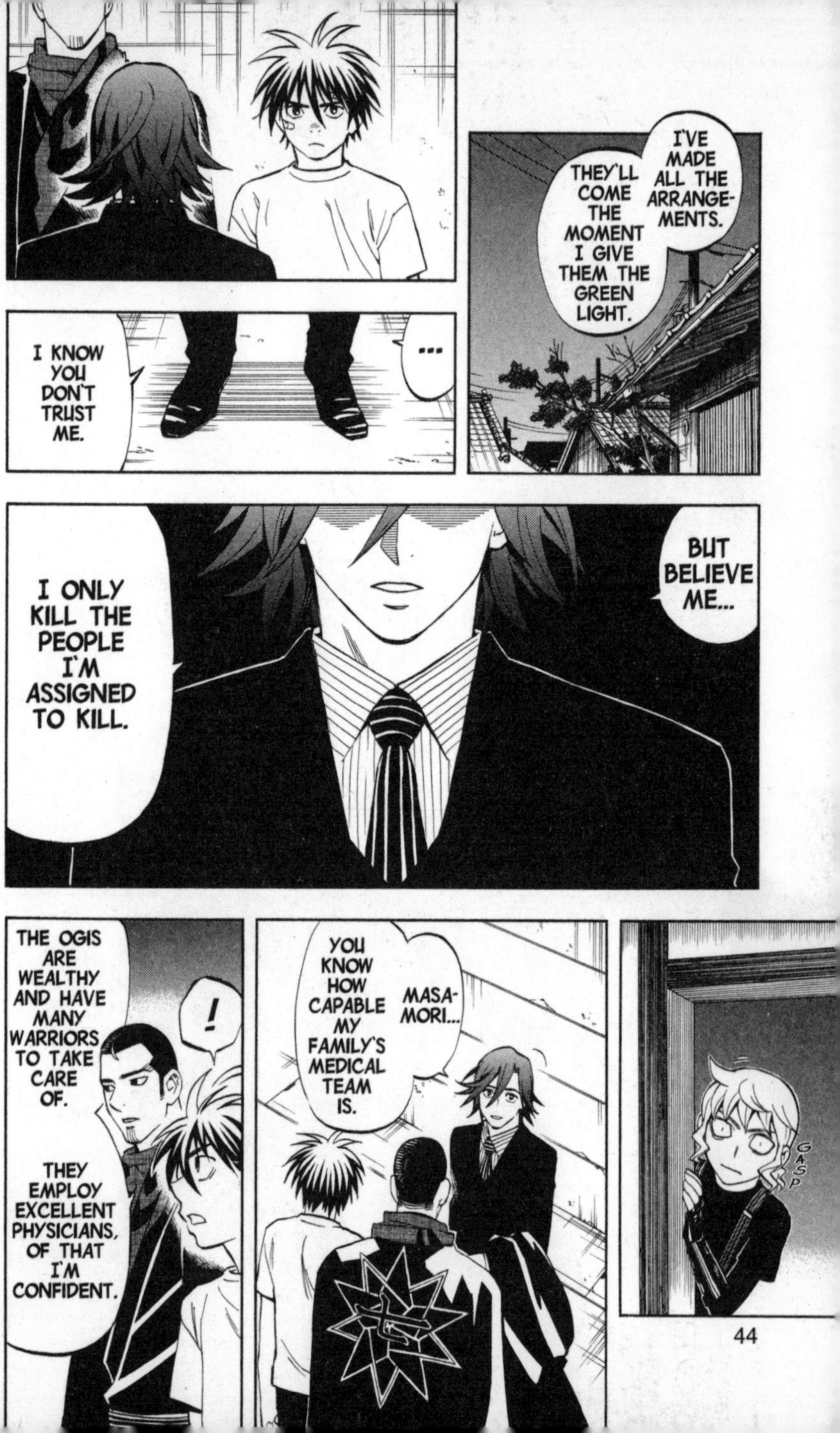
I'VE MADE ALL THE ARRANGEMENTS.
THEY'LL COME THE MOMENT I GIVE THEM THE GREEN LIGHT.
...
I KNOW YOU DON'T TRUST ME.
BUT BELIEVE ME...
I ONLY KILL THE PEOPLE I'M ASSIGNED TO KILL.
GASP
MASAMORI...
YOU KNOW HOW CAPABLE MY FAMILY'S MEDICAL TEAM IS.
!
THE OGIS ARE WEALTHY AND HAVE MANY WARRIORS TO TAKE CARE OF.
THEY EMPLOY EXCELLENT PHYSICIANS, OF THAT I'M CONFIDENT.

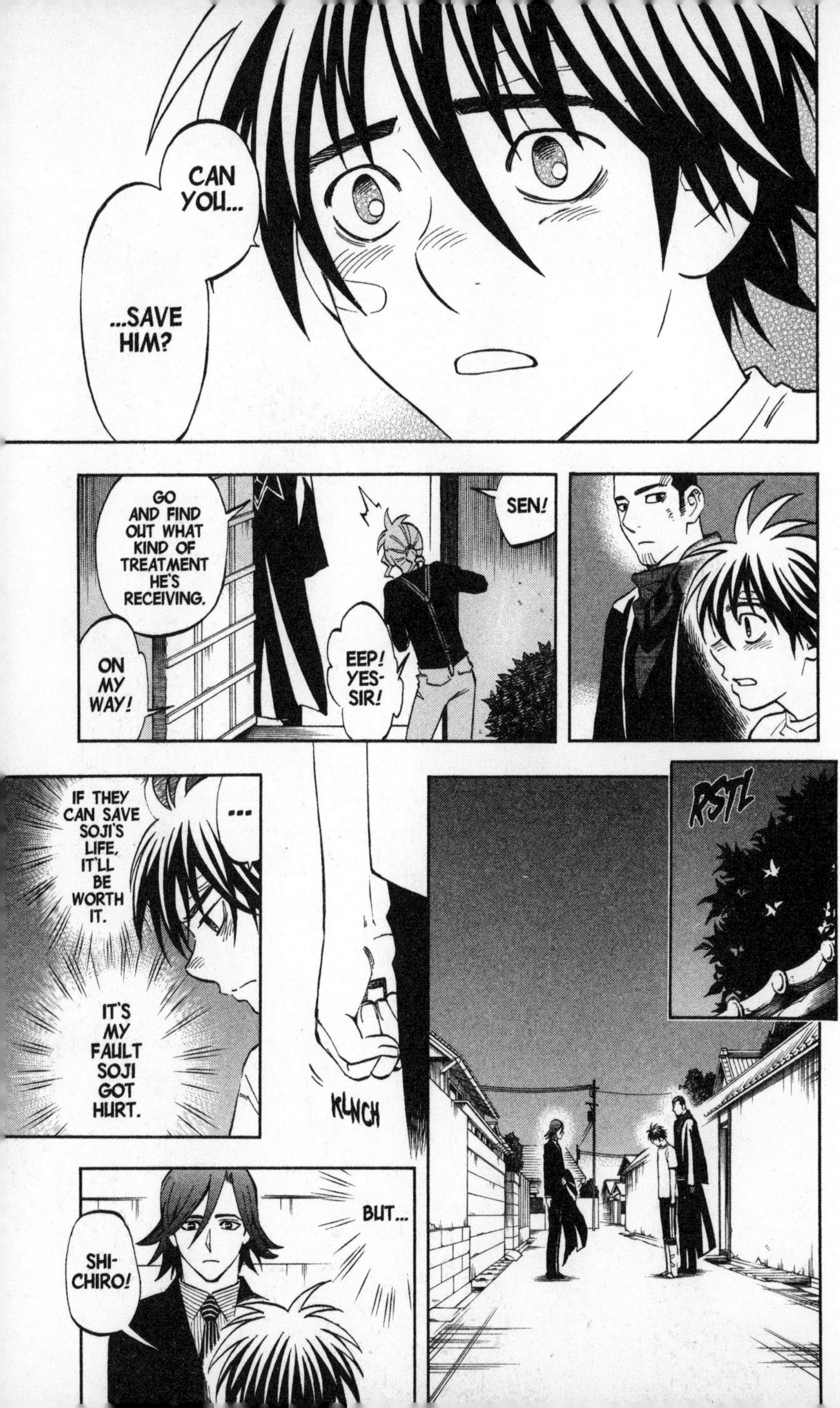
CAN YOU...
...SAVE HIM?
SEN!
EEP! YES-SIR!
GO AND FIND OUT WHAT KIND OF TREATMENT HE'S RECEIVING.
ON MY WAY!
RSTL
KLNCH
...
IF THEY CAN SAVE SOJI'S LIFE, IT'LL BE WORTH IT.
IT'S MY FAULT SOJI GOT HURT.
BUT...
SHI-CHIRO!

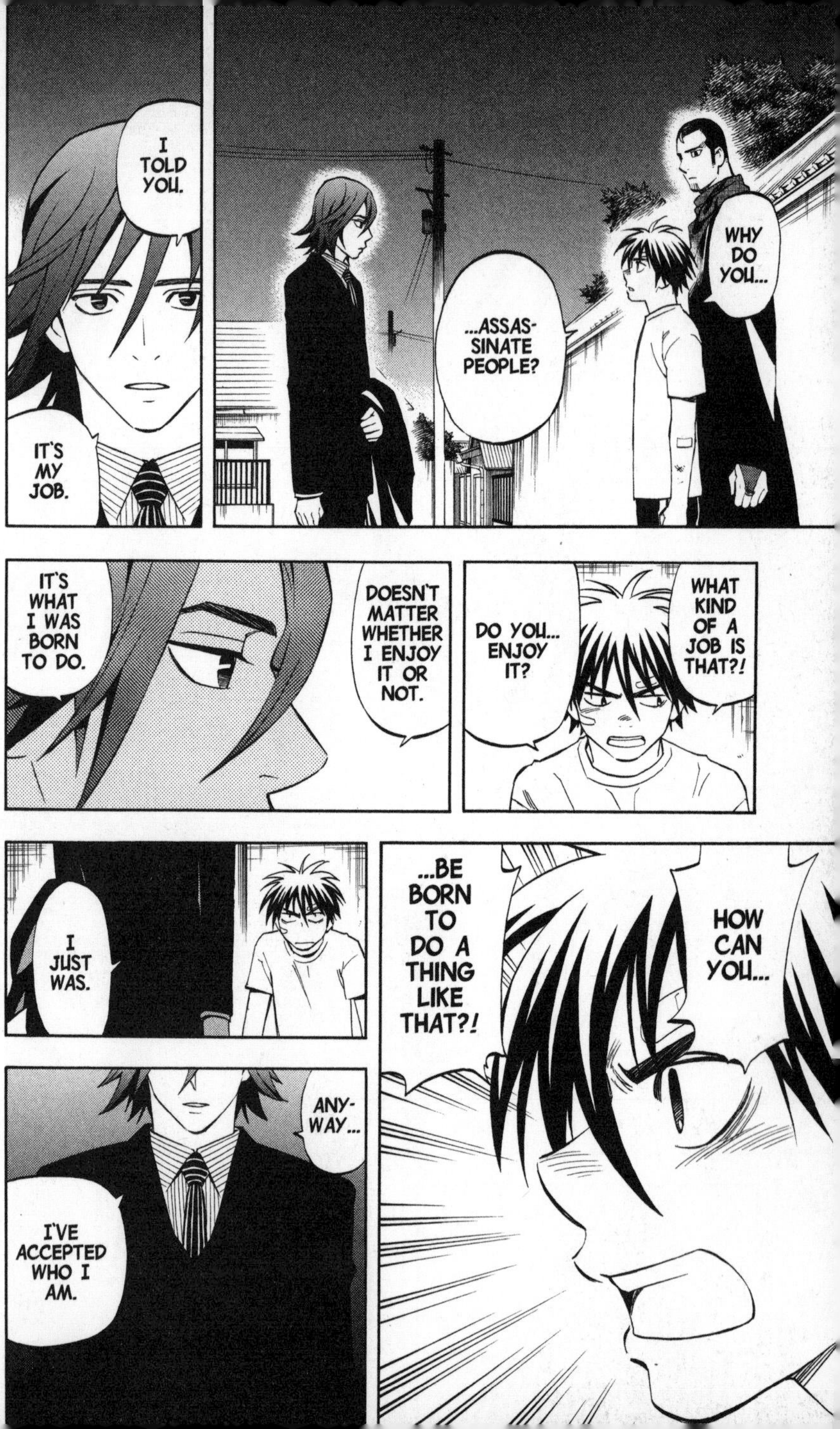
WHY DO YOU...
...ASSAS-SINATE PEOPLE?
I TOLD YOU.
IT'S MY JOB.
WHAT KIND OF A JOB IS THAT?!
DO YOU... ENJOY IT?
DOESN'T MATTER WHETHER I ENJOY IT OR NOT.
IT'S WHAT I WAS BORN TO DO.
HOW CAN YOU...
...BE BORN TO DO A THING LIKE THAT?!
I JUST WAS.
ANY-WAY...
I'VE ACCEPTED WHO I AM.

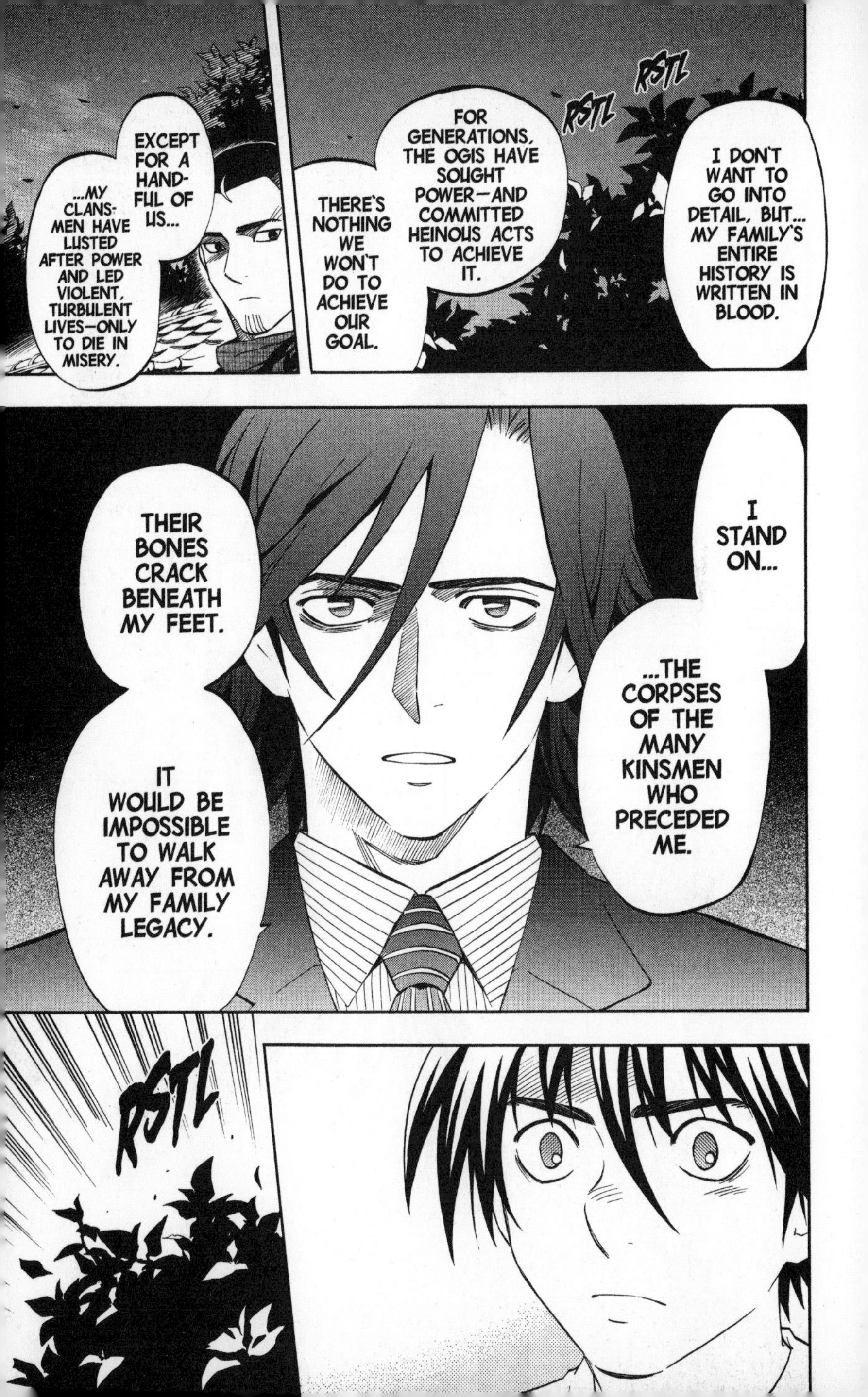
RSTL
RSTL
I DON'T WANT TO GO INTO DETAIL, BUT... MY FAMILY'S ENTIRE HISTORY IS WRITTEN IN BLOOD.
FOR GENERATIONS, THE OGIS HAVE SOUGHT POWER—AND COMMITTED HEINOUS ACTS TO ACHIEVE IT.
THERE'S NOTHING WE WON'T DO TO ACHIEVE OUR GOAL.
EXCEPT FOR A HANDFUL OF US...
...MY CLANSMEN HAVE LUSTED AFTER POWER AND LED VIOLENT, TURBULENT LIVES—ONLY TO DIE IN MISERY.
I STAND ON...
...THE CORPSES OF THE MANY KINSMEN WHO PRECEDED ME.
THEIR BONES CRACK BENEATH MY FEET.
IT WOULD BE IMPOSSIBLE TO WALK AWAY FROM MY FAMILY LEGACY.
RSTL

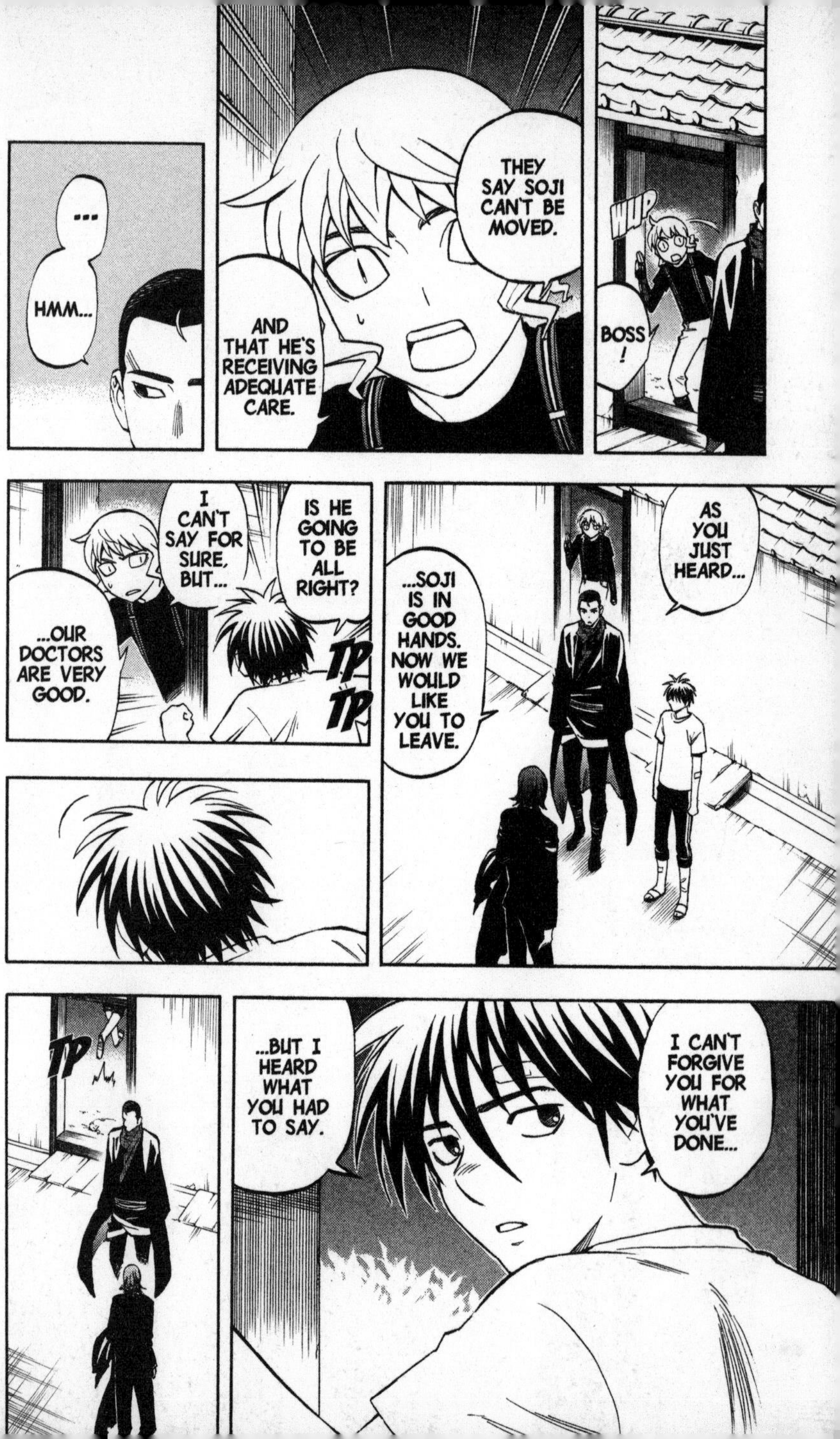
WUP
BOSS!
THEY SAY SOJI CAN'T BE MOVED.
AND THAT HE'S RECEIVING ADEQUATE CARE.
...
HMM...
AS YOU JUST HEARD...
...SOJI IS IN GOOD HANDS. NOW WE WOULD LIKE YOU TO LEAVE.
IS HE GOING TO BE ALL RIGHT?
I CAN'T SAY FOR SURE, BUT...
...OUR DOCTORS ARE VERY GOOD.
TP
TP
I CAN'T FORGIVE YOU FOR WHAT YOU'VE DONE...
...BUT I HEARD WHAT YOU HAD TO SAY.
TP

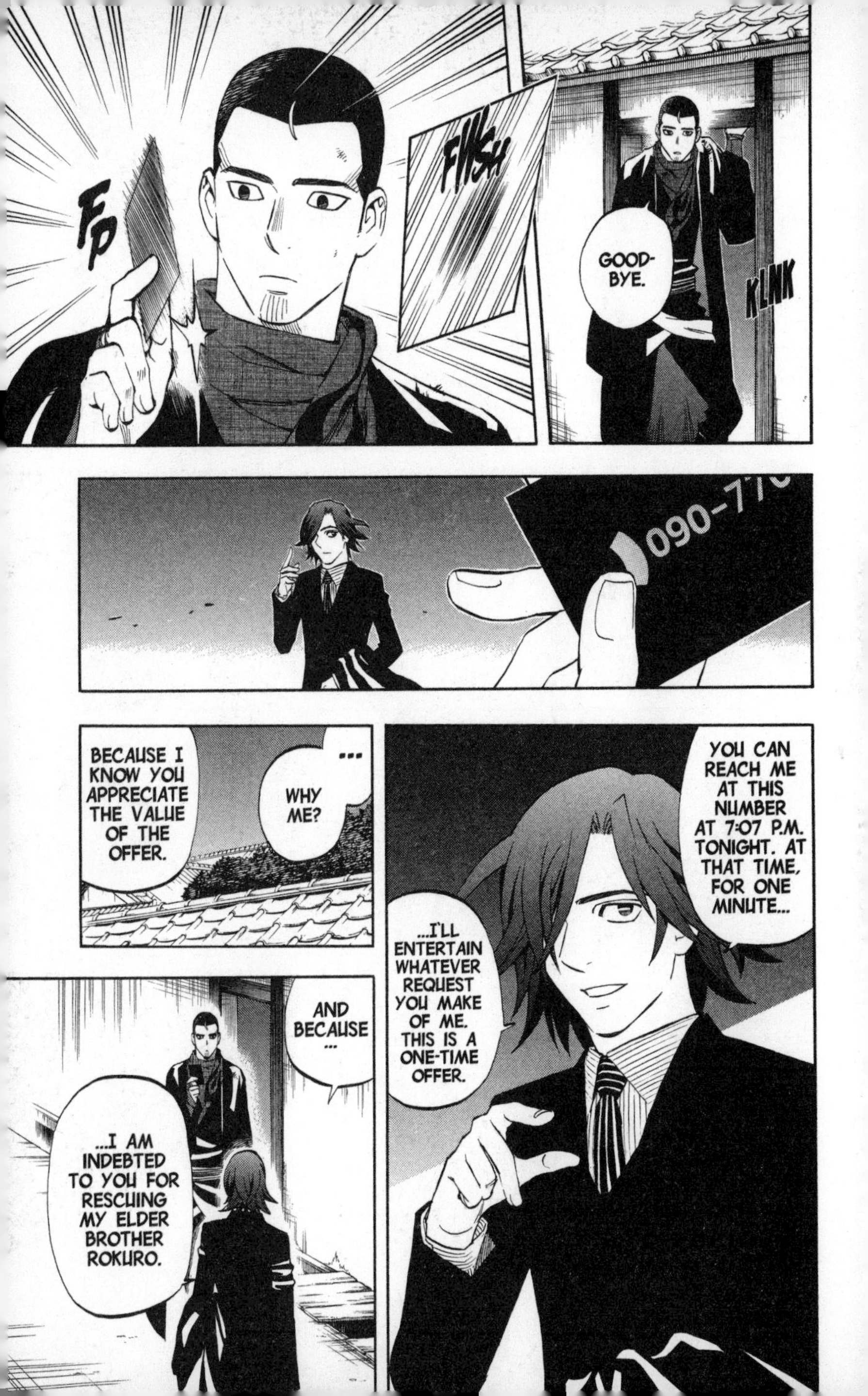
GOOD-BYE.
KLNK
FWSH
FP
090-77
YOU CAN REACH ME AT THIS NUMBER AT 7:07 P.M. TONIGHT. AT THAT TIME, FOR ONE MINUTE...
...I'LL ENTERTAIN WHATEVER REQUEST YOU MAKE OF ME. THIS IS A ONE-TIME OFFER.
...
WHY ME?
BECAUSE I KNOW YOU APPRECIATE THE VALUE OF THE OFFER.
AND BECAUSE ...
...I AM INDEBTED TO YOU FOR RESCUING MY ELDER BROTHER ROKURO.

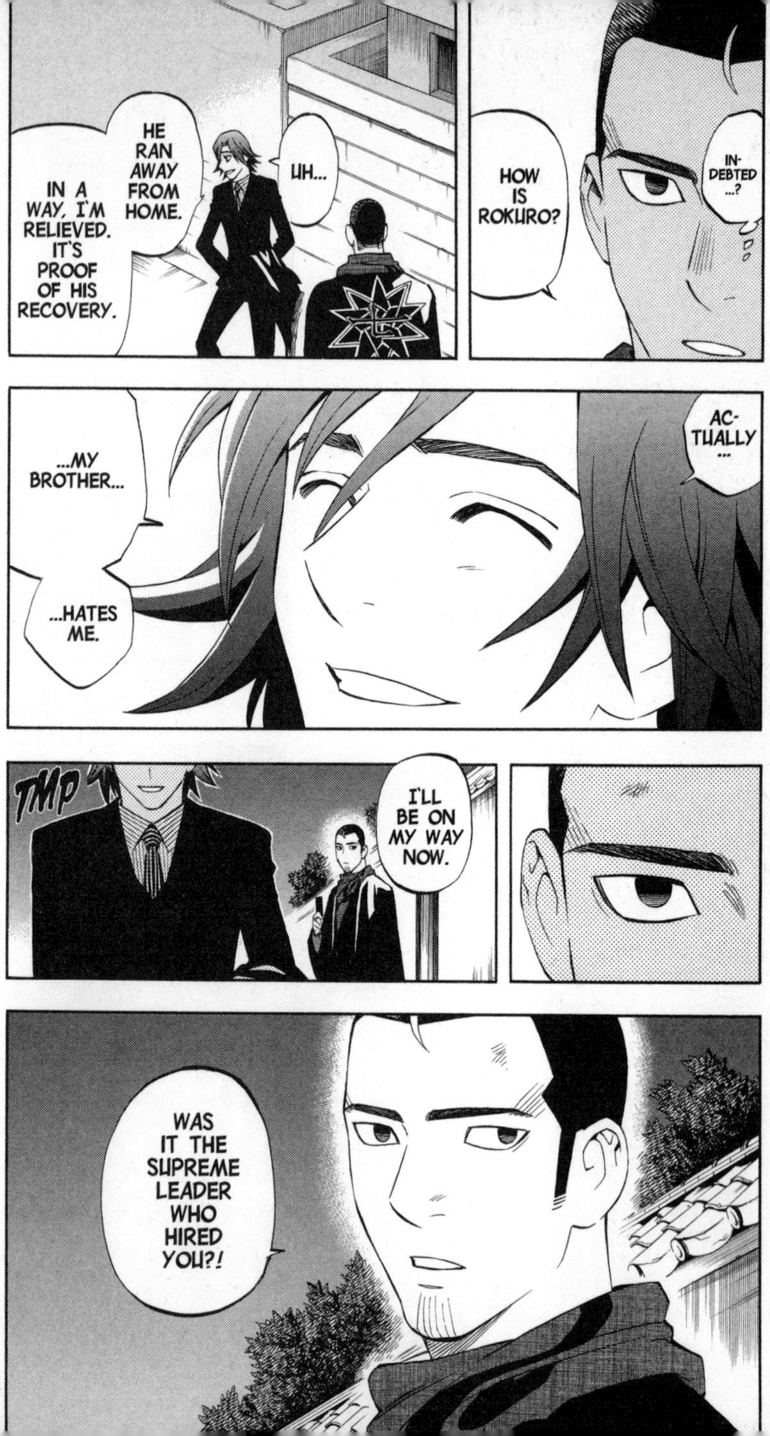
IN-DEBTED ...?
HOW IS ROKURO?
UH...
HE RAN AWAY FROM HOME.
IN A WAY, I'M RELIEVED. IT'S PROOF OF HIS RECOVERY.
ACTUALLY ...
...MY BROTHER...
...HATES ME.
I'LL BE ON MY WAY NOW.
TMP
WAS IT THE SUPREME LEADER WHO HIRED YOU?!

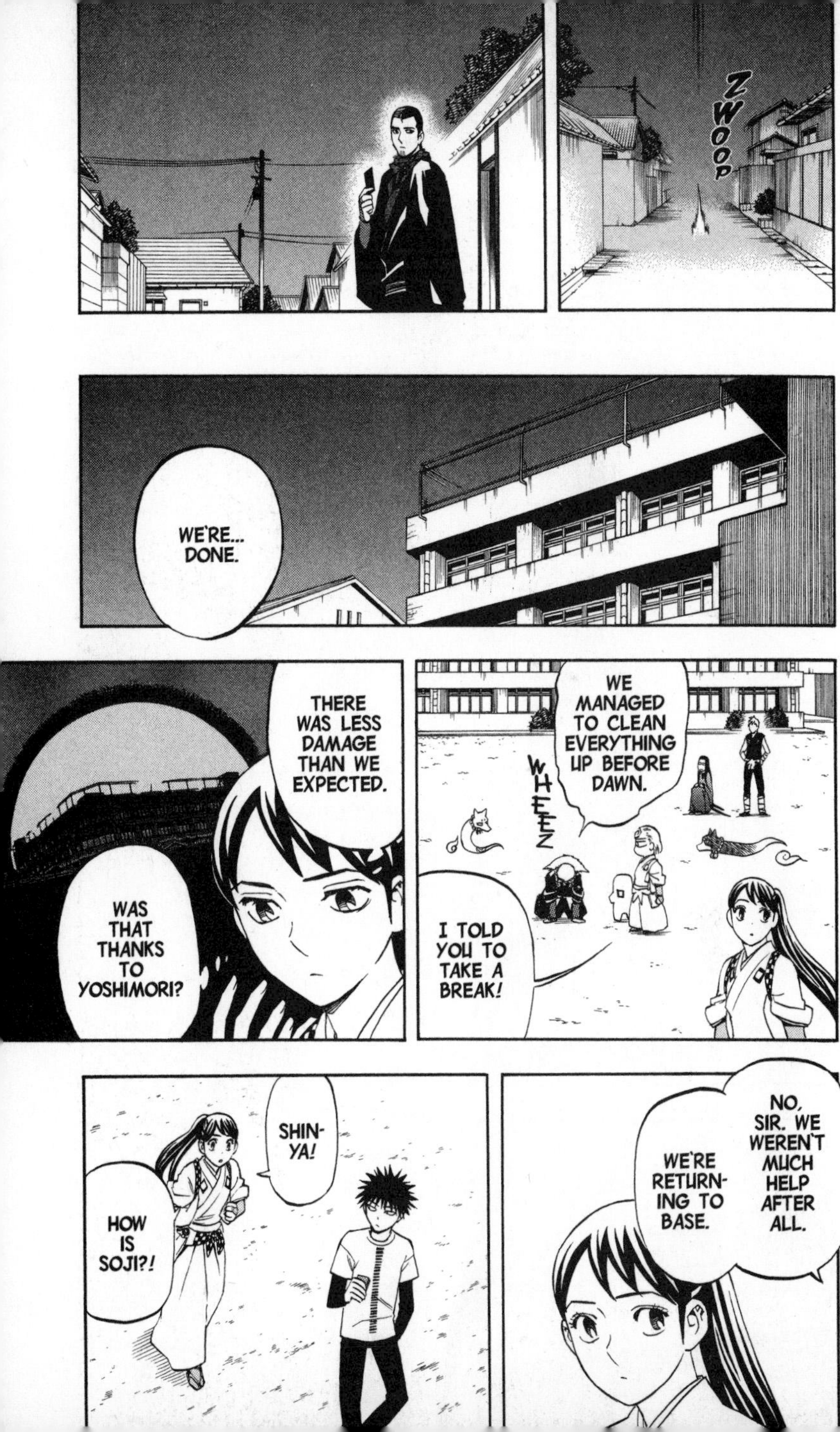
ZWOOP
WE'RE... DONE.
WE MANAGED TO CLEAN EVERYTHING UP BEFORE DAWN.
WHEEZ
I TOLD YOU TO TAKE A BREAK!
THERE WAS LESS DAMAGE THAN WE EXPECTED.
WAS THAT THANKS TO YOSHIMORI?
NO, SIR. WE WEREN'T MUCH HELP AFTER ALL.
WE'RE RETURNING TO BASE.
SHIN-YA!
HOW IS SOJI?!

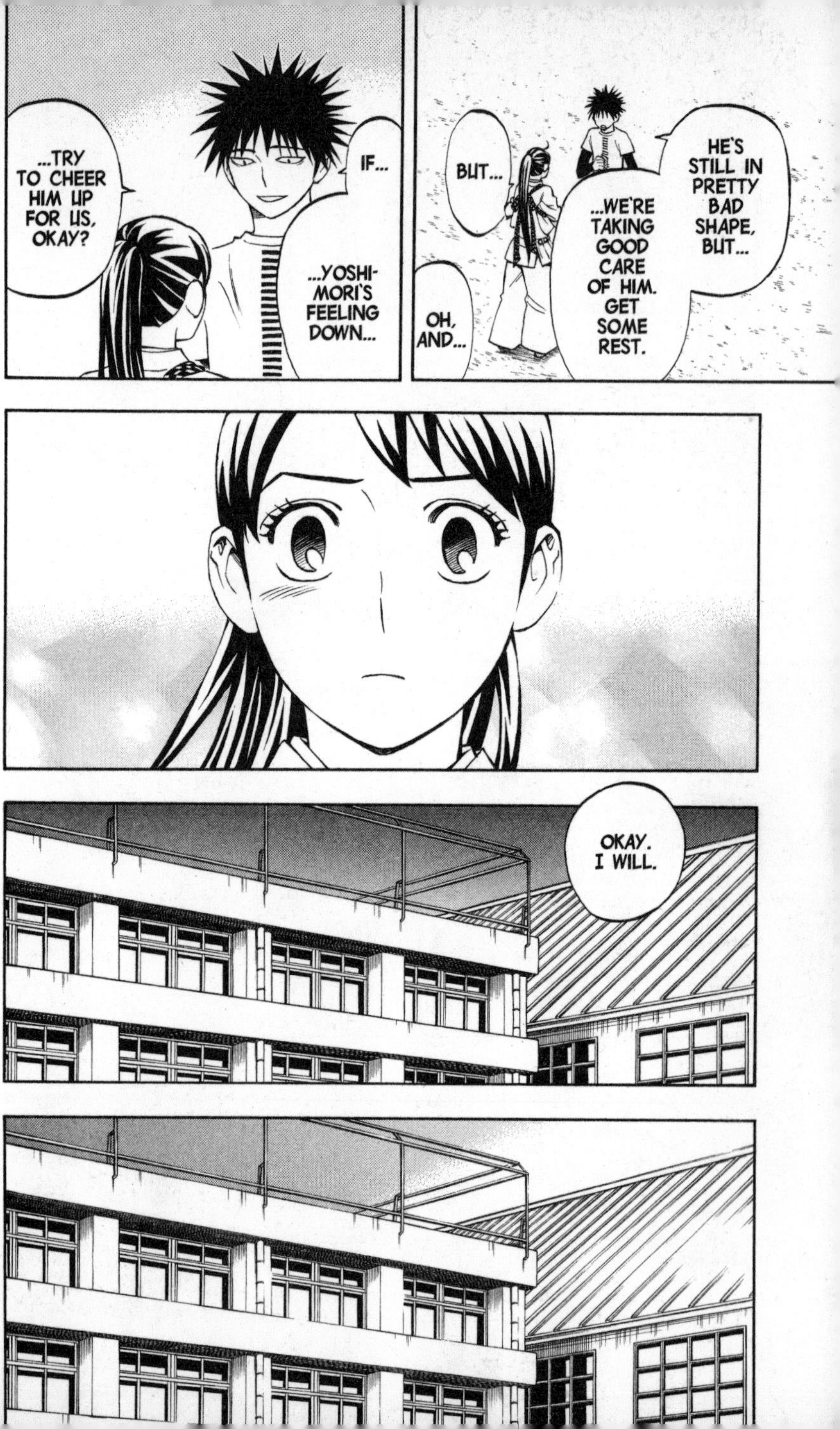
HE'S STILL IN PRETTY BAD SHAPE, BUT...
...WE'RE TAKING GOOD CARE OF HIM. GET SOME REST.
BUT...
OH, AND...
IF...
...YOSHIMORI'S FEELING DOWN...
...TRY TO CHEER HIM UP FOR US, OKAY?
OKAY. I WILL.

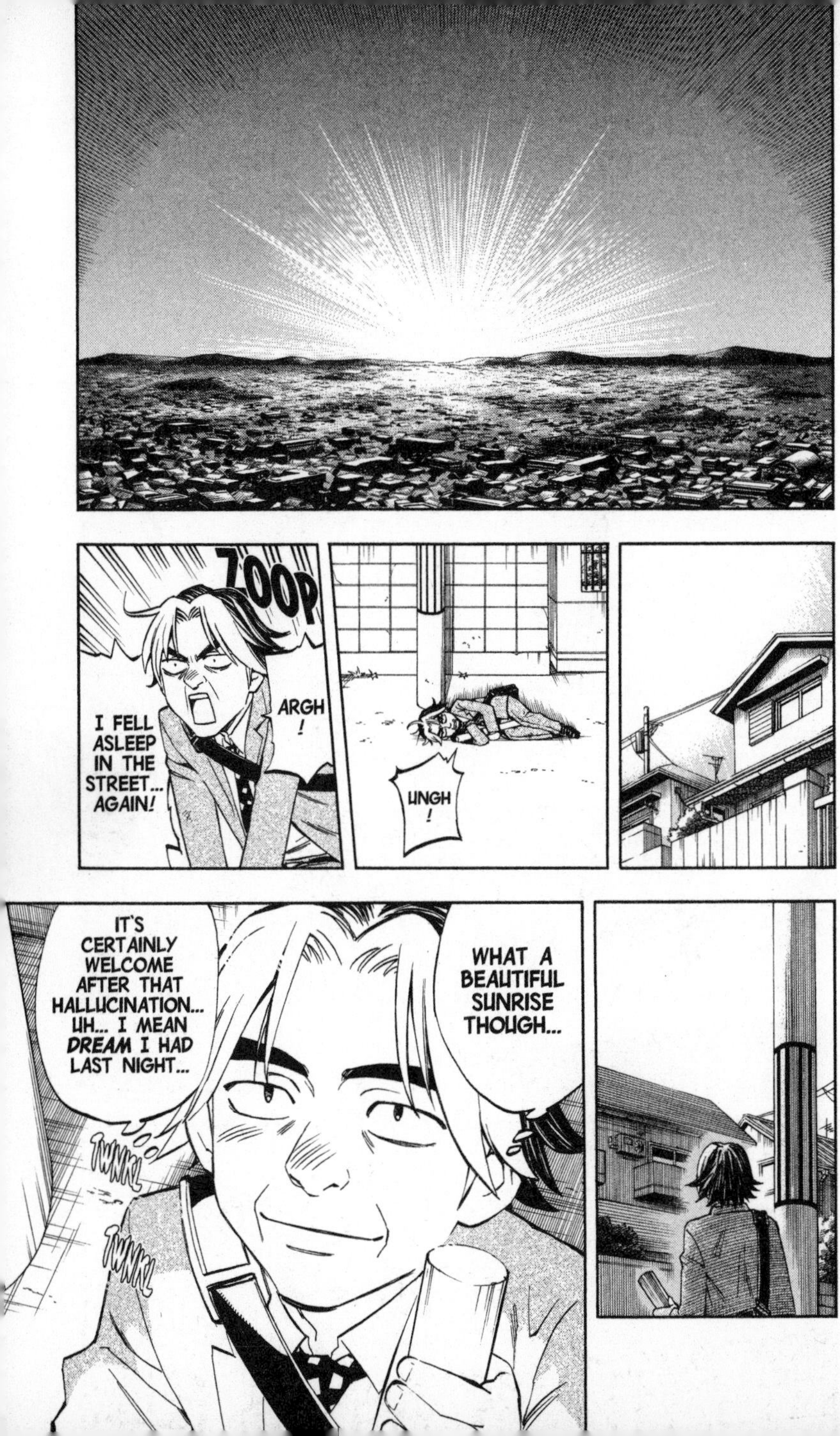
UNGH!
ZOOP
ARGH!
I FELL ASLEEP IN THE STREET... AGAIN!
WHAT A BEAUTIFUL SUNRISE THOUGH...
IT'S CERTAINLY WELCOME AFTER THAT HALLUCINATION... UH... I MEAN *DREAM* I HAD LAST NIGHT...
TWNKL
TWNKL

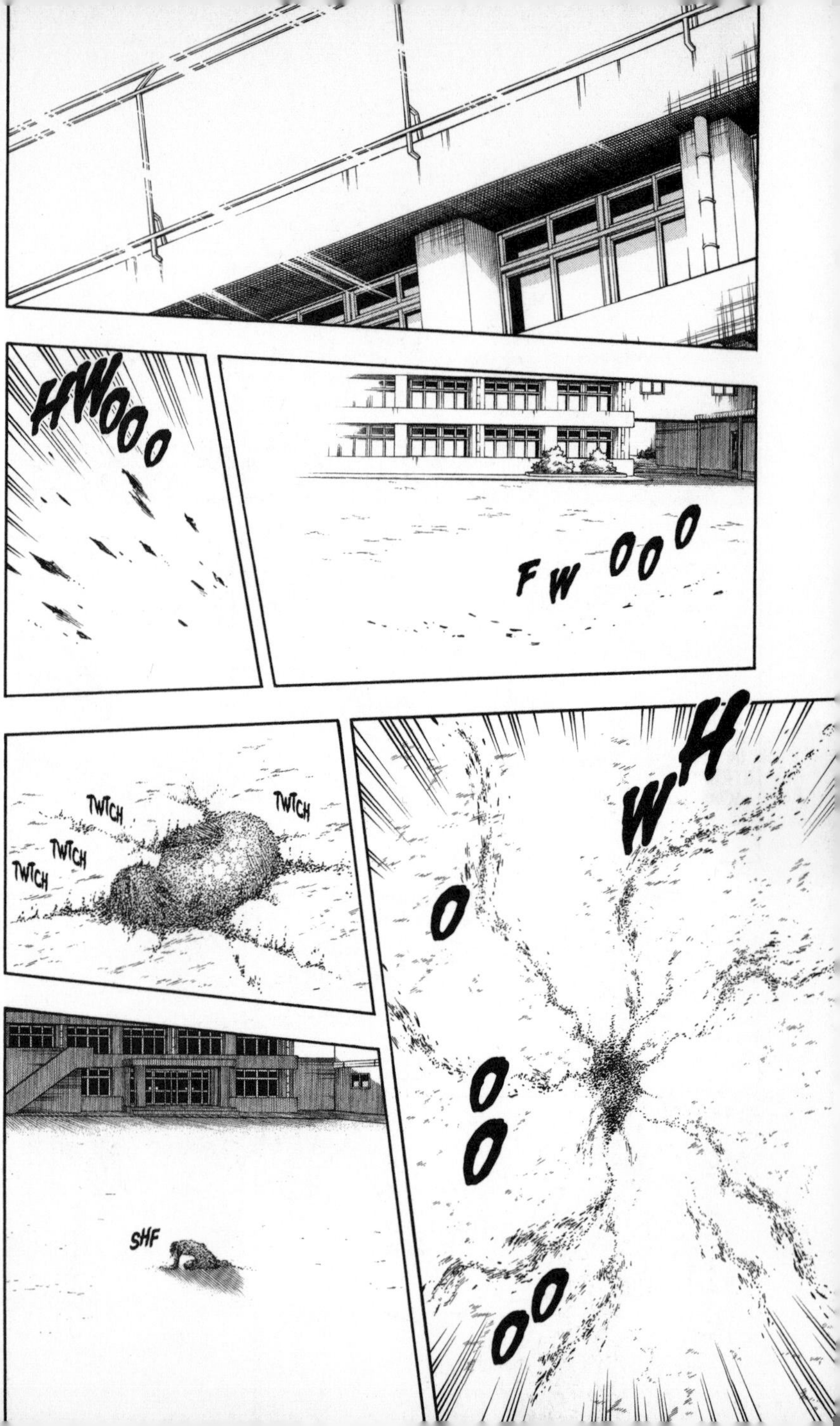
FWOOO
HWOOO
WHOOOOO
TWITCH
TWITCH
TWITCH
TWITCH
SHF

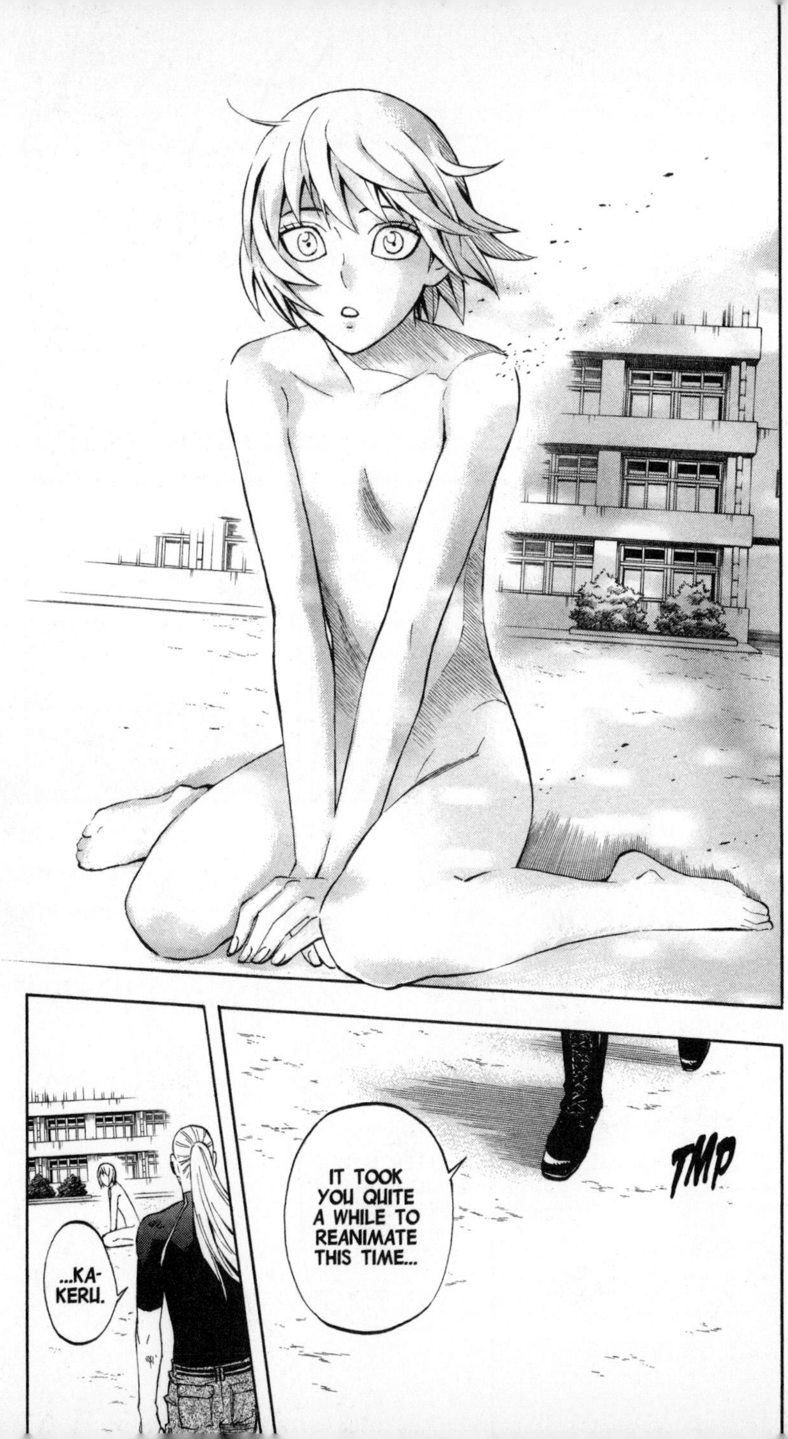
TMP
IT TOOK YOU QUITE A WHILE TO REANIMATE THIS TIME...
...KA-KERU.

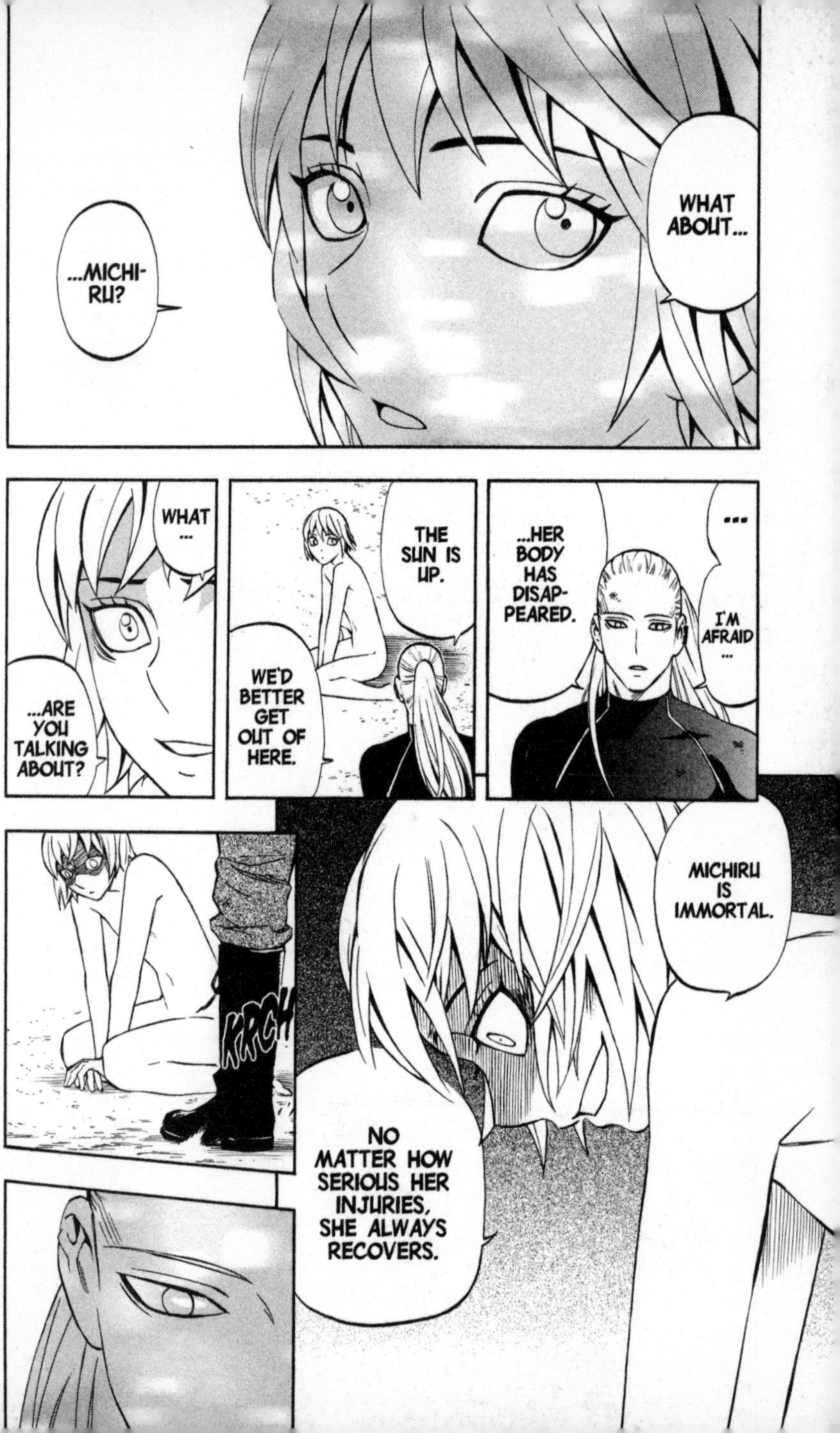
WHAT ABOUT...
...MICHIRU?
...
I'M AFRAID ...
...HER BODY HAS DISAPPEARED.
THE SUN IS UP.
WE'D BETTER GET OUT OF HERE.
WHAT ...
...ARE YOU TALKING ABOUT?
MICHIRU IS IMMORTAL.
NO MATTER HOW SERIOUS HER INJURIES, SHE ALWAYS RECOVERS.
KRCH

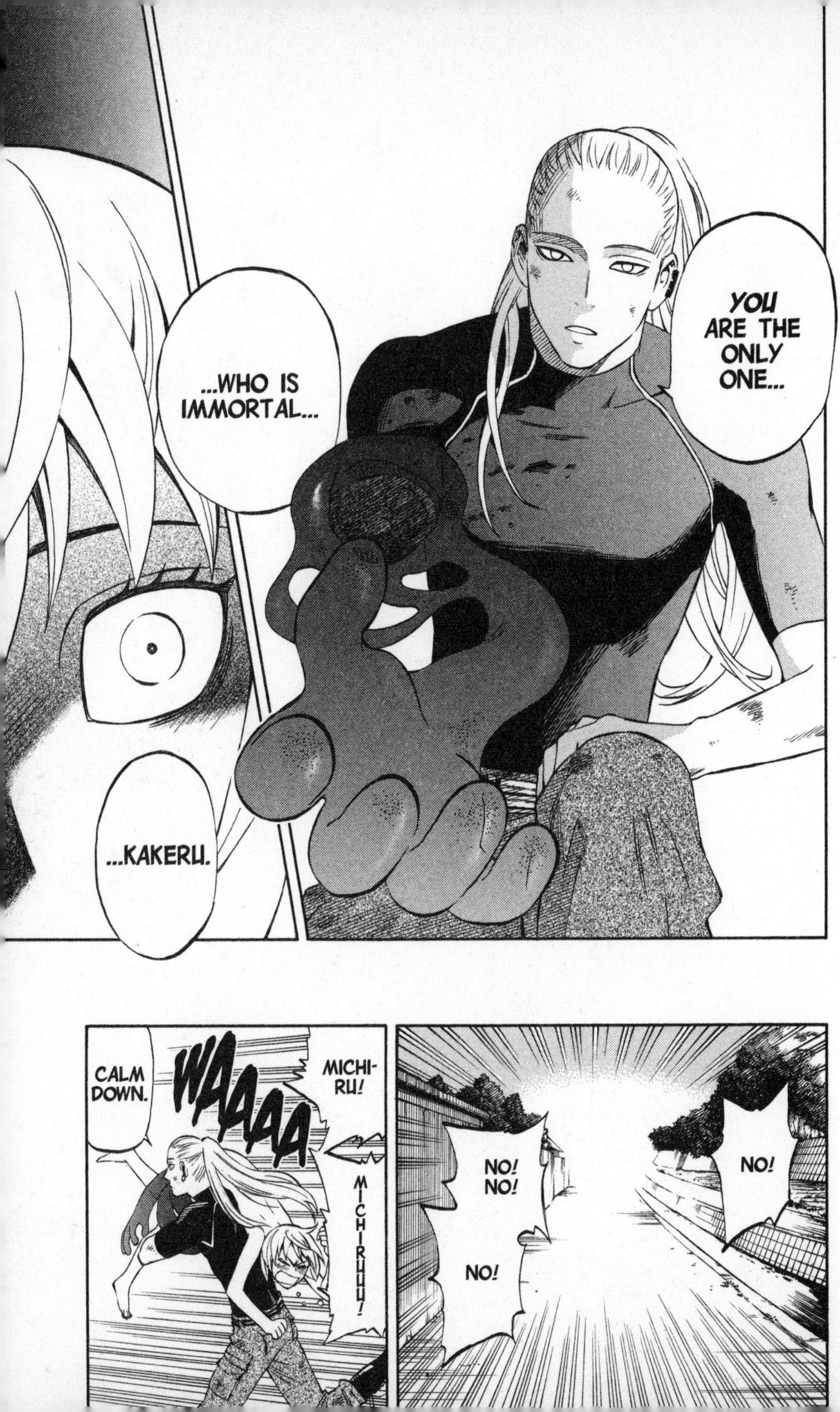
YOU ARE THE ONLY ONE...
...WHO IS IMMORTAL...
...KAKERU.
NO!
NO! NO!
NO!
MICHI-RU!
WAAAAA
CALM DOWN.
MICHIRUUU!

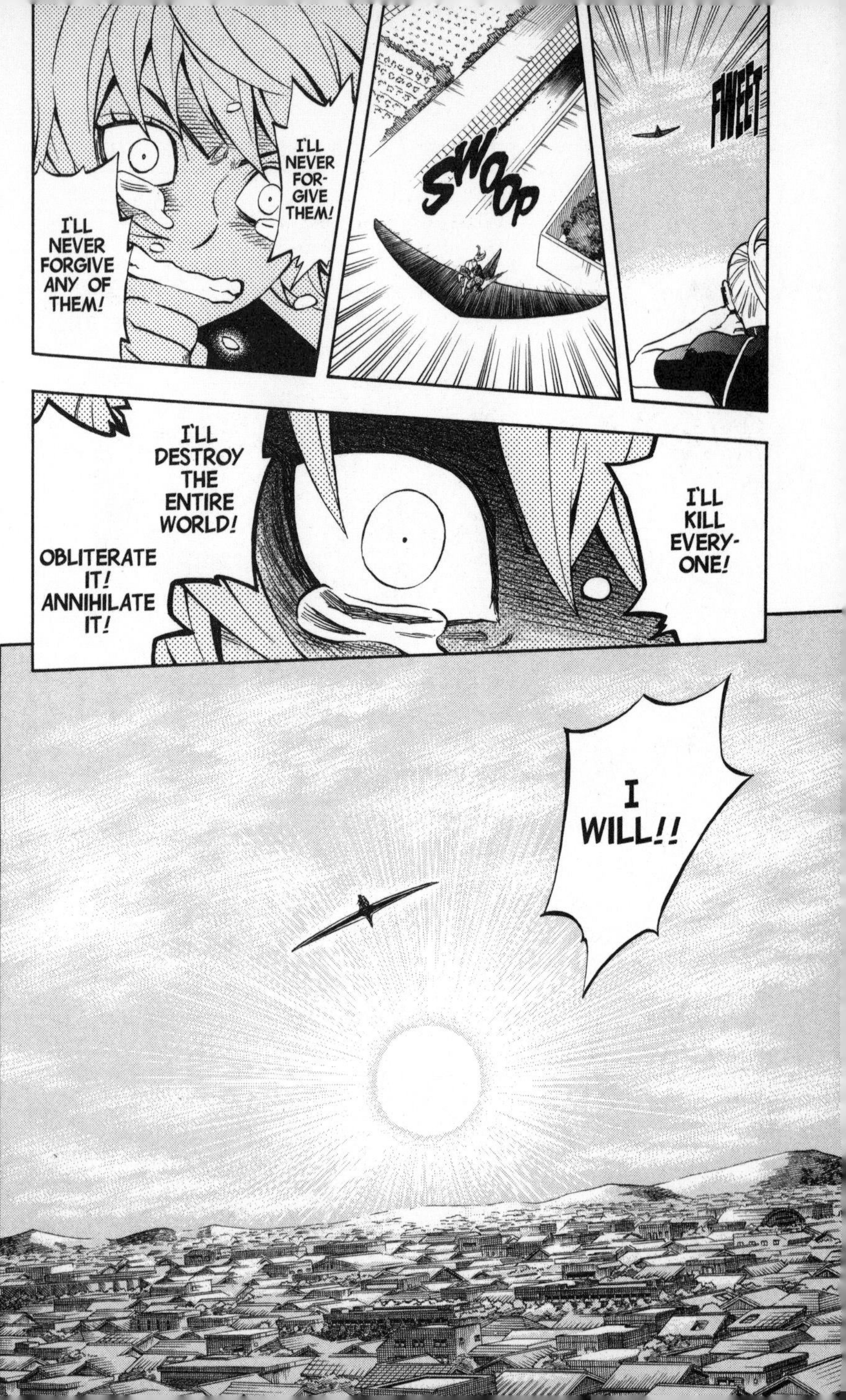
FWEET
SWOOP
I'LL NEVER FOR-GIVE THEM!
I'LL NEVER FORGIVE ANY OF THEM!
I'LL KILL EVERY-ONE!
I'LL DESTROY THE ENTIRE WORLD!
OBLITERATE IT! ANNIHILATE IT!
I WILL!!

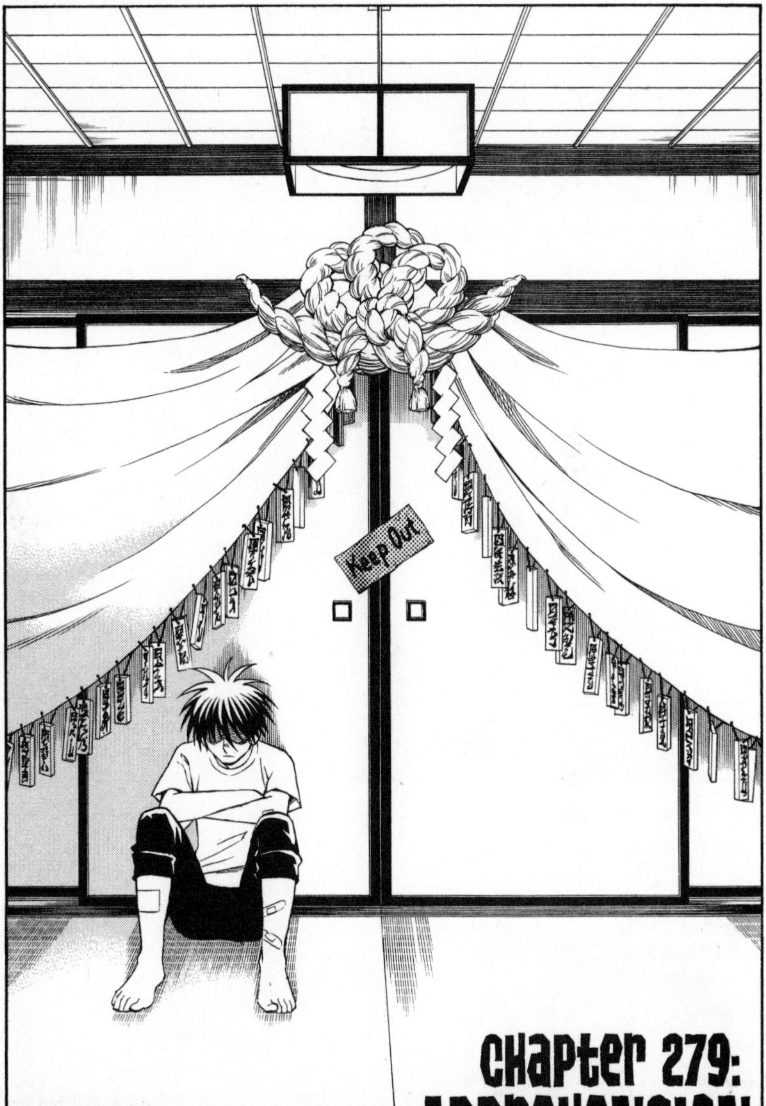
Keep Out
Chapter 279:
Apprehension

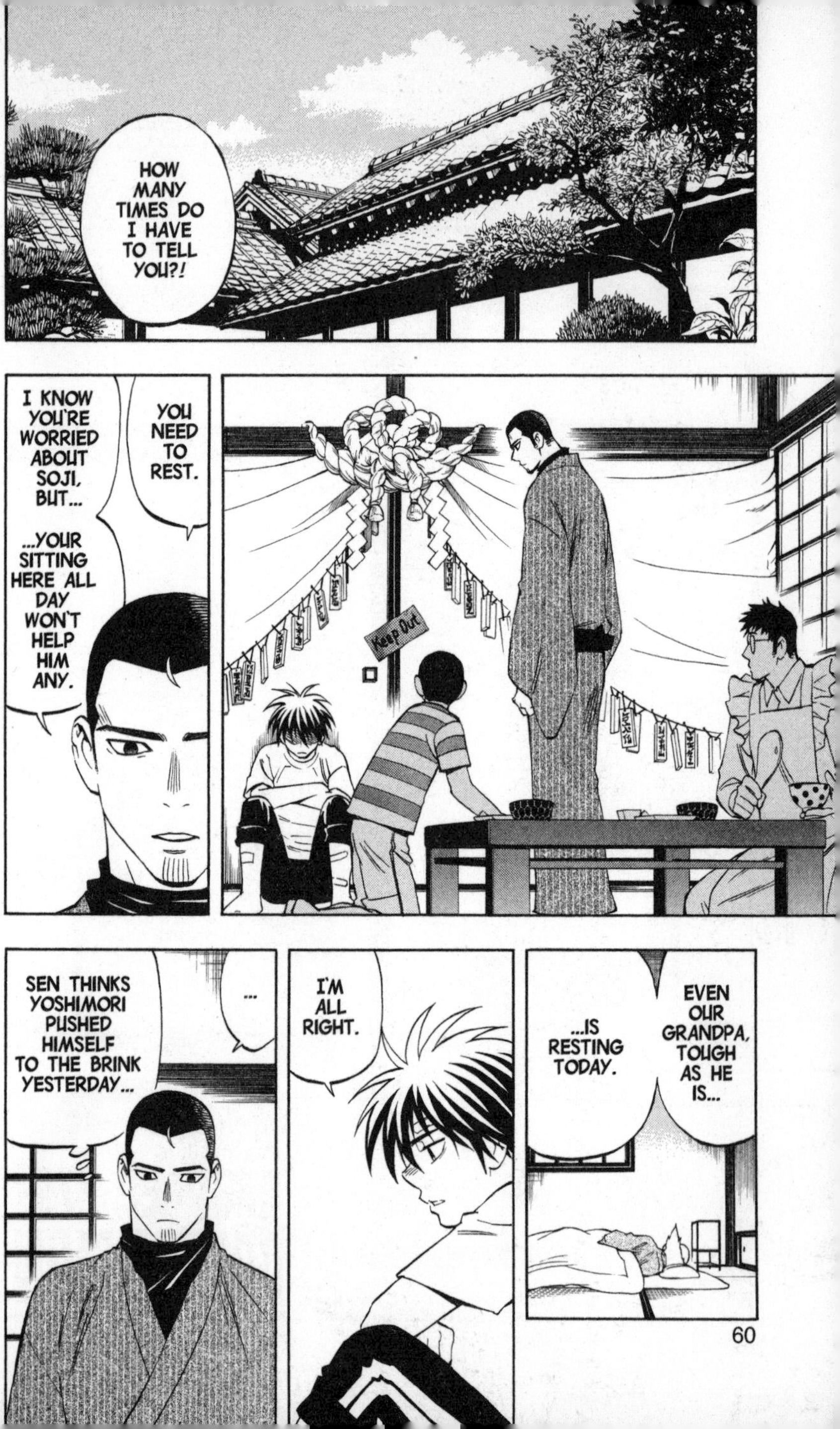
HOW MANY TIMES DO I HAVE TO TELL YOU?!
Keep Out
YOU NEED TO REST.
I KNOW YOU'RE WORRIED ABOUT SOJI, BUT...
...YOUR SITTING HERE ALL DAY WON'T HELP HIM ANY.
EVEN OUR GRANDPA, TOUGH AS HE IS...
...IS RESTING TODAY.
I'M ALL RIGHT.
...
SEN THINKS YOSHIMORI PUSHED HIMSELF TO THE BRINK YESTERDAY...

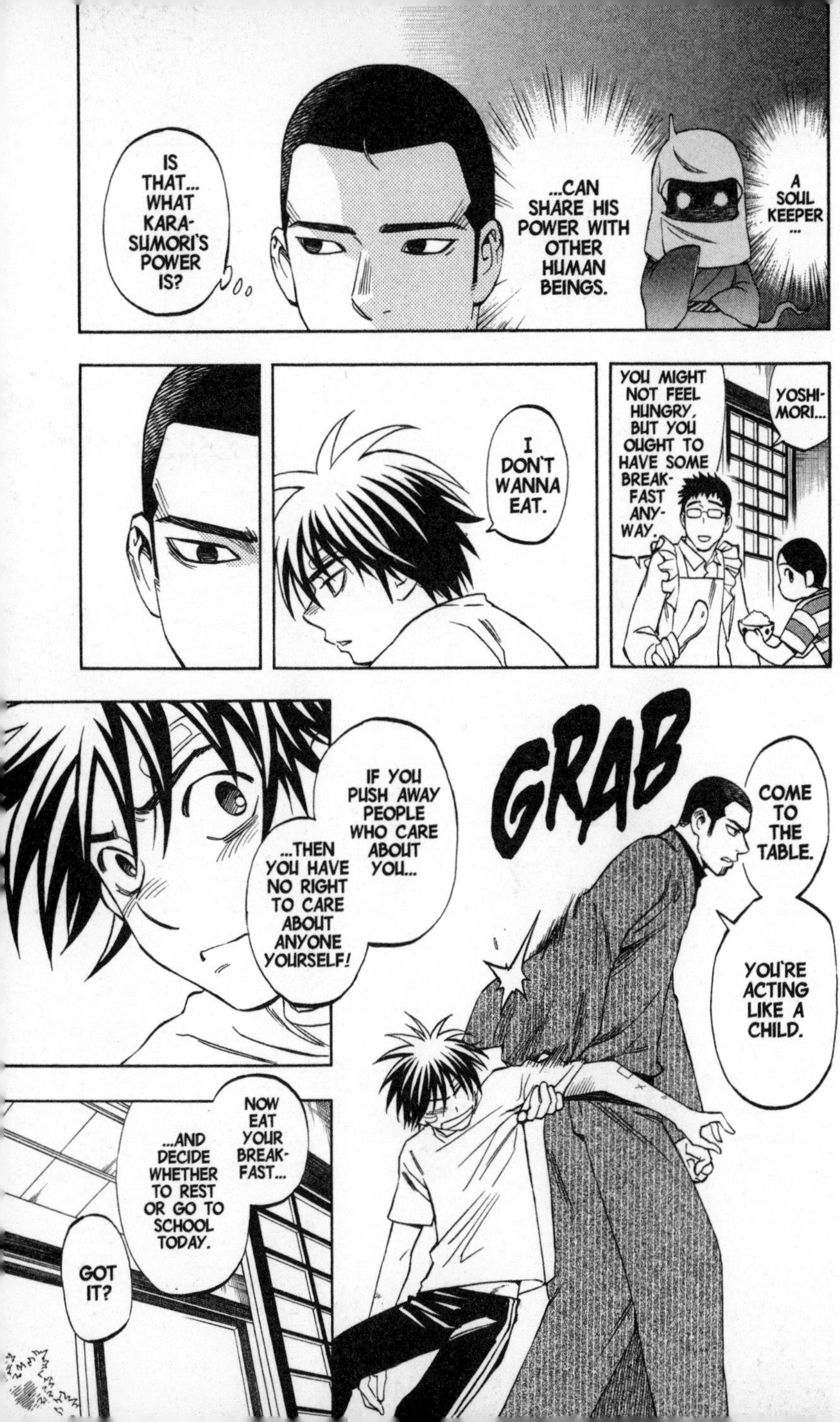
A SOUL KEEPER...
...CAN SHARE HIS POWER WITH OTHER HUMAN BEINGS.
IS THAT... WHAT KARASUMORI'S POWER IS?
YOSHIMORI...
YOU MIGHT NOT FEEL HUNGRY, BUT YOU OUGHT TO HAVE SOME BREAKFAST ANYWAY.
I DON'T WANNA EAT.
GRAB
COME TO THE TABLE.
YOU'RE ACTING LIKE A CHILD.
IF YOU PUSH AWAY PEOPLE WHO CARE ABOUT YOU...
...THEN YOU HAVE NO RIGHT TO CARE ABOUT ANYONE YOURSELF!
NOW EAT YOUR BREAKFAST...
...AND DECIDE WHETHER TO REST OR GO TO SCHOOL TODAY.
GOT IT?

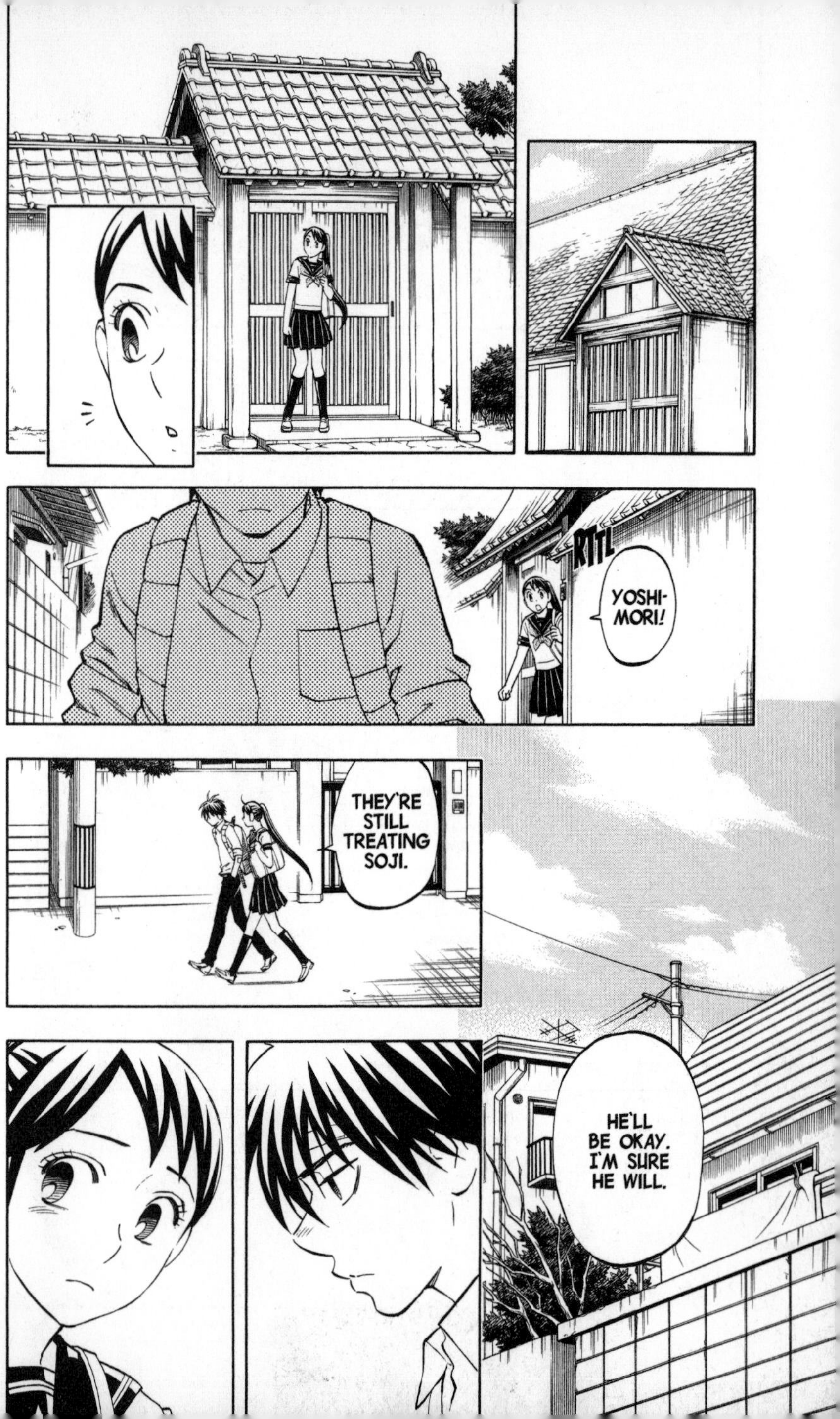
RTTL
YOSHI-MORI!
THEY'RE STILL TREATING SOJI.
HE'LL BE OKAY. I'M SURE HE WILL.

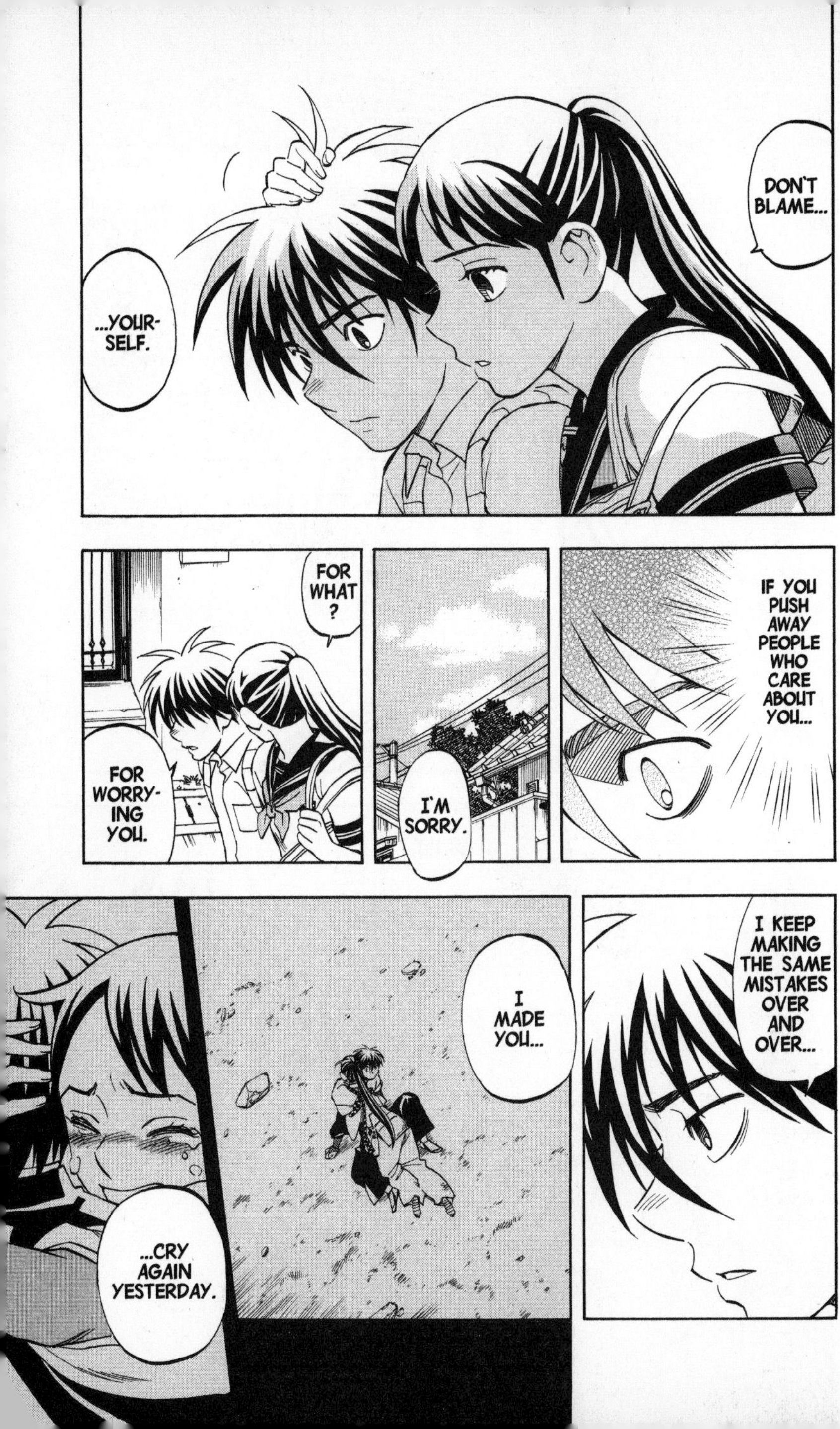
DON'T BLAME...
...YOUR-SELF.
IF YOU PUSH AWAY PEOPLE WHO CARE ABOUT YOU...
I'M SORRY.
FOR WHAT?
FOR WORRY-ING YOU.
I KEEP MAKING THE SAME MISTAKES OVER AND OVER...
I MADE YOU...
...CRY AGAIN YESTERDAY.

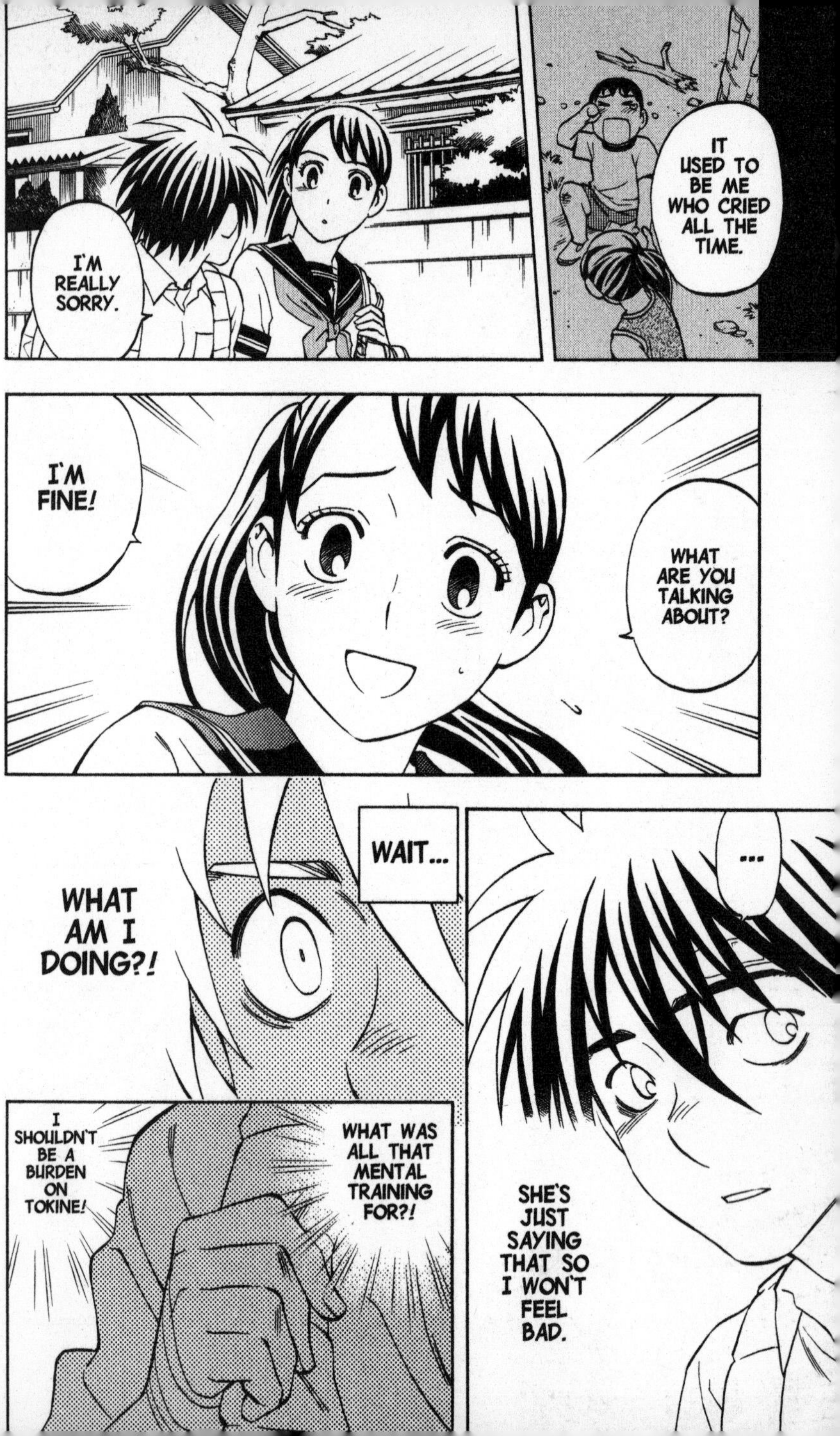
IT USED TO BE ME WHO CRIED ALL THE TIME.
I'M REALLY SORRY.
WHAT ARE YOU TALKING ABOUT?
I'M FINE!
...
SHE'S JUST SAYING THAT SO I WON'T FEEL BAD.
WAIT...
WHAT AM I DOING?!
WHAT WAS ALL THAT MENTAL TRAINING FOR?!
I SHOULDN'T BE A BURDEN ON TOKINE!

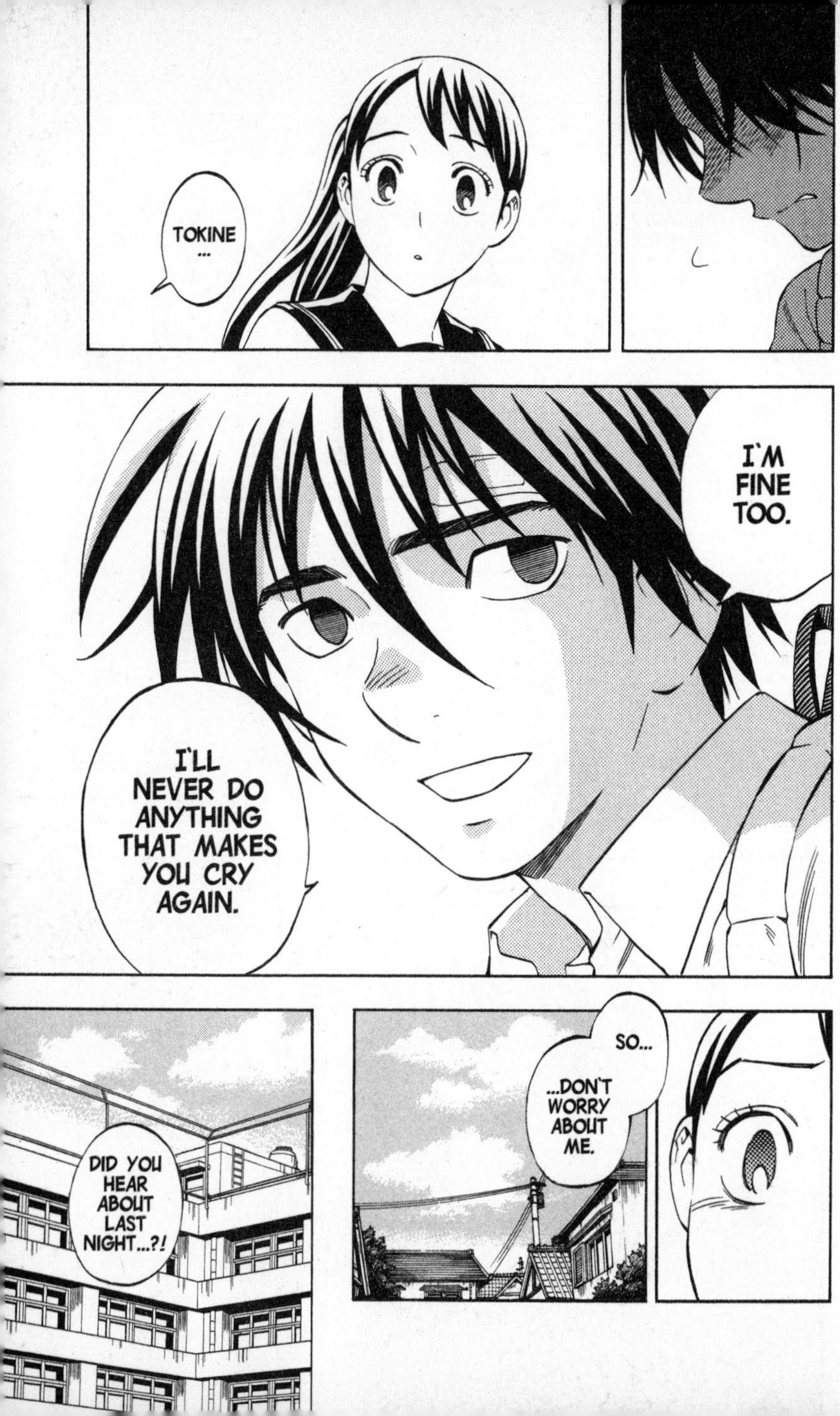
TOKINE ...
I'M FINE TOO.
I'LL NEVER DO ANYTHING THAT MAKES YOU CRY AGAIN.
SO...
...DON'T WORRY ABOUT ME.
DID YOU HEAR ABOUT LAST NIGHT...?!

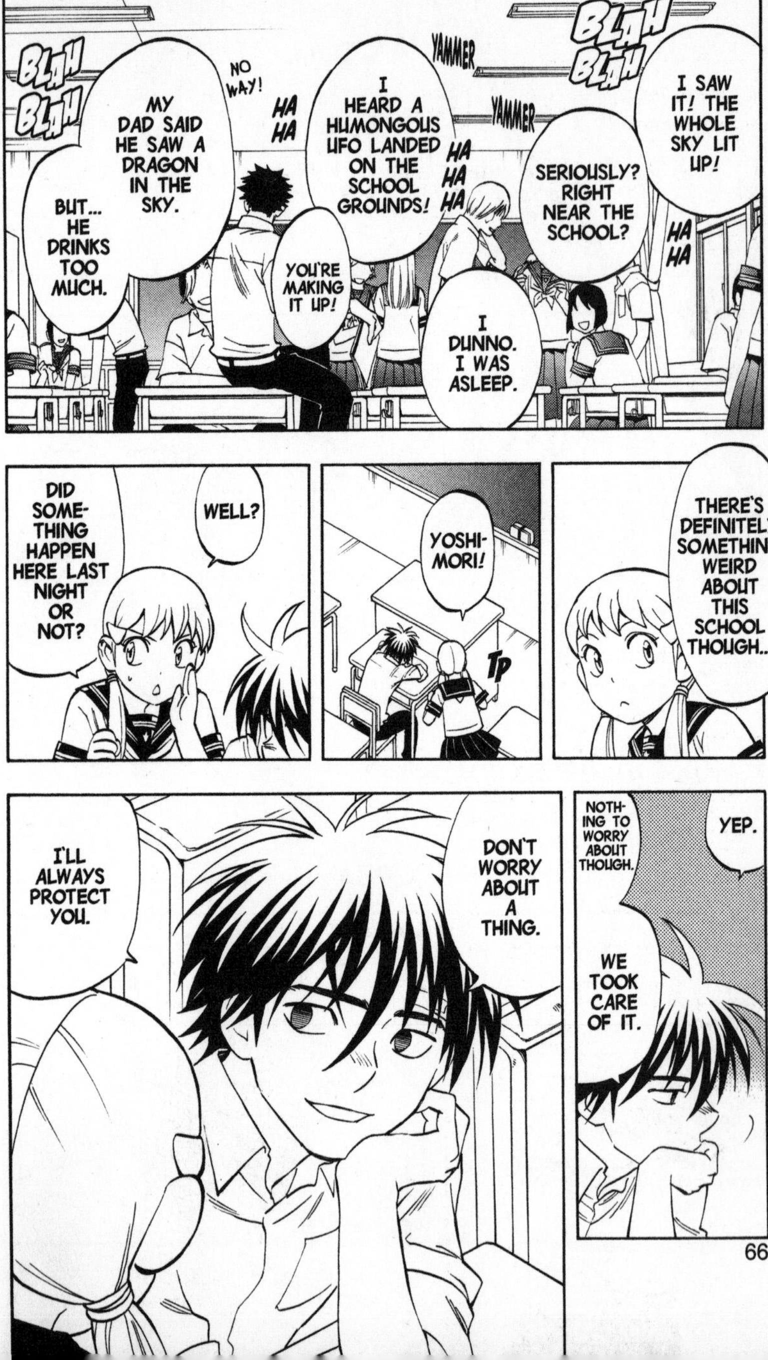
BLAH BLAH
I SAW IT! THE WHOLE SKY LIT UP!
SERIOUSLY? RIGHT NEAR THE SCHOOL?
HA HA
YAMMER
YAMMER
I HEARD A HUMONGOUS UFO LANDED ON THE SCHOOL GROUNDS!
HA HA HA
I DUNNO. I WAS ASLEEP.
YOU'RE MAKING IT UP!
HA HA
NO WAY!
MY DAD SAID HE SAW A DRAGON IN THE SKY.
BUT... HE DRINKS TOO MUCH.
BLAH BLAH
THERE'S DEFINITELY SOMETHING WEIRD ABOUT THIS SCHOOL THOUGH...
YOSHIMORI!
TP
WELL?
DID SOMETHING HAPPEN HERE LAST NIGHT OR NOT?
YEP.
NOTHING TO WORRY ABOUT THOUGH.
WE TOOK CARE OF IT.
DON'T WORRY ABOUT A THING.
I'LL ALWAYS PROTECT YOU.

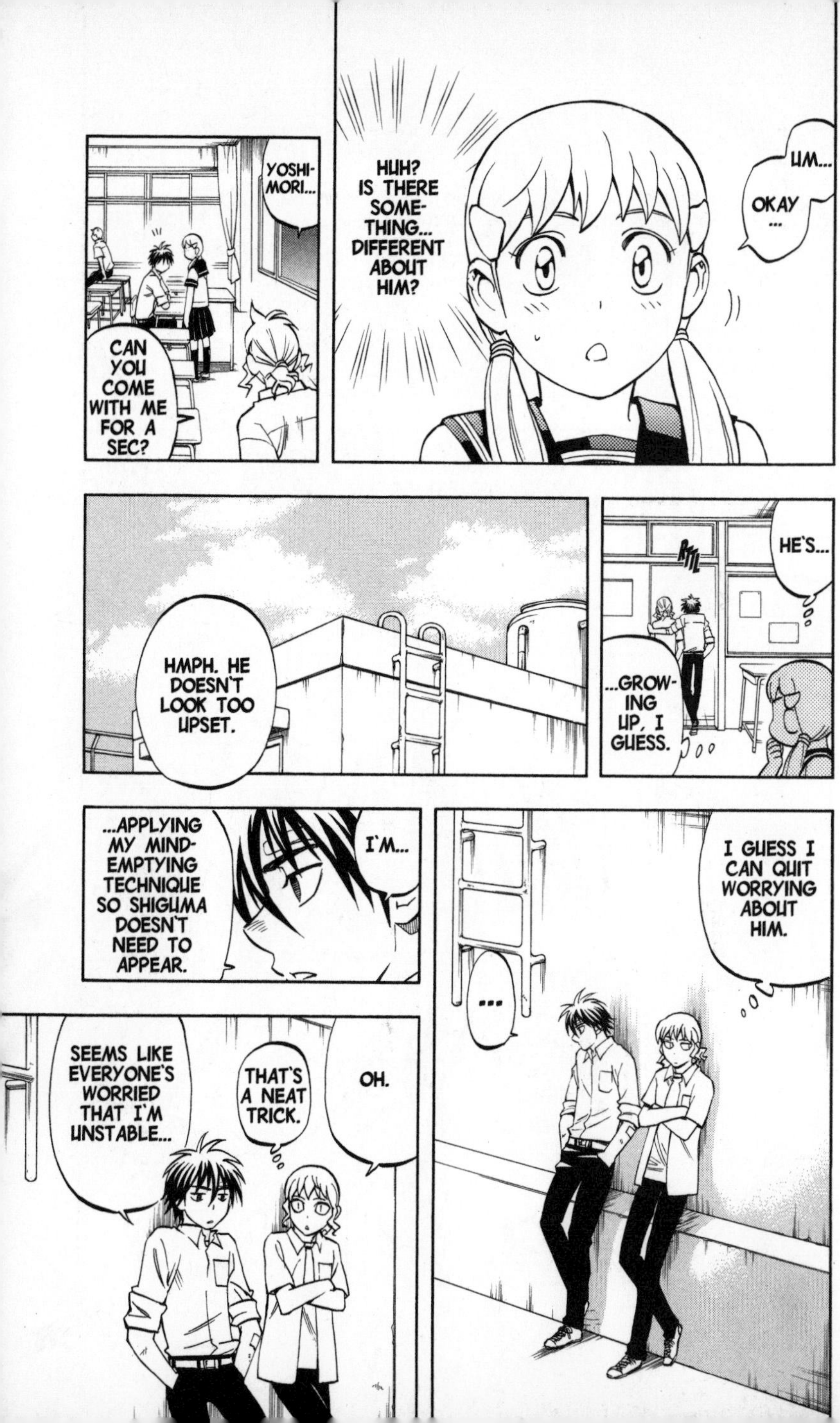
UM... OKAY...
HUH? IS THERE SOMETHING... DIFFERENT ABOUT HIM?
YOSHIMORI...
CAN YOU COME WITH ME FOR A SEC?
HE'S...
...GROWING UP, I GUESS.
HMPH. HE DOESN'T LOOK TOO UPSET.
I GUESS I CAN QUIT WORRYING ABOUT HIM.
...
I'M...
...APPLYING MY MIND-EMPTYING TECHNIQUE SO SHIGUMA DOESN'T NEED TO APPEAR.
OH.
THAT'S A NEAT TRICK.
SEEMS LIKE EVERYONE'S WORRIED THAT I'M UNSTABLE...

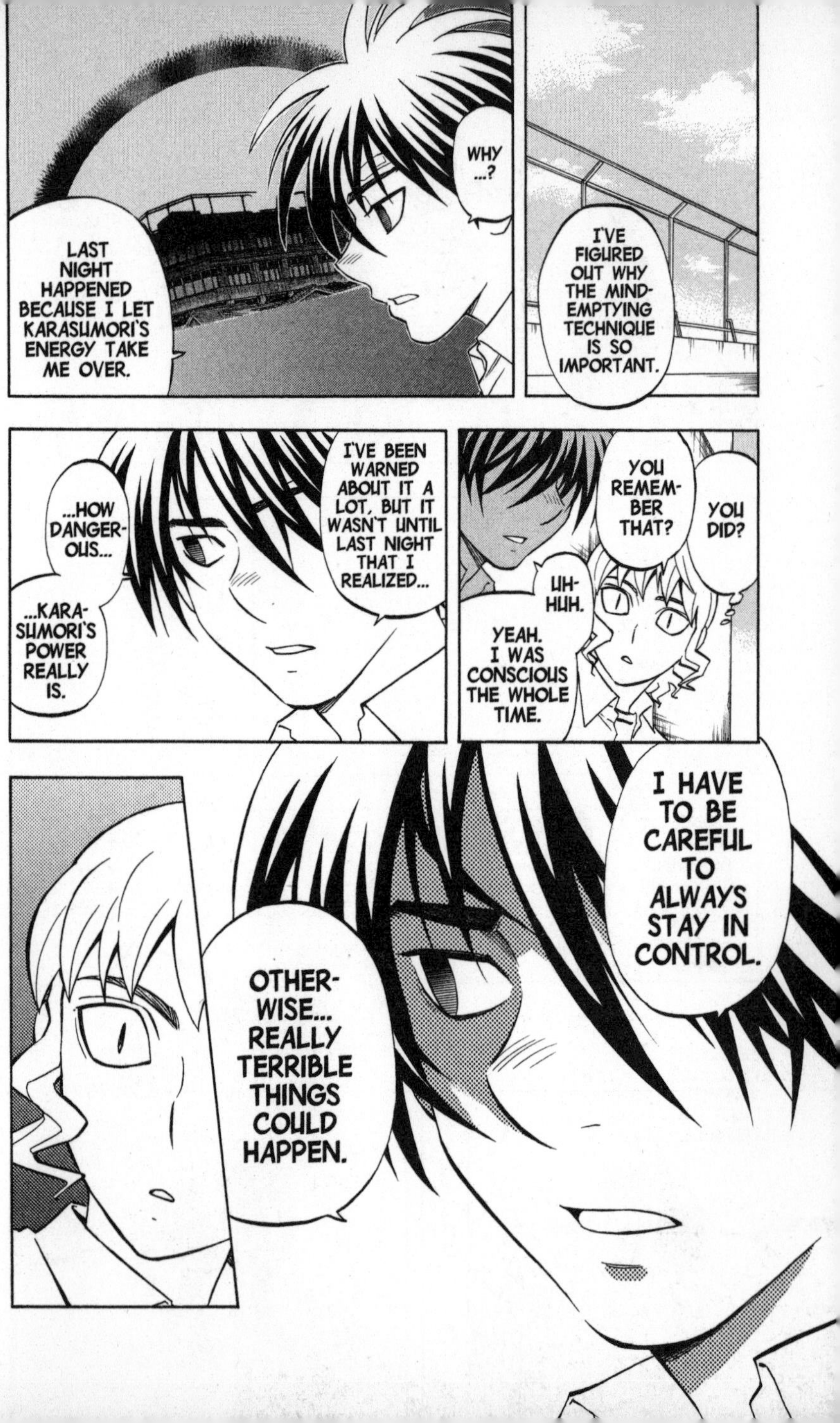
I'VE FIGURED OUT WHY THE MIND-EMPTYING TECHNIQUE IS SO IMPORTANT.
WHY ...?
LAST NIGHT HAPPENED BECAUSE I LET KARASUMORI'S ENERGY TAKE ME OVER.
YOU DID?
YOU REMEMBER THAT?
UH-HUH.
YEAH. I WAS CONSCIOUS THE WHOLE TIME.
I'VE BEEN WARNED ABOUT IT A LOT, BUT IT WASN'T UNTIL LAST NIGHT THAT I REALIZED...
...HOW DANGEROUS...
...KARASUMORI'S POWER REALLY IS.
I HAVE TO BE CAREFUL TO ALWAYS STAY IN CONTROL.
OTHERWISE... REALLY TERRIBLE THINGS COULD HAPPEN.

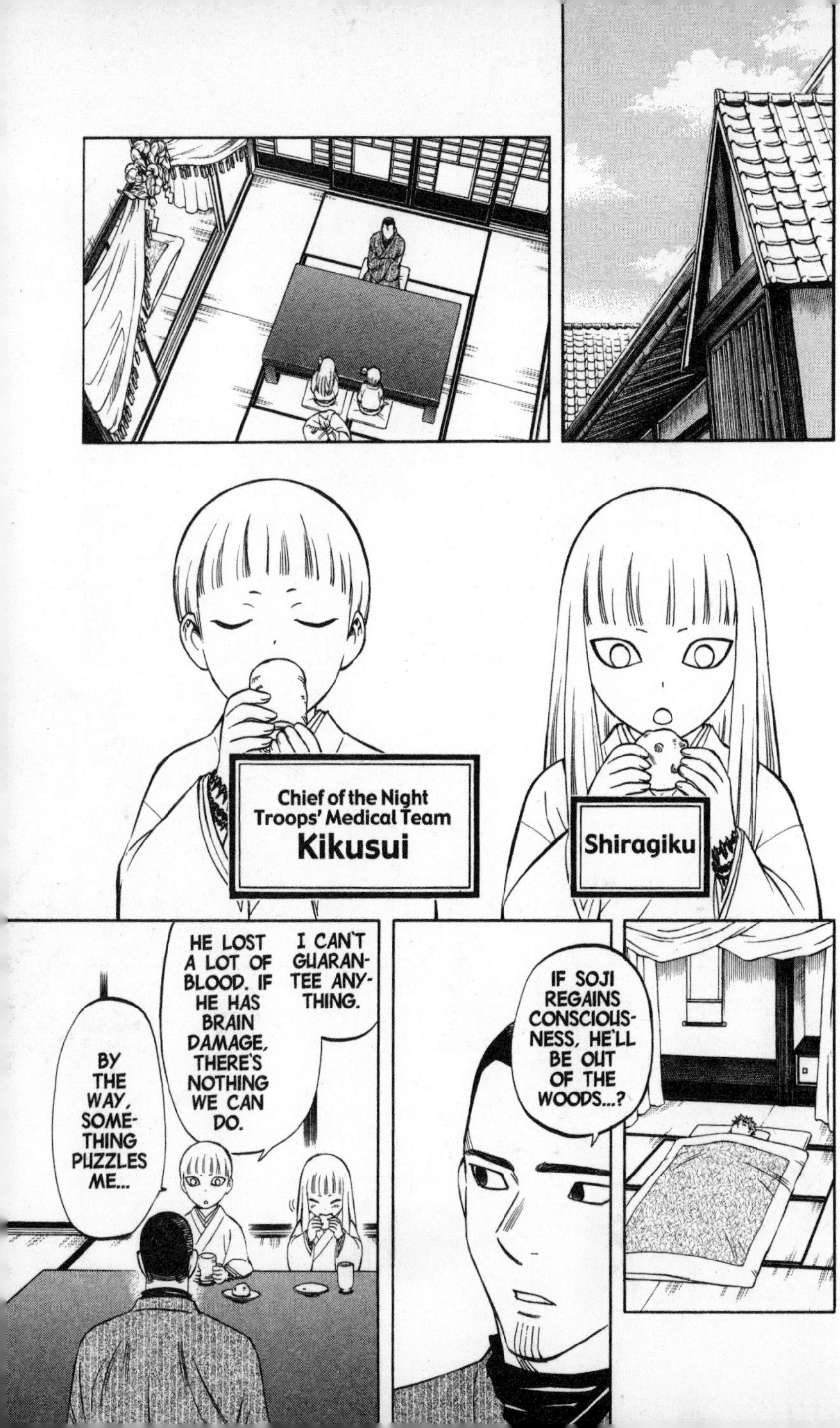
Shiragiku
Chief of the Night Troops' Medical Team Kikusui
IF SOJI REGAINS CONSCIOUSNESS, HE'LL BE OUT OF THE WOODS...?
I CAN'T GUARANTEE ANYTHING.
HE LOST A LOT OF BLOOD. IF HE HAS BRAIN DAMAGE, THERE'S NOTHING WE CAN DO.
BY THE WAY, SOMETHING PUZZLES ME...

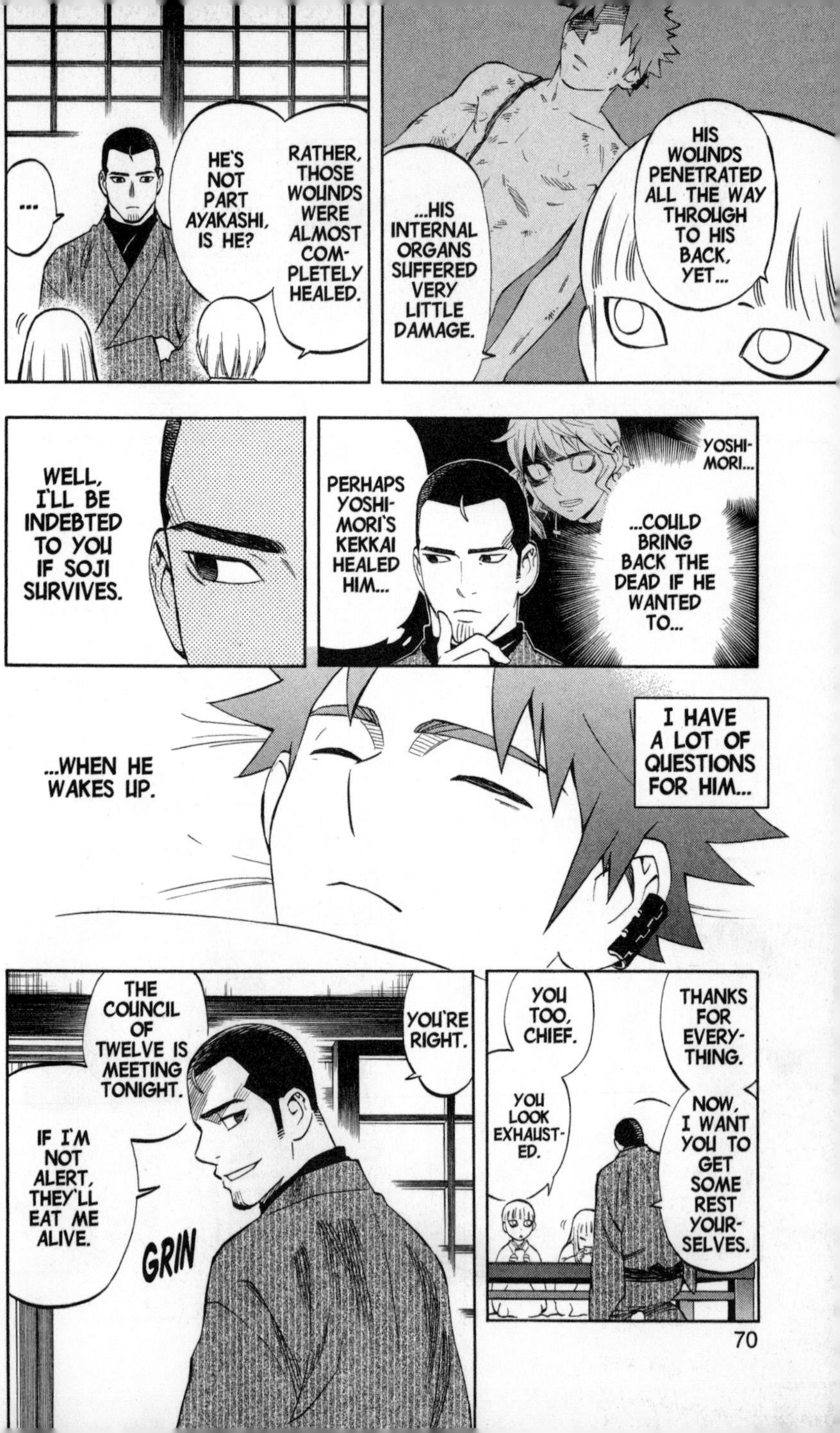
HIS WOUNDS PENETRATED ALL THE WAY THROUGH TO HIS BACK, YET...
...HIS INTERNAL ORGANS SUFFERED VERY LITTLE DAMAGE.
RATHER, THOSE WOUNDS WERE ALMOST COMPLETELY HEALED.
HE'S NOT PART AYAKASHI, IS HE?
...
YOSHIMORI...
...COULD BRING BACK THE DEAD IF HE WANTED TO...
PERHAPS YOSHIMORI'S KEKKAI HEALED HIM...
WELL, I'LL BE INDEBTED TO YOU IF SOJI SURVIVES.
I HAVE A LOT OF QUESTIONS FOR HIM...
...WHEN HE WAKES UP.
THANKS FOR EVERYTHING.
NOW, I WANT YOU TO GET SOME REST YOURSELVES.
YOU TOO, CHIEF.
YOU LOOK EXHAUSTED.
YOU'RE RIGHT.
THE COUNCIL OF TWELVE IS MEETING TONIGHT.
IF I'M NOT ALERT, THEY'LL EAT ME ALIVE.
GRIN

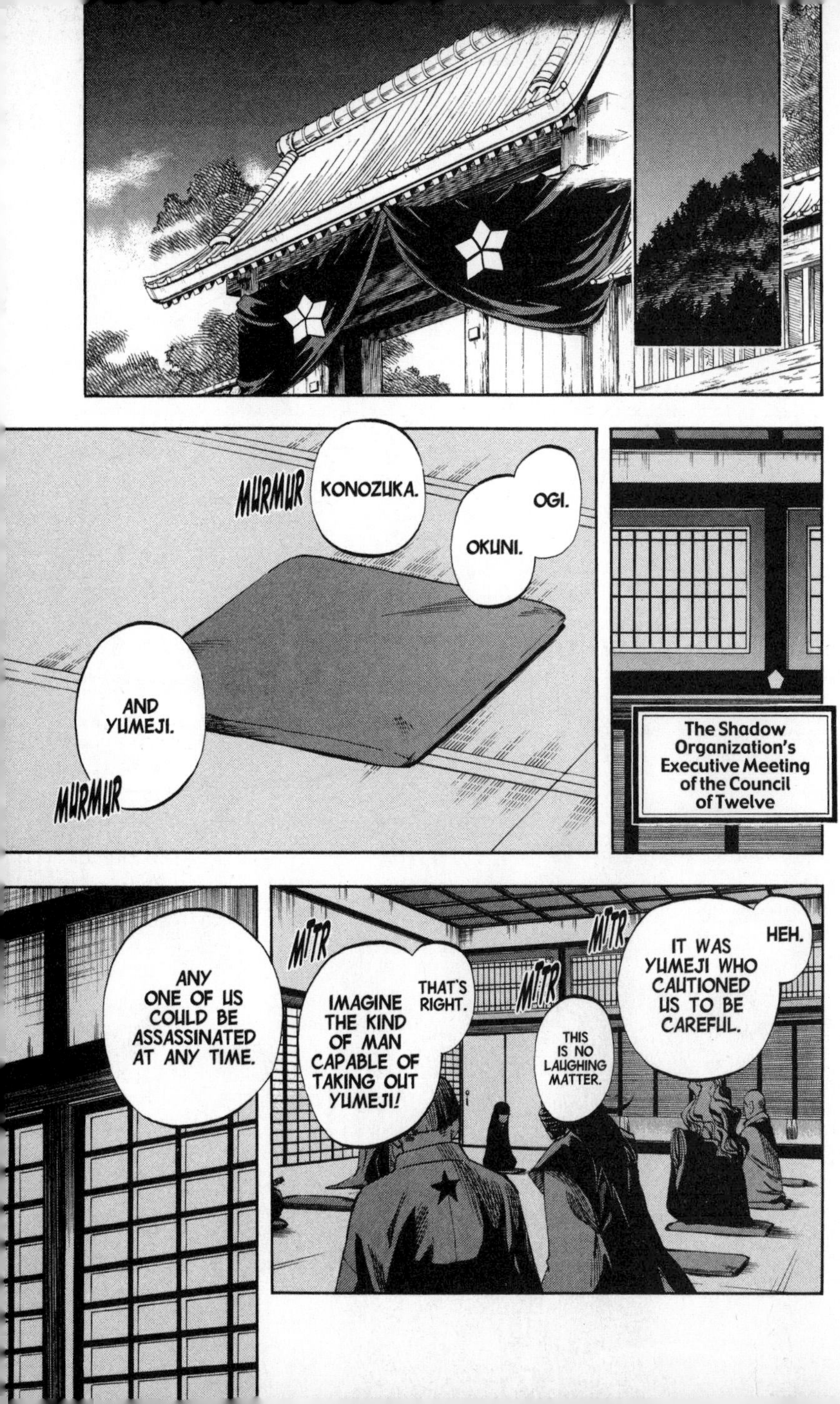
The Shadow Organization's Executive Meeting of the Council of Twelve
OGI.
KONOZUKA.
MURMUR
OKUNI.
AND YUMEJI.
MURMUR
HEH.
IT WAS YUMEJI WHO CAUTIONED US TO BE CAREFUL.
MITR
MITR
THIS IS NO LAUGHING MATTER.
THAT'S RIGHT.
IMAGINE THE KIND OF MAN CAPABLE OF TAKING OUT YUMEJI!
MITR
ANY ONE OF US COULD BE ASSASSINATED AT ANY TIME.

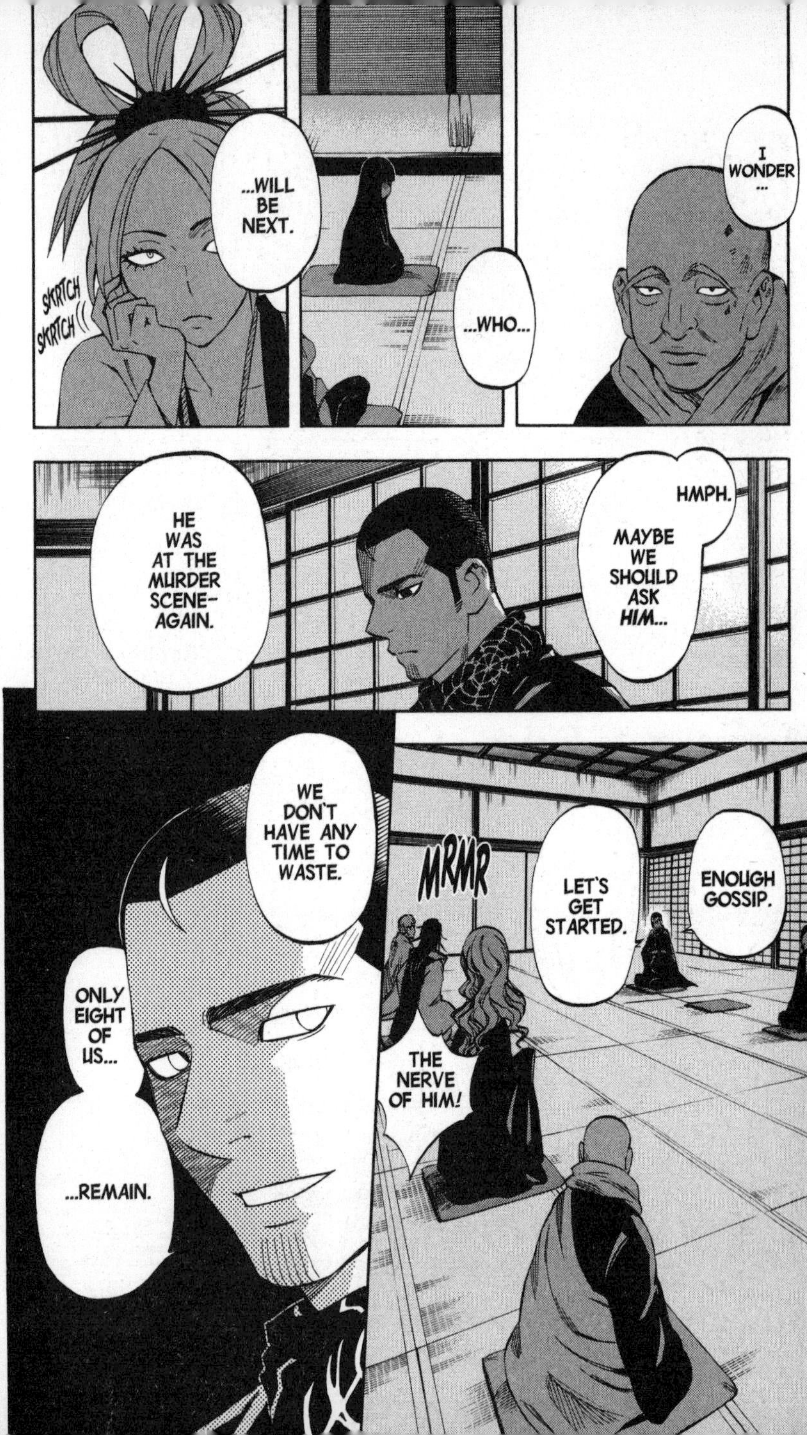
I WONDER...
...WHO...
...WILL BE NEXT.
SKRTCH SKRTCH
HMPH.
MAYBE WE SHOULD ASK HIM...
HE WAS AT THE MURDER SCENE-AGAIN.
ENOUGH GOSSIP.
LET'S GET STARTED.
MRMR
THE NERVE OF HIM!
WE DON'T HAVE ANY TIME TO WASTE.
ONLY EIGHT OF US...
...REMAIN.

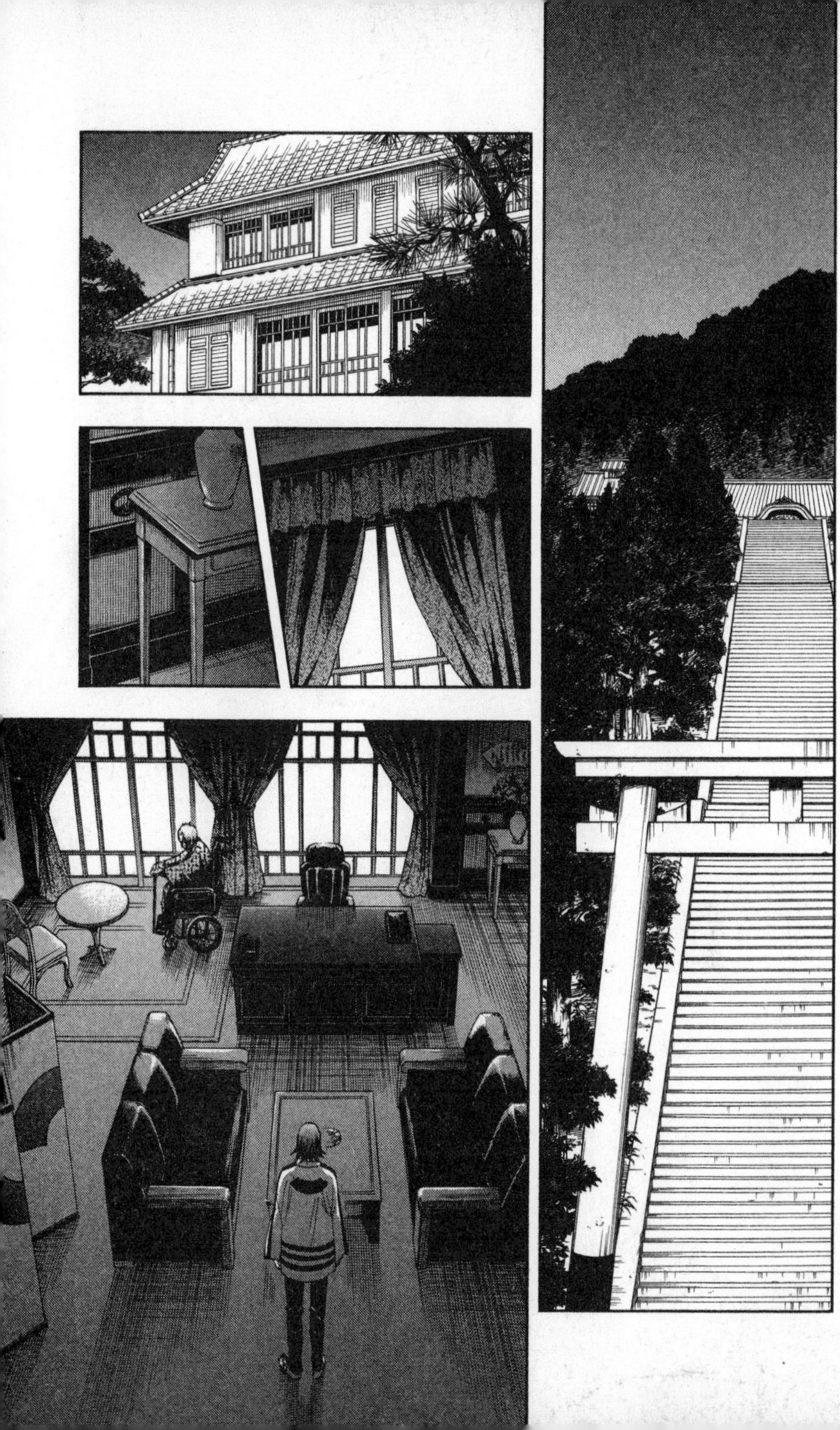

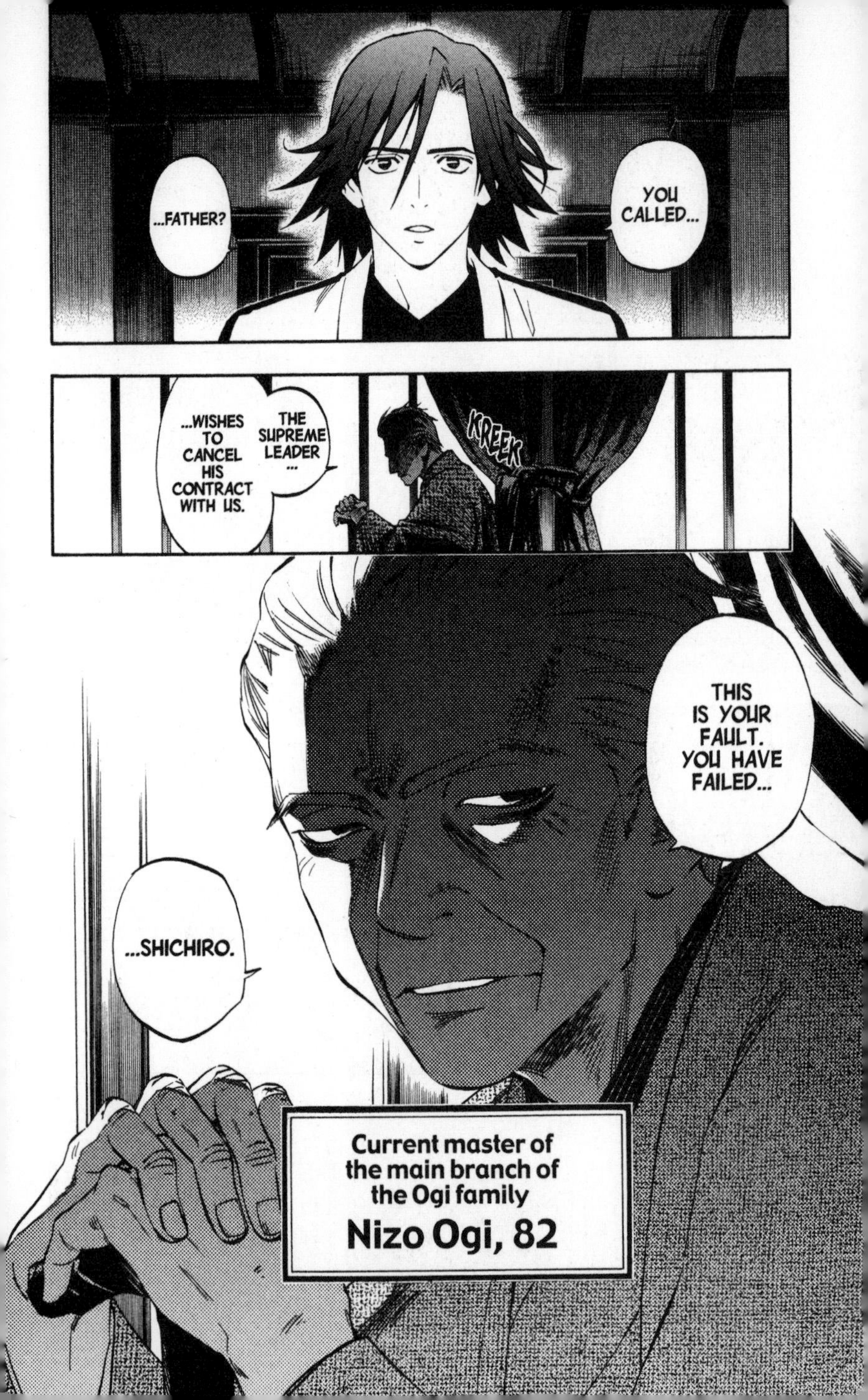

YOU CALLED...
...FATHER?
KREEK
THE SUPREME LEADER...
...WISHES TO CANCEL HIS CONTRACT WITH US.
THIS IS YOUR FAULT. YOU HAVE FAILED...
...SHICHIRO.
Current master of the main branch of the Ogi family
Nizo Ogi, 82

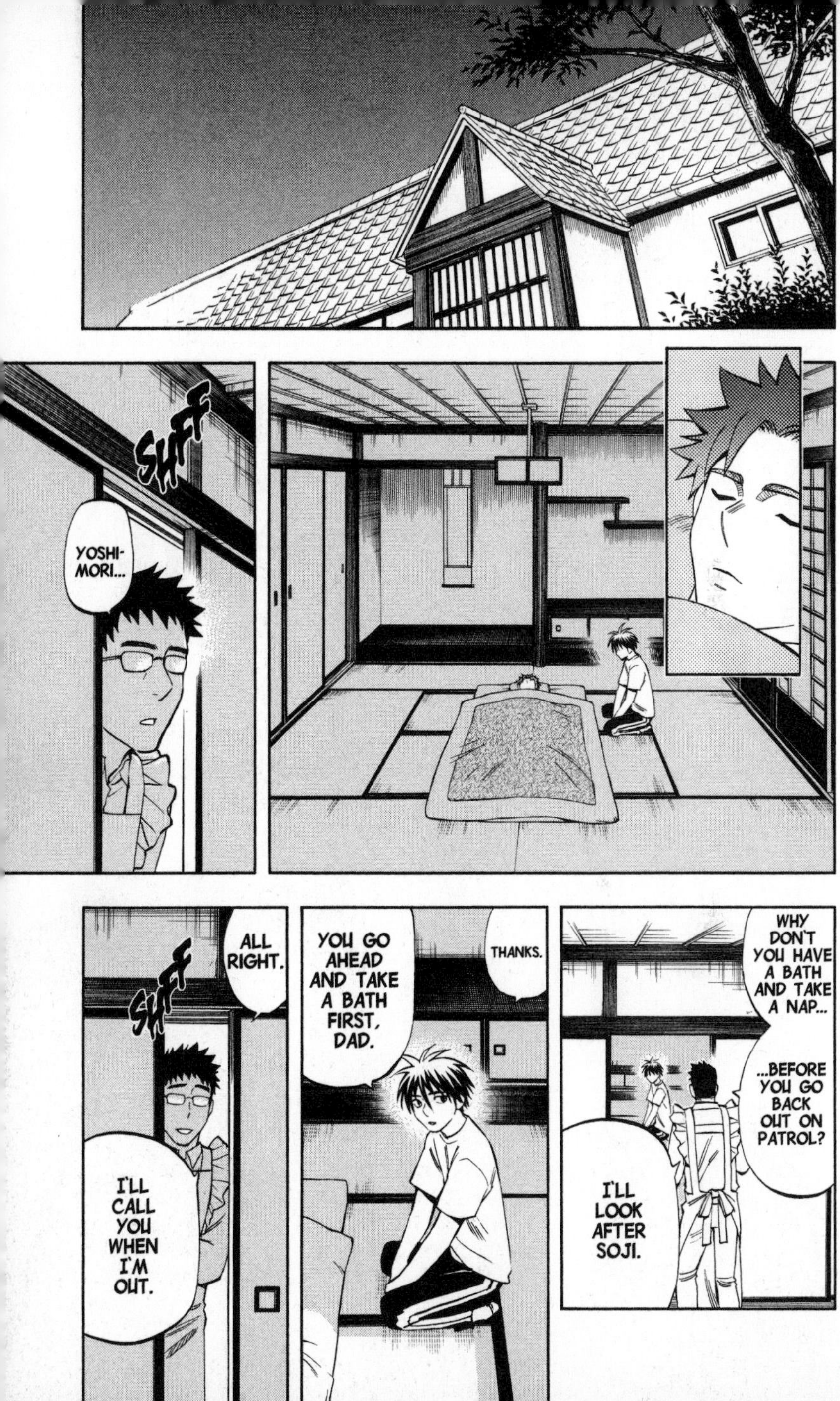
SHFF
YOSHIMORI...
WHY DON'T YOU HAVE A BATH AND TAKE A NAP...
...BEFORE YOU GO BACK OUT ON PATROL?
I'LL LOOK AFTER SOJI.
THANKS.
YOU GO AHEAD AND TAKE A BATH FIRST, DAD.
ALL RIGHT.
SHFF
I'LL CALL YOU WHEN I'M OUT.

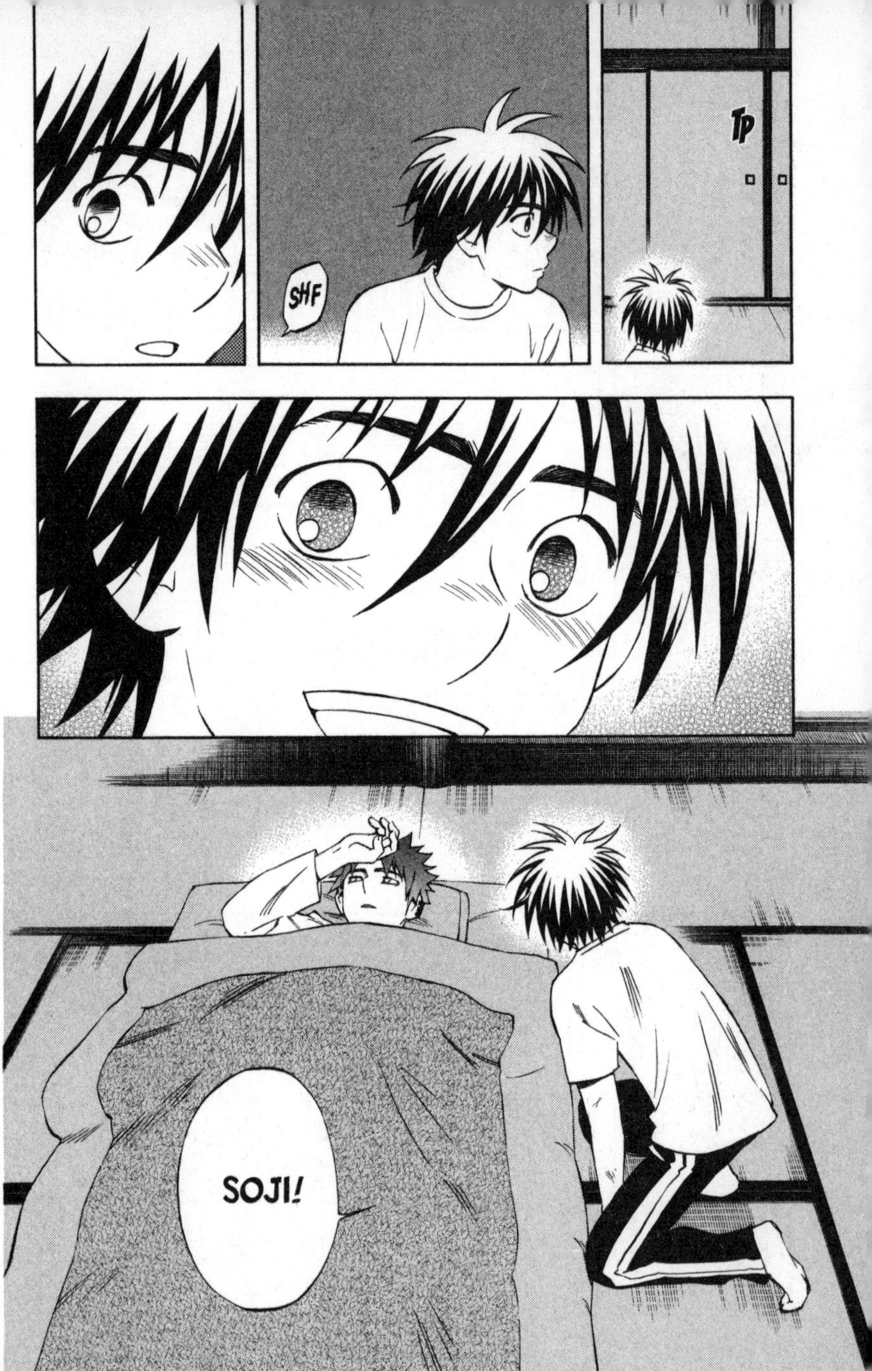
TP
SHF
SOJI!

Chapter 280:

Awakening

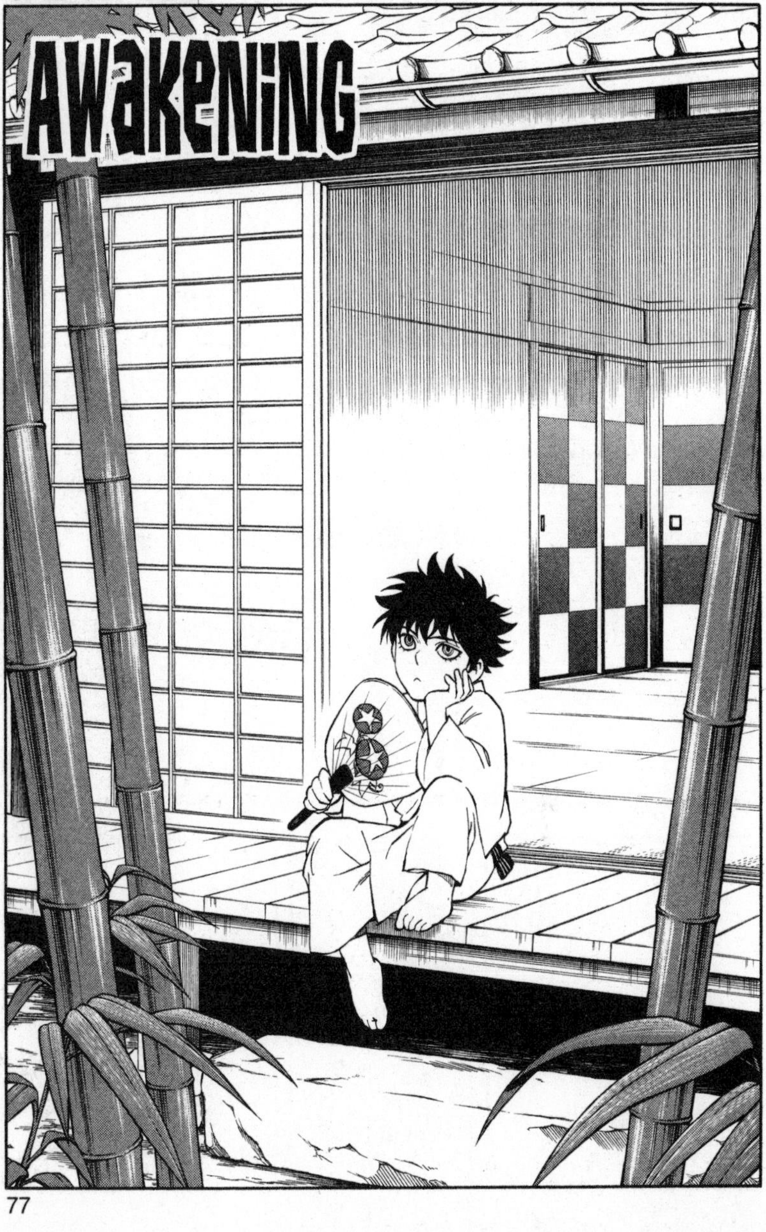

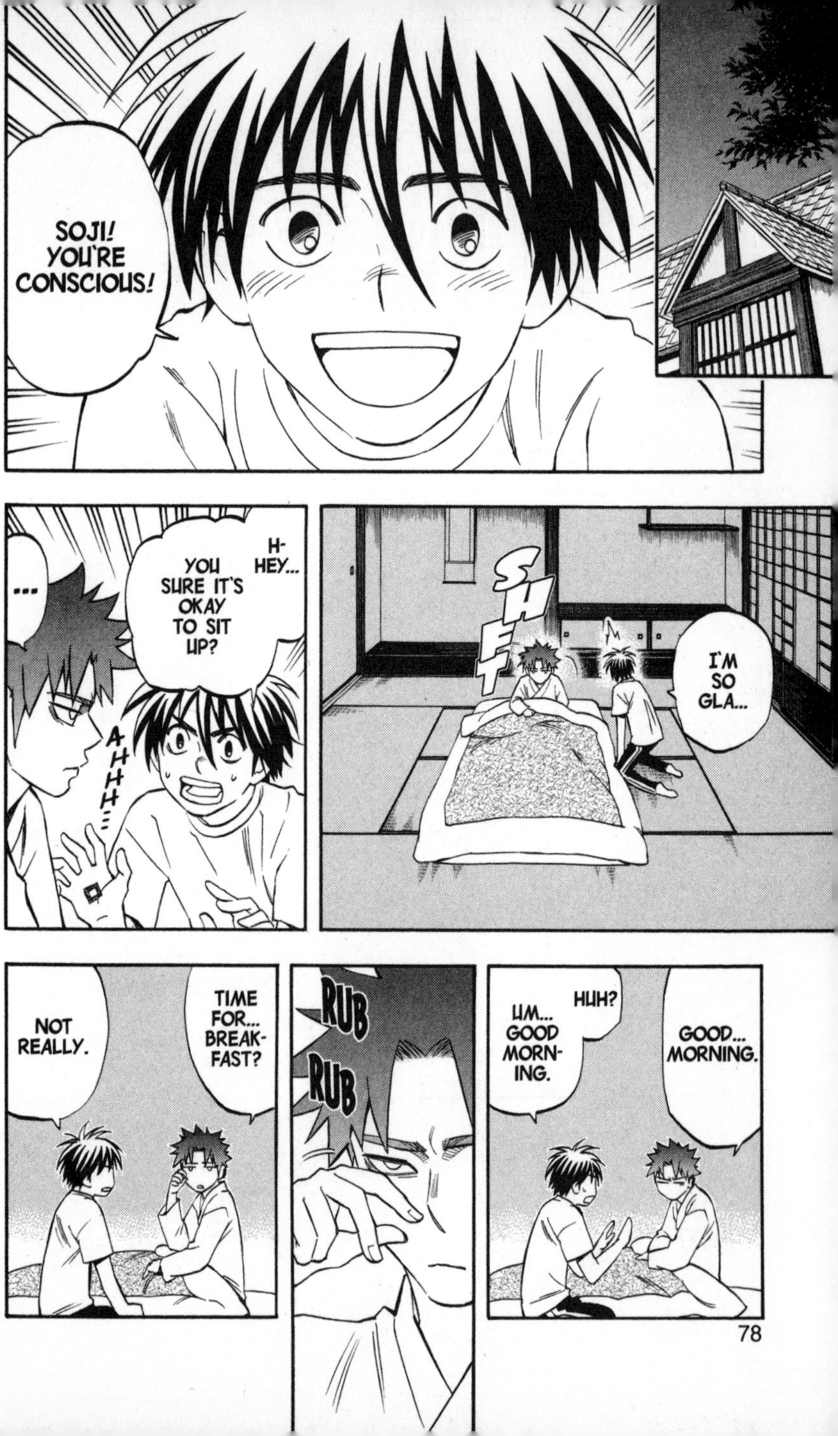
SOJI! YOU'RE CONSCIOUS!
SHFT
I'M SO GLA...
H- HEY... YOU SURE IT'S OKAY TO SIT UP?
...
AHHHH...
GOOD... MORNING.
HUH?
UM... GOOD MORNING.
RUB RUB
TIME FOR... BREAKFAST?
NOT REALLY.

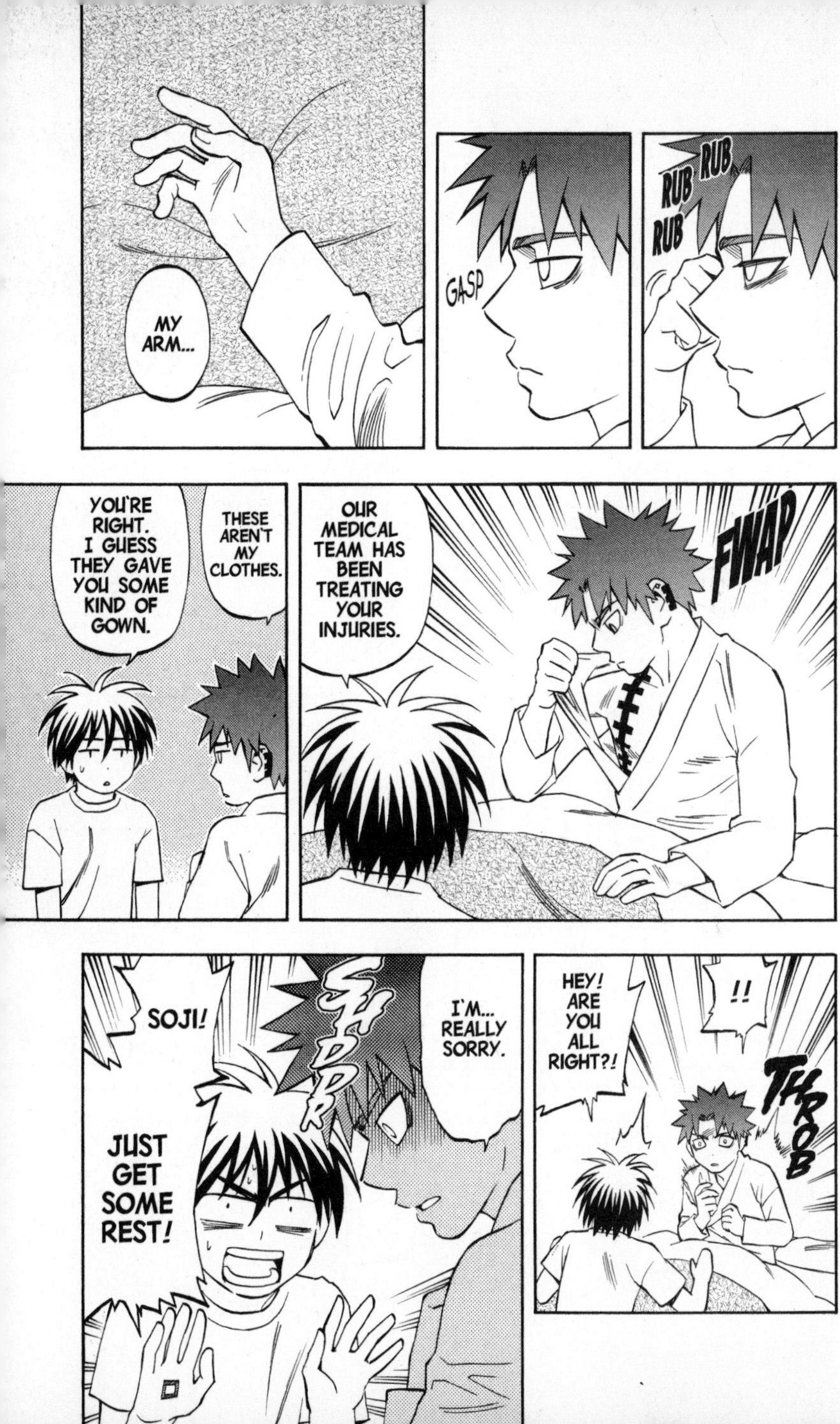
RUB
RUB
RUB
GASP
MY ARM...
FWAP
OUR MEDICAL TEAM HAS BEEN TREATING YOUR INJURIES.
THESE AREN'T MY CLOTHES.
YOU'RE RIGHT. I GUESS THEY GAVE YOU SOME KIND OF GOWN.
!!
HEY! ARE YOU ALL RIGHT?!
THROB
I'M... REALLY SORRY.
SHDDR
SOJI!
JUST GET SOME REST!

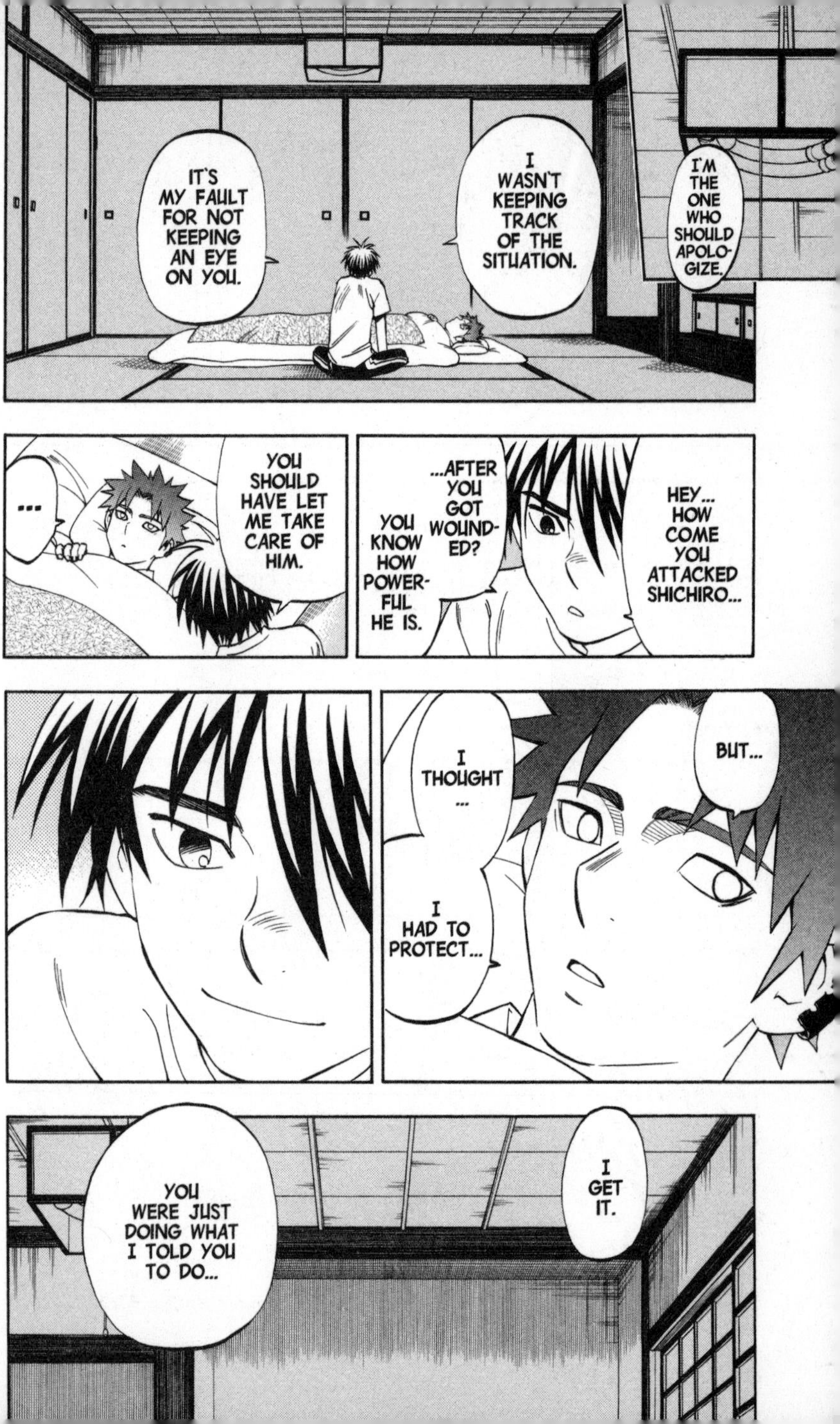
I'M THE ONE WHO SHOULD APOLOGIZE.
I WASN'T KEEPING TRACK OF THE SITUATION.
IT'S MY FAULT FOR NOT KEEPING AN EYE ON YOU.
HEY... HOW COME YOU ATTACKED SHICHIRO...
...AFTER YOU GOT WOUNDED?
YOU KNOW HOW POWERFUL HE IS.
YOU SHOULD HAVE LET ME TAKE CARE OF HIM.
...
BUT...
I THOUGHT...
I HAD TO PROTECT...
I GET IT.
YOU WERE JUST DOING WHAT I TOLD YOU TO DO...

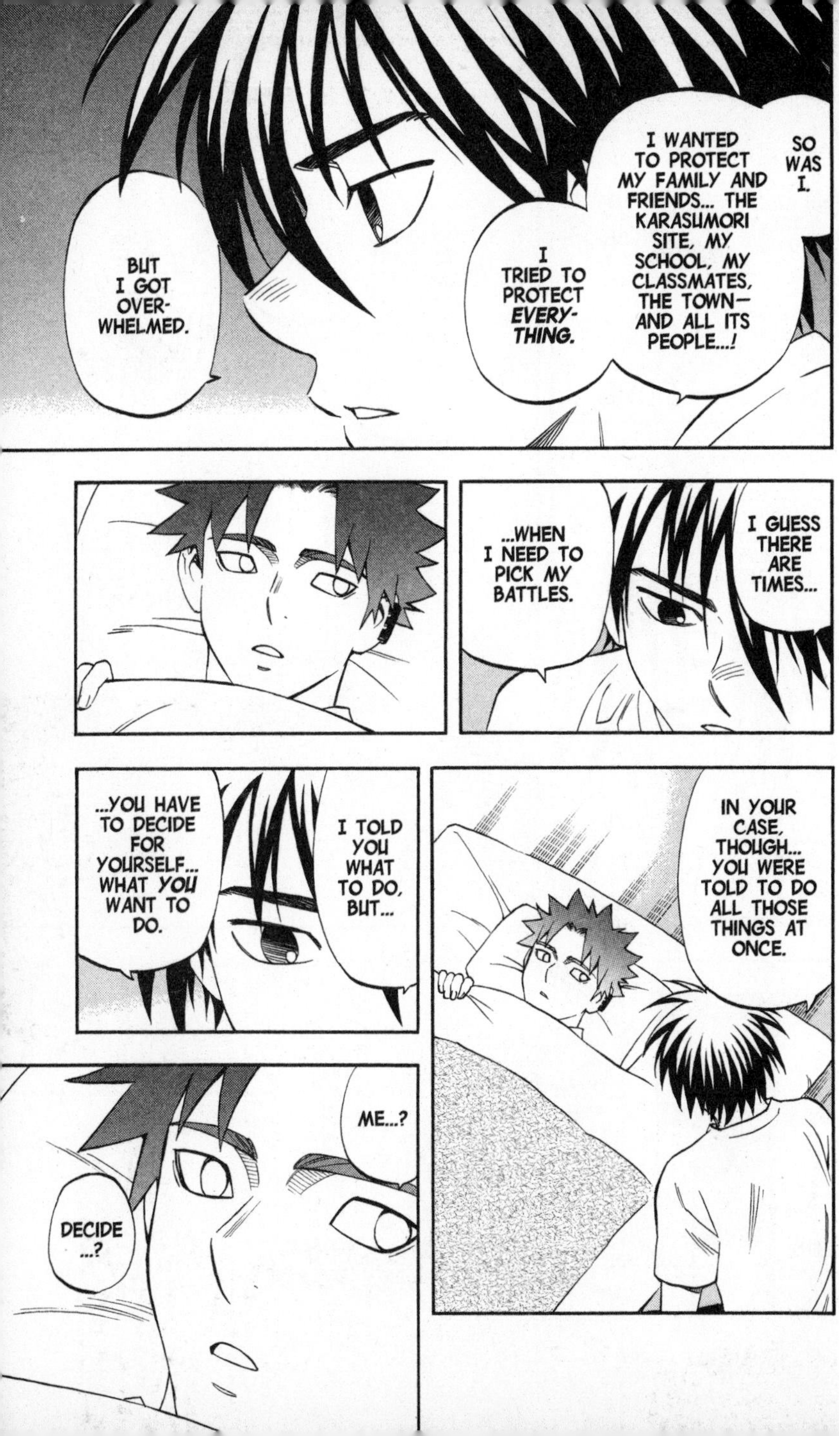
SO WAS I.
I WANTED TO PROTECT MY FAMILY AND FRIENDS... THE KARASUMORI SITE, MY SCHOOL, MY CLASSMATES, THE TOWN—AND ALL ITS PEOPLE...!
I TRIED TO PROTECT *EVERYTHING.*
BUT I GOT OVERWHELMED.
I GUESS THERE ARE TIMES...
...WHEN I NEED TO PICK MY BATTLES.
IN YOUR CASE, THOUGH... YOU WERE TOLD TO DO ALL THOSE THINGS AT ONCE.
I TOLD YOU WHAT TO DO, BUT...
...YOU HAVE TO DECIDE FOR YOURSELF... WHAT *YOU* WANT TO DO.
ME...?
DECIDE ...?

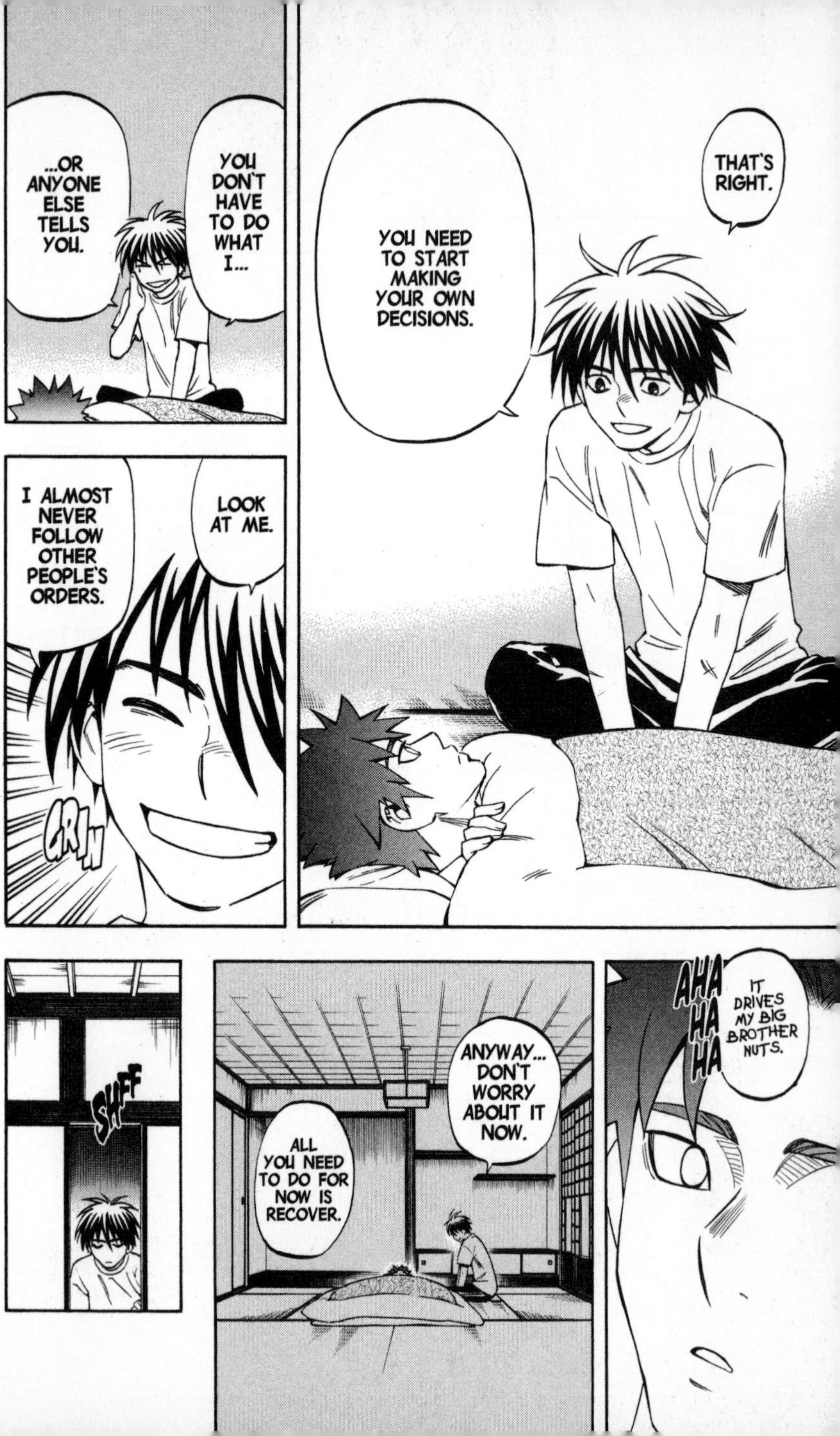
THAT'S RIGHT.
YOU NEED TO START MAKING YOUR OWN DECISIONS.
YOU DON'T HAVE TO DO WHAT I...
...OR ANYONE ELSE TELLS YOU.
LOOK AT ME.
I ALMOST NEVER FOLLOW OTHER PEOPLE'S ORDERS.
GRIN
AHAHAHA
IT DRIVES MY BIG BROTHER NUTS.
ANYWAY... DON'T WORRY ABOUT IT NOW.
ALL YOU NEED TO DO FOR NOW IS RECOVER.
SHFF

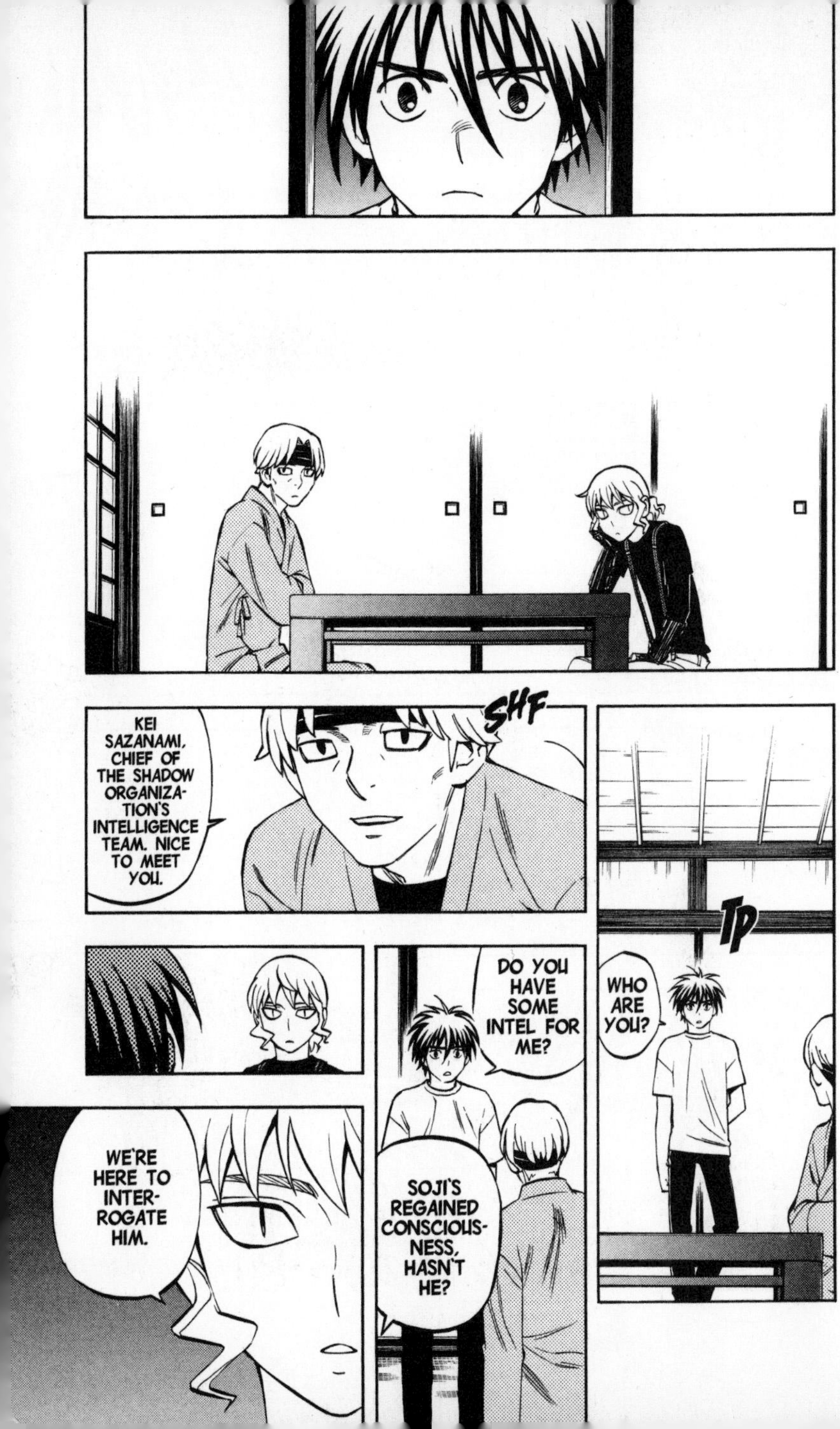
TP
WHO ARE YOU?
SHF
KEI SAZANAMI, CHIEF OF THE SHADOW ORGANIZATION'S INTELLIGENCE TEAM. NICE TO MEET YOU.
DO YOU HAVE SOME INTEL FOR ME?
SOJI'S REGAINED CONSCIOUSNESS, HASN'T HE?
WE'RE HERE TO INTERROGATE HIM.

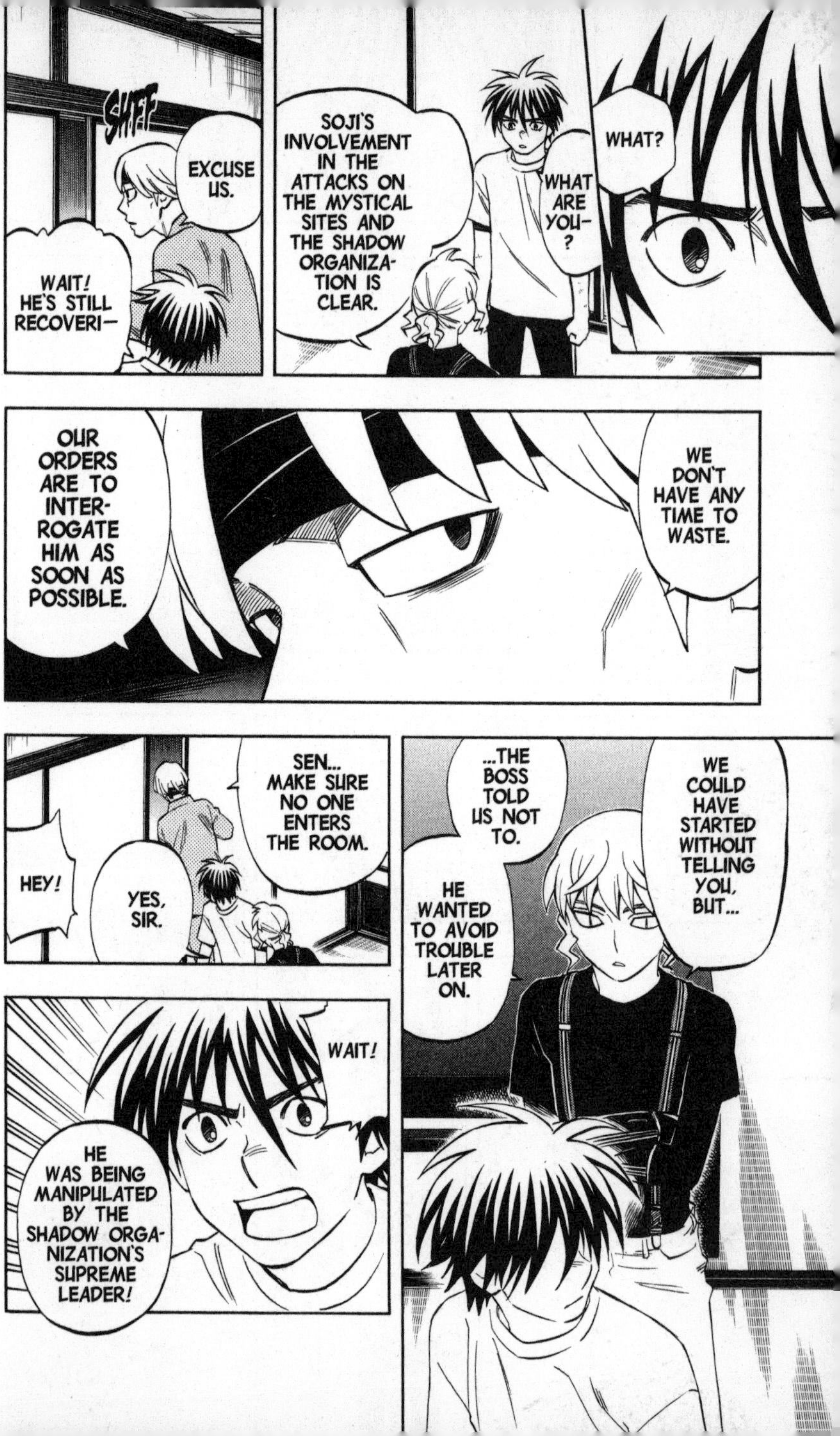
WHAT?
WHAT ARE YOU—?
SOJI'S INVOLVEMENT IN THE ATTACKS ON THE MYSTICAL SITES AND THE SHADOW ORGANIZATION IS CLEAR.
SHFF
EXCUSE US.
WAIT! HE'S STILL RECOVERI—
WE DON'T HAVE ANY TIME TO WASTE.
OUR ORDERS ARE TO INTERROGATE HIM AS SOON AS POSSIBLE.
WE COULD HAVE STARTED WITHOUT TELLING YOU, BUT...
...THE BOSS TOLD US NOT TO.
HE WANTED TO AVOID TROUBLE LATER ON.
SEN... MAKE SURE NO ONE ENTERS THE ROOM.
YES, SIR.
HEY!
WAIT!
HE WAS BEING MANIPULATED BY THE SHADOW ORGANIZATION'S SUPREME LEADER!

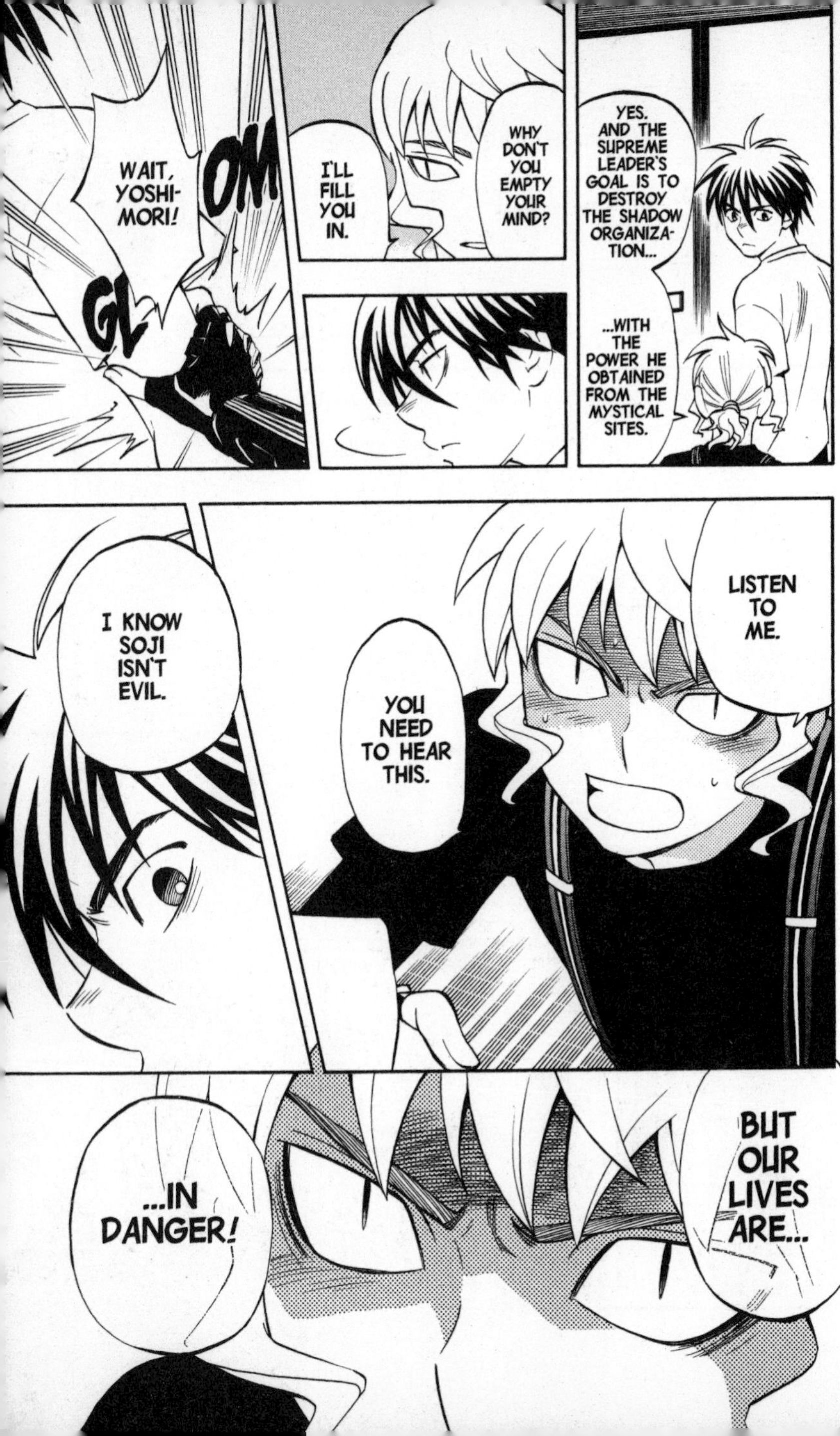
YES. AND THE SUPREME LEADER'S GOAL IS TO DESTROY THE SHADOW ORGANIZATION...
...WITH THE POWER HE OBTAINED FROM THE MYSTICAL SITES.
WHY DON'T YOU EMPTY YOUR MIND?
I'LL FILL YOU IN.
OM
WAIT, YOSHIMORI!
GL
LISTEN TO ME.
YOU NEED TO HEAR THIS.
I KNOW SOJI ISN'T EVIL.
BUT OUR LIVES ARE...
...IN DANGER!

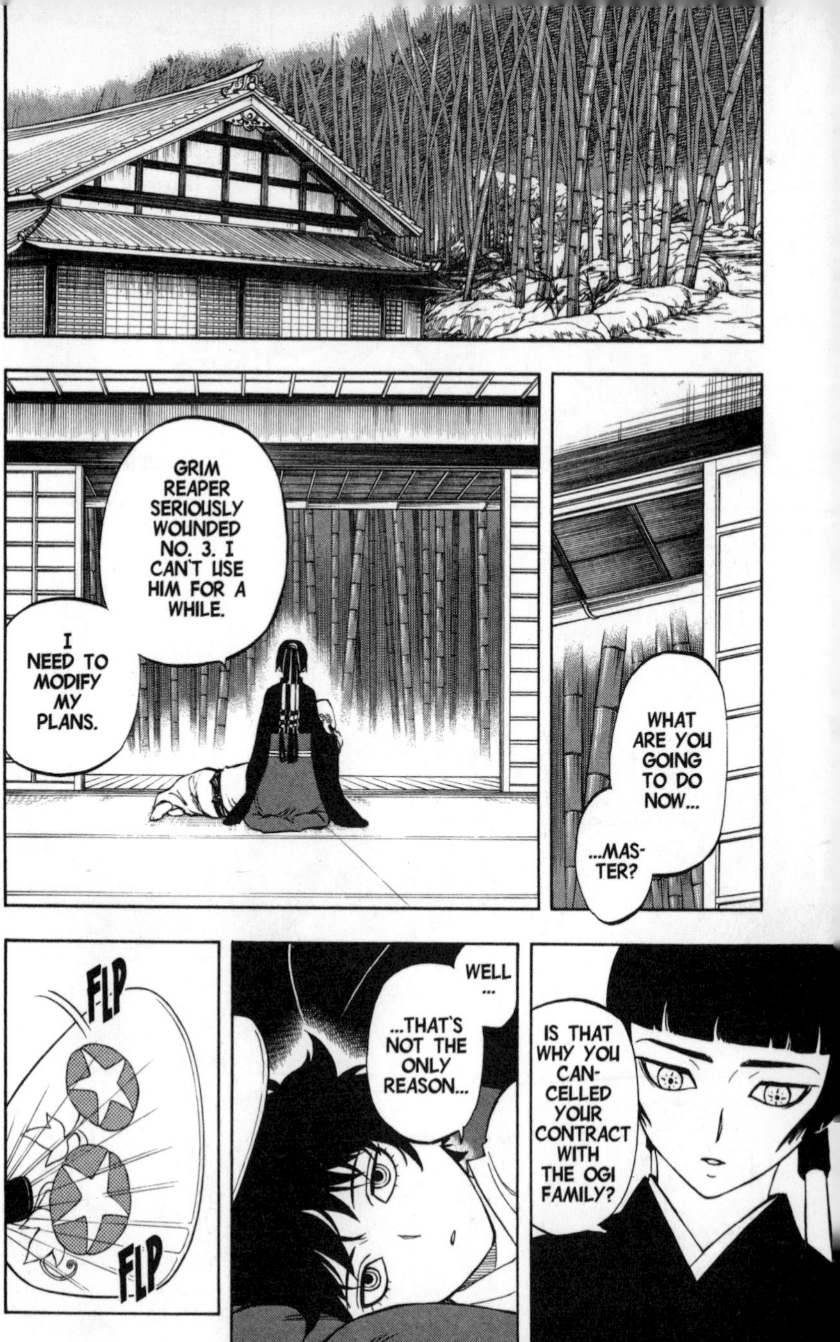
WHAT ARE YOU GOING TO DO NOW...
...MASTER?
GRIM REAPER SERIOUSLY WOUNDED NO. 3. I CAN'T USE HIM FOR A WHILE.
I NEED TO MODIFY MY PLANS.
IS THAT WHY YOU CANCELLED YOUR CONTRACT WITH THE OGI FAMILY?
WELL...
...THAT'S NOT THE ONLY REASON...
FLP
FLP

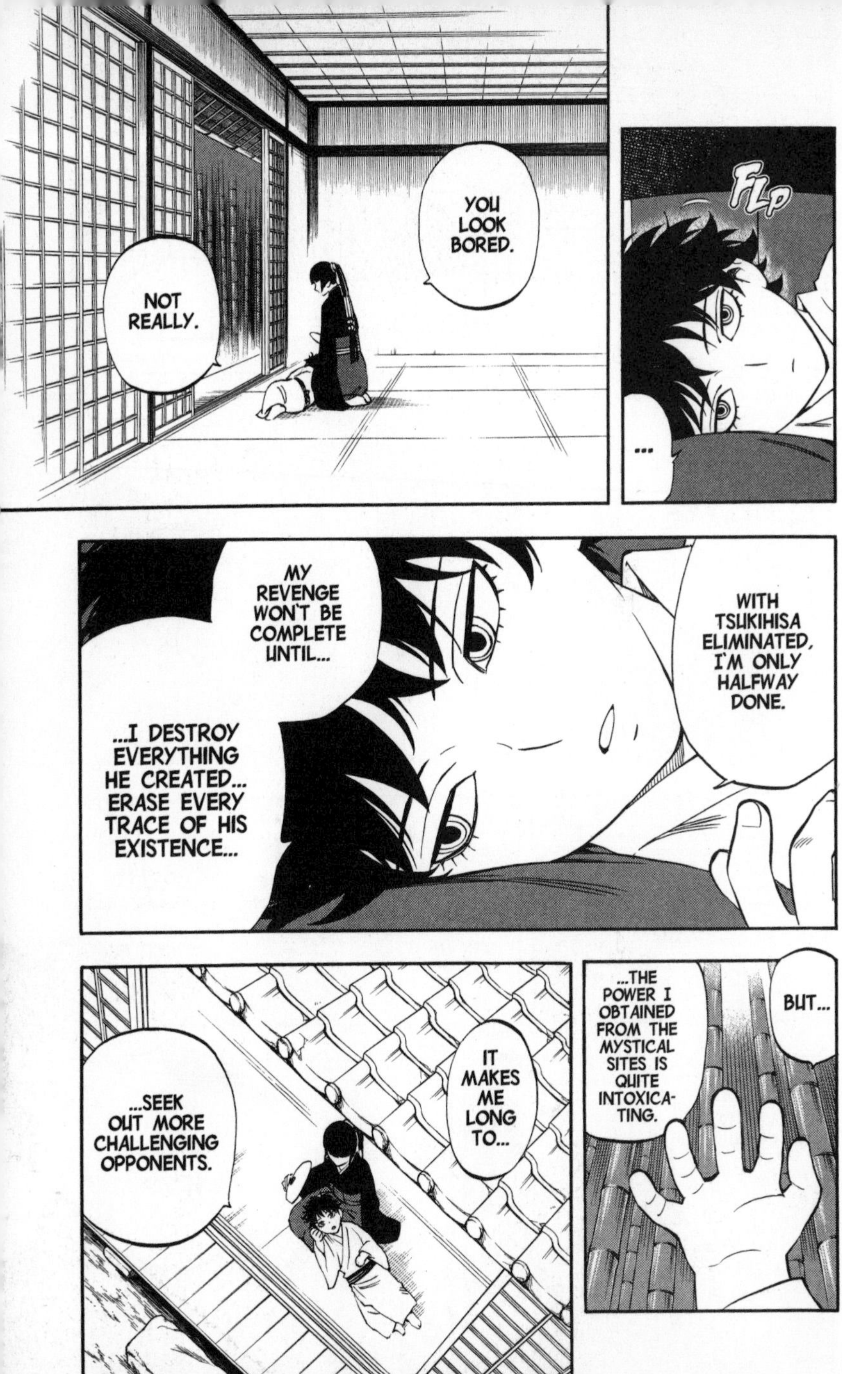
FLP
...
YOU LOOK BORED.
NOT REALLY.
WITH TSUKIHISA ELIMINATED, I'M ONLY HALFWAY DONE.
MY REVENGE WON'T BE COMPLETE UNTIL...
...I DESTROY EVERYTHING HE CREATED... ERASE EVERY TRACE OF HIS EXISTENCE...
BUT...
...THE POWER I OBTAINED FROM THE MYSTICAL SITES IS QUITE INTOXICATING.
IT MAKES ME LONG TO...
...SEEK OUT MORE CHALLENGING OPPONENTS.

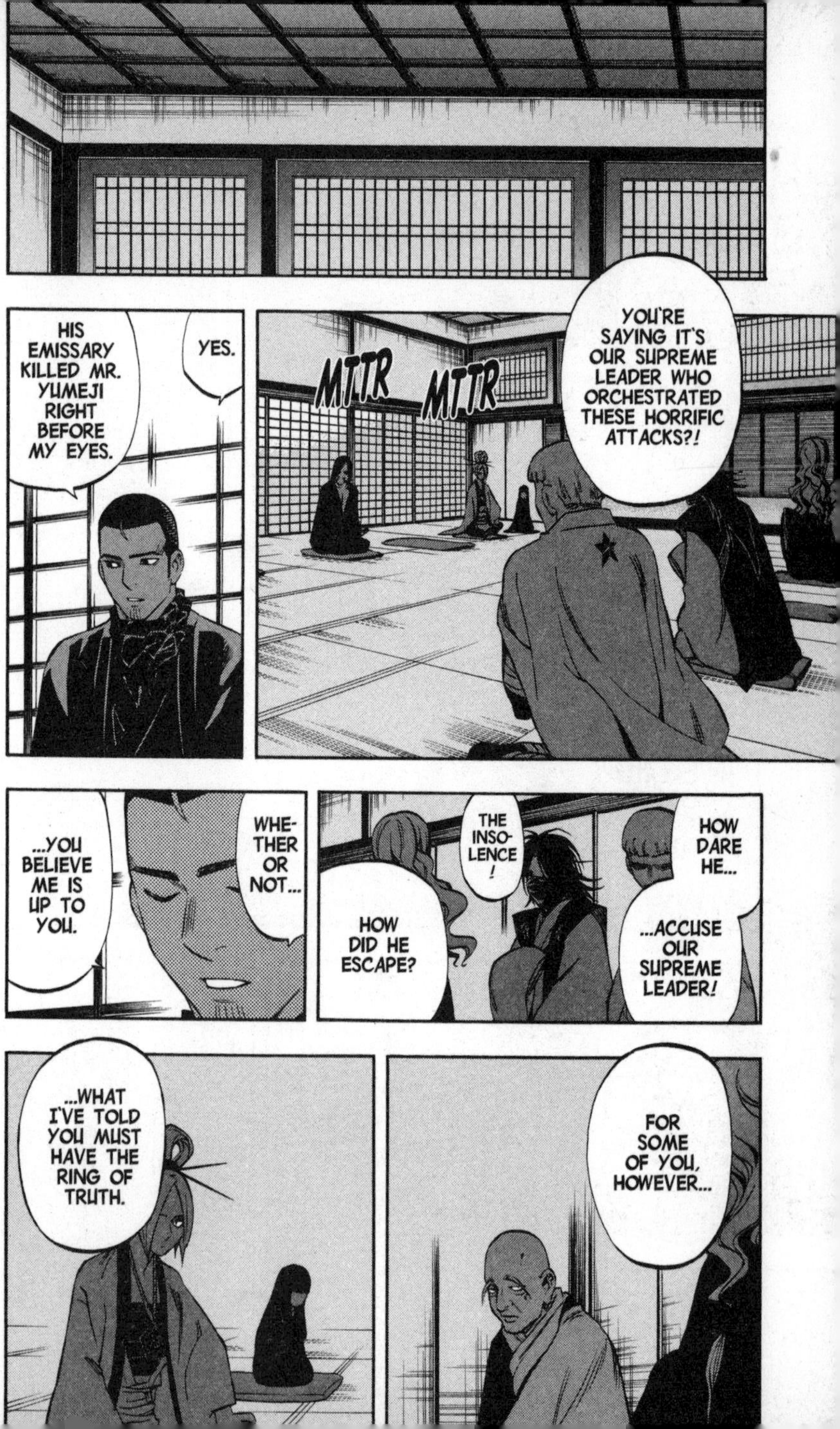
YOU'RE SAYING IT'S OUR SUPREME LEADER WHO ORCHESTRATED THESE HORRIFIC ATTACKS?!
MTTR MTTR
YES.
HIS EMISSARY KILLED MR. YUMEJI RIGHT BEFORE MY EYES.
HOW DARE HE...
...ACCUSE OUR SUPREME LEADER!
THE INSOLENCE!
HOW DID HE ESCAPE?
WHETHER OR NOT...
...YOU BELIEVE ME IS UP TO YOU.
FOR SOME OF YOU, HOWEVER...
...WHAT I'VE TOLD YOU MUST HAVE THE RING OF TRUTH.

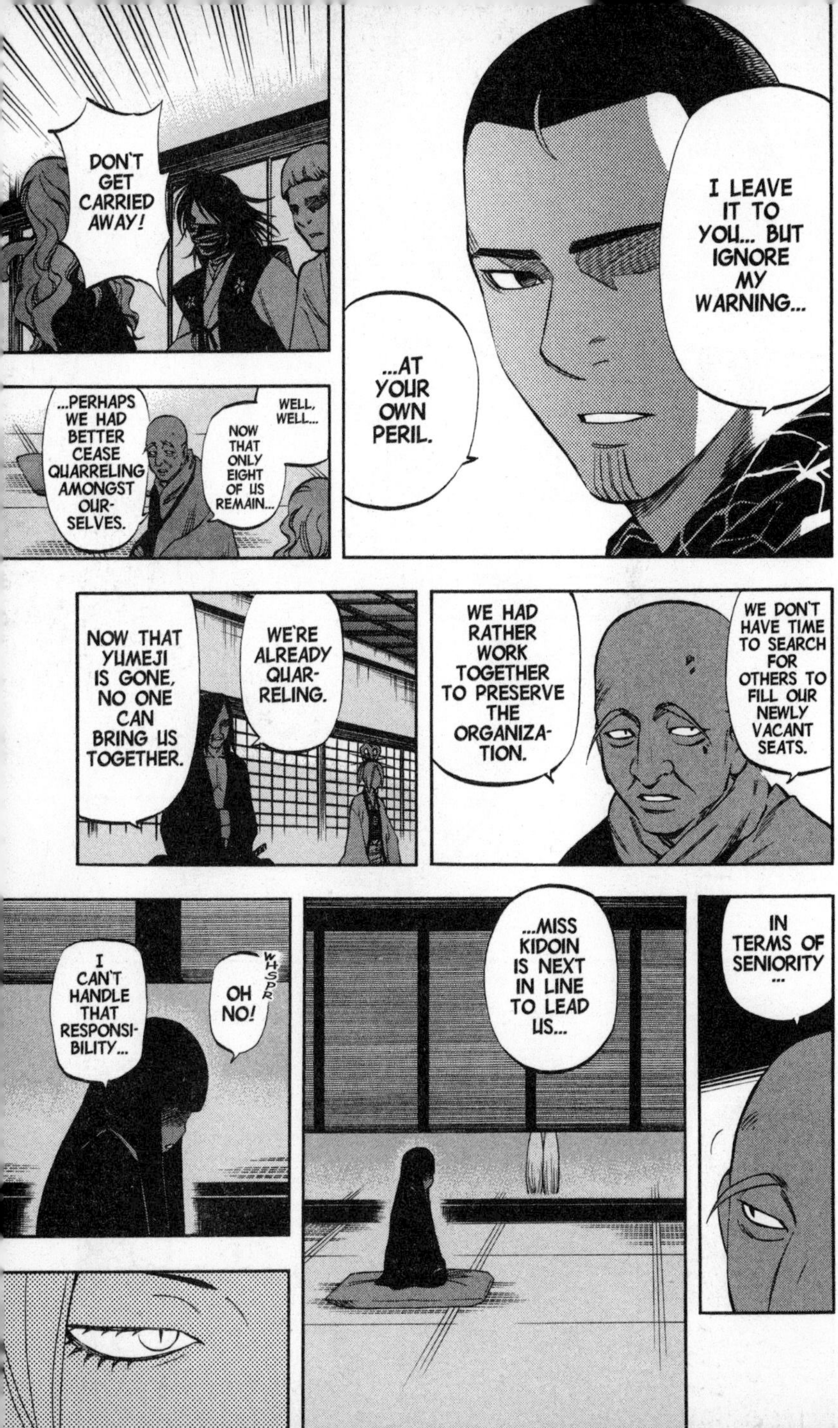
I LEAVE IT TO YOU... BUT IGNORE MY WARNING...
...AT YOUR OWN PERIL.
DON'T GET CARRIED AWAY!
WELL, WELL...
NOW THAT ONLY EIGHT OF US REMAIN...
...PERHAPS WE HAD BETTER CEASE QUARRELING AMONGST OUR-SELVES.
WE DON'T HAVE TIME TO SEARCH FOR OTHERS TO FILL OUR NEWLY VACANT SEATS.
WE HAD RATHER WORK TOGETHER TO PRESERVE THE ORGANIZA-TION.
WE'RE ALREADY QUAR-RELING.
NOW THAT YUMEJI IS GONE, NO ONE CAN BRING US TOGETHER.
IN TERMS OF SENIORITY...
...MISS KIDOIN IS NEXT IN LINE TO LEAD US...
WHSPR
OH NO!
I CAN'T HANDLE THAT RESPONSI-BILITY...

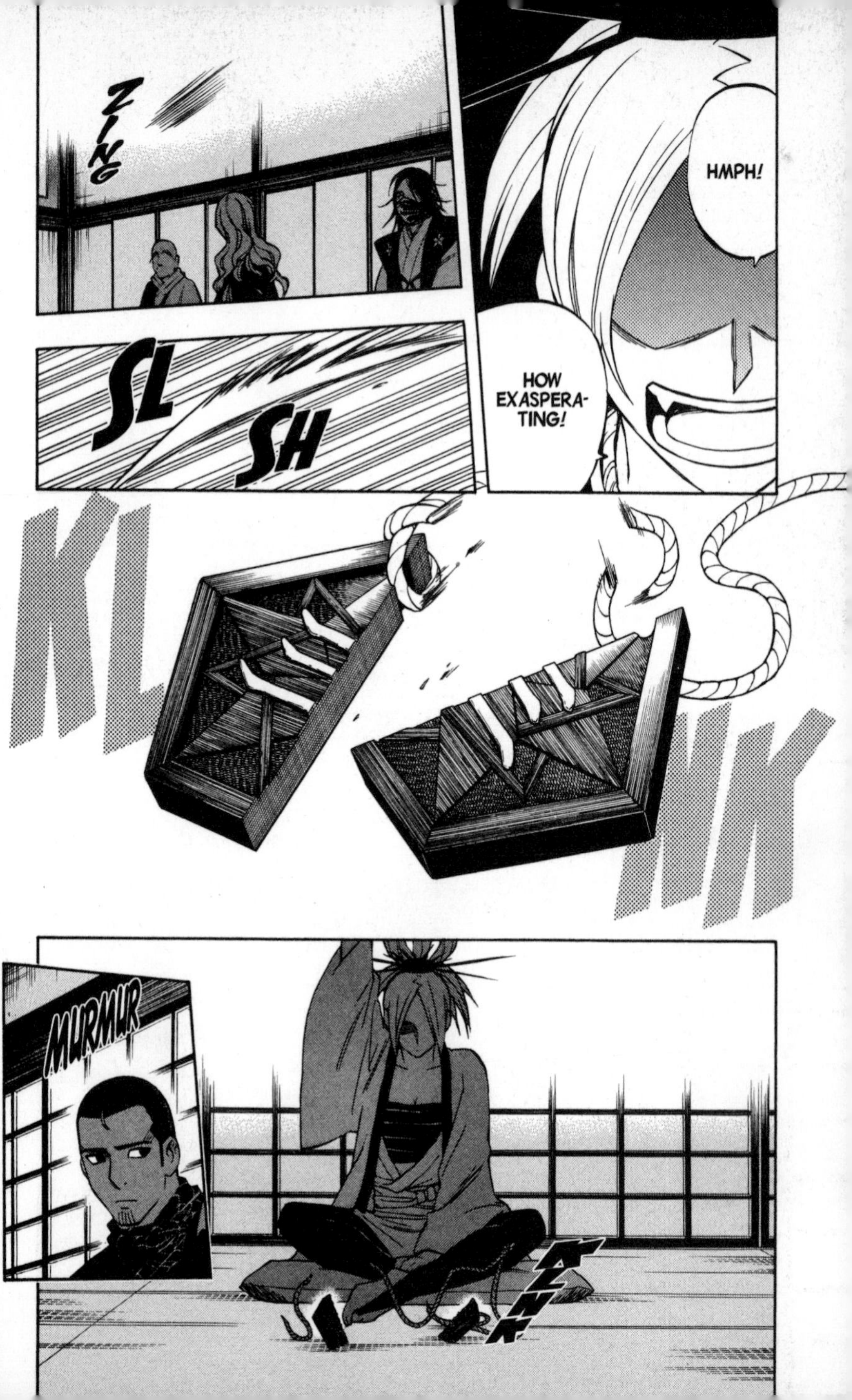
HMPH!
HOW EXASPERA-TING!
ZING
SL SH
KL NK
KLINK
MURMUR

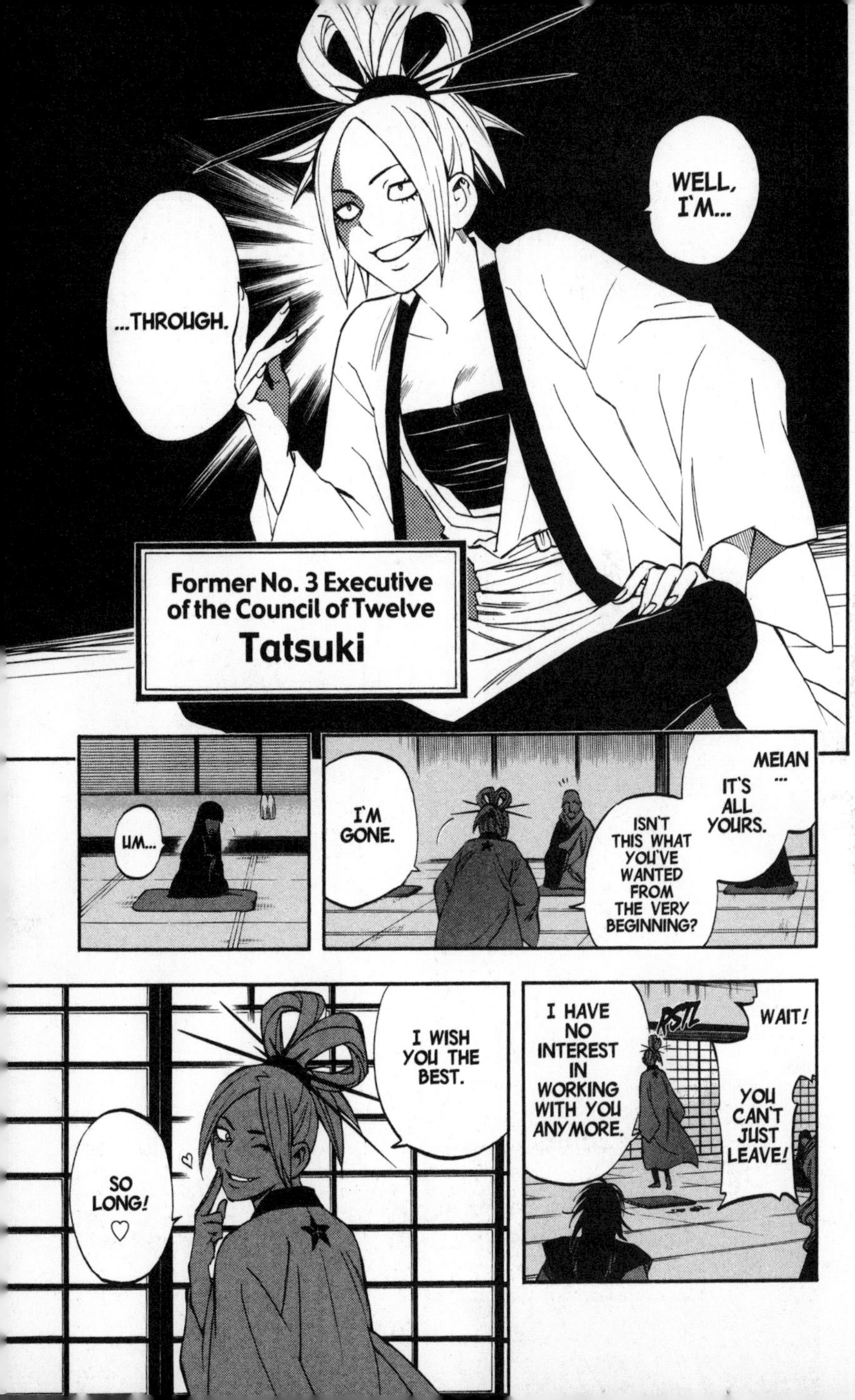
WELL, I'M...
...THROUGH.
Former No. 3 Executive of the Council of Twelve
Tatsuki
MEIAN...
IT'S ALL YOURS.
ISN'T THIS WHAT YOU'VE WANTED FROM THE VERY BEGINNING?
I'M GONE.
UM...
WAIT!
YOU CAN'T JUST LEAVE!
RSTL
I HAVE NO INTEREST IN WORKING WITH YOU ANYMORE.
I WISH YOU THE BEST.
SO LONG! ♡

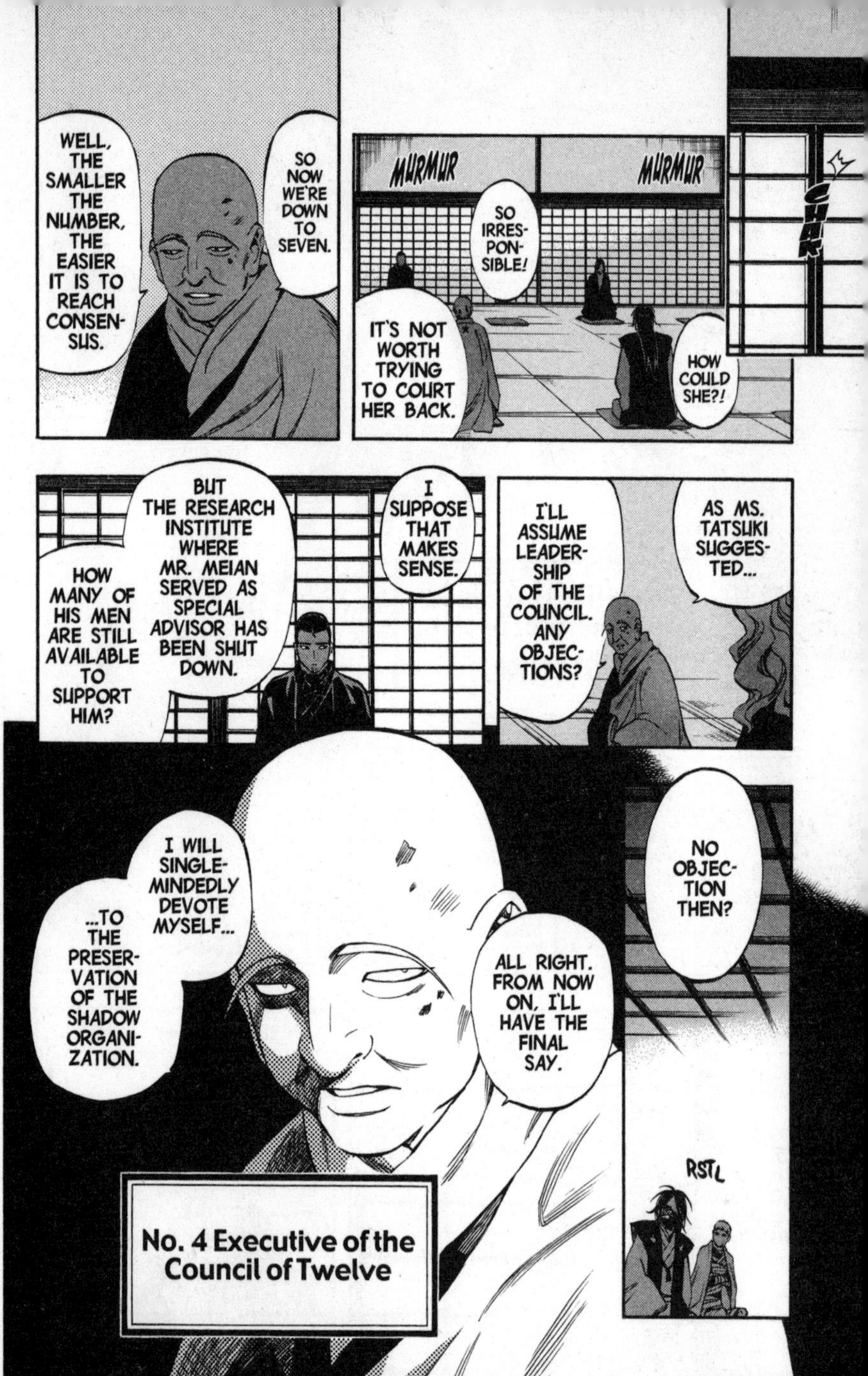
CHAK
MURMUR
MURMUR
SO IRRESPONSIBLE!
HOW COULD SHE?!
IT'S NOT WORTH TRYING TO COURT HER BACK.
SO NOW WE'RE DOWN TO SEVEN.
WELL, THE SMALLER THE NUMBER, THE EASIER IT IS TO REACH CONSENSUS.
AS MS. TATSUKI SUGGESTED...
I'LL ASSUME LEADERSHIP OF THE COUNCIL. ANY OBJECTIONS?
I SUPPOSE THAT MAKES SENSE.
BUT THE RESEARCH INSTITUTE WHERE MR. MEIAN SERVED AS SPECIAL ADVISOR HAS BEEN SHUT DOWN.
HOW MANY OF HIS MEN ARE STILL AVAILABLE TO SUPPORT HIM?
NO OBJECTION THEN?
RSTL
ALL RIGHT. FROM NOW ON, I'LL HAVE THE FINAL SAY.
I WILL SINGLE-MINDEDLY DEVOTE MYSELF...
...TO THE PRESERVATION OF THE SHADOW ORGANIZATION.
No. 4 Executive of the Council of Twelve

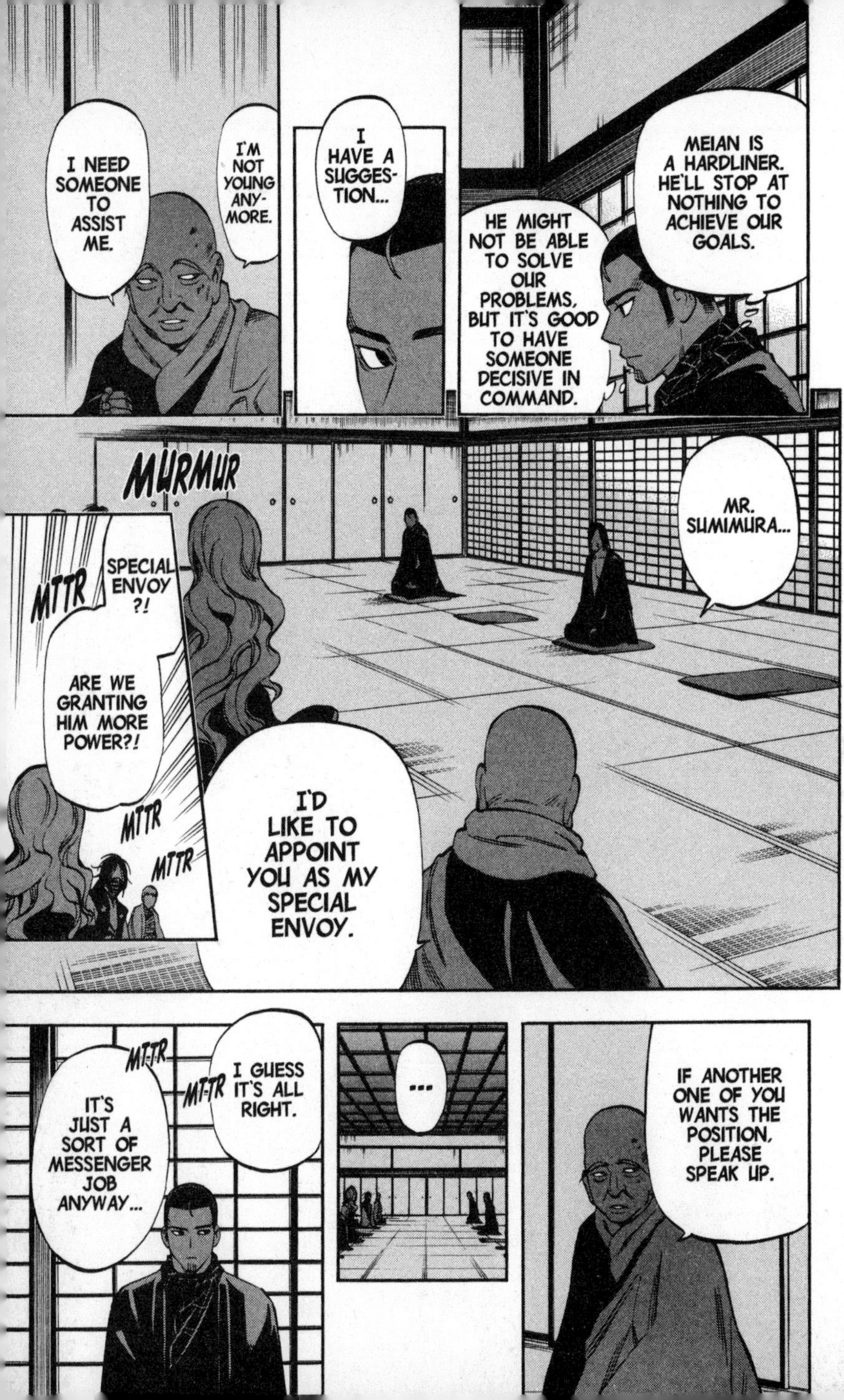
MEIAN IS A HARDLINER. HE'LL STOP AT NOTHING TO ACHIEVE OUR GOALS.
HE MIGHT NOT BE ABLE TO SOLVE OUR PROBLEMS, BUT IT'S GOOD TO HAVE SOMEONE DECISIVE IN COMMAND.
I HAVE A SUGGESTION...
I'M NOT YOUNG ANYMORE.
I NEED SOMEONE TO ASSIST ME.
MR. SUMIMURA...
MURMUR
I'D LIKE TO APPOINT YOU AS MY SPECIAL ENVOY.
SPECIAL ENVOY?!
MTTR
ARE WE GRANTING HIM MORE POWER?!
MTTR
MTTR
IF ANOTHER ONE OF YOU WANTS THE POSITION, PLEASE SPEAK UP.
...
I GUESS IT'S ALL RIGHT.
MT-TR
IT'S JUST A SORT OF MESSENGER JOB ANYWAY...
MT-TR

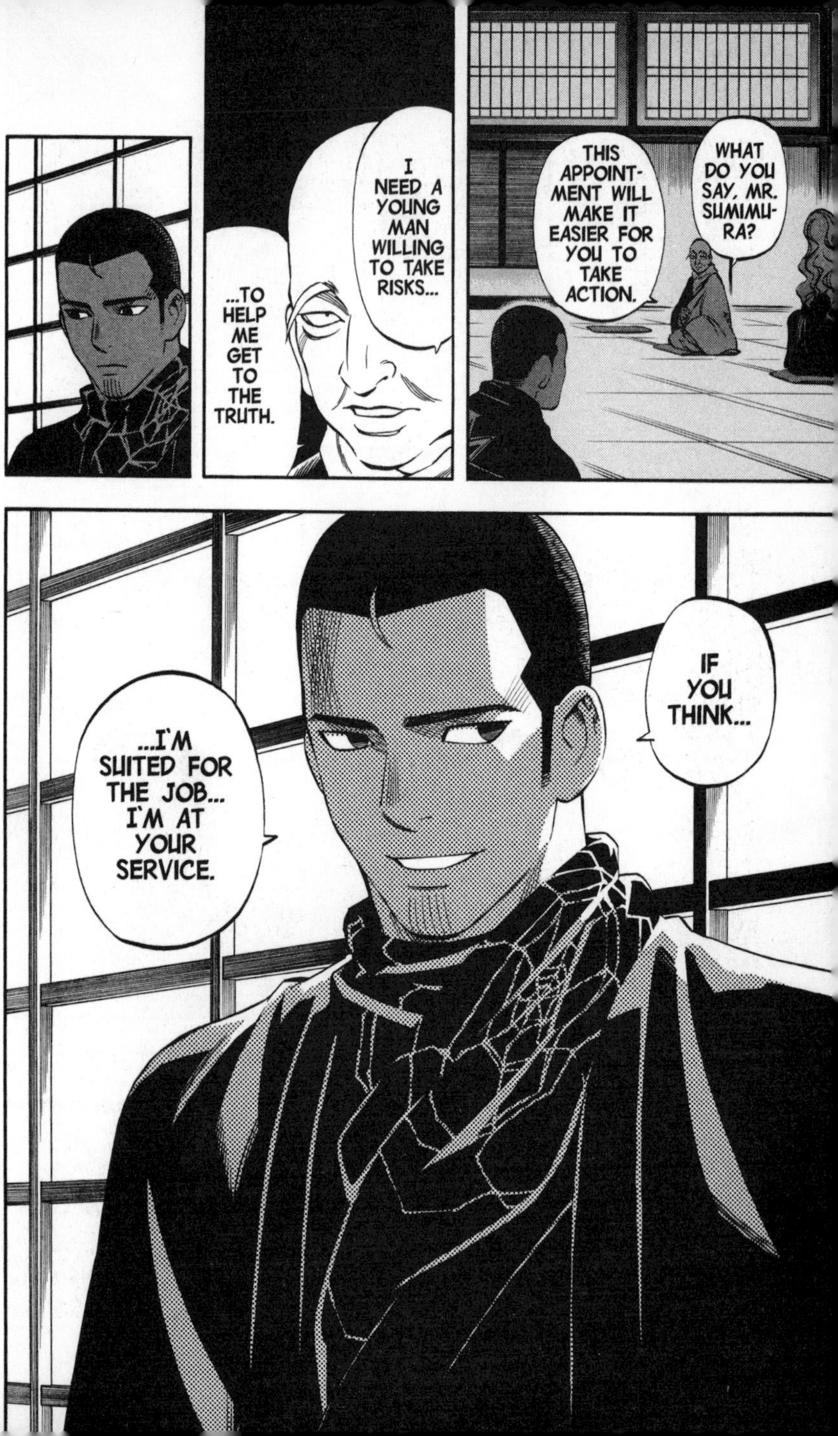
WHAT DO YOU SAY, MR. SUMIMURA?
THIS APPOINTMENT WILL MAKE IT EASIER FOR YOU TO TAKE ACTION.
I NEED A YOUNG MAN WILLING TO TAKE RISKS...
...TO HELP ME GET TO THE TRUTH.
IF YOU THINK...
...I'M SUITED FOR THE JOB... I'M AT YOUR SERVICE.

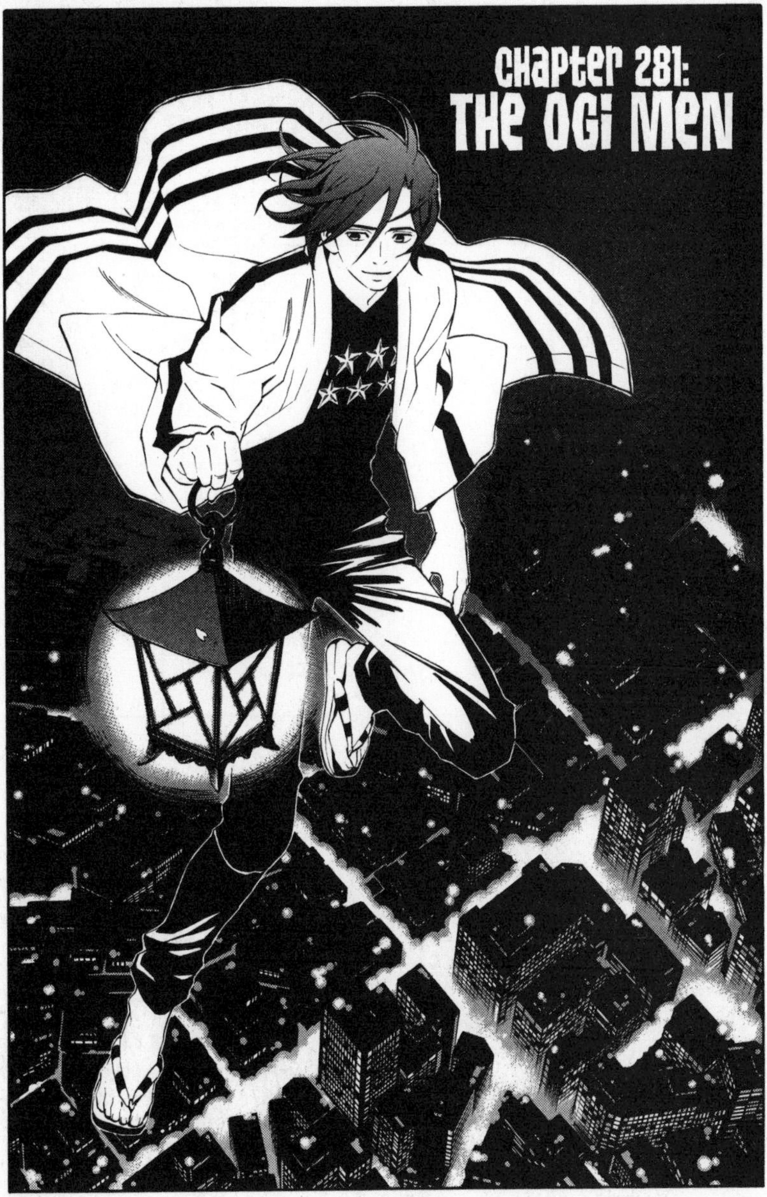
Chapter 281:
The Ogi Men

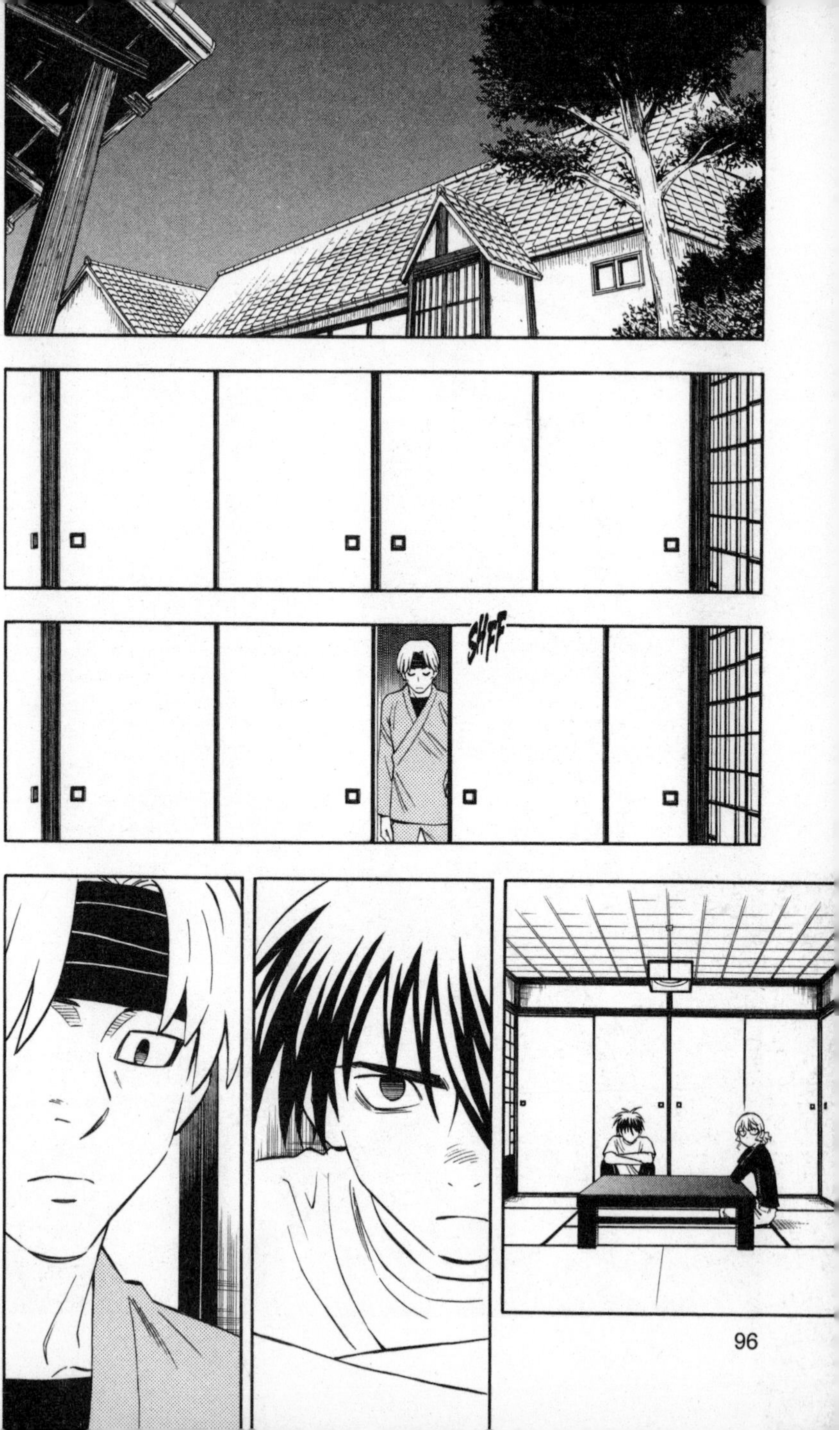
SHFF

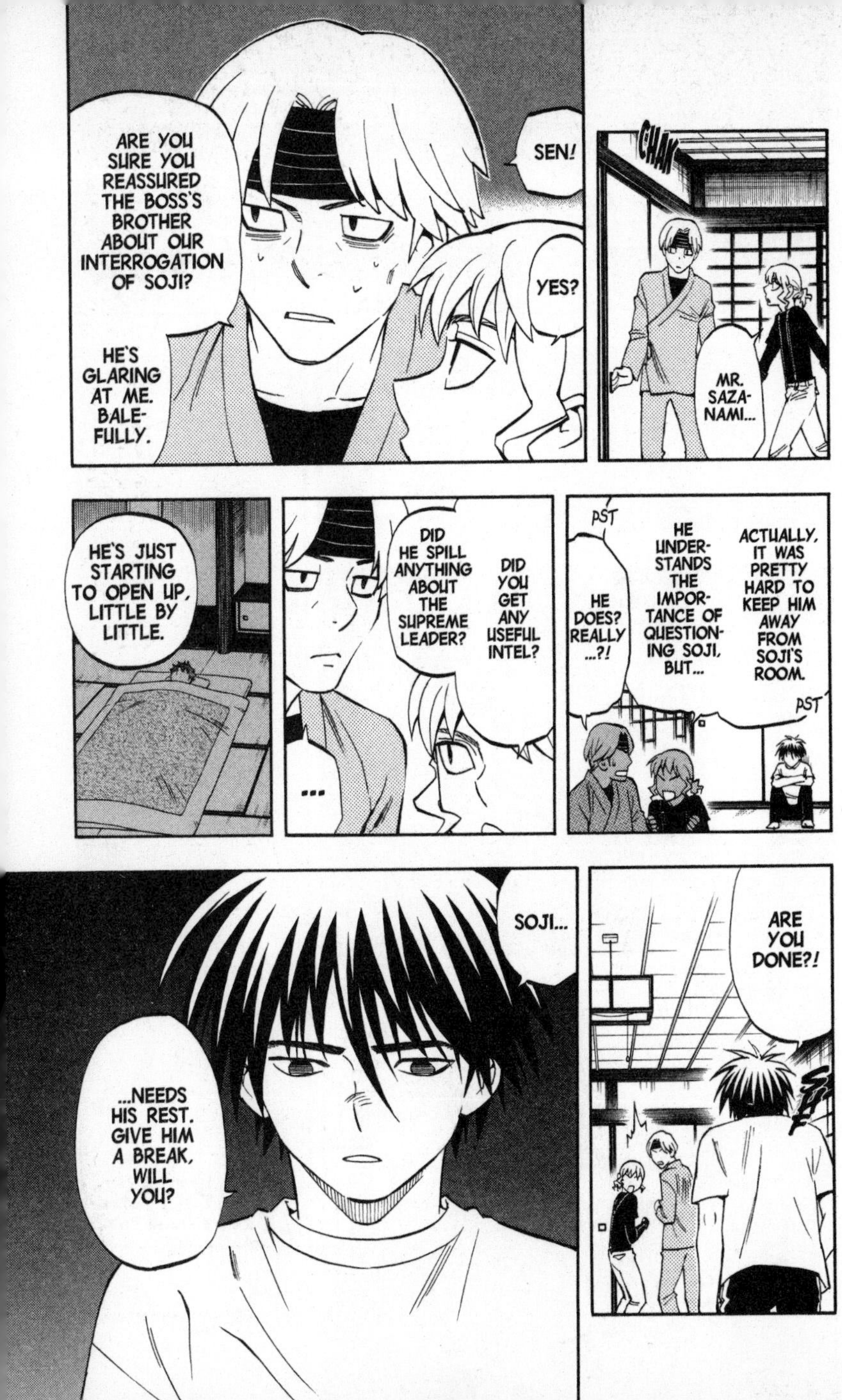
CHAK
MR. SAZANAMI...
SEN!
YES?
ARE YOU SURE YOU REASSURED THE BOSS'S BROTHER ABOUT OUR INTERROGATION OF SOJI?
HE'S GLARING AT ME. BALEFULLY.
PST
ACTUALLY, IT WAS PRETTY HARD TO KEEP HIM AWAY FROM SOJI'S ROOM.
HE UNDERSTANDS THE IMPORTANCE OF QUESTIONING SOJI, BUT...
HE DOES? REALLY ...?!
PST
DID YOU GET ANY USEFUL INTEL?
DID HE SPILL ANYTHING ABOUT THE SUPREME LEADER?
...
HE'S JUST STARTING TO OPEN UP, LITTLE BY LITTLE.
ARE YOU DONE?!
SOJI...
...NEEDS HIS REST. GIVE HIM A BREAK, WILL YOU?

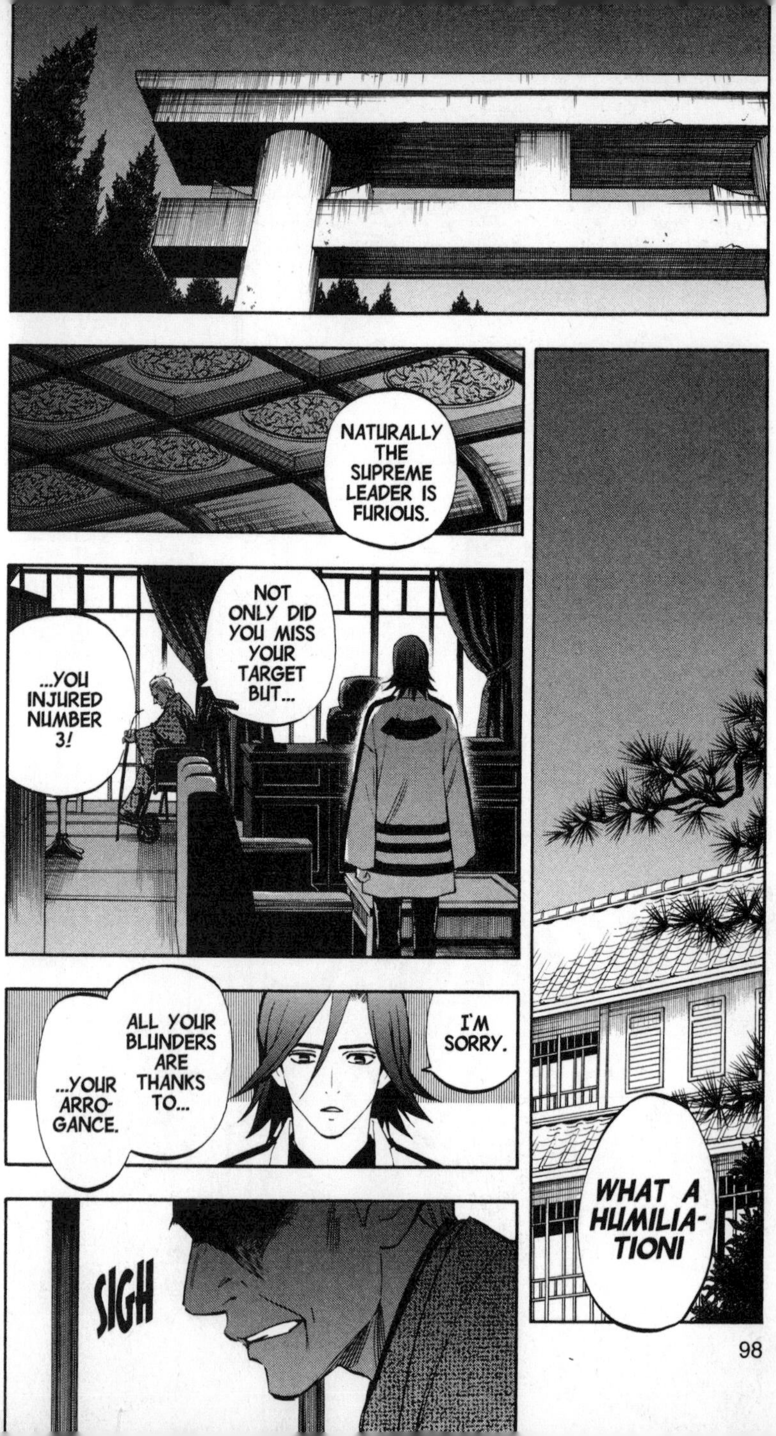
WHAT A HUMILIATION!
NATURALLY THE SUPREME LEADER IS FURIOUS.
NOT ONLY DID YOU MISS YOUR TARGET BUT...
...YOU INJURED NUMBER 3!
I'M SORRY.
ALL YOUR BLUNDERS ARE THANKS TO...
...YOUR ARROGANCE.
SIGH

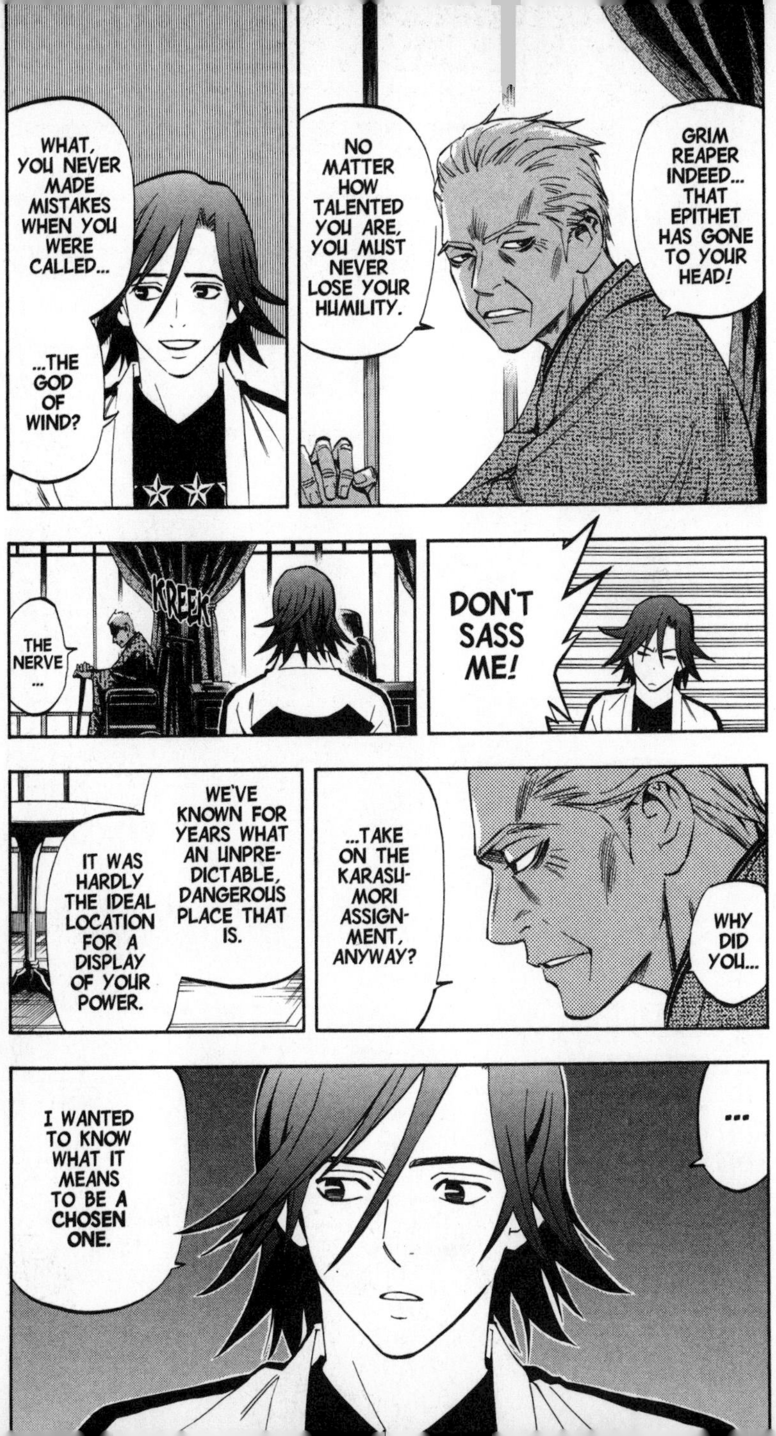
GRIM REAPER INDEED... THAT EPITHET HAS GONE TO YOUR HEAD!
NO MATTER HOW TALENTED YOU ARE, YOU MUST NEVER LOSE YOUR HUMILITY.
WHAT, YOU NEVER MADE MISTAKES WHEN YOU WERE CALLED...
...THE GOD OF WIND?
DON'T SASS ME!
KREEK
THE NERVE...
WHY DID YOU...
...TAKE ON THE KARASU-MORI ASSIGN-MENT, ANYWAY?
WE'VE KNOWN FOR YEARS WHAT AN UNPRE-DICTABLE, DANGEROUS PLACE THAT IS.
IT WAS HARDLY THE IDEAL LOCATION FOR A DISPLAY OF YOUR POWER.
...
I WANTED TO KNOW WHAT IT MEANS TO BE A CHOSEN ONE.

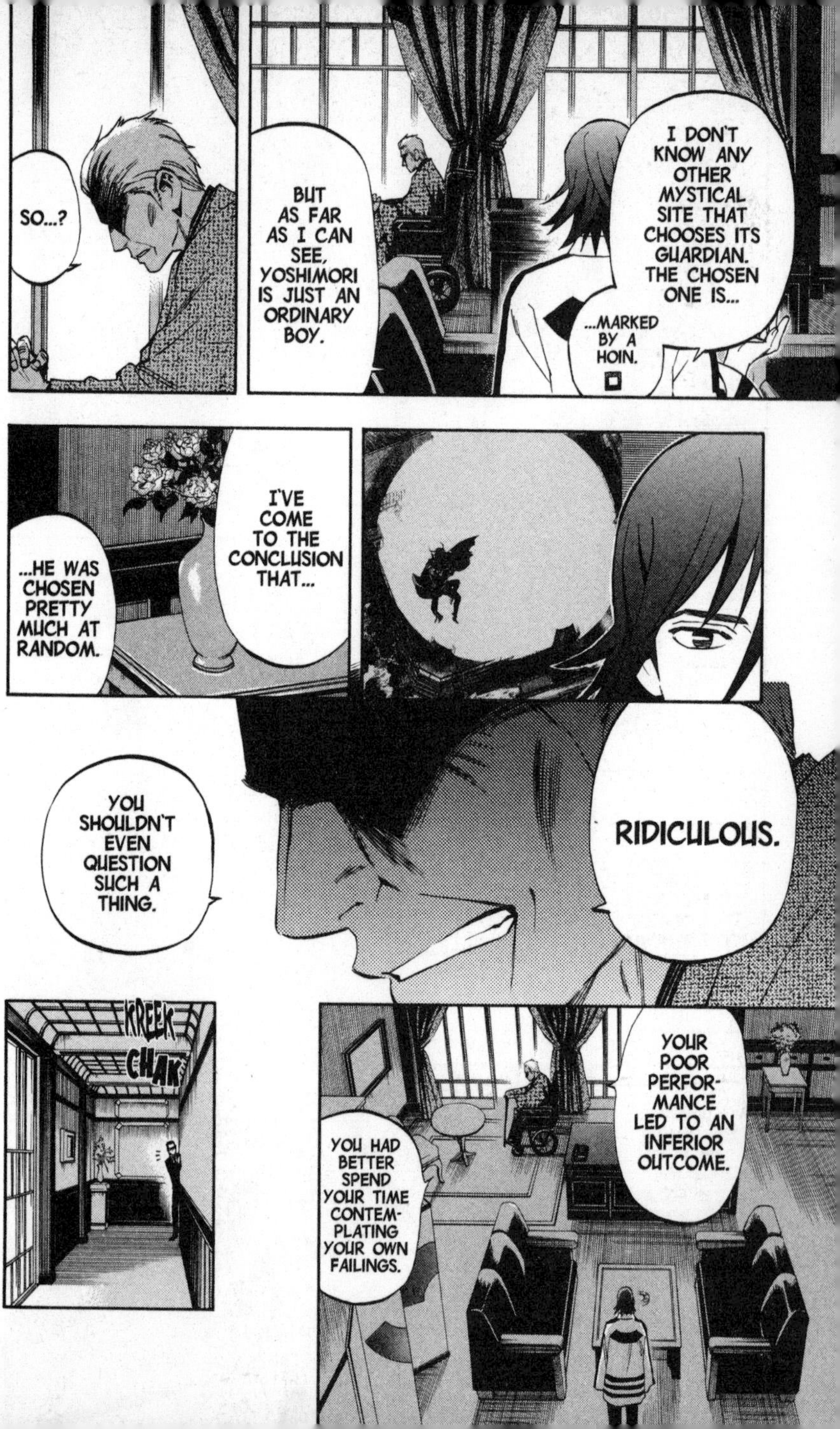
I DON'T KNOW ANY OTHER MYSTICAL SITE THAT CHOOSES ITS GUARDIAN. THE CHOSEN ONE IS...
...MARKED BY A HOIN.
BUT AS FAR AS I CAN SEE, YOSHIMORI IS JUST AN ORDINARY BOY.
SO...?
I'VE COME TO THE CONCLUSION THAT...
...HE WAS CHOSEN PRETTY MUCH AT RANDOM.
RIDICULOUS.
YOU SHOULDN'T EVEN QUESTION SUCH A THING.
YOUR POOR PERFORMANCE LED TO AN INFERIOR OUTCOME.
YOU HAD BETTER SPEND YOUR TIME CONTEMPLATING YOUR OWN FAILINGS.
KREEK
CHAK

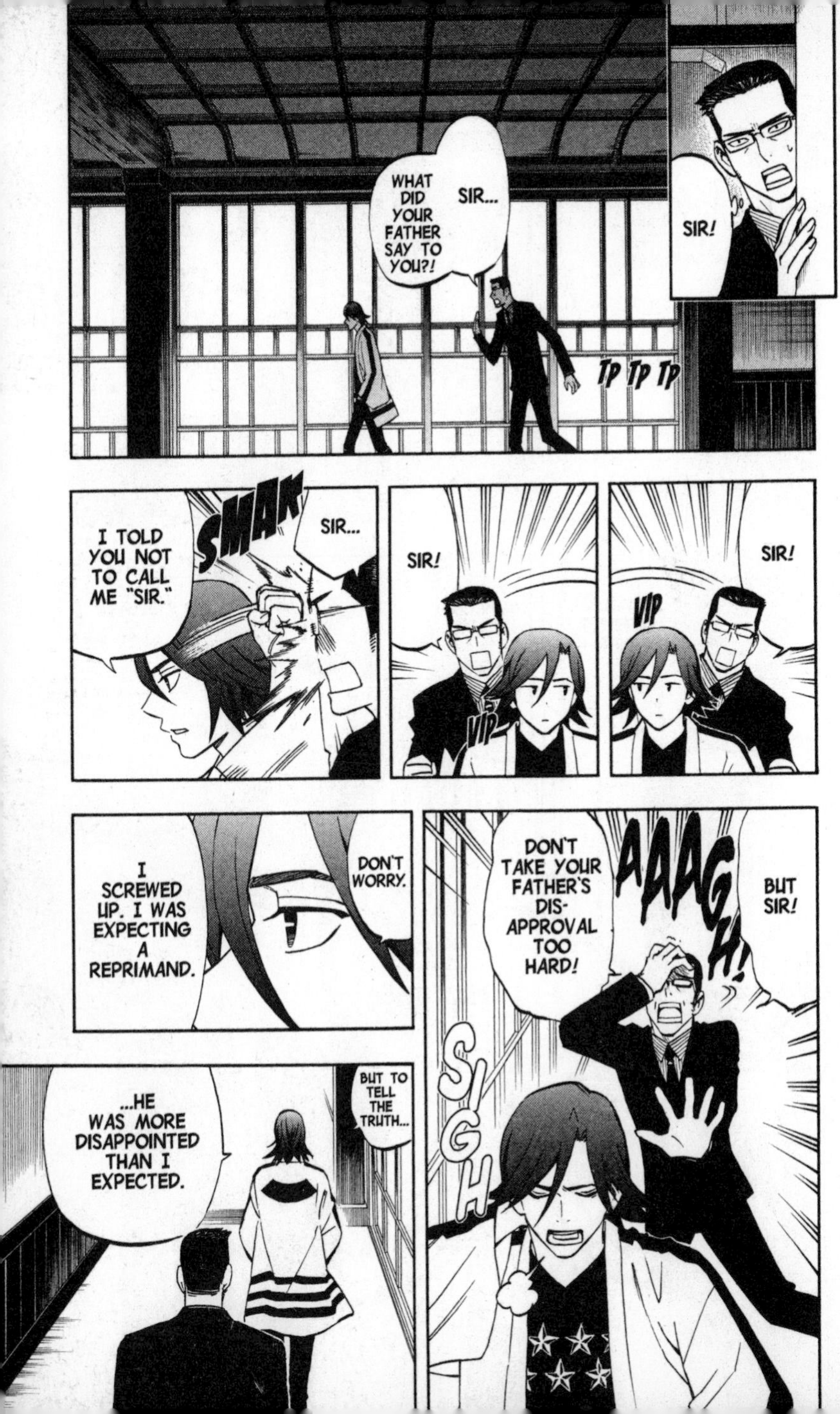
SIR!
SIR...
WHAT DID YOUR FATHER SAY TO YOU?!
Tp Tp Tp
SIR!
VIP
SIR!
VIP
SIR...
SMAK
I TOLD YOU NOT TO CALL ME "SIR."
BUT SIR!
AAAGH!
DON'T TAKE YOUR FATHER'S DIS-APPROVAL TOO HARD!
SIGH
DON'T WORRY.
I SCREWED UP. I WAS EXPECTING A REPRIMAND.
BUT TO TELL THE TRUTH...
...HE WAS MORE DISAPPOINTED THAN I EXPECTED.

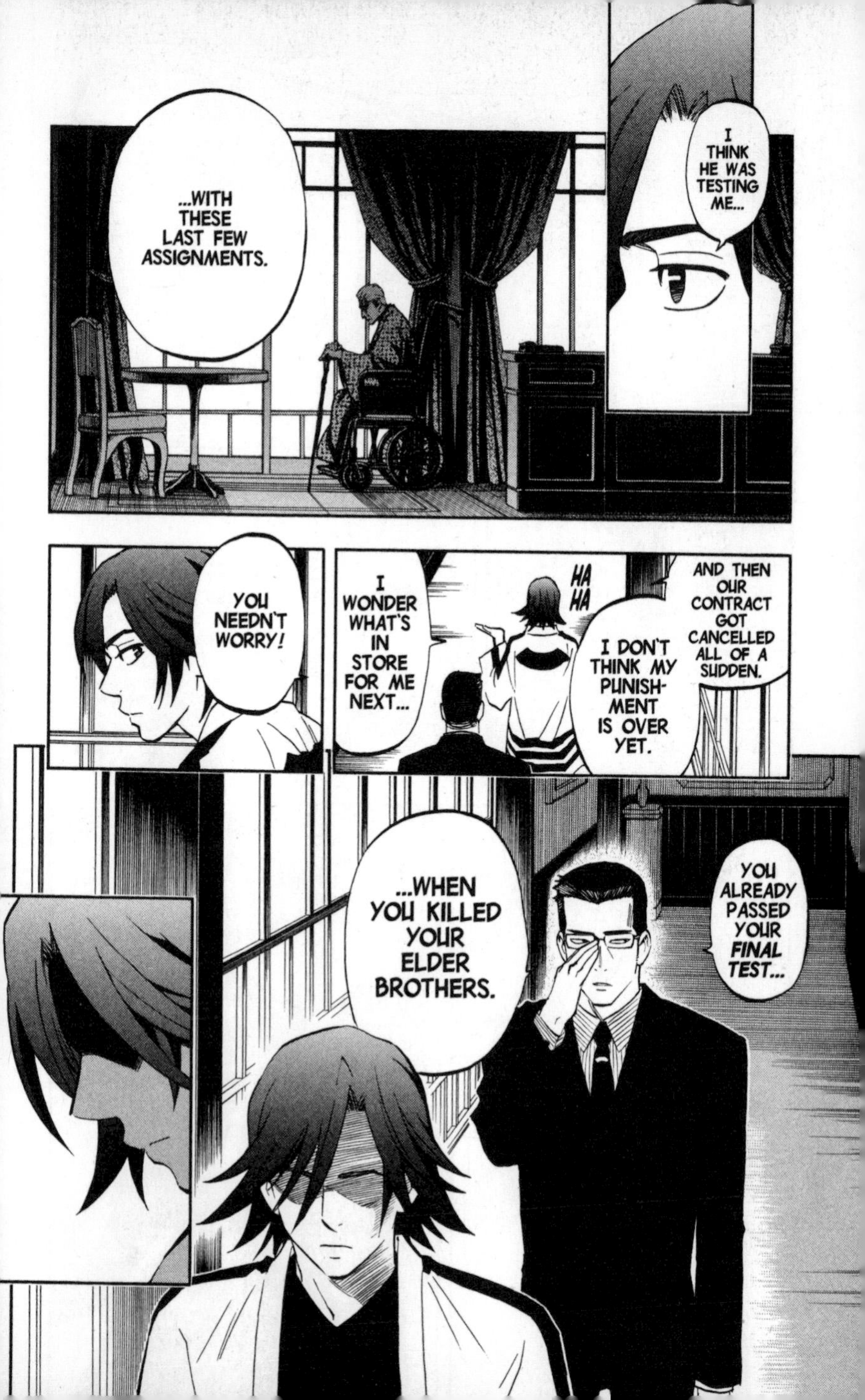
I THINK HE WAS TESTING ME...
...WITH THESE LAST FEW ASSIGNMENTS.
AND THEN OUR CONTRACT GOT CANCELLED ALL OF A SUDDEN.
HA HA
I DON'T THINK MY PUNISHMENT IS OVER YET.
I WONDER WHAT'S IN STORE FOR ME NEXT...
YOU NEEDN'T WORRY!
YOU ALREADY PASSED YOUR *FINAL TEST*...
...WHEN YOU KILLED YOUR ELDER BROTHERS.

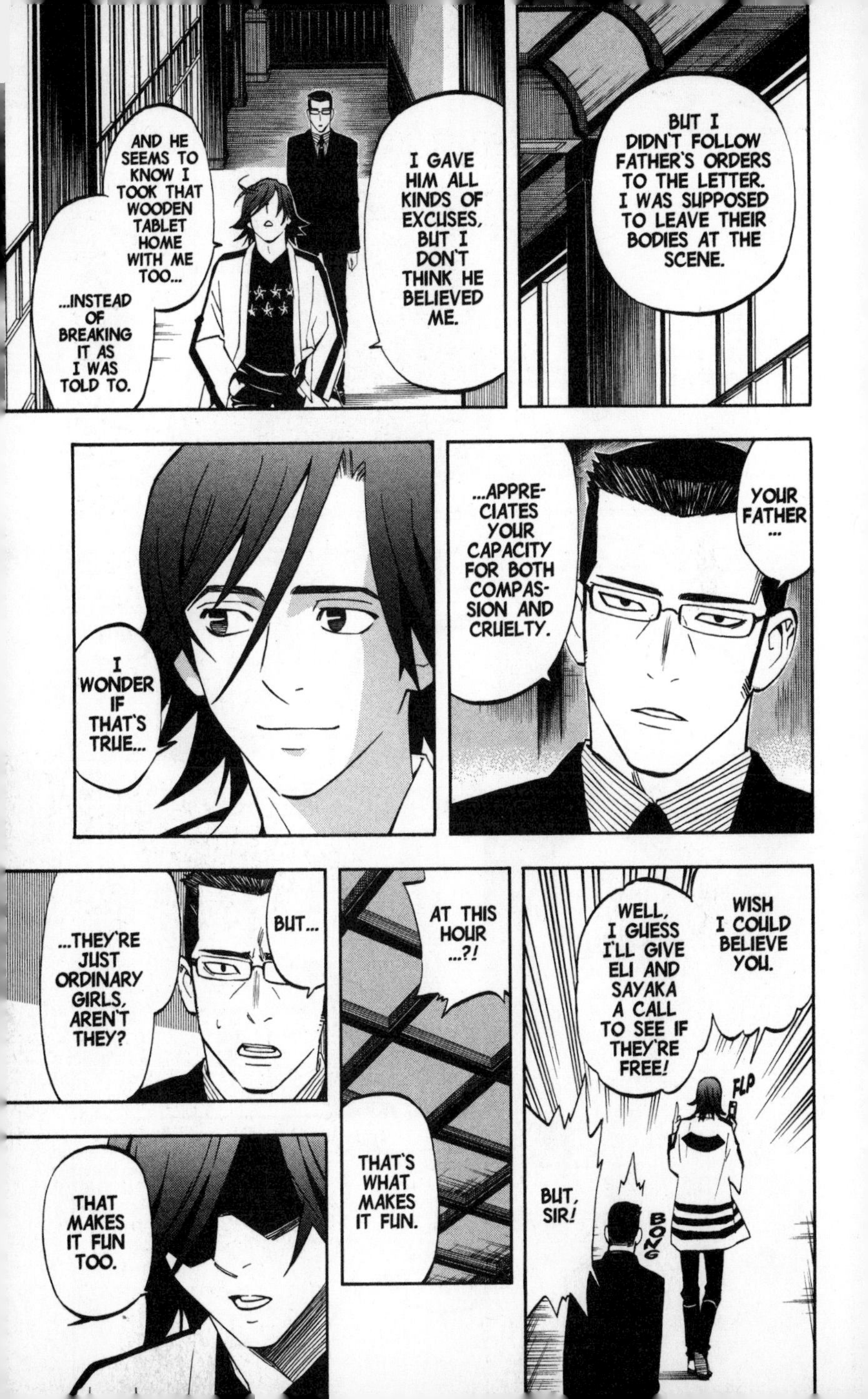
BUT I DIDN'T FOLLOW FATHER'S ORDERS TO THE LETTER. I WAS SUPPOSED TO LEAVE THEIR BODIES AT THE SCENE.
I GAVE HIM ALL KINDS OF EXCUSES, BUT I DON'T THINK HE BELIEVED ME.
AND HE SEEMS TO KNOW I TOOK THAT WOODEN TABLET HOME WITH ME TOO...
...INSTEAD OF BREAKING IT AS I WAS TOLD TO.
YOUR FATHER ...
...APPRECIATES YOUR CAPACITY FOR BOTH COMPASSION AND CRUELTY.
I WONDER IF THAT'S TRUE...
WISH I COULD BELIEVE YOU.
WELL, I GUESS I'LL GIVE ELI AND SAYAKA A CALL TO SEE IF THEY'RE FREE!
FLP
BUT, SIR!
BONG
AT THIS HOUR ...?!
THAT'S WHAT MAKES IT FUN.
BUT...
...THEY'RE JUST ORDINARY GIRLS, AREN'T THEY?
THAT MAKES IT FUN TOO.

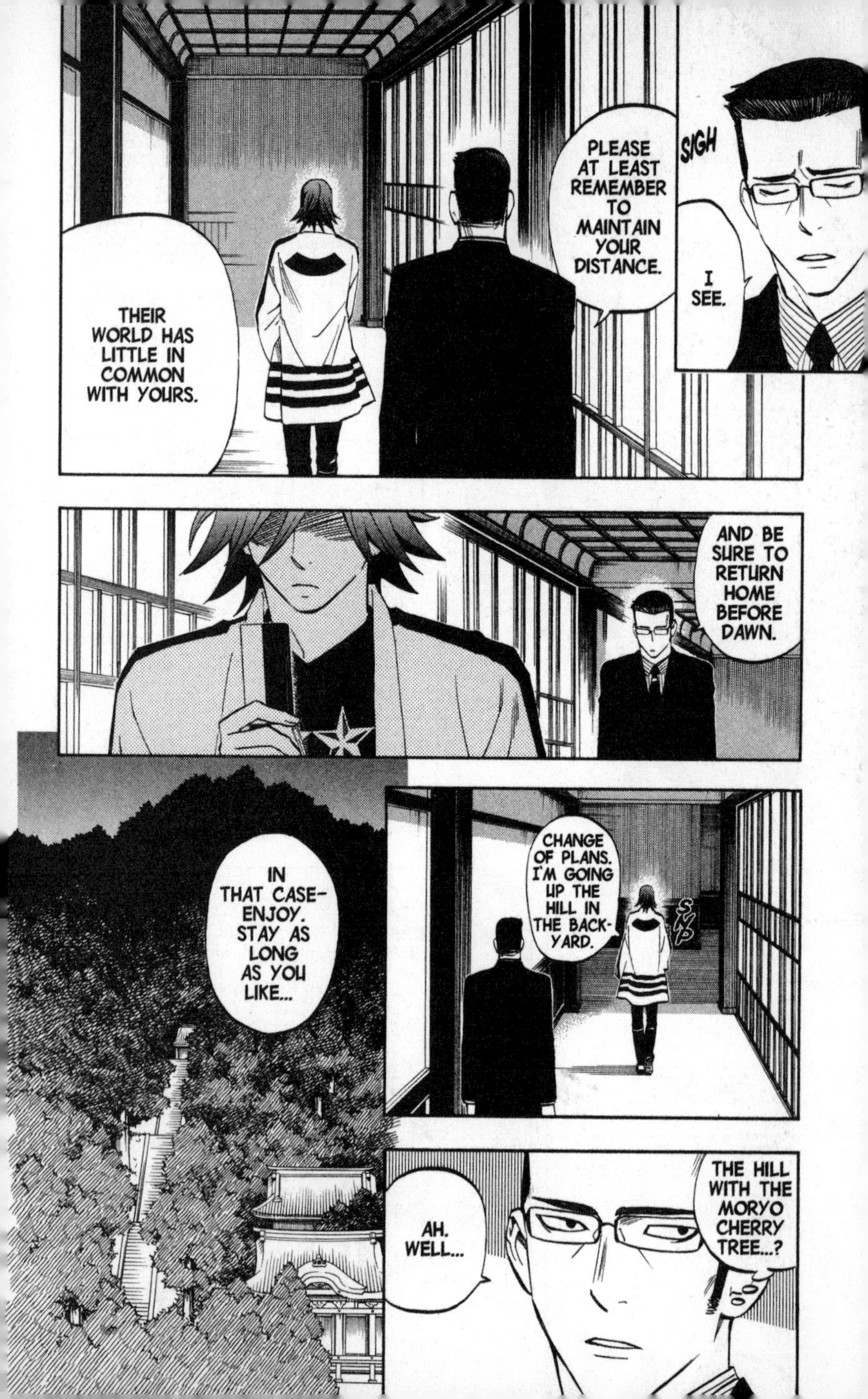
SIGH
I SEE.
PLEASE AT LEAST REMEMBER TO MAINTAIN YOUR DISTANCE.
THEIR WORLD HAS LITTLE IN COMMON WITH YOURS.
AND BE SURE TO RETURN HOME BEFORE DAWN.
CHANGE OF PLANS. I'M GOING UP THE HILL IN THE BACK-YARD.
SNAP
THE HILL WITH THE MORYO CHERRY TREE...?
AH. WELL...
IN THAT CASE-ENJOY. STAY AS LONG AS YOU LIKE...

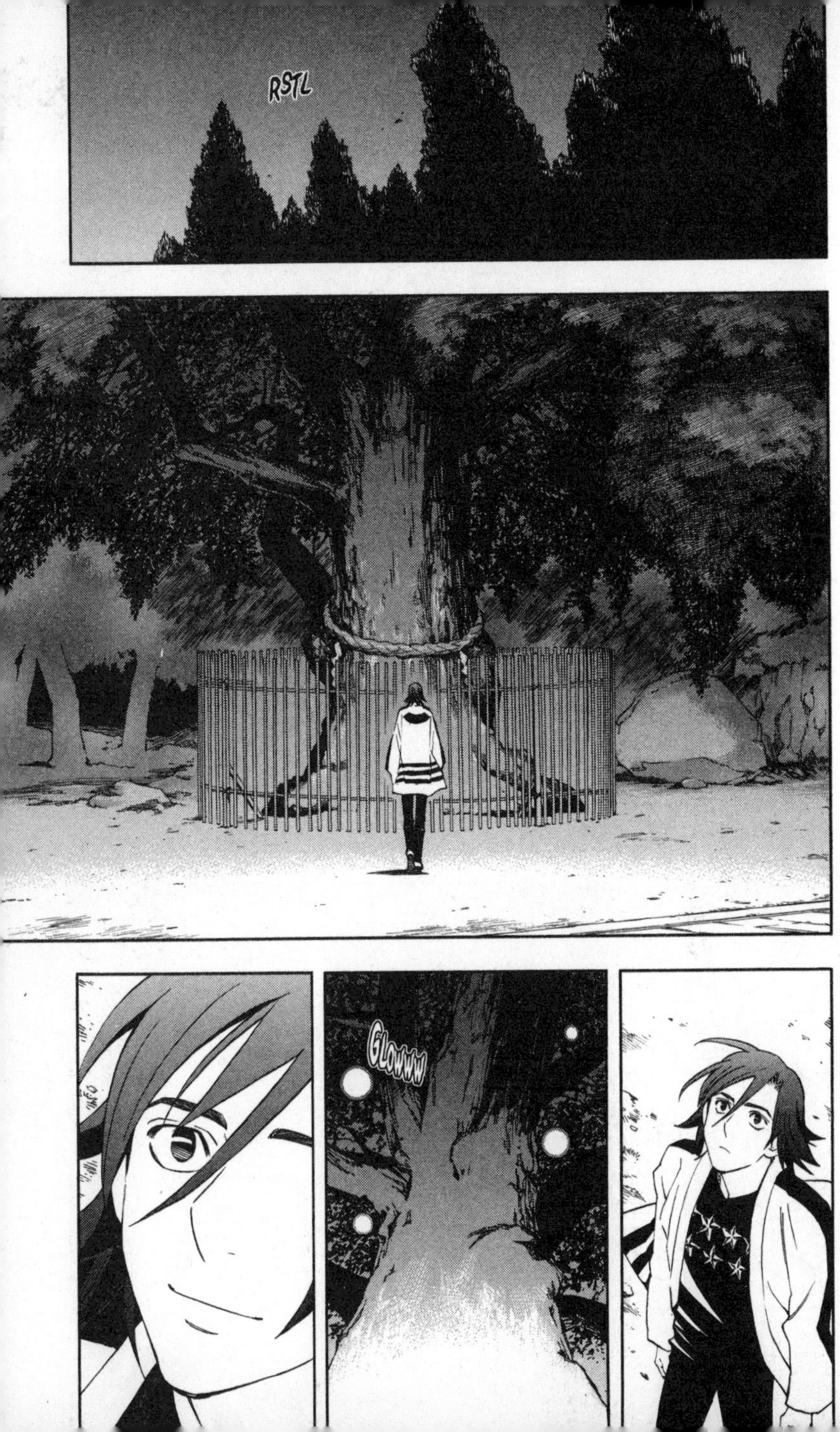
RSTL
GLOWWW

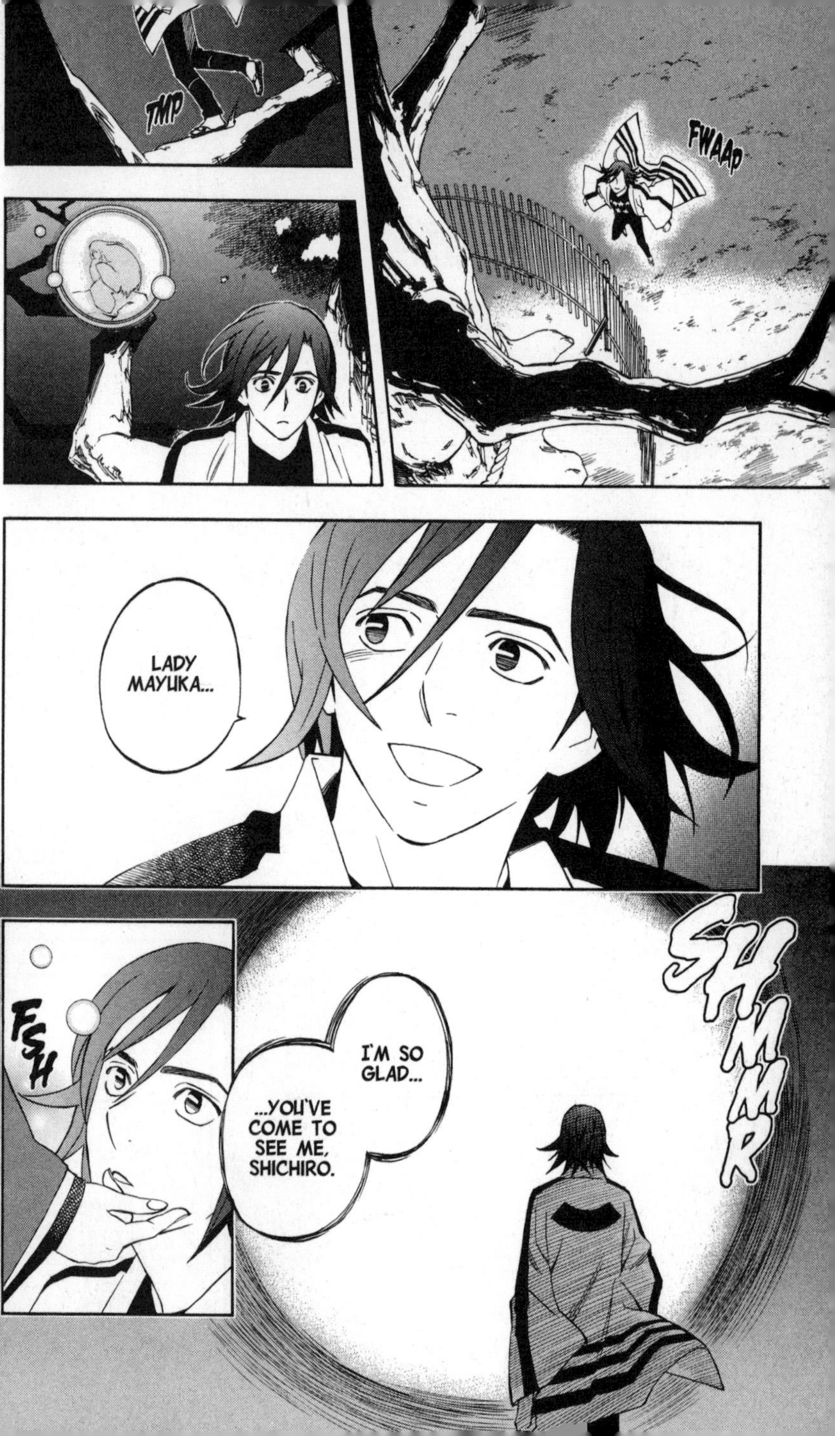
FWAAP
TMP
LADY MAYUKA...
SHMMR
I'M SO GLAD...
...YOU'VE COME TO SEE ME, SHICHIRO.
FSH

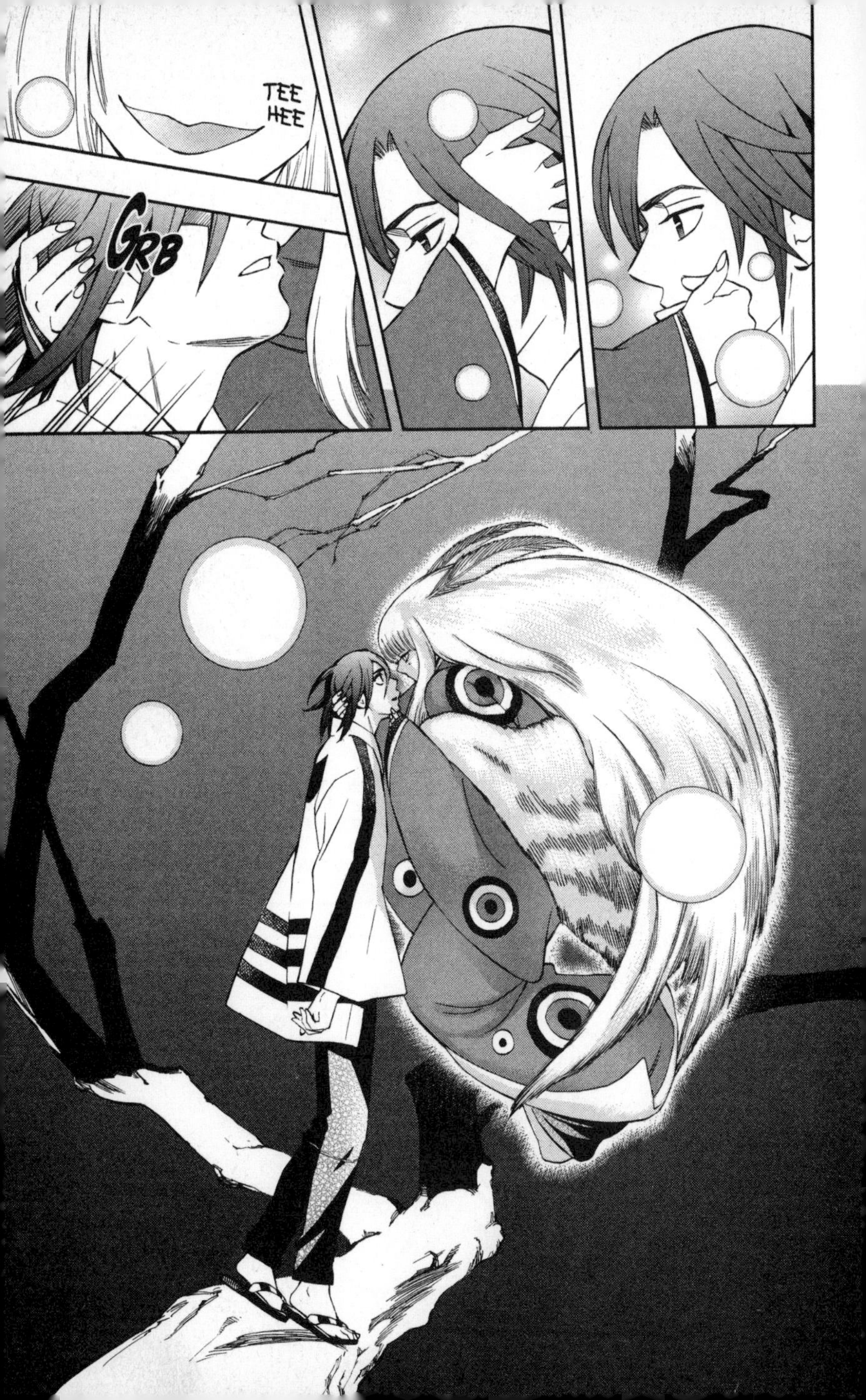
TEE HEE
GRB

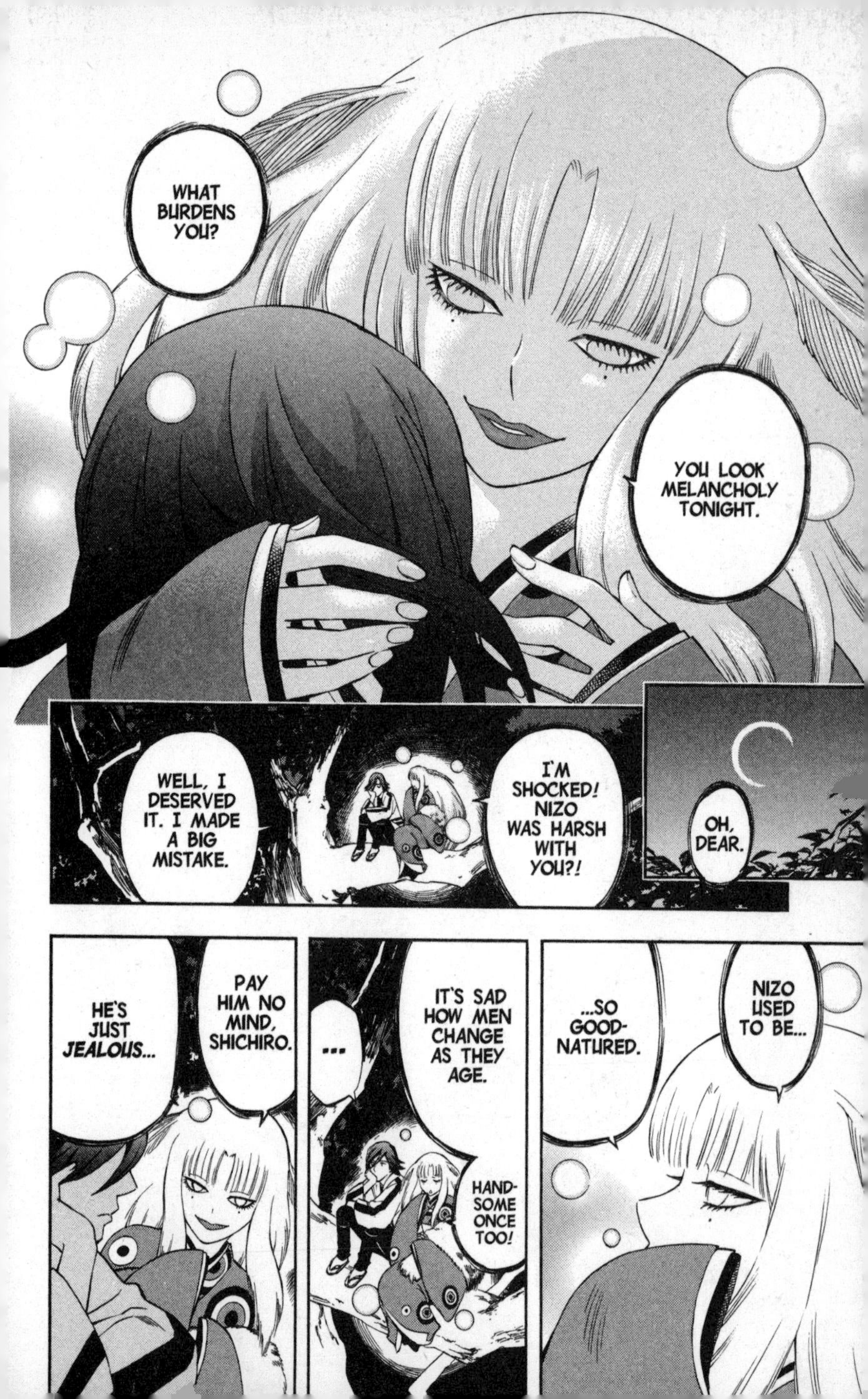
YOU LOOK MELANCHOLY TONIGHT.
WHAT BURDENS YOU?
OH, DEAR.
I'M SHOCKED! NIZO WAS HARSH WITH YOU?!
WELL, I DESERVED IT. I MADE A BIG MISTAKE.
NIZO USED TO BE...
...SO GOOD-NATURED.
IT'S SAD HOW MEN CHANGE AS THEY AGE.
HAND-SOME ONCE TOO!
...
PAY HIM NO MIND, SHICHIRO.
HE'S JUST *JEALOUS*...

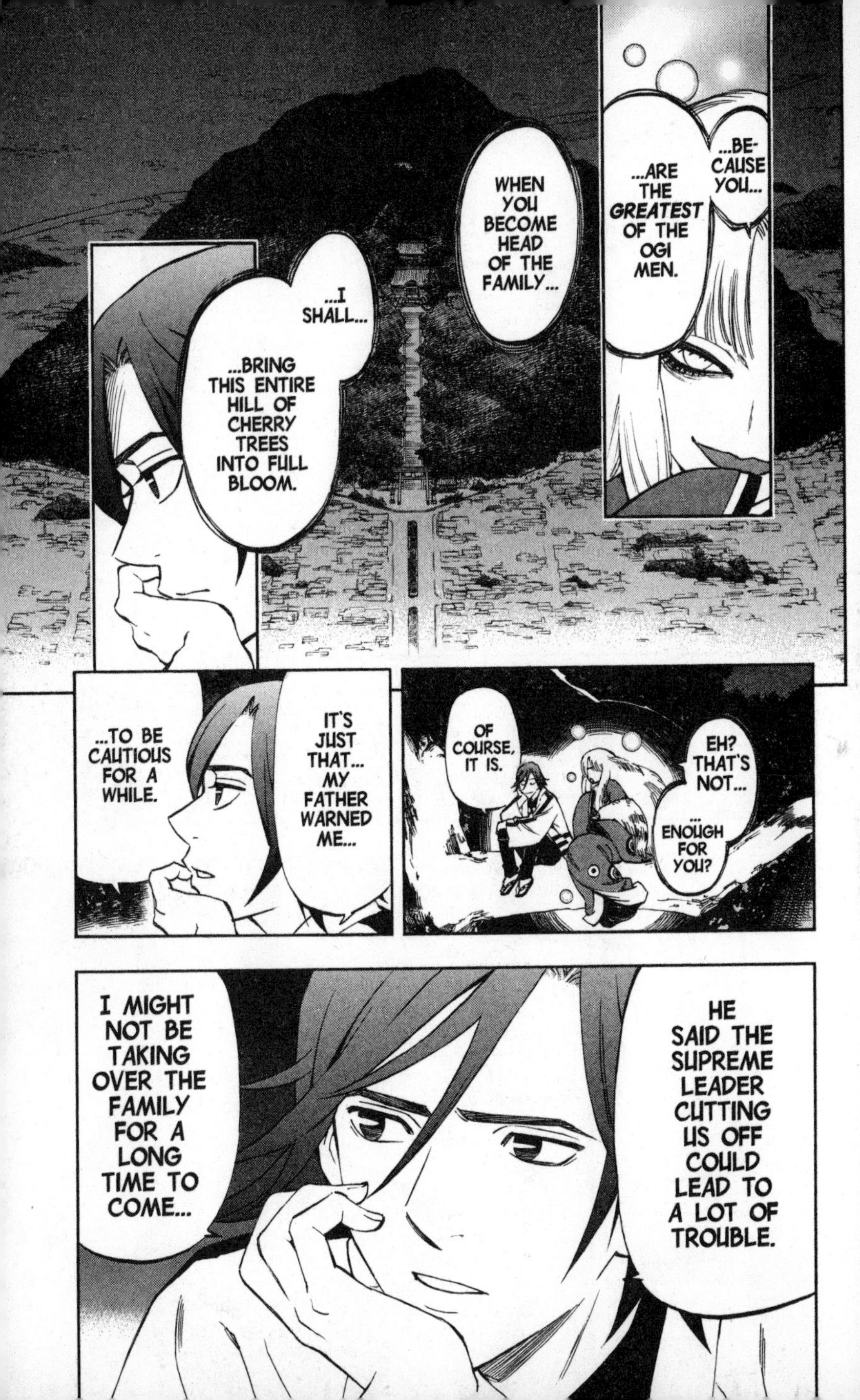
...BE-CAUSE YOU...
...ARE THE *GREATEST* OF THE OGI MEN.
WHEN YOU BECOME HEAD OF THE FAMILY...
...I SHALL...
...BRING THIS ENTIRE HILL OF CHERRY TREES INTO FULL BLOOM.
EH? THAT'S NOT...
...ENOUGH FOR YOU?
OF COURSE, IT IS.
IT'S JUST THAT... MY FATHER WARNED ME...
...TO BE CAUTIOUS FOR A WHILE.
HE SAID THE SUPREME LEADER CUTTING US OFF COULD LEAD TO A LOT OF TROUBLE.
I MIGHT NOT BE TAKING OVER THE FAMILY FOR A LONG TIME TO COME...

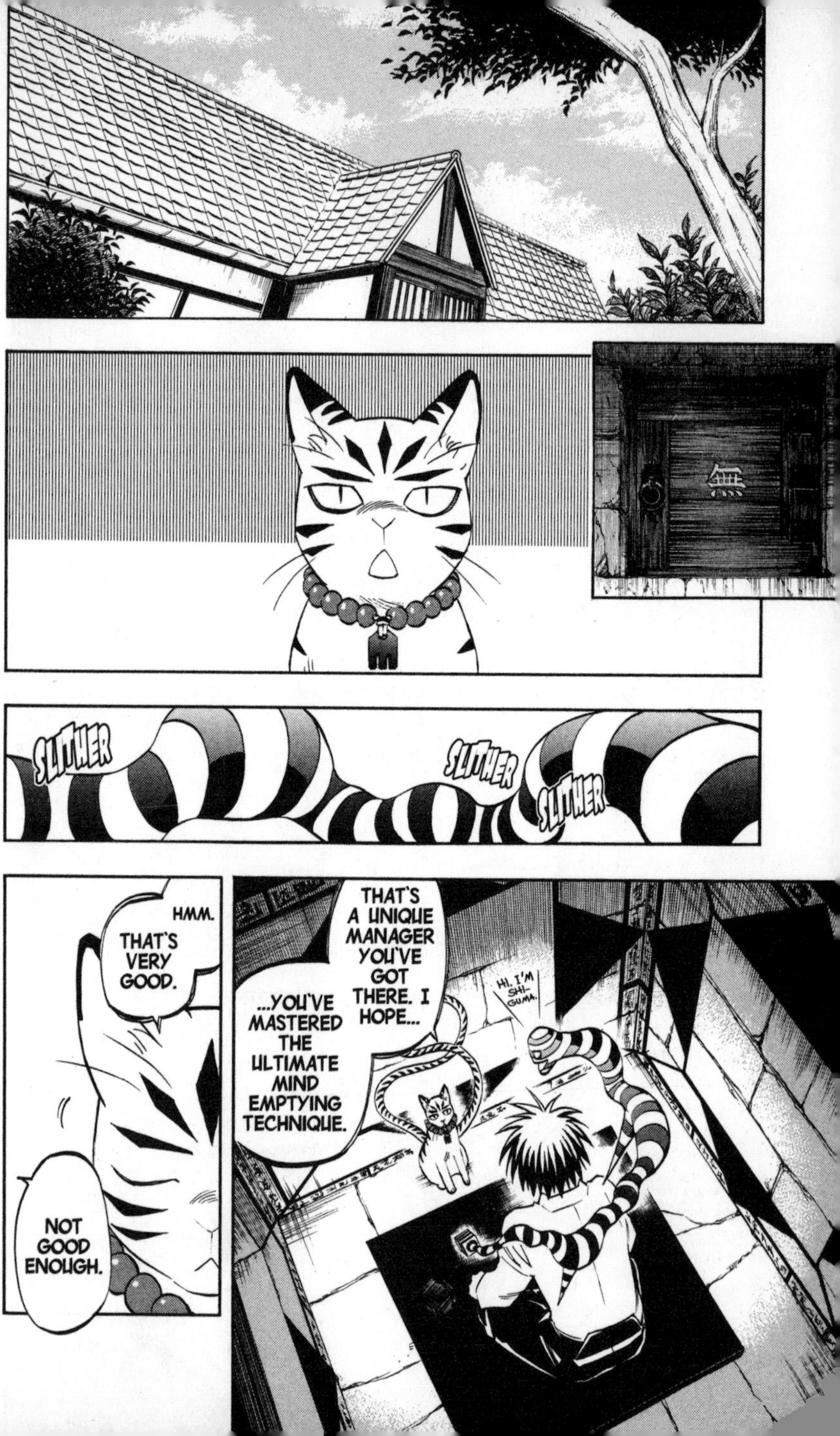
無
SLITHER
SLITHER
SLITHER
THAT'S A UNIQUE MANAGER YOU'VE GOT THERE. I HOPE...
...YOU'VE MASTERED THE ULTIMATE MIND EMPTYING TECHNIQUE.
HI, I'M SHI-GUMA.
HMM. THAT'S VERY GOOD.
NOT GOOD ENOUGH.

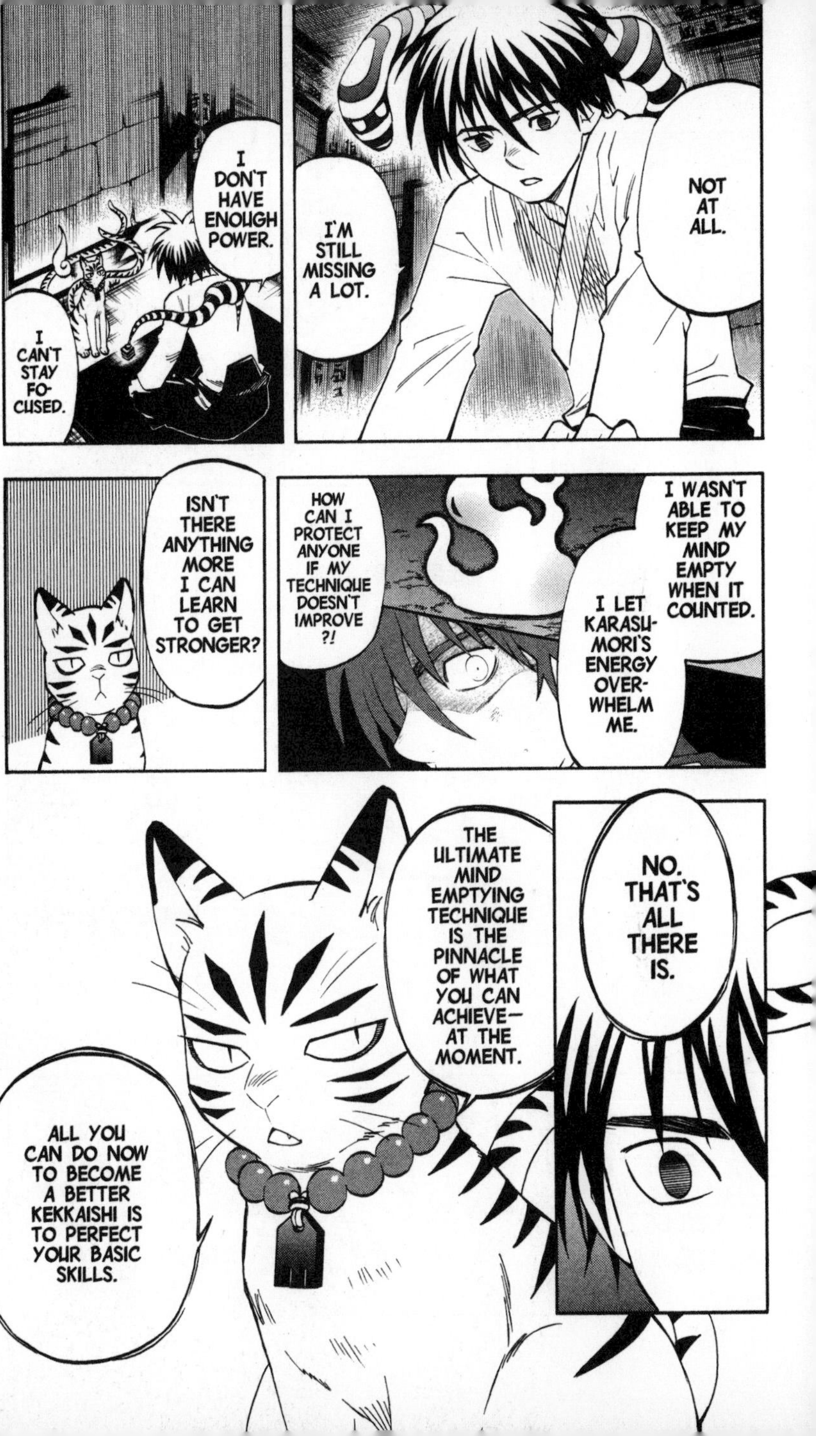
NOT AT ALL.
I'M STILL MISSING A LOT.
I DON'T HAVE ENOUGH POWER.
I CAN'T STAY FOCUSED.
I WASN'T ABLE TO KEEP MY MIND EMPTY WHEN IT COUNTED.
I LET KARASUMORI'S ENERGY OVERWHELM ME.
HOW CAN I PROTECT ANYONE IF MY TECHNIQUE DOESN'T IMPROVE?!
ISN'T THERE ANYTHING MORE I CAN LEARN TO GET STRONGER?
NO. THAT'S ALL THERE IS.
THE ULTIMATE MIND EMPTYING TECHNIQUE IS THE PINNACLE OF WHAT YOU CAN ACHIEVE—AT THE MOMENT.
ALL YOU CAN DO NOW TO BECOME A BETTER KEKKAISHI IS TO PERFECT YOUR BASIC SKILLS.

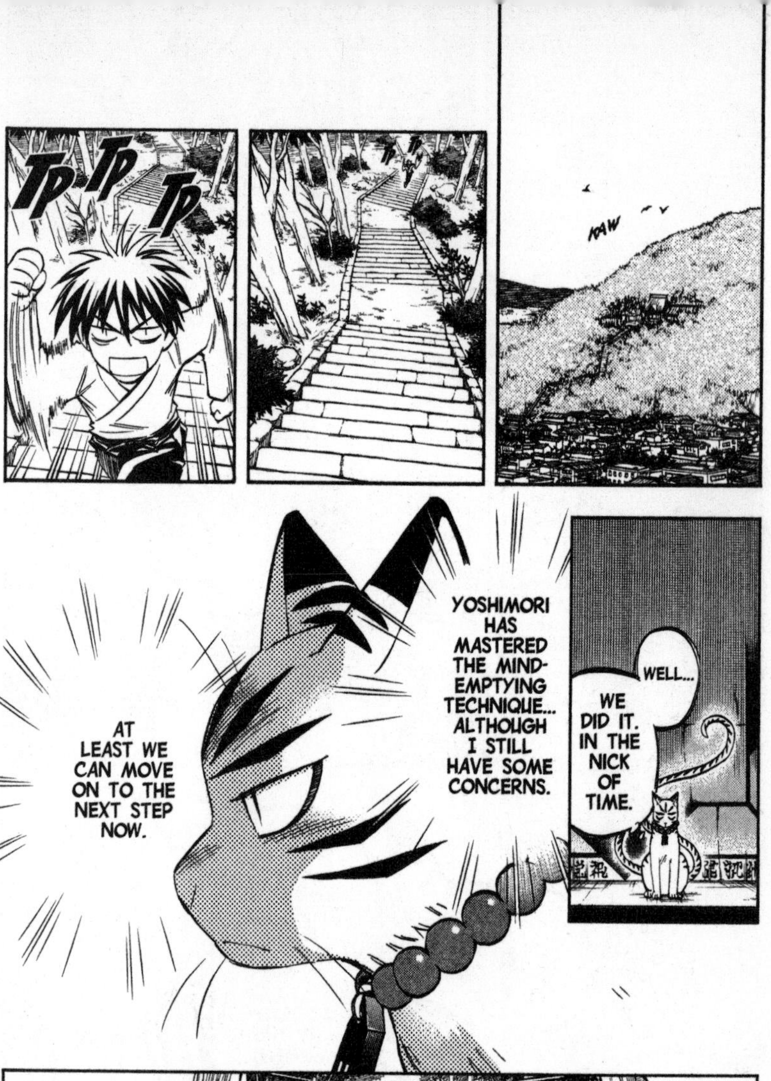
KAW
TP TP
TP TP TP
WELL...
WE DID IT. IN THE NICK OF TIME.
YOSHIMORI HAS MASTERED THE MIND-EMPTYING TECHNIQUE... ALTHOUGH I STILL HAVE SOME CONCERNS.
AT LEAST WE CAN MOVE ON TO THE NEXT STEP NOW.
ALL RIGHT. HOW DO I...
...PERFECT MY BASIC SKILLS?!

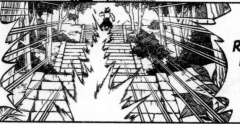

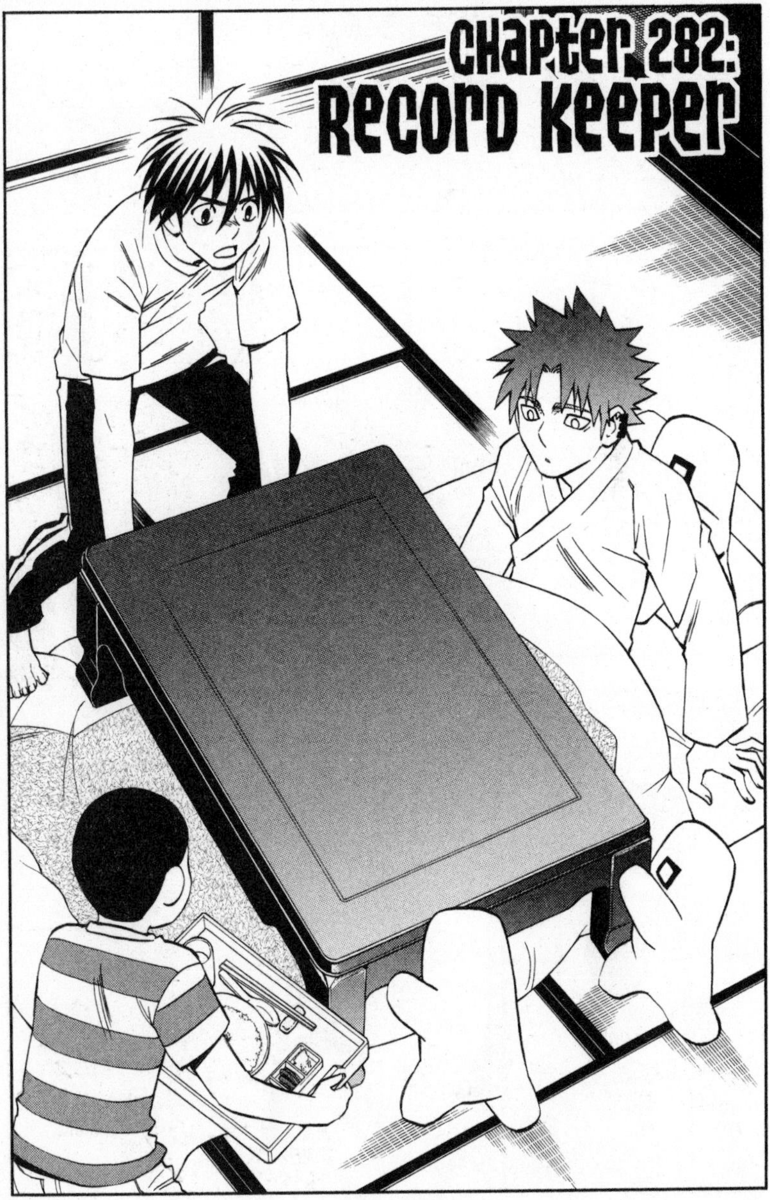
Chapter 282:
Record Keeper

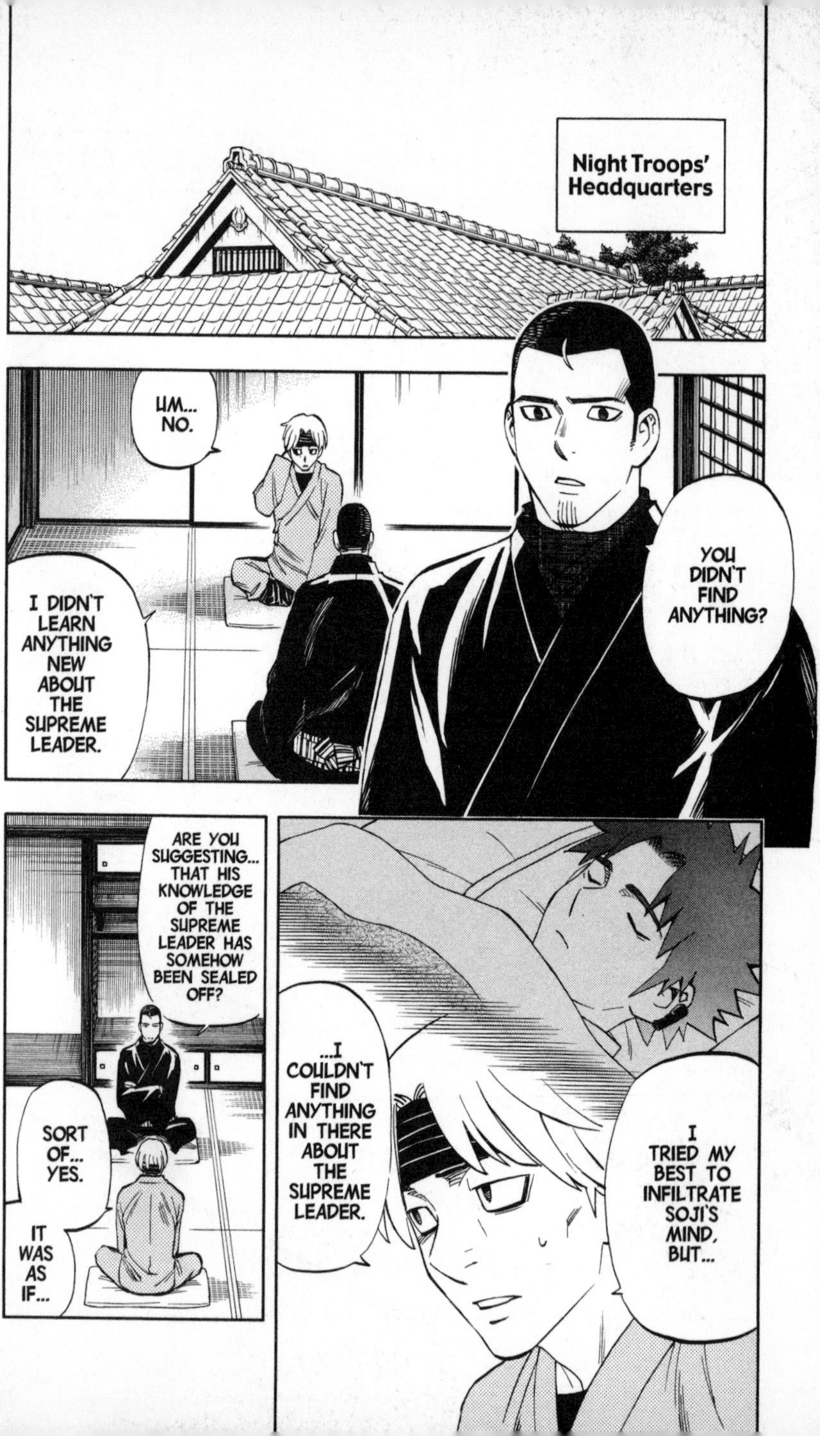
Night Troops' Headquarters
YOU DIDN'T FIND ANYTHING?
UM... NO.
I DIDN'T LEARN ANYTHING NEW ABOUT THE SUPREME LEADER.
I TRIED MY BEST TO INFILTRATE SOJI'S MIND, BUT...
...I COULDN'T FIND ANYTHING IN THERE ABOUT THE SUPREME LEADER.
ARE YOU SUGGESTING... THAT HIS KNOWLEDGE OF THE SUPREME LEADER HAS SOMEHOW BEEN SEALED OFF?
SORT OF... YES.
IT WAS AS IF...

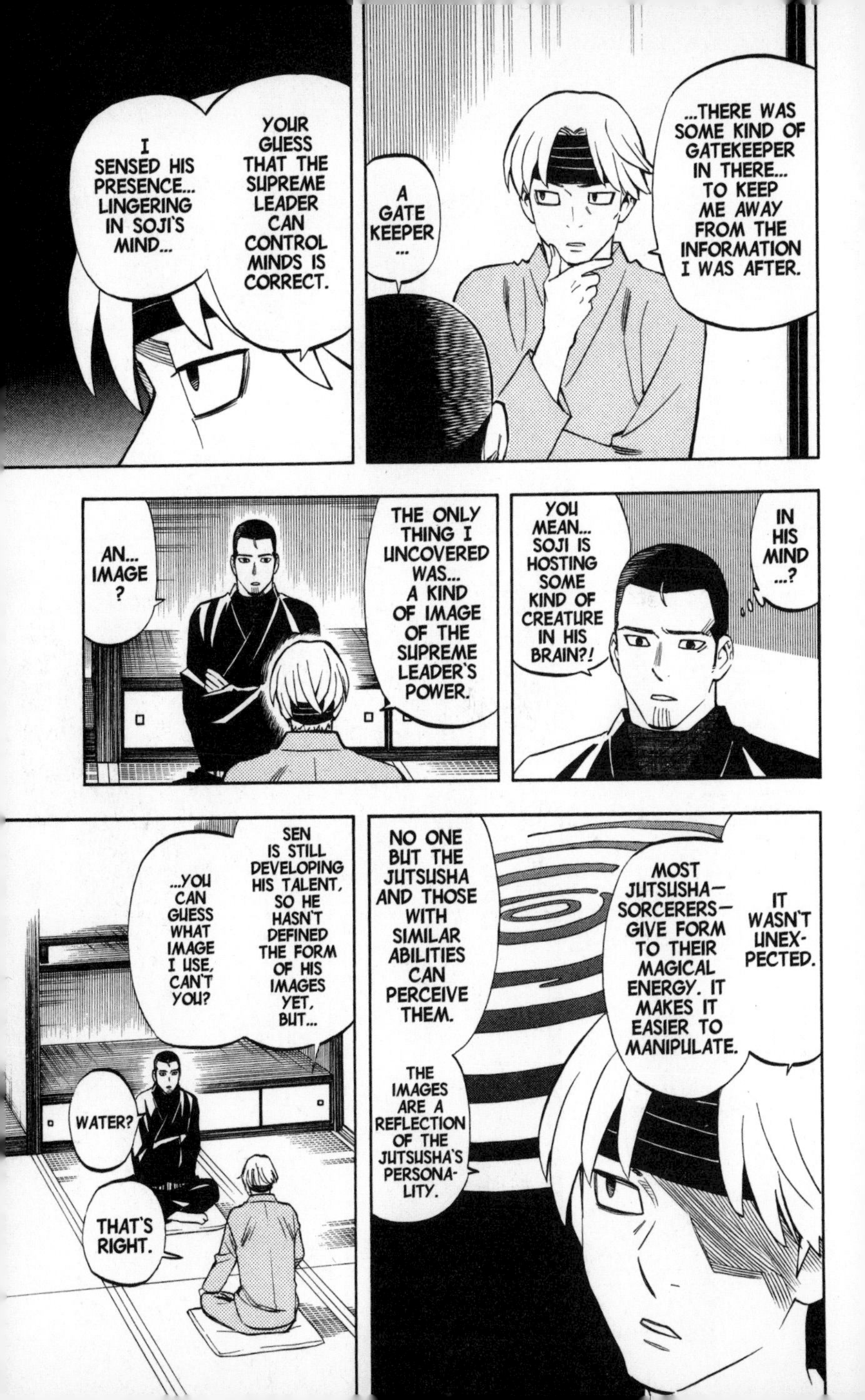
...THERE WAS SOME KIND OF GATEKEEPER IN THERE... TO KEEP ME AWAY FROM THE INFORMATION I WAS AFTER.
A GATE KEEPER ...
YOUR GUESS THAT THE SUPREME LEADER CAN CONTROL MINDS IS CORRECT.
I SENSED HIS PRESENCE... LINGERING IN SOJI'S MIND...
IN HIS MIND ...?
YOU MEAN... SOJI IS HOSTING SOME KIND OF CREATURE IN HIS BRAIN?!
THE ONLY THING I UNCOVERED WAS... A KIND OF IMAGE OF THE SUPREME LEADER'S POWER.
AN... IMAGE ?
IT WASN'T UNEX-PECTED.
MOST JUTSUSHA— SORCERERS— GIVE FORM TO THEIR MAGICAL ENERGY. IT MAKES IT EASIER TO MANIPULATE.
NO ONE BUT THE JUTSUSHA AND THOSE WITH SIMILAR ABILITIES CAN PERCEIVE THEM.
THE IMAGES ARE A REFLECTION OF THE JUTSUSHA'S PERSONA-LITY.
SEN IS STILL DEVELOPING HIS TALENT, SO HE HASN'T DEFINED THE FORM OF HIS IMAGES YET, BUT...
...YOU CAN GUESS WHAT IMAGE I USE, CAN'T YOU?
WATER?
THAT'S RIGHT.

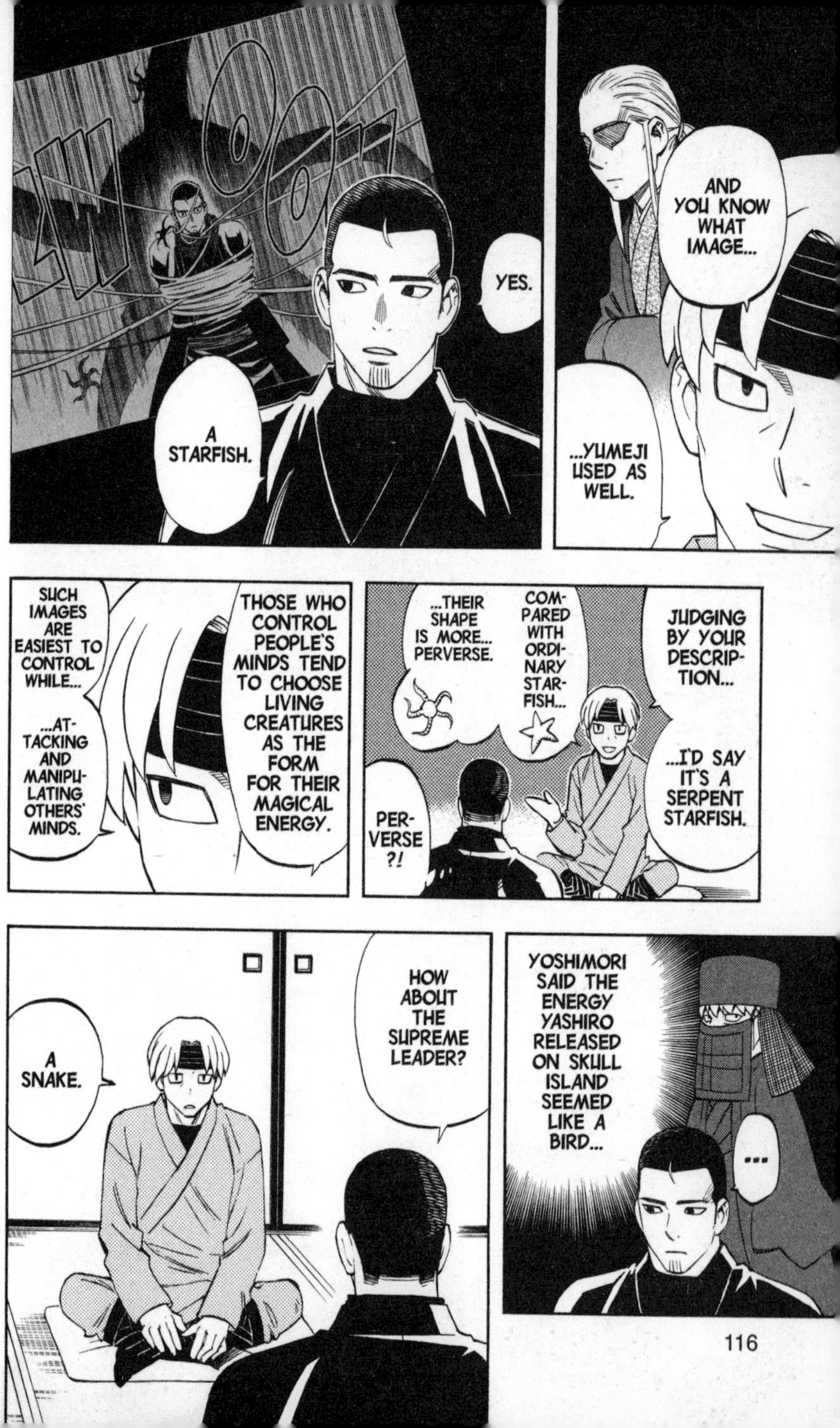
AND YOU KNOW WHAT IMAGE...
...YUMEJI USED AS WELL.
YES.
A STARFISH.
JUDGING BY YOUR DESCRIPTION...
...I'D SAY IT'S A SERPENT STARFISH.
COMPARED WITH ORDINARY STARFISH...
...THEIR SHAPE IS MORE... PERVERSE.
PERVERSE?!
THOSE WHO CONTROL PEOPLE'S MINDS TEND TO CHOOSE LIVING CREATURES AS THE FORM FOR THEIR MAGICAL ENERGY.
SUCH IMAGES ARE EASIEST TO CONTROL WHILE...
...ATTACKING AND MANIPULATING OTHERS' MINDS.
YOSHIMORI SAID THE ENERGY YASHIRO RELEASED ON SKULL ISLAND SEEMED LIKE A BIRD...
...
HOW ABOUT THE SUPREME LEADER?
A SNAKE.

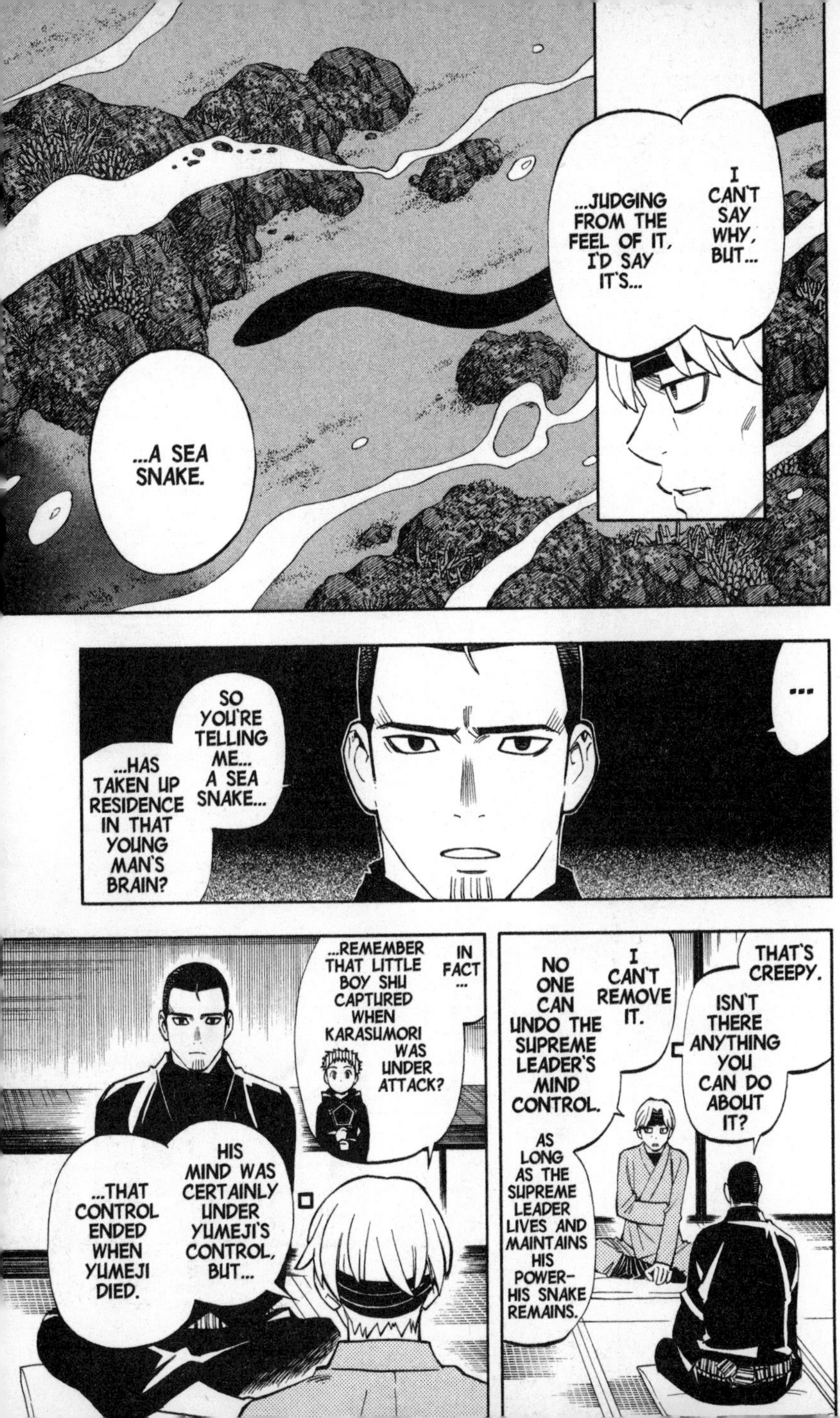
I CAN'T SAY WHY, BUT...
...JUDGING FROM THE FEEL OF IT, I'D SAY IT'S...
...A SEA SNAKE.
...
SO YOU'RE TELLING ME... A SEA SNAKE...
...HAS TAKEN UP RESIDENCE IN THAT YOUNG MAN'S BRAIN?
THAT'S CREEPY.
ISN'T THERE ANYTHING YOU CAN DO ABOUT IT?
I CAN'T REMOVE IT.
NO ONE CAN UNDO THE SUPREME LEADER'S MIND CONTROL.
AS LONG AS THE SUPREME LEADER LIVES AND MAINTAINS HIS POWER-HIS SNAKE REMAINS.
IN FACT...
...REMEMBER THAT LITTLE BOY SHU CAPTURED WHEN KARASUMORI WAS UNDER ATTACK?
HIS MIND WAS CERTAINLY UNDER YUMEJI'S CONTROL, BUT...
...THAT CONTROL ENDED WHEN YUMEJI DIED.

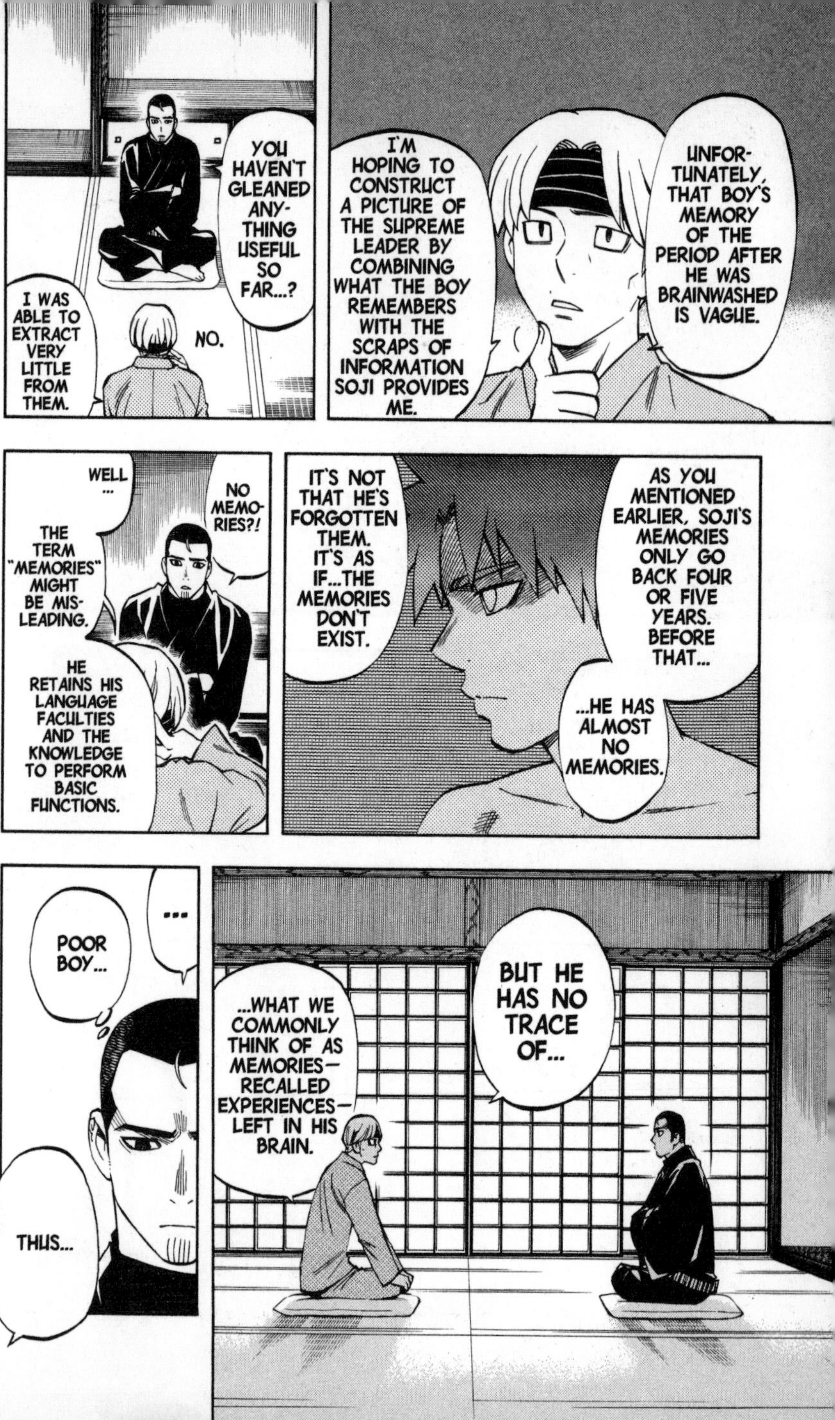
UNFORTUNATELY, THAT BOY'S MEMORY OF THE PERIOD AFTER HE WAS BRAINWASHED IS VAGUE.
I'M HOPING TO CONSTRUCT A PICTURE OF THE SUPREME LEADER BY COMBINING WHAT THE BOY REMEMBERS WITH THE SCRAPS OF INFORMATION SOJI PROVIDES ME.
YOU HAVEN'T GLEANED ANYTHING USEFUL SO FAR...?
NO.
I WAS ABLE TO EXTRACT VERY LITTLE FROM THEM.
AS YOU MENTIONED EARLIER, SOJI'S MEMORIES ONLY GO BACK FOUR OR FIVE YEARS. BEFORE THAT...
...HE HAS ALMOST NO MEMORIES.
IT'S NOT THAT HE'S FORGOTTEN THEM. IT'S AS IF...THE MEMORIES DON'T EXIST.
NO MEMORIES?!
WELL...
THE TERM "MEMORIES" MIGHT BE MISLEADING.
HE RETAINS HIS LANGUAGE FACULTIES AND THE KNOWLEDGE TO PERFORM BASIC FUNCTIONS.
BUT HE HAS NO TRACE OF...
...WHAT WE COMMONLY THINK OF AS MEMORIES—RECALLED EXPERIENCES—LEFT IN HIS BRAIN.
...
POOR BOY...
THUS...

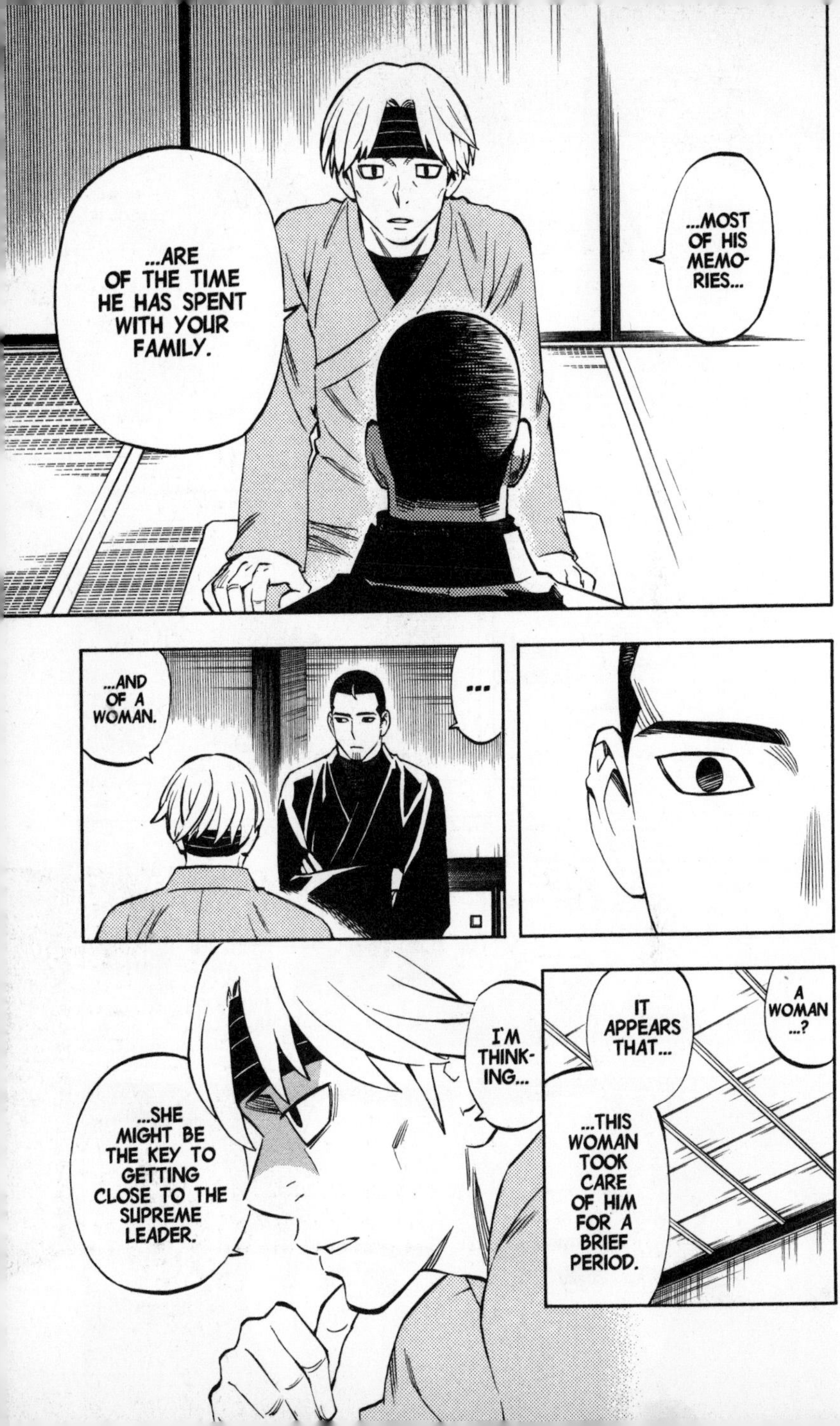
...MOST OF HIS MEMORIES...
...ARE OF THE TIME HE HAS SPENT WITH YOUR FAMILY.
...
...AND OF A WOMAN.
A WOMAN ...?
IT APPEARS THAT...
...THIS WOMAN TOOK CARE OF HIM FOR A BRIEF PERIOD.
I'M THINKING...
...SHE MIGHT BE THE KEY TO GETTING CLOSE TO THE SUPREME LEADER.

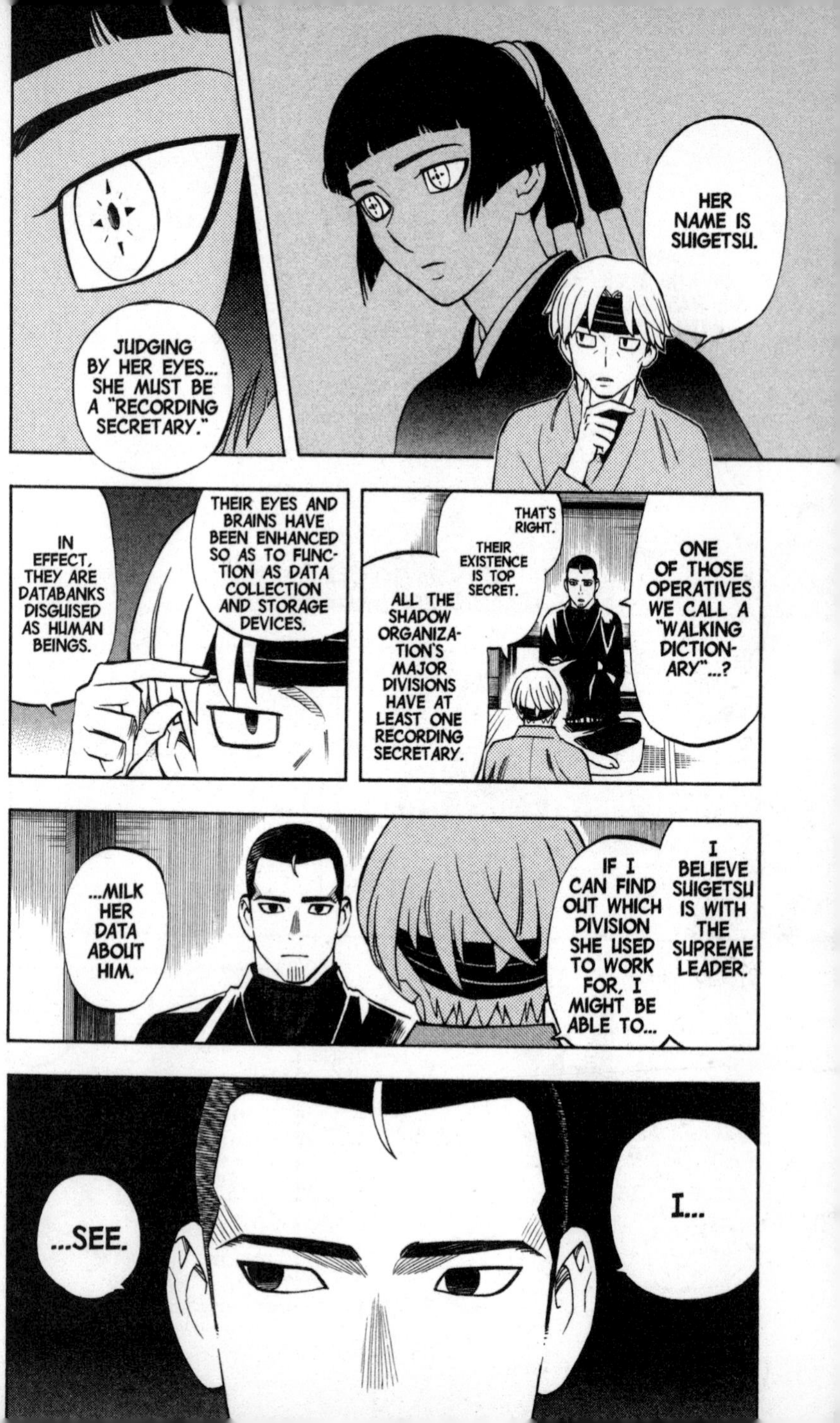
HER NAME IS SUIGETSU.
JUDGING BY HER EYES... SHE MUST BE A "RECORDING SECRETARY."
ONE OF THOSE OPERATIVES WE CALL A "WALKING DICTIONARY"...?
THAT'S RIGHT.
THEIR EXISTENCE IS TOP SECRET.
ALL THE SHADOW ORGANIZATION'S MAJOR DIVISIONS HAVE AT LEAST ONE RECORDING SECRETARY.
THEIR EYES AND BRAINS HAVE BEEN ENHANCED SO AS TO FUNCTION AS DATA COLLECTION AND STORAGE DEVICES.
IN EFFECT, THEY ARE DATABANKS DISGUISED AS HUMAN BEINGS.
I BELIEVE SUIGETSU IS WITH THE SUPREME LEADER.
IF I CAN FIND OUT WHICH DIVISION SHE USED TO WORK FOR, I MIGHT BE ABLE TO...
...MILK HER DATA ABOUT HIM.
I...
...SEE.

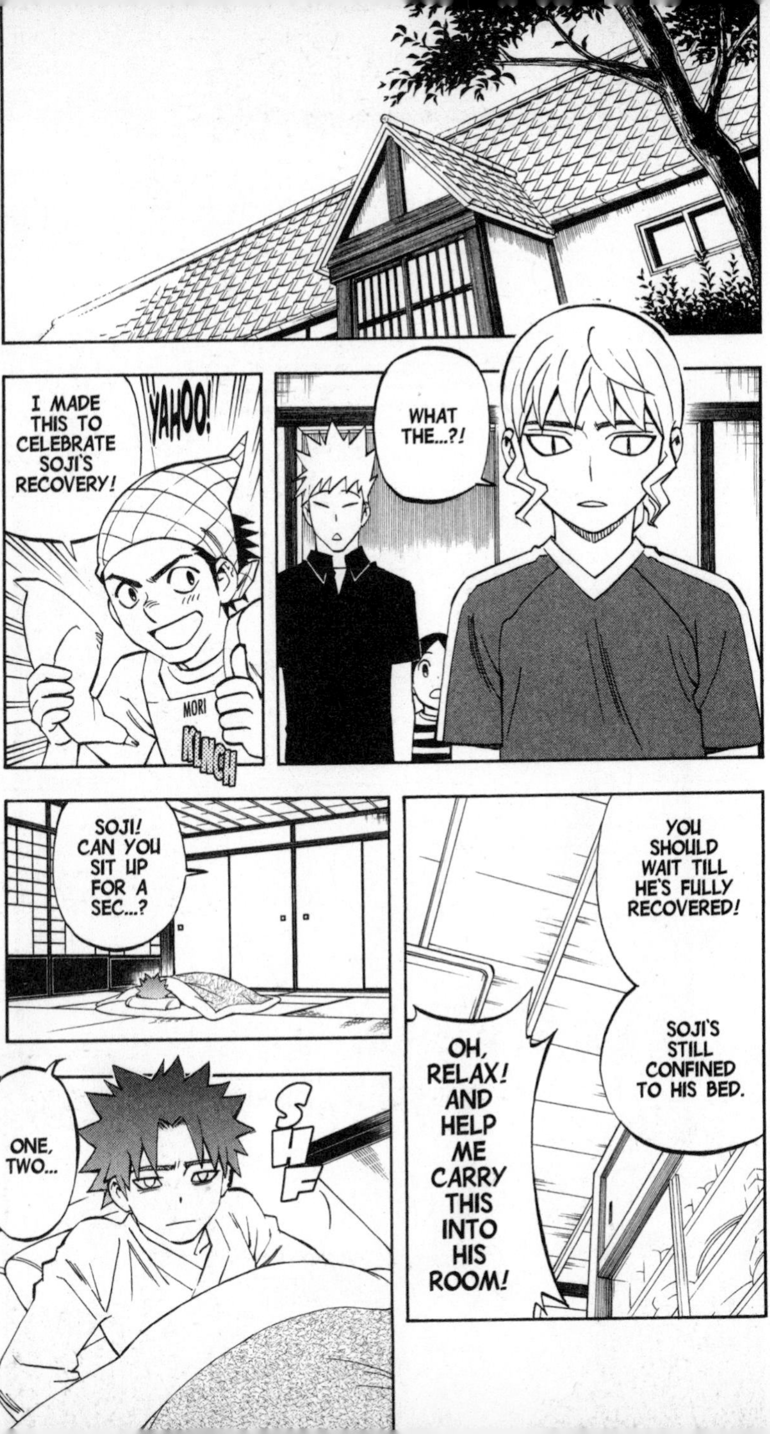
WHAT THE...?!
YAHOO!
I MADE THIS TO CELEBRATE SOJI'S RECOVERY!
YOU SHOULD WAIT TILL HE'S FULLY RECOVERED!
SOJI'S STILL CONFINED TO HIS BED.
OH, RELAX! AND HELP ME CARRY THIS INTO HIS ROOM!
SOJI! CAN YOU SIT UP FOR A SEC...?
SHF
ONE, TWO...

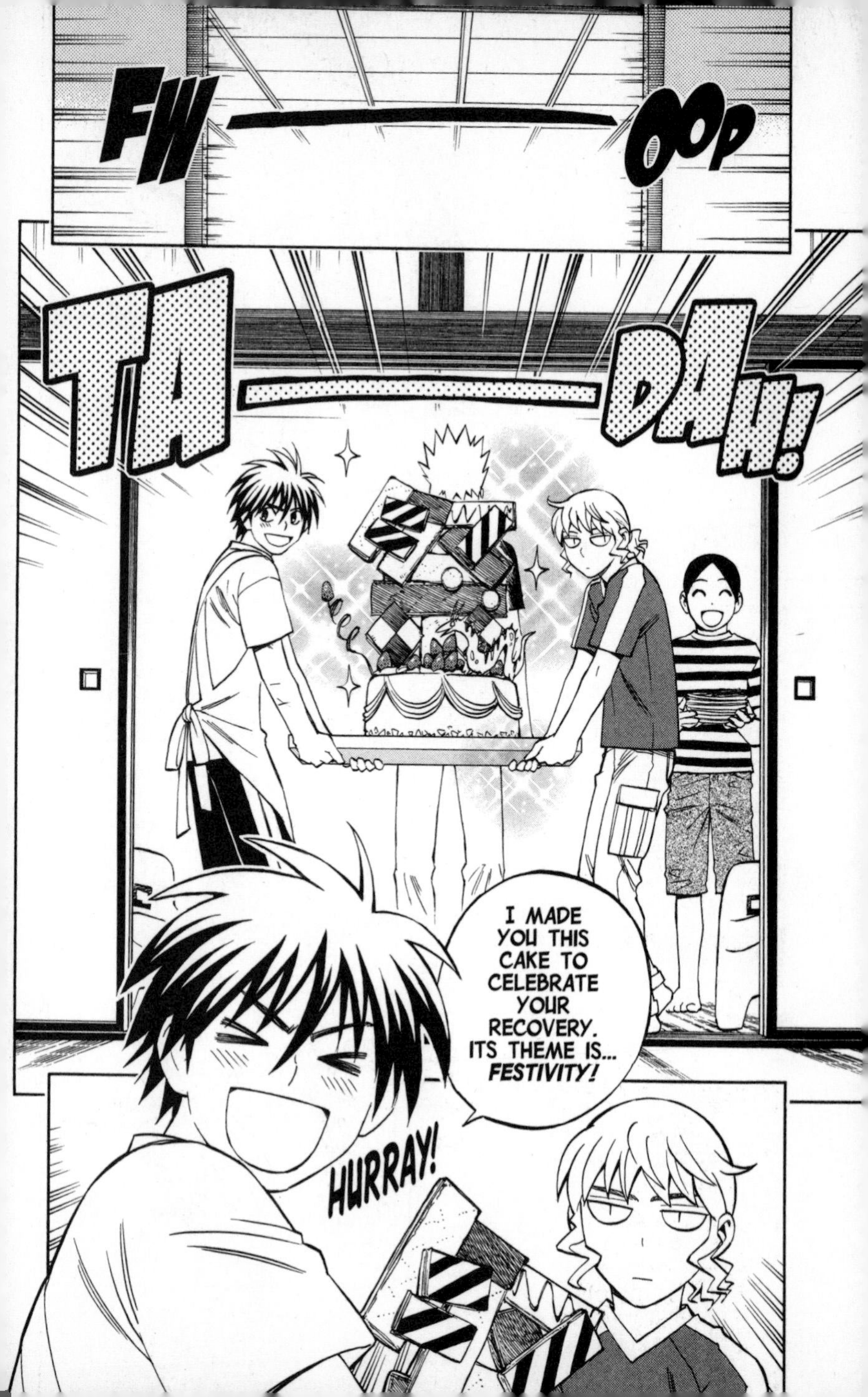
FW————OOP
TA————DAH!
I MADE YOU THIS CAKE TO CELEBRATE YOUR RECOVERY. ITS THEME IS... FESTIVITY!
HURRAY!

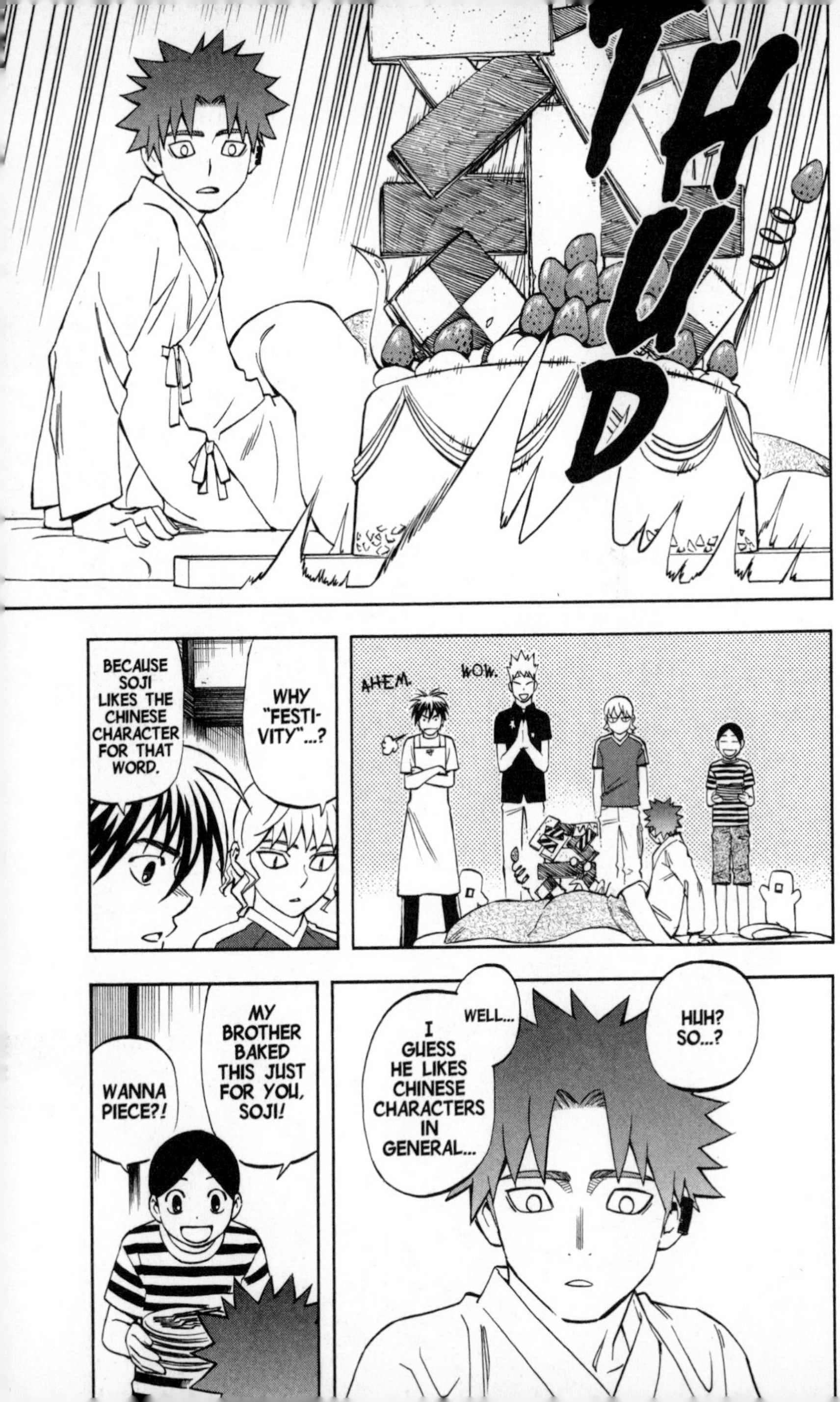
THUD
AHEM.
WOW.
WHY "FESTI-VITY"...?
BECAUSE SOJI LIKES THE CHINESE CHARACTER FOR THAT WORD.
HUH? SO...?
WELL...
I GUESS HE LIKES CHINESE CHARACTERS IN GENERAL...
MY BROTHER BAKED THIS JUST FOR YOU, SOJI!
WANNA PIECE?!

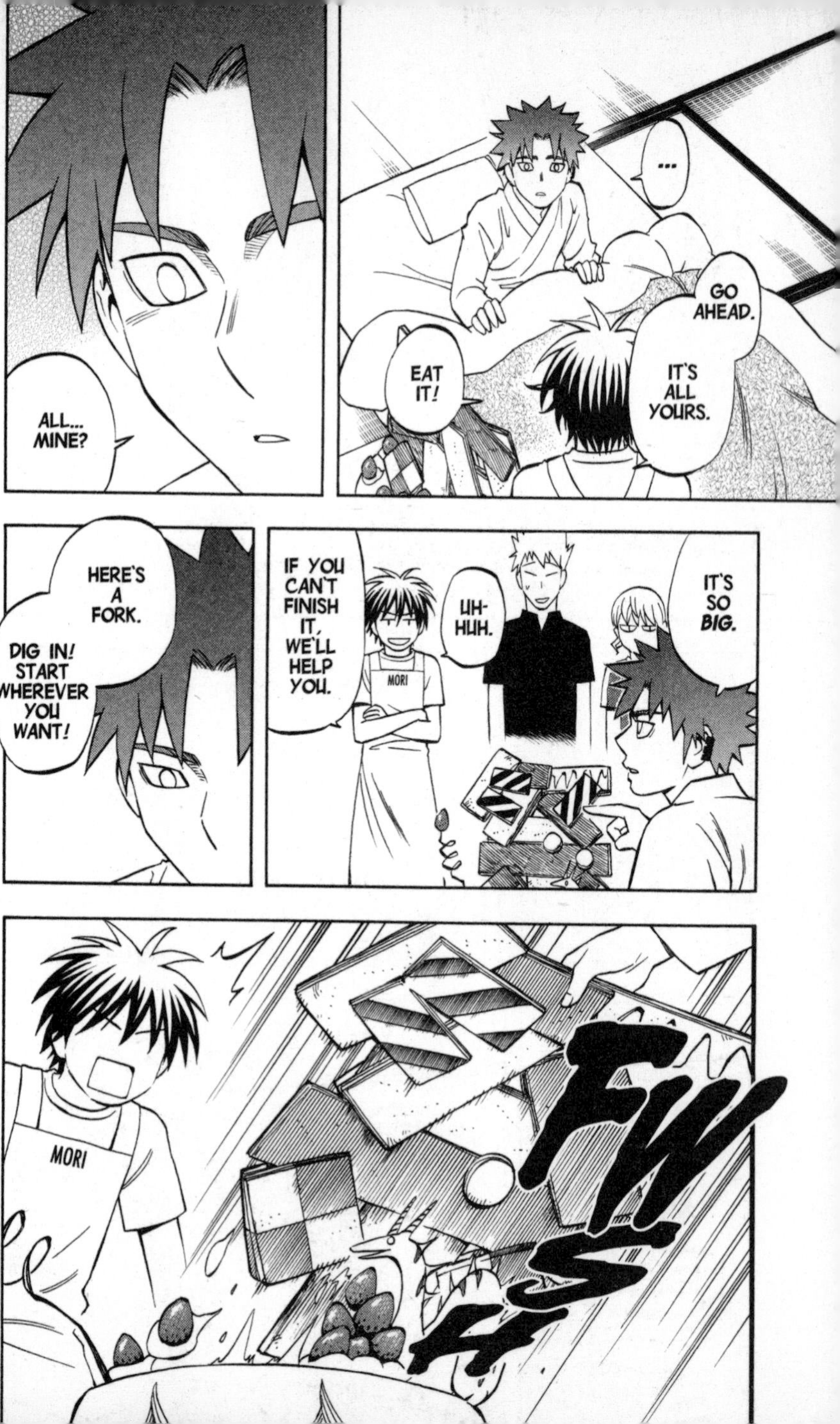
...
GO AHEAD.
IT'S ALL YOURS.
EAT IT!
ALL... MINE?
IT'S SO BIG.
UH-HUH.
IF YOU CAN'T FINISH IT, WE'LL HELP YOU.
MORI
HERE'S A FORK.
DIG IN! START WHEREVER YOU WANT!
MORI
FWSH

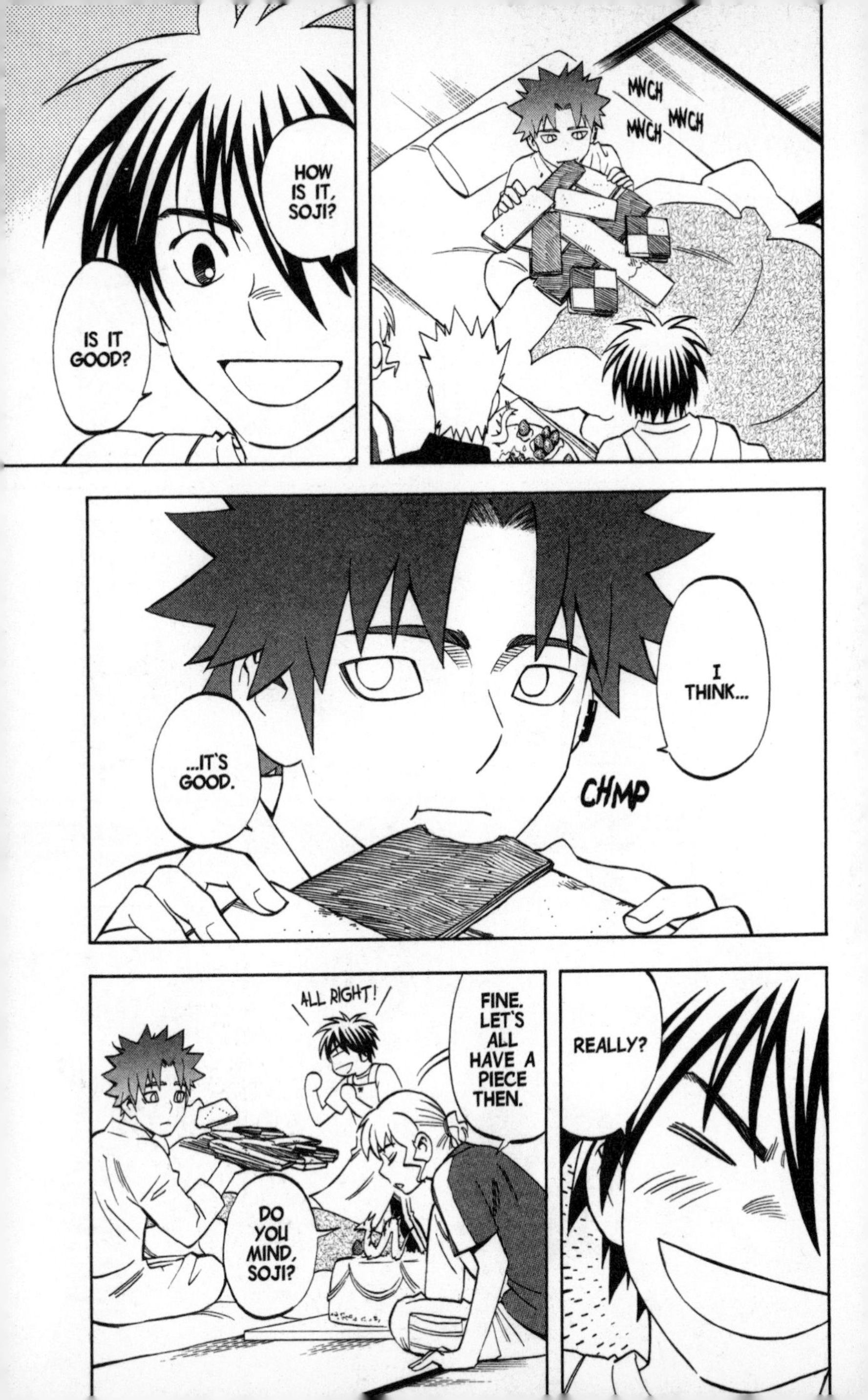
MNCH
MNCH
MNCH
HOW IS IT, SOJI?
IS IT GOOD?
I THINK...
CHMP
...IT'S GOOD.
REALLY?
FINE. LET'S ALL HAVE A PIECE THEN.
ALL RIGHT!
DO YOU MIND, SOJI?

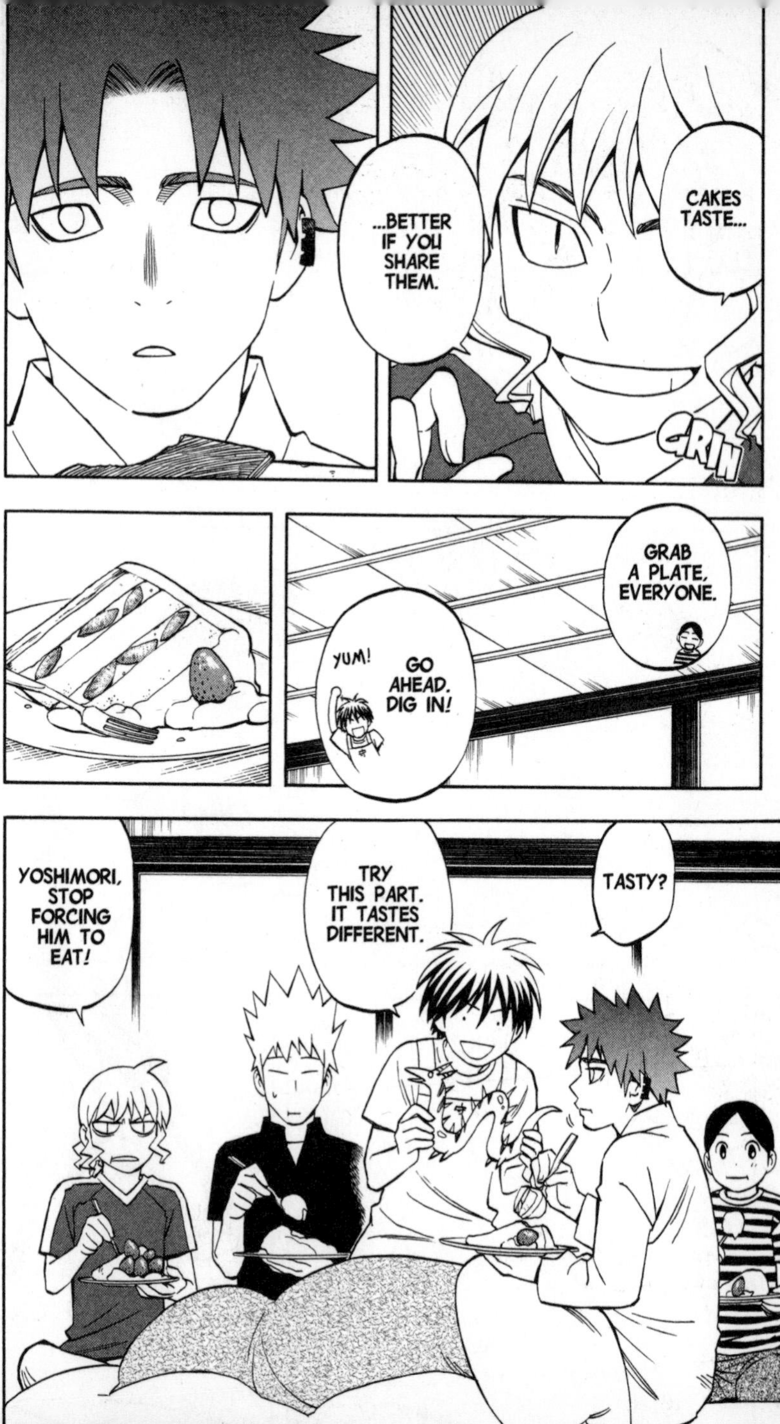
CAKES TASTE...
...BETTER IF YOU SHARE THEM.
GRIN
GRAB A PLATE, EVERYONE.
GO AHEAD. DIG IN!
YUM!
TASTY?
TRY THIS PART. IT TASTES DIFFERENT.
YOSHIMORI, STOP FORCING HIM TO EAT!

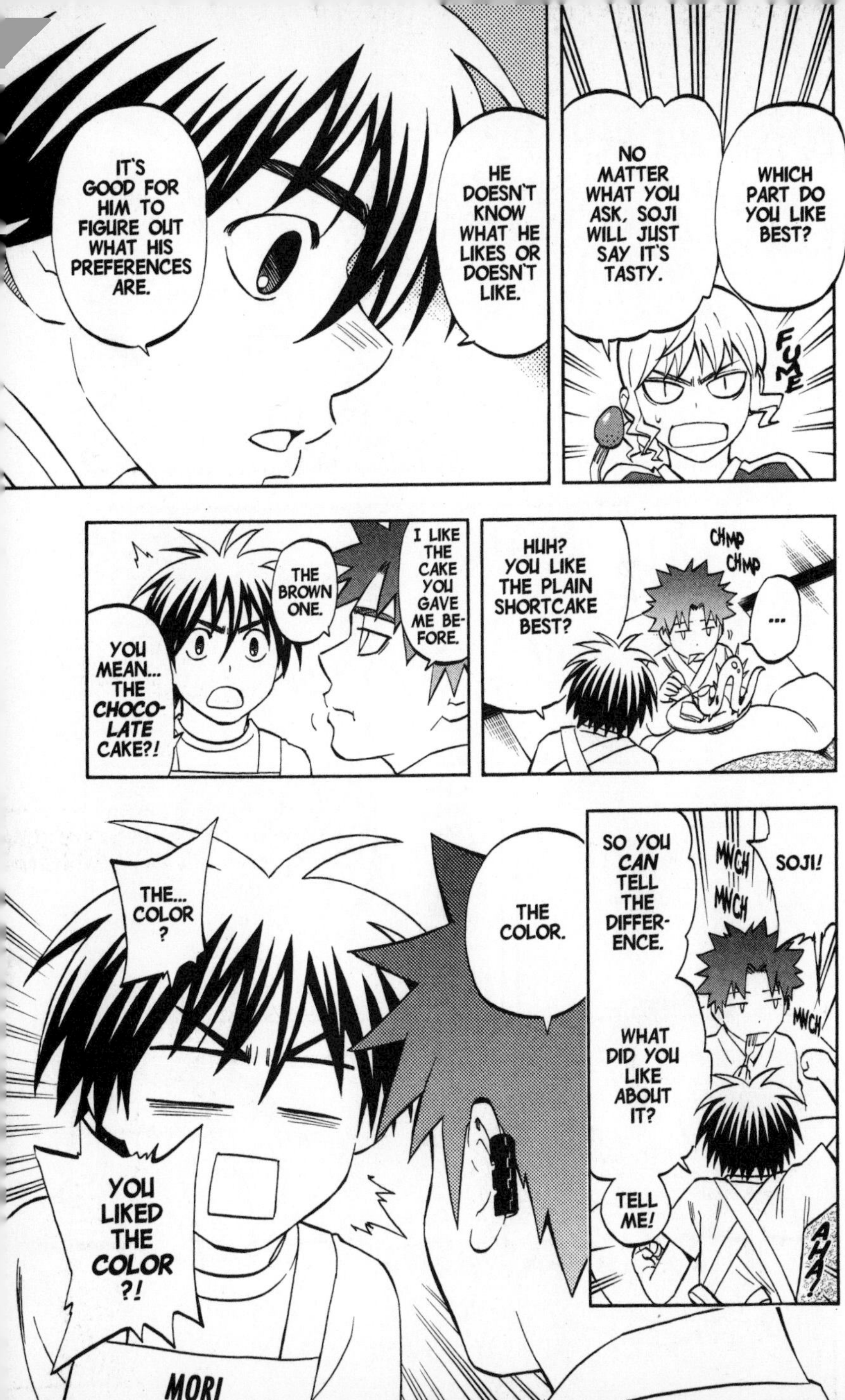
WHICH PART DO YOU LIKE BEST?
NO MATTER WHAT YOU ASK, SOJI WILL JUST SAY IT'S TASTY.
FUME
HE DOESN'T KNOW WHAT HE LIKES OR DOESN'T LIKE.
IT'S GOOD FOR HIM TO FIGURE OUT WHAT HIS PREFERENCES ARE.
CHMP CHMP
...
HUH? YOU LIKE THE PLAIN SHORTCAKE BEST?
I LIKE THE CAKE YOU GAVE ME BEFORE.
THE BROWN ONE.
YOU MEAN... THE *CHOCOLATE* CAKE?!
SOJI!
MNCH MNCH
SO YOU *CAN* TELL THE DIFFERENCE.
MNCH
WHAT DID YOU LIKE ABOUT IT?
TELL ME!
AHA!
THE COLOR.
THE... COLOR?
YOU LIKED THE *COLOR*?!
MORI

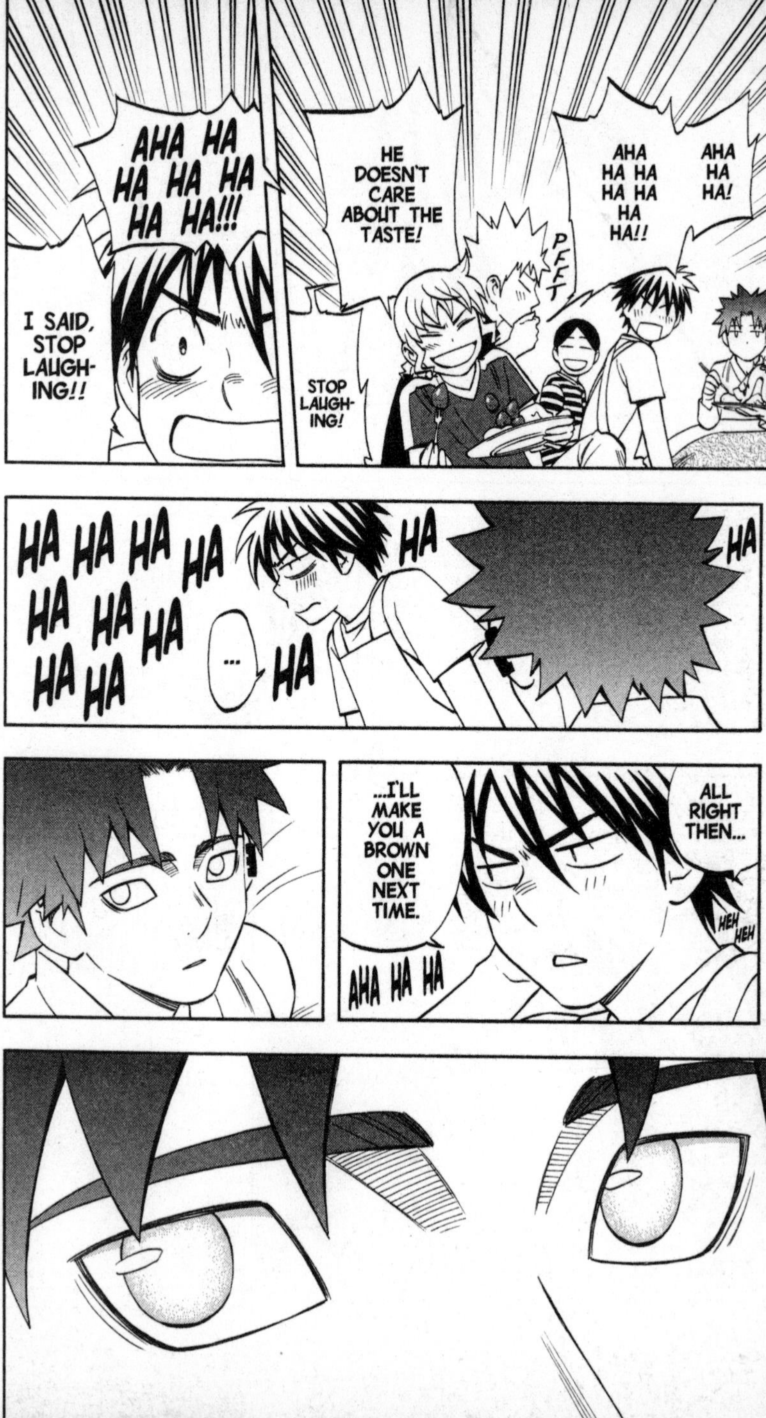
AHA HA HA!
AHA HA HA HA HA HA HA!!
PFFT
HE DOESN'T CARE ABOUT THE TASTE!
STOP LAUGHING!
AHA HA HA HA HA HA HA!!!
I SAID, STOP LAUGHING!!
HA
HA
HA HA HA HA HA HA HA HA HA HA
...
ALL RIGHT THEN...
HEH HEH
...I'LL MAKE YOU A BROWN ONE NEXT TIME.
AHA HA HA

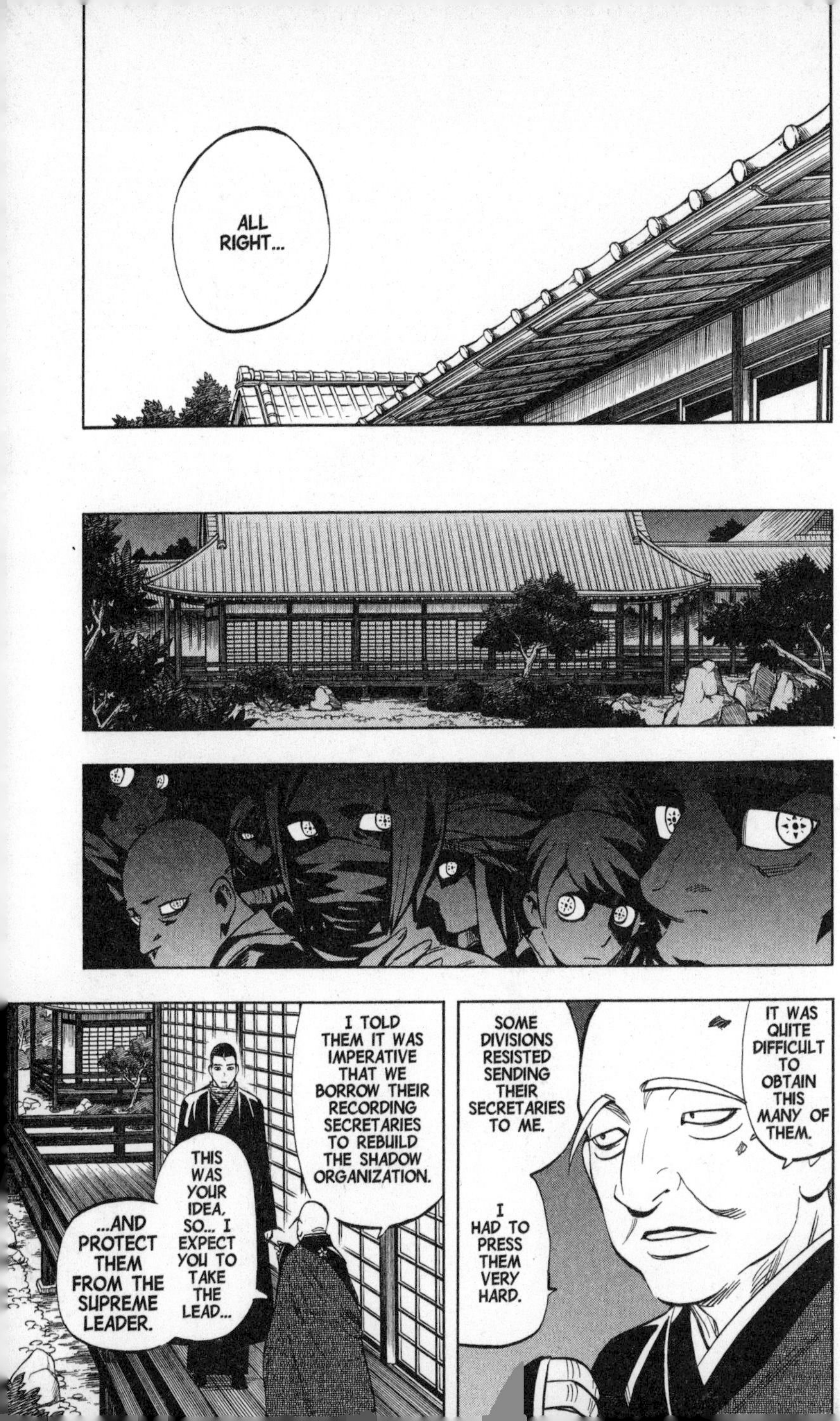
ALL RIGHT...
IT WAS QUITE DIFFICULT TO OBTAIN THIS MANY OF THEM.
SOME DIVISIONS RESISTED SENDING THEIR SECRETARIES TO ME.
I HAD TO PRESS THEM VERY HARD.
I TOLD THEM IT WAS IMPERATIVE THAT WE BORROW THEIR RECORDING SECRETARIES TO REBUILD THE SHADOW ORGANIZATION.
THIS WAS YOUR IDEA, SO... I EXPECT YOU TO TAKE THE LEAD...
...AND PROTECT THEM FROM THE SUPREME LEADER.

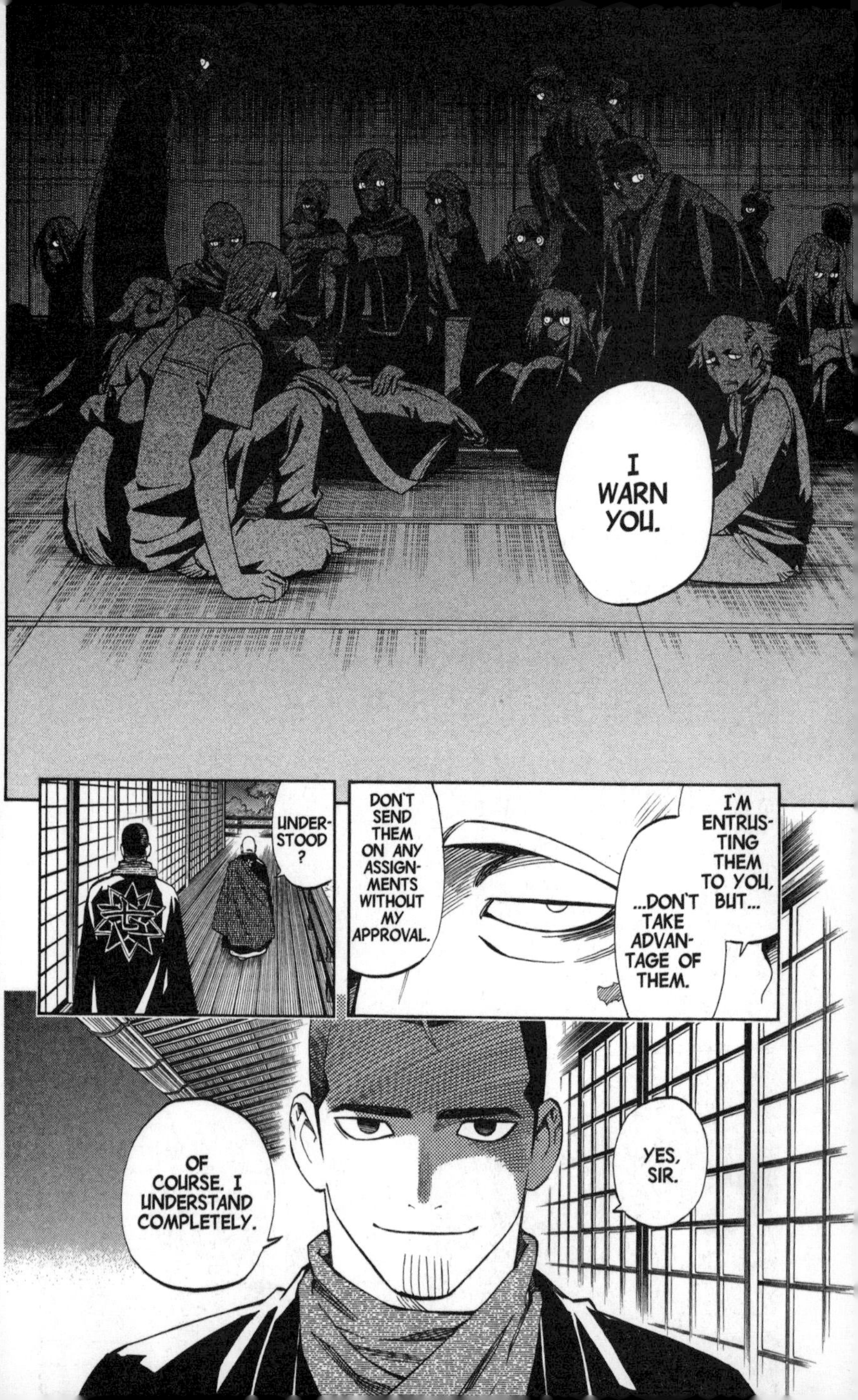
I WARN YOU.
I'M ENTRUS-TING THEM TO YOU, BUT...
...DON'T TAKE ADVAN-TAGE OF THEM.
DON'T SEND THEM ON ANY ASSIGN-MENTS WITHOUT MY APPROVAL.
UNDER-STOOD?
YES, SIR.
OF COURSE. I UNDERSTAND COMPLETELY.

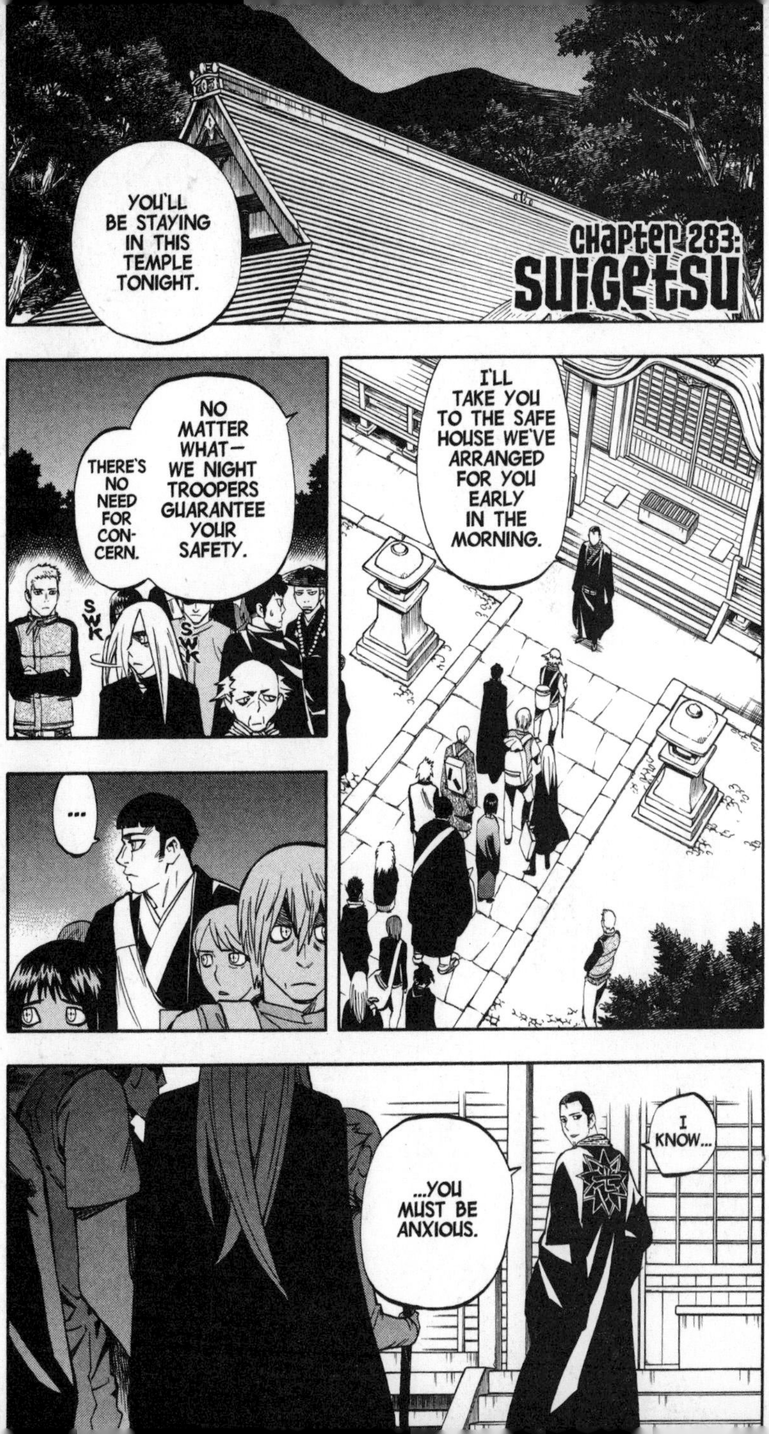

Chapter 283:
Suigetsu
YOU'LL BE STAYING IN THIS TEMPLE TONIGHT.
I'LL TAKE YOU TO THE SAFE HOUSE WE'VE ARRANGED FOR YOU EARLY IN THE MORNING.
NO MATTER WHAT— WE NIGHT TROOPERS GUARANTEE YOUR SAFETY.
THERE'S NO NEED FOR CON- CERN.
SWK
SWK
...
I KNOW...
...YOU MUST BE ANXIOUS.

Chapter 283: Suigetsu

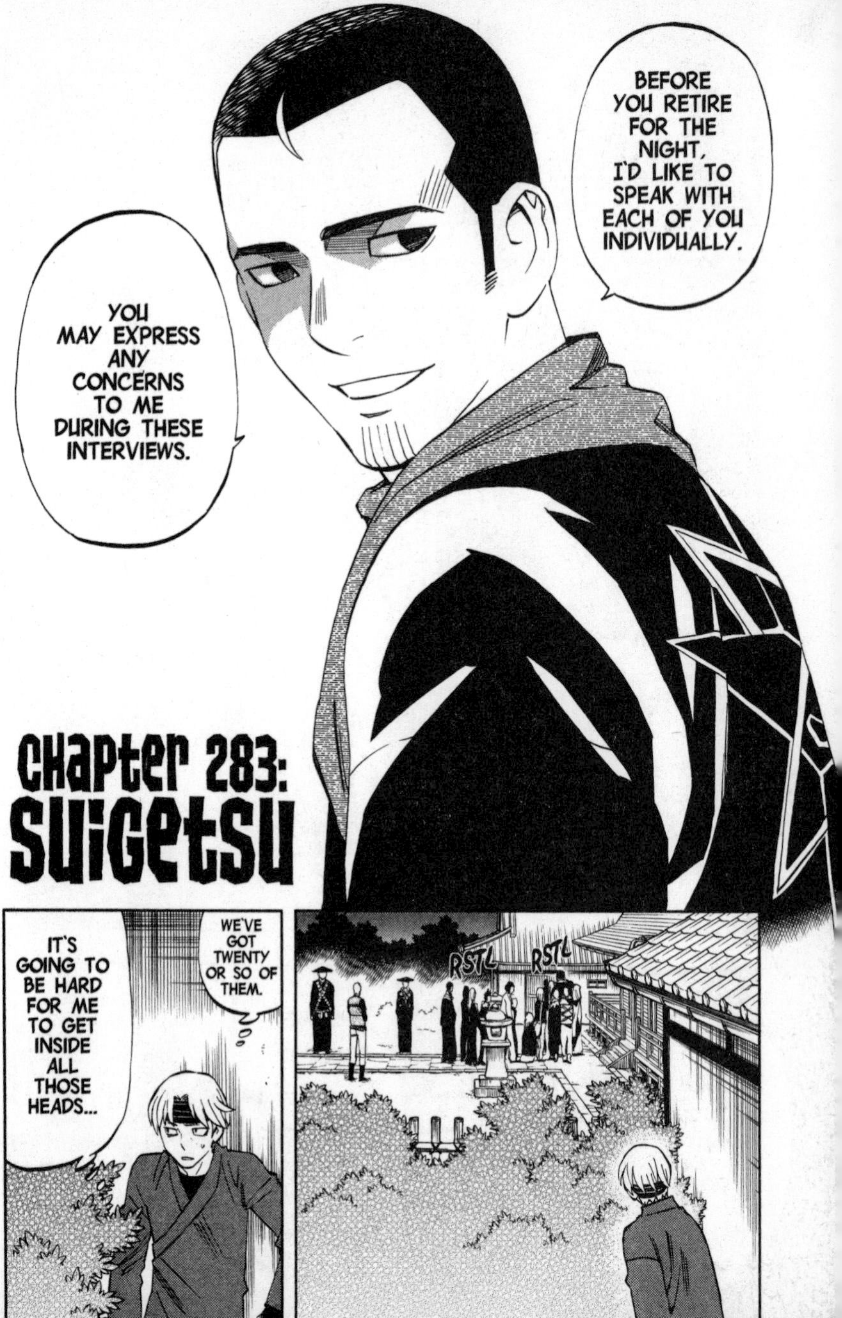
BEFORE YOU RETIRE FOR THE NIGHT, I'D LIKE TO SPEAK WITH EACH OF YOU INDIVIDUALLY.
YOU MAY EXPRESS ANY CONCERNS TO ME DURING THESE INTERVIEWS.
RSTL
RSTL
WE'VE GOT TWENTY OR SO OF THEM.
IT'S GOING TO BE HARD FOR ME TO GET INSIDE ALL THOSE HEADS...

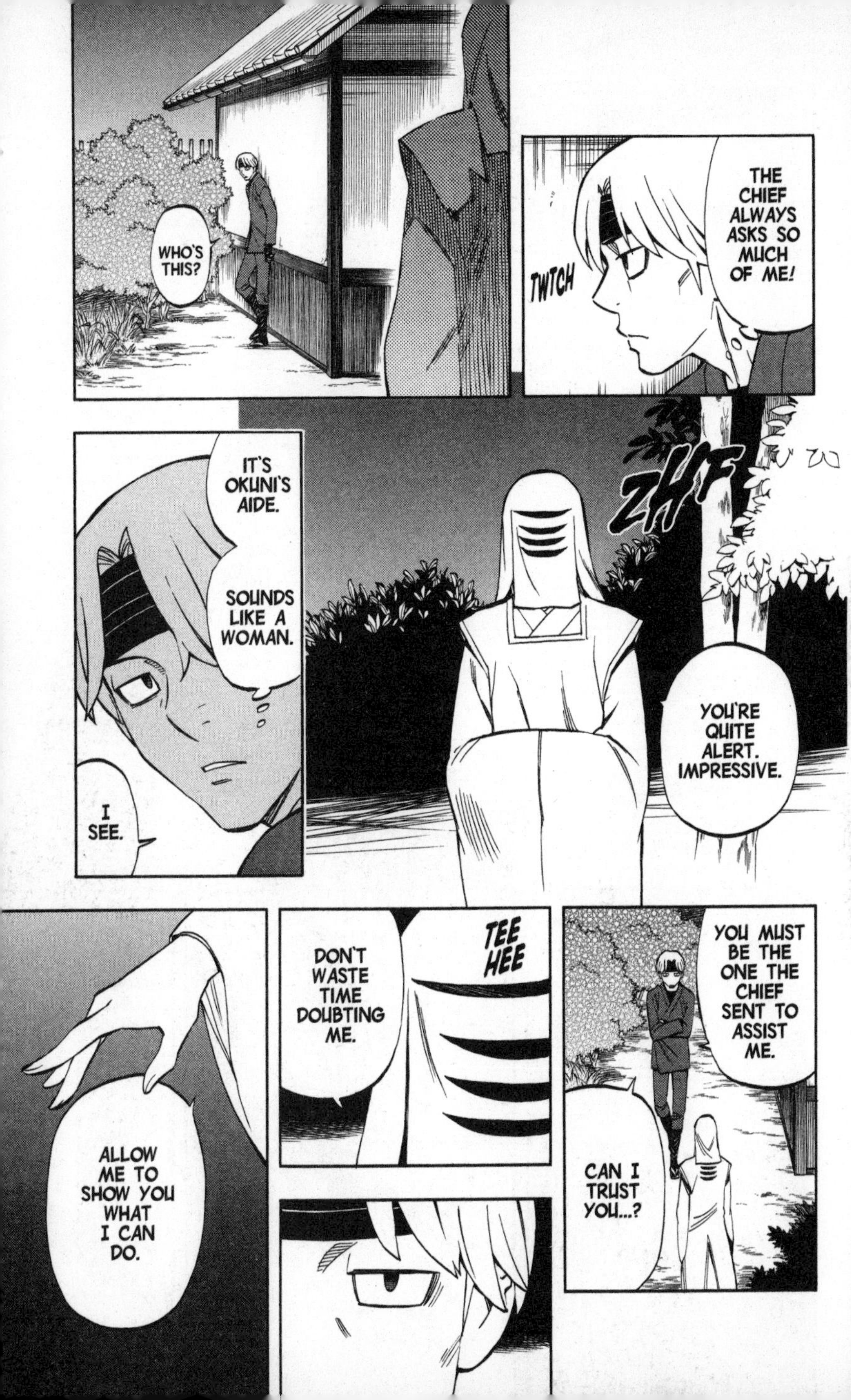
THE CHIEF ALWAYS ASKS SO MUCH OF ME!
TWTCH
WHO'S THIS?
ZHF
YOU'RE QUITE ALERT. IMPRESSIVE.
IT'S OKUNI'S AIDE.
SOUNDS LIKE A WOMAN.
I SEE.
YOU MUST BE THE ONE THE CHIEF SENT TO ASSIST ME.
CAN I TRUST YOU...?
TEE HEE
DON'T WASTE TIME DOUBTING ME.
ALLOW ME TO SHOW YOU WHAT I CAN DO.

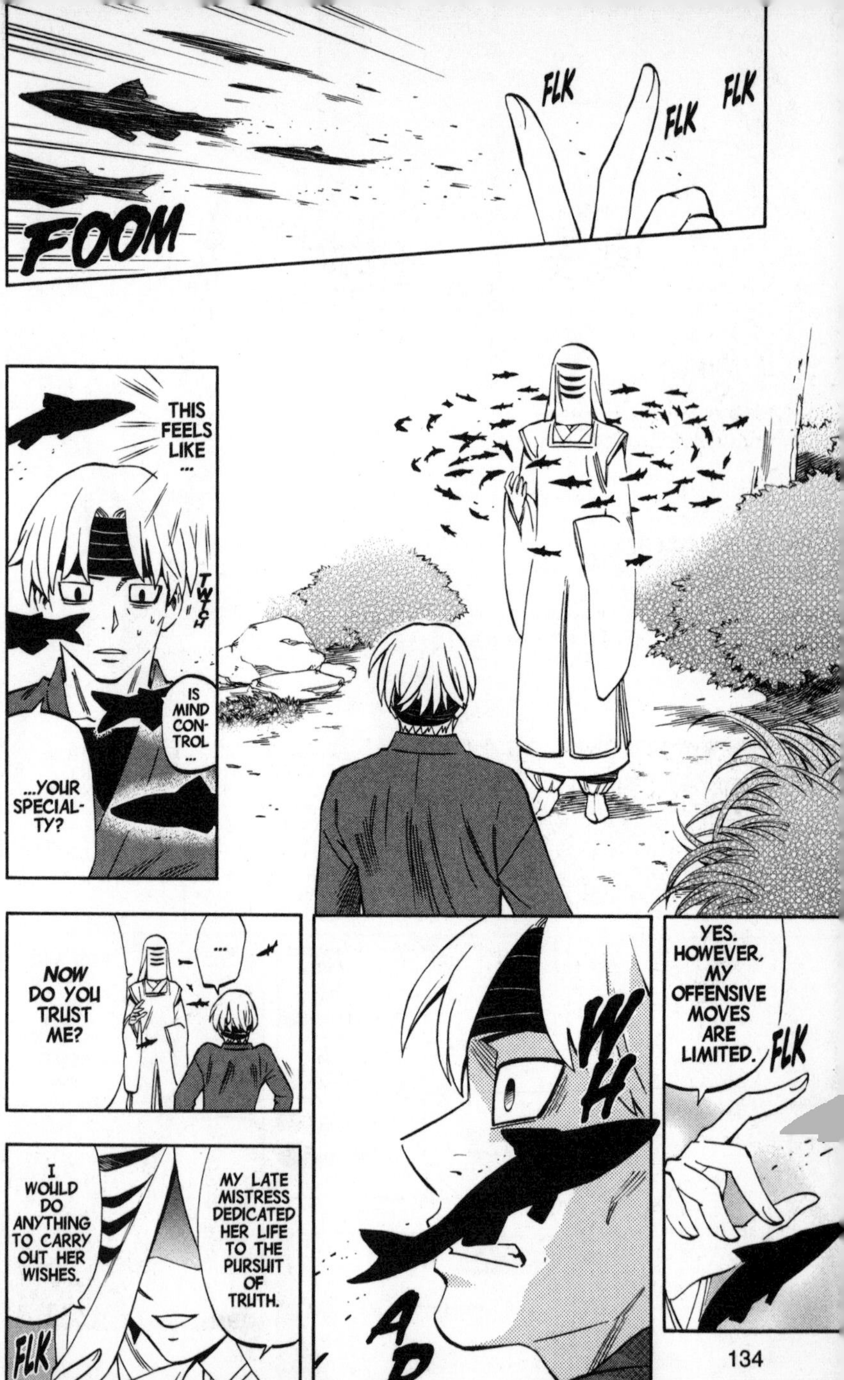
FLK
FLK
FLK
FOOM
THIS FEELS LIKE...
TWITCH
IS MIND CONTROL...
...YOUR SPECIALTY?
YES. HOWEVER, MY OFFENSIVE MOVES ARE LIMITED.
FLK
WHAP
NOW DO YOU TRUST ME?
...
MY LATE MISTRESS DEDICATED HER LIFE TO THE PURSUIT OF TRUTH.
I WOULD DO ANYTHING TO CARRY OUT HER WISHES.
FLK

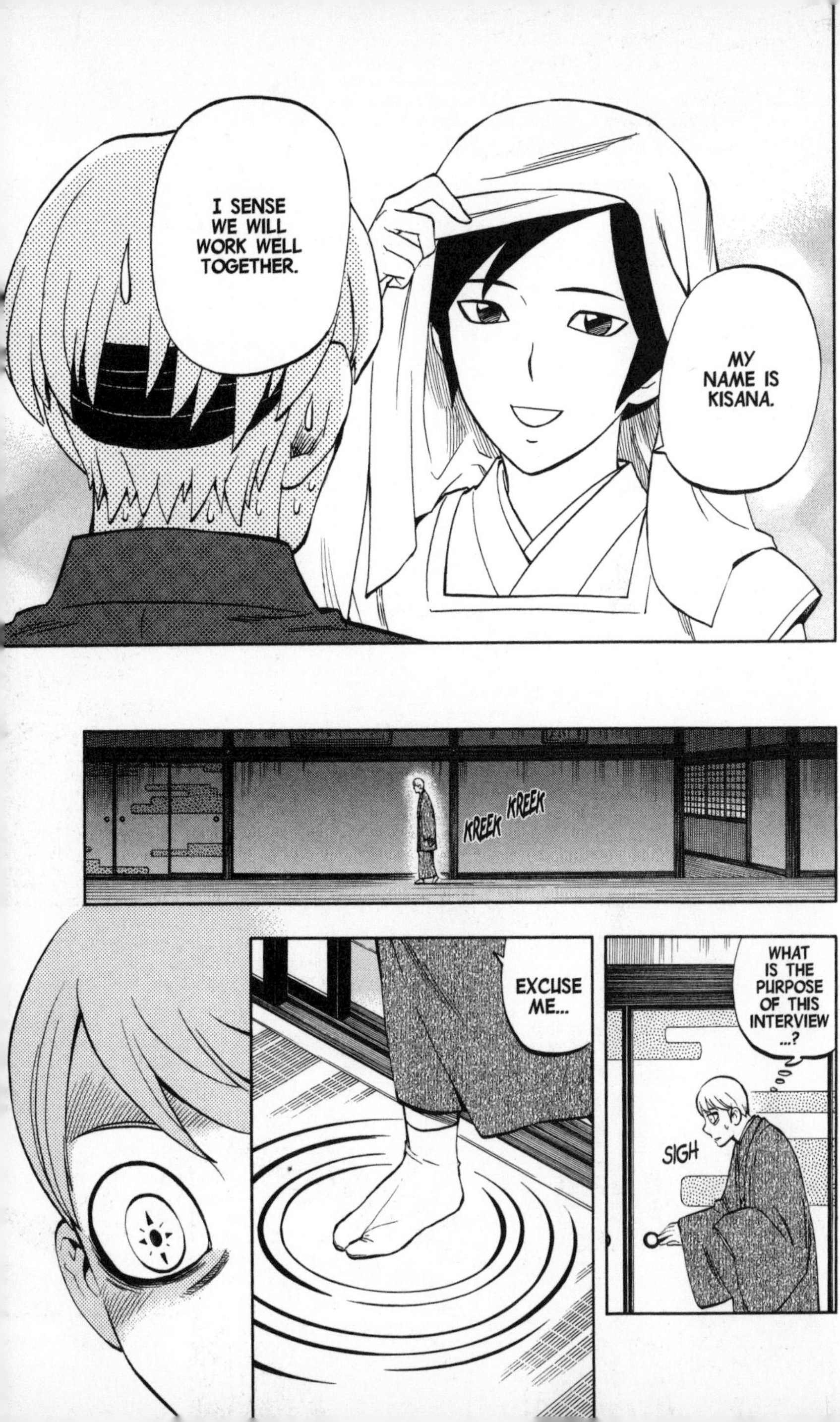
MY NAME IS KISANA.
I SENSE WE WILL WORK WELL TOGETHER.
KREEK
KREEK
WHAT IS THE PURPOSE OF THIS INTERVIEW ...?
SIGH
EXCUSE ME...

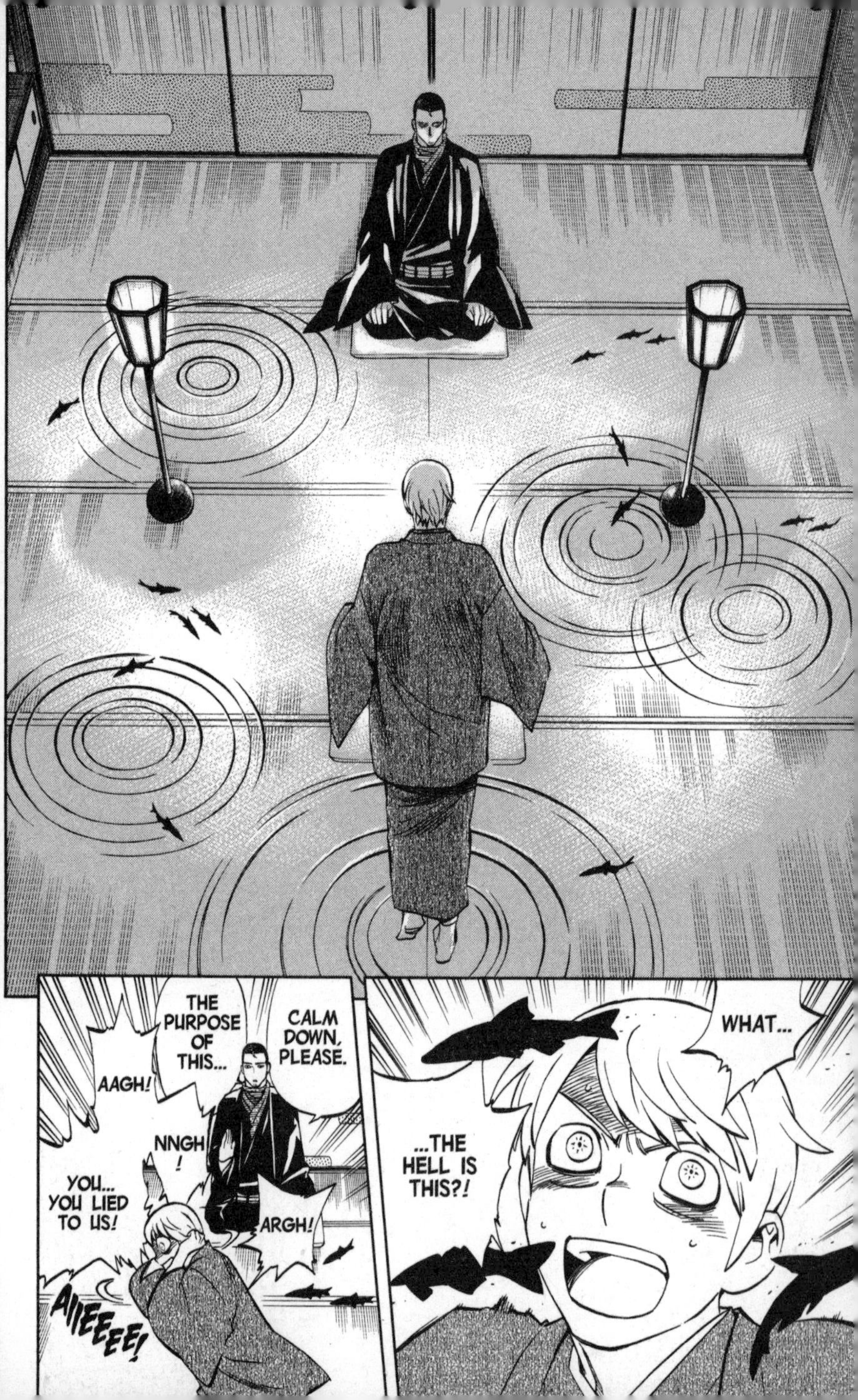
WHAT...
...THE HELL IS THIS?!
CALM DOWN, PLEASE.
THE PURPOSE OF THIS...
AAGH!
NNGH!
ARGH!
YOU... YOU LIED TO US!
AIIEEEEE!

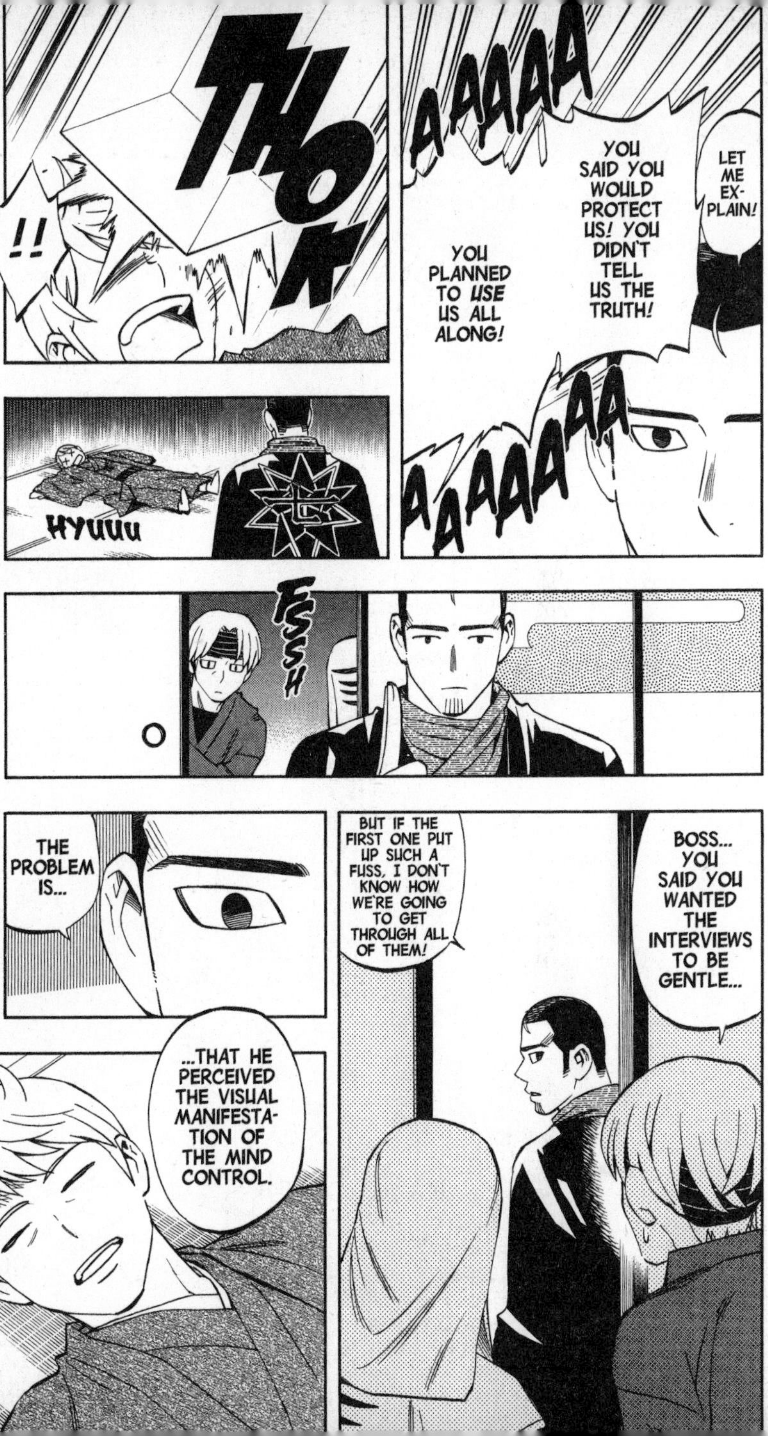
AAAAAA
LET ME EX-PLAIN!
YOU SAID YOU WOULD PROTECT US! YOU DIDN'T TELL US THE TRUTH!
YOU PLANNED TO *USE* US ALL ALONG!
AAAAAAA
THOK
!!
HYUUU
FSSSH
BOSS... YOU SAID YOU WANTED THE INTERVIEWS TO BE GENTLE...
BUT IF THE FIRST ONE PUT UP SUCH A FUSS, I DON'T KNOW HOW WE'RE GOING TO GET THROUGH ALL OF THEM!
THE PROBLEM IS...
...THAT HE PERCEIVED THE VISUAL MANIFESTATION OF THE MIND CONTROL.

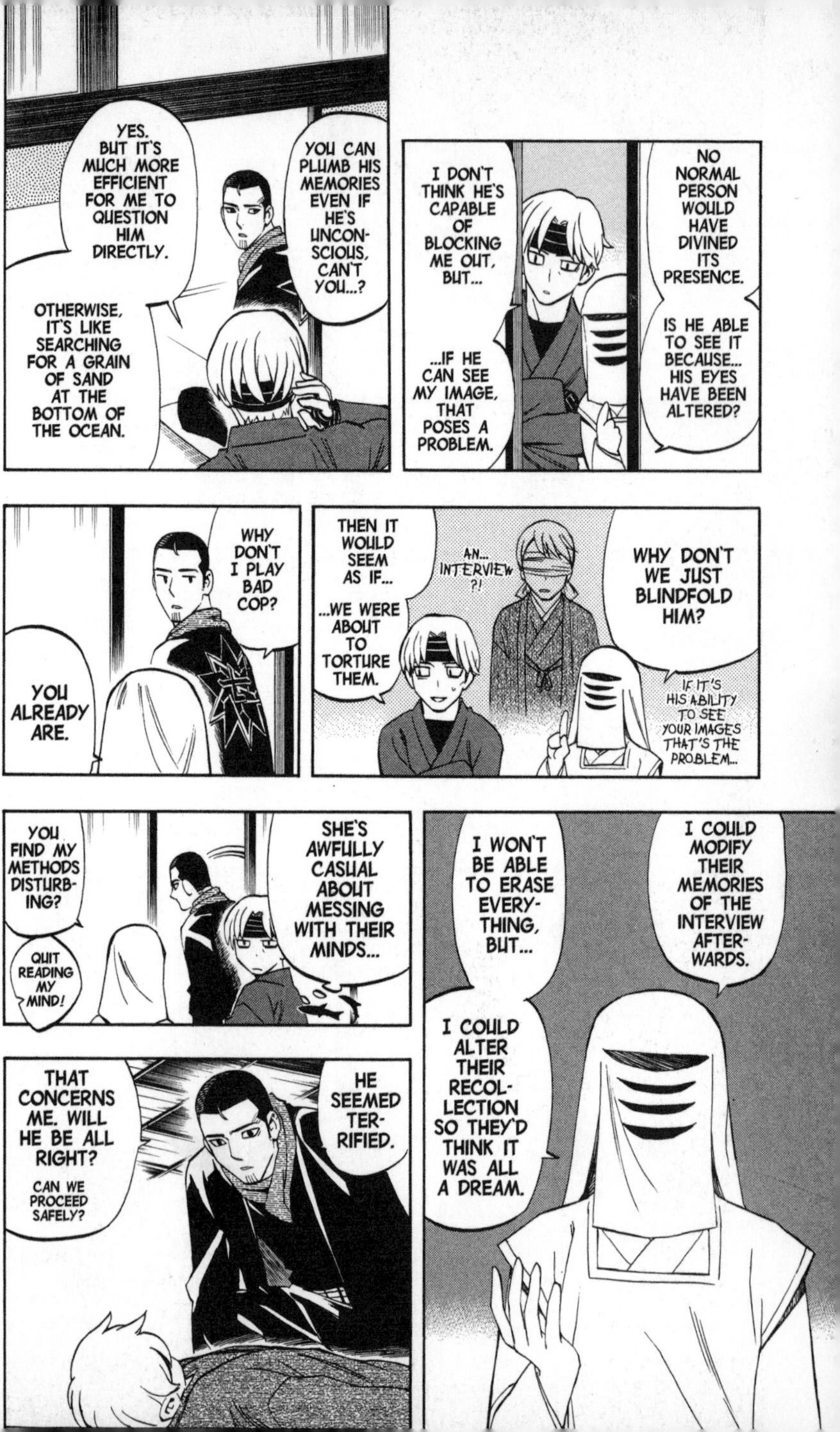
NO NORMAL PERSON WOULD HAVE DIVINED ITS PRESENCE.
IS HE ABLE TO SEE IT BECAUSE... HIS EYES HAVE BEEN ALTERED?
I DON'T THINK HE'S CAPABLE OF BLOCKING ME OUT, BUT...
...IF HE CAN SEE MY IMAGE, THAT POSES A PROBLEM.
YOU CAN PLUMB HIS MEMORIES EVEN IF HE'S UNCON-SCIOUS, CAN'T YOU...?
YES. BUT IT'S MUCH MORE EFFICIENT FOR ME TO QUESTION HIM DIRECTLY.
OTHERWISE, IT'S LIKE SEARCHING FOR A GRAIN OF SAND AT THE BOTTOM OF THE OCEAN.
WHY DON'T WE JUST BLINDFOLD HIM?
IF IT'S HIS ABILITY TO SEE YOUR IMAGES THAT'S THE PROBLEM...
AN... INTERVIEW?!
THEN IT WOULD SEEM AS IF...
...WE WERE ABOUT TO TORTURE THEM.
WHY DON'T I PLAY BAD COP?
YOU ALREADY ARE.
I COULD MODIFY THEIR MEMORIES OF THE INTERVIEW AFTER-WARDS.
I WON'T BE ABLE TO ERASE EVERY-THING, BUT...
I COULD ALTER THEIR RECOL-LECTION SO THEY'D THINK IT WAS ALL A DREAM.
SHE'S AWFULLY CASUAL ABOUT MESSING WITH THEIR MINDS...
YOU FIND MY METHODS DISTURB-ING?
QUIT READING MY MIND!
HE SEEMED TER-RIFIED.
THAT CONCERNS ME. WILL HE BE ALL RIGHT?
CAN WE PROCEED SAFELY?

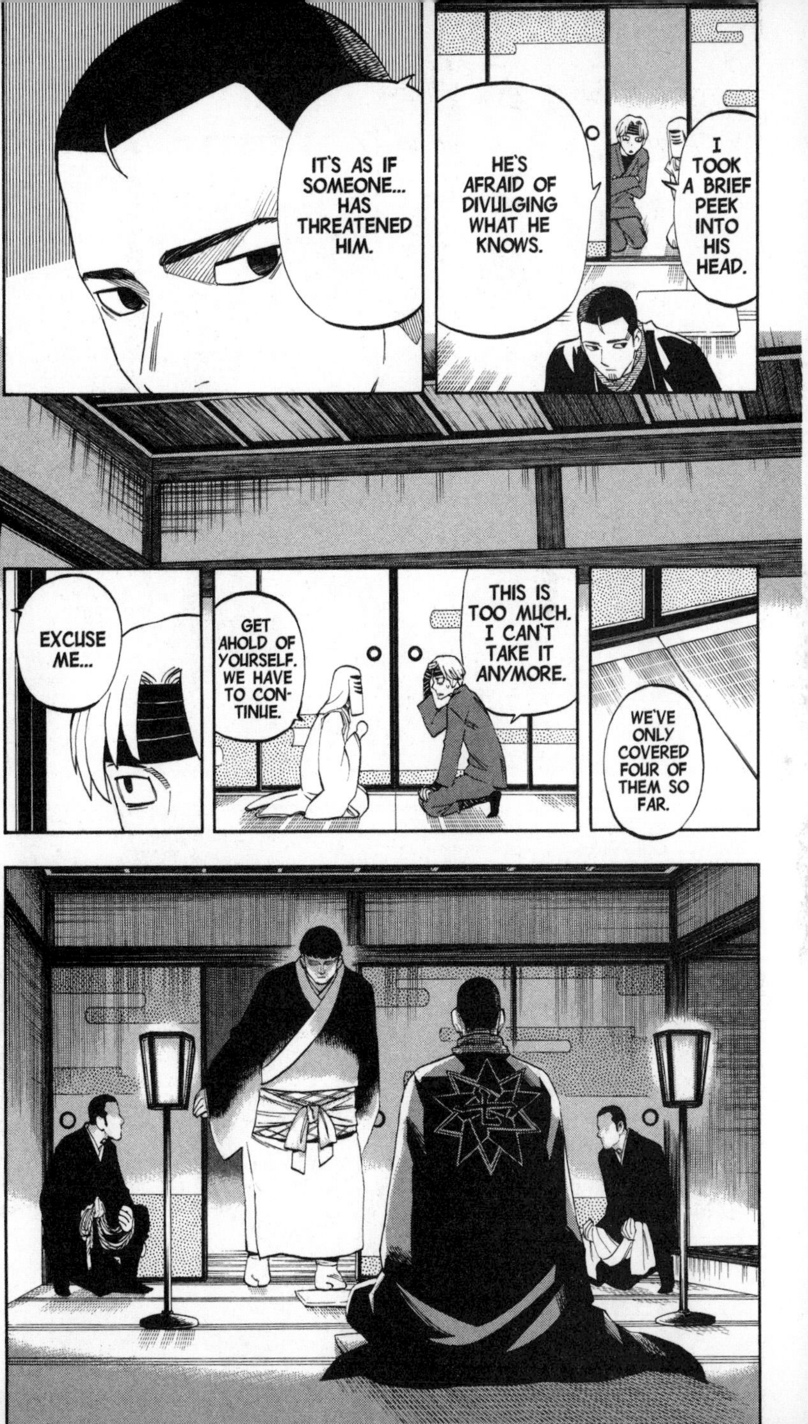
I TOOK A BRIEF PEEK INTO HIS HEAD.
HE'S AFRAID OF DIVULGING WHAT HE KNOWS.
IT'S AS IF SOMEONE... HAS THREATENED HIM.
WE'VE ONLY COVERED FOUR OF THEM SO FAR.
THIS IS TOO MUCH. I CAN'T TAKE IT ANYMORE.
GET AHOLD OF YOURSELF. WE HAVE TO CON-TINUE.
EXCUSE ME...

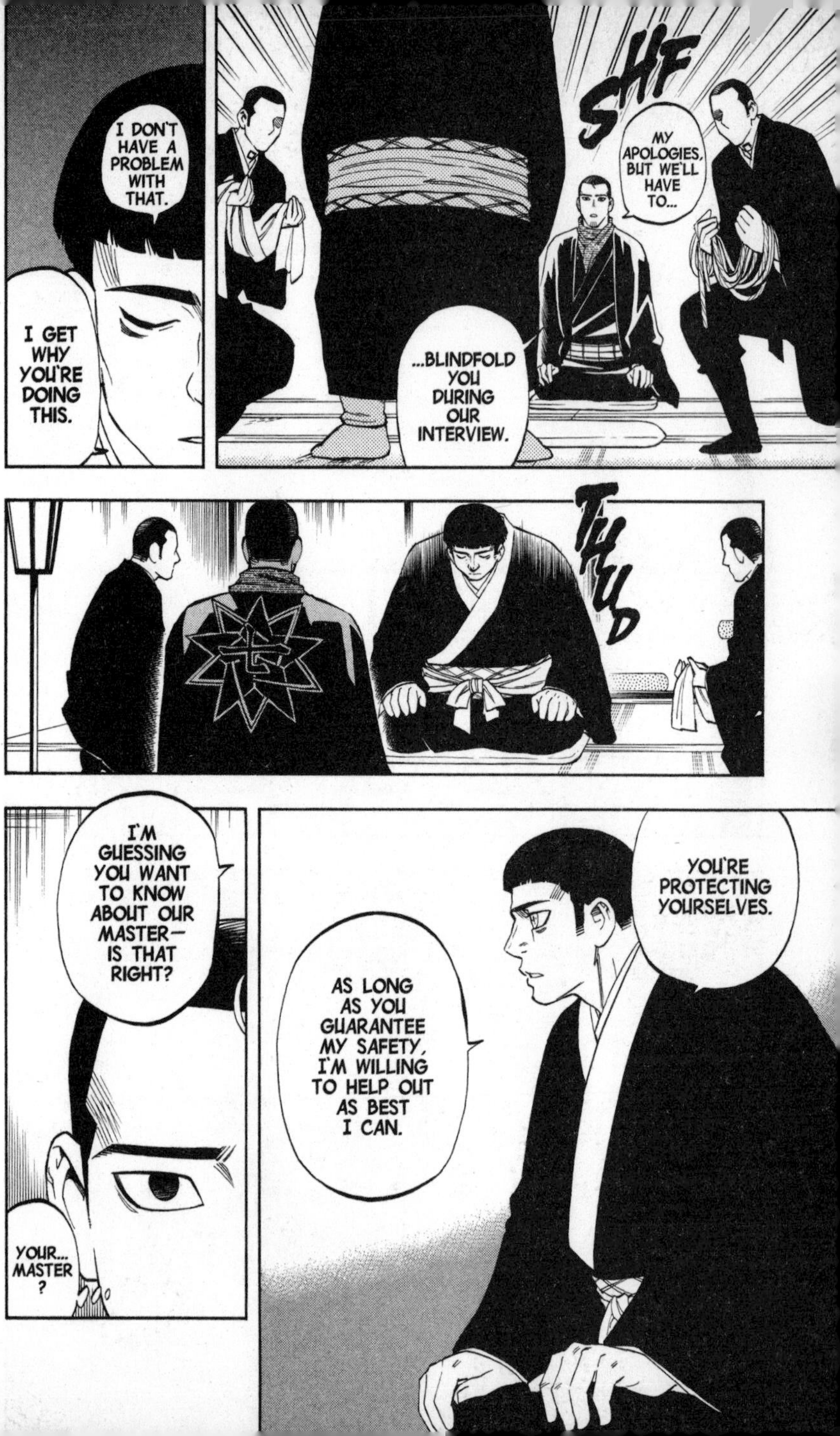
SHF
MY APOLOGIES, BUT WE'LL HAVE TO...
...BLINDFOLD YOU DURING OUR INTERVIEW.
I DON'T HAVE A PROBLEM WITH THAT.
I GET WHY YOU'RE DOING THIS.
THUD
YOU'RE PROTECTING YOURSELVES.
AS LONG AS YOU GUARANTEE MY SAFETY, I'M WILLING TO HELP OUT AS BEST I CAN.
I'M GUESSING YOU WANT TO KNOW ABOUT OUR MASTER— IS THAT RIGHT?
YOUR... MASTER ?

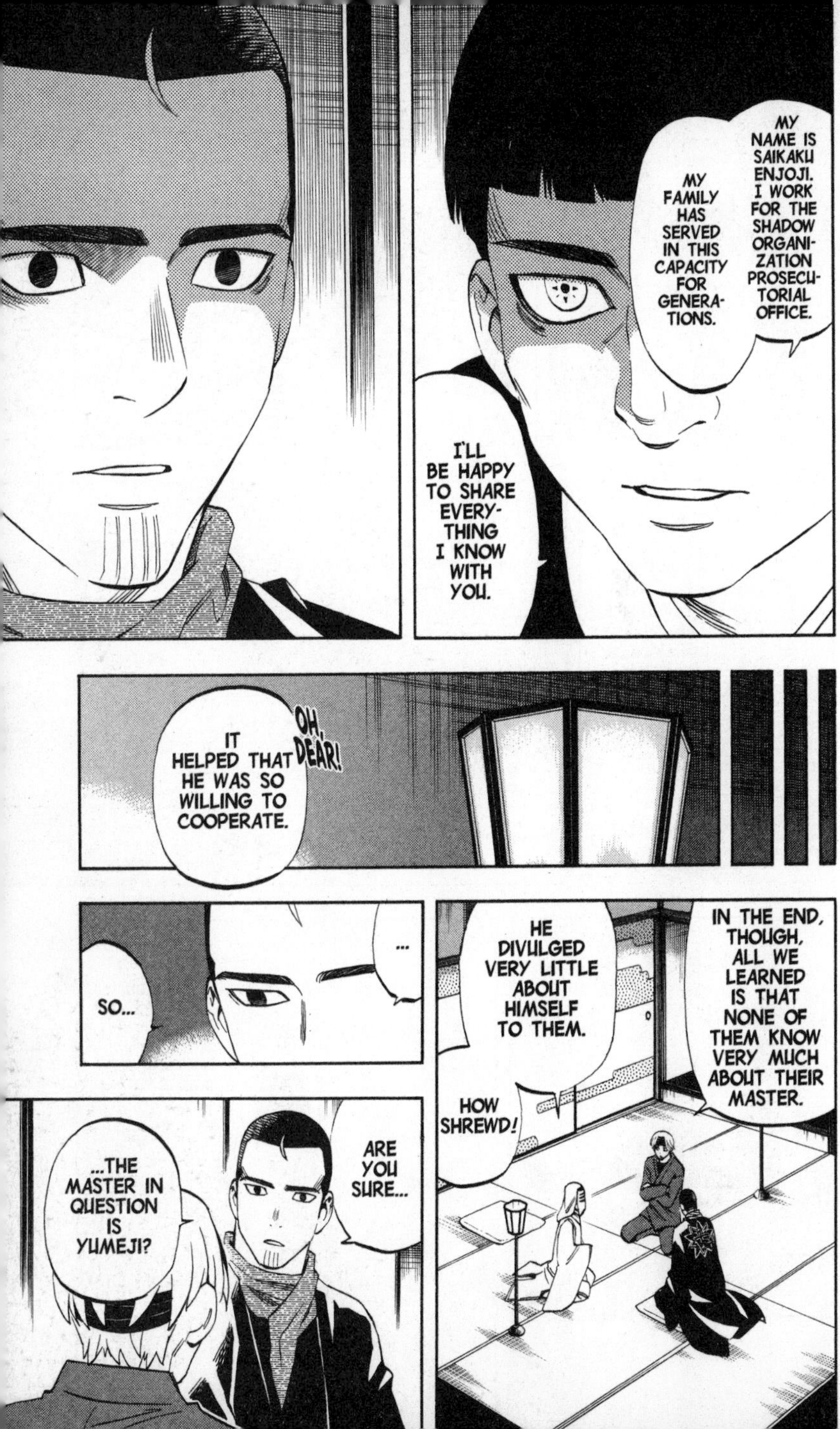
MY NAME IS SAIKAKU ENJOJI. I WORK FOR THE SHADOW ORGANIZATION PROSECUTORIAL OFFICE.
MY FAMILY HAS SERVED IN THIS CAPACITY FOR GENERATIONS.
I'LL BE HAPPY TO SHARE EVERYTHING I KNOW WITH YOU.
OH, DEAR!
IT HELPED THAT HE WAS SO WILLING TO COOPERATE.
IN THE END, THOUGH, ALL WE LEARNED IS THAT NONE OF THEM KNOW VERY MUCH ABOUT THEIR MASTER.
HE DIVULGED VERY LITTLE ABOUT HIMSELF TO THEM.
HOW SHREWD!
...
SO...
ARE YOU SURE...
...THE MASTER IN QUESTION IS YUMEJI?

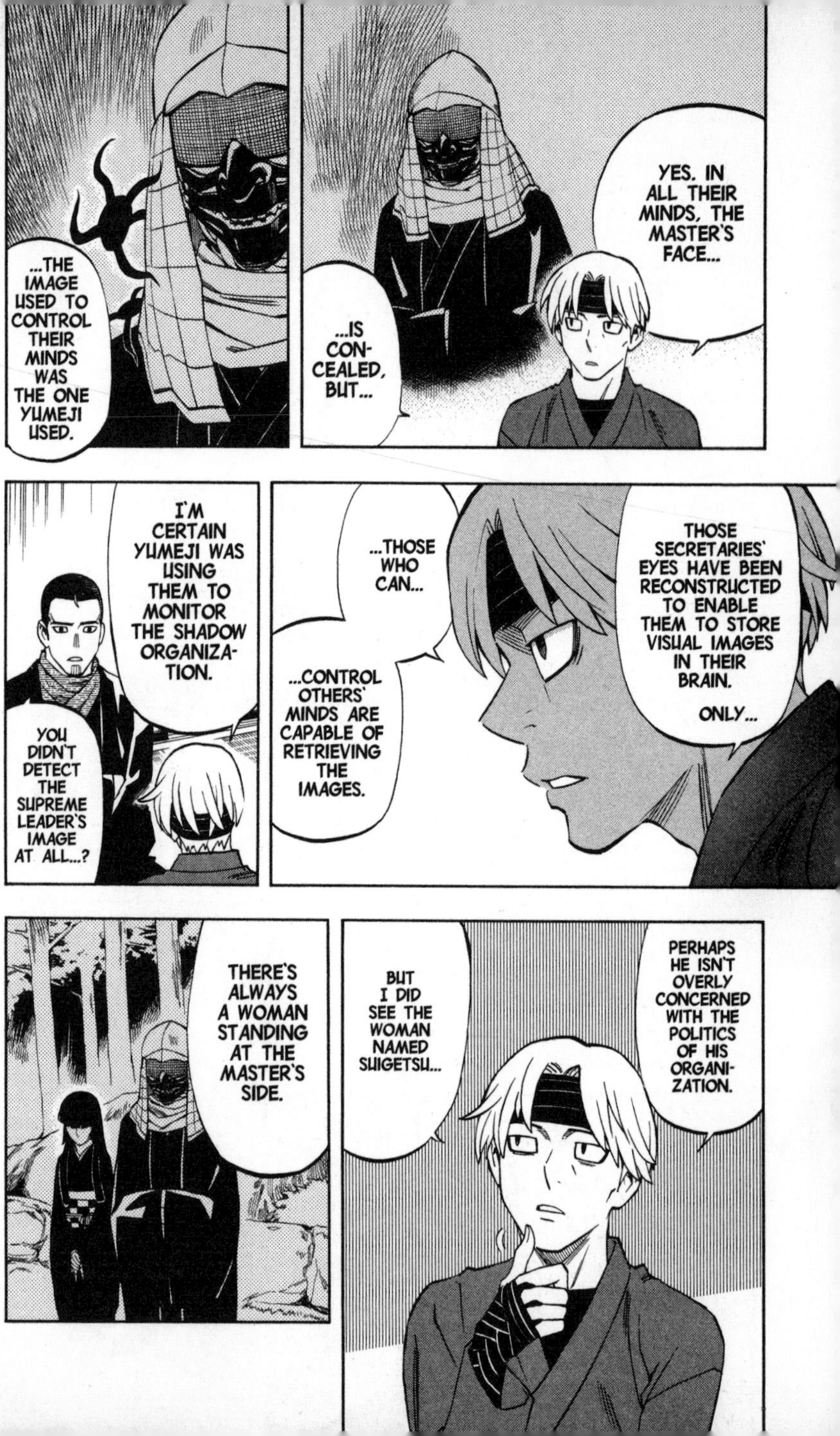
YES. IN ALL THEIR MINDS, THE MASTER'S FACE...
...IS CONCEALED, BUT...
...THE IMAGE USED TO CONTROL THEIR MINDS WAS THE ONE YUMEJI USED.
THOSE SECRETARIES' EYES HAVE BEEN RECONSTRUCTED TO ENABLE THEM TO STORE VISUAL IMAGES IN THEIR BRAIN.
ONLY...
...THOSE WHO CAN...
...CONTROL OTHERS' MINDS ARE CAPABLE OF RETRIEVING THE IMAGES.
I'M CERTAIN YUMEJI WAS USING THEM TO MONITOR THE SHADOW ORGANIZATION.
YOU DIDN'T DETECT THE SUPREME LEADER'S IMAGE AT ALL...?
PERHAPS HE ISN'T OVERLY CONCERNED WITH THE POLITICS OF HIS ORGANIZATION.
BUT I DID SEE THE WOMAN NAMED SUIGETSU...
THERE'S ALWAYS A WOMAN STANDING AT THE MASTER'S SIDE.

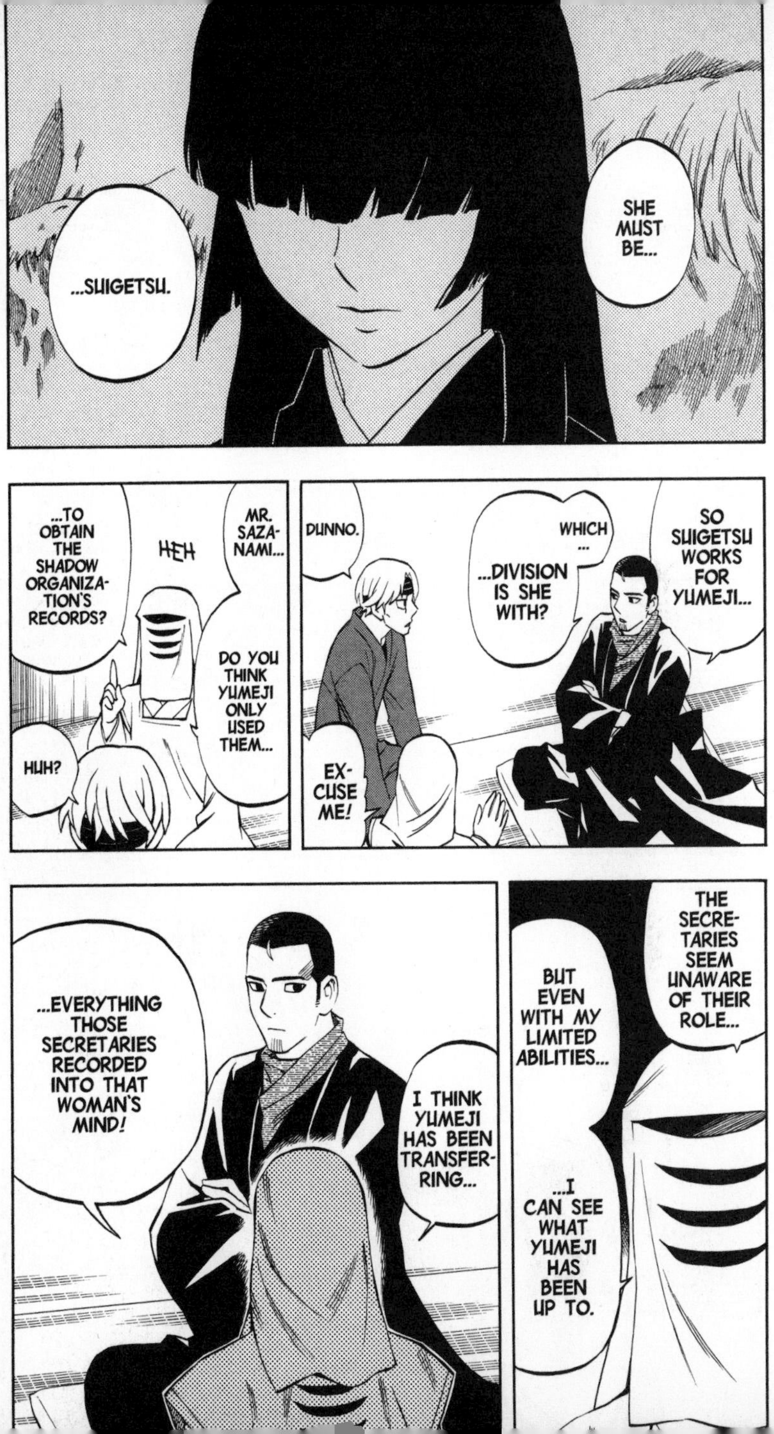
SHE MUST BE...
...SHIGETSU.
SO SHIGETSU WORKS FOR YUMEJI...
WHICH ...
...DIVISION IS SHE WITH?
DUNNO.
EXCUSE ME!
MR. SAZANAMI...
DO YOU THINK YUMEJI ONLY USED THEM...
...TO OBTAIN THE SHADOW ORGANIZATION'S RECORDS?
HEH
HUH?
THE SECRETARIES SEEM UNAWARE OF THEIR ROLE...
BUT EVEN WITH MY LIMITED ABILITIES...
...I CAN SEE WHAT YUMEJI HAS BEEN UP TO.
I THINK YUMEJI HAS BEEN TRANSFERRING...
...EVERYTHING THOSE SECRETARIES RECORDED INTO THAT WOMAN'S MIND!

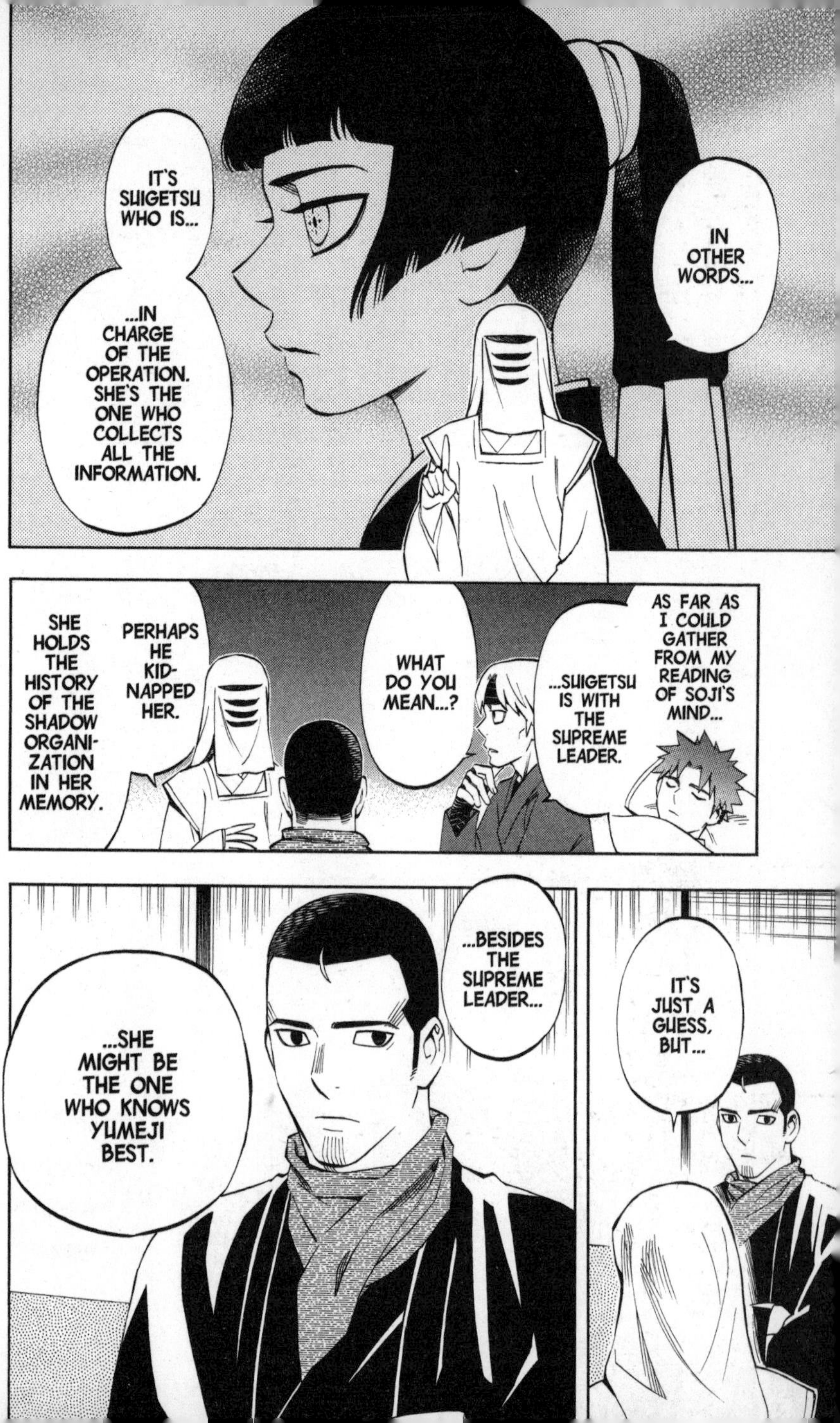
IN OTHER WORDS...
IT'S SHIGETSU WHO IS...
...IN CHARGE OF THE OPERATION. SHE'S THE ONE WHO COLLECTS ALL THE INFORMATION.
AS FAR AS I COULD GATHER FROM MY READING OF SOJI'S MIND...
...SHIGETSU IS WITH THE SUPREME LEADER.
WHAT DO YOU MEAN...?
PERHAPS HE KIDNAPPED HER.
SHE HOLDS THE HISTORY OF THE SHADOW ORGANIZATION IN HER MEMORY.
IT'S JUST A GUESS, BUT...
...BESIDES THE SUPREME LEADER...
...SHE MIGHT BE THE ONE WHO KNOWS YUMEJI BEST.

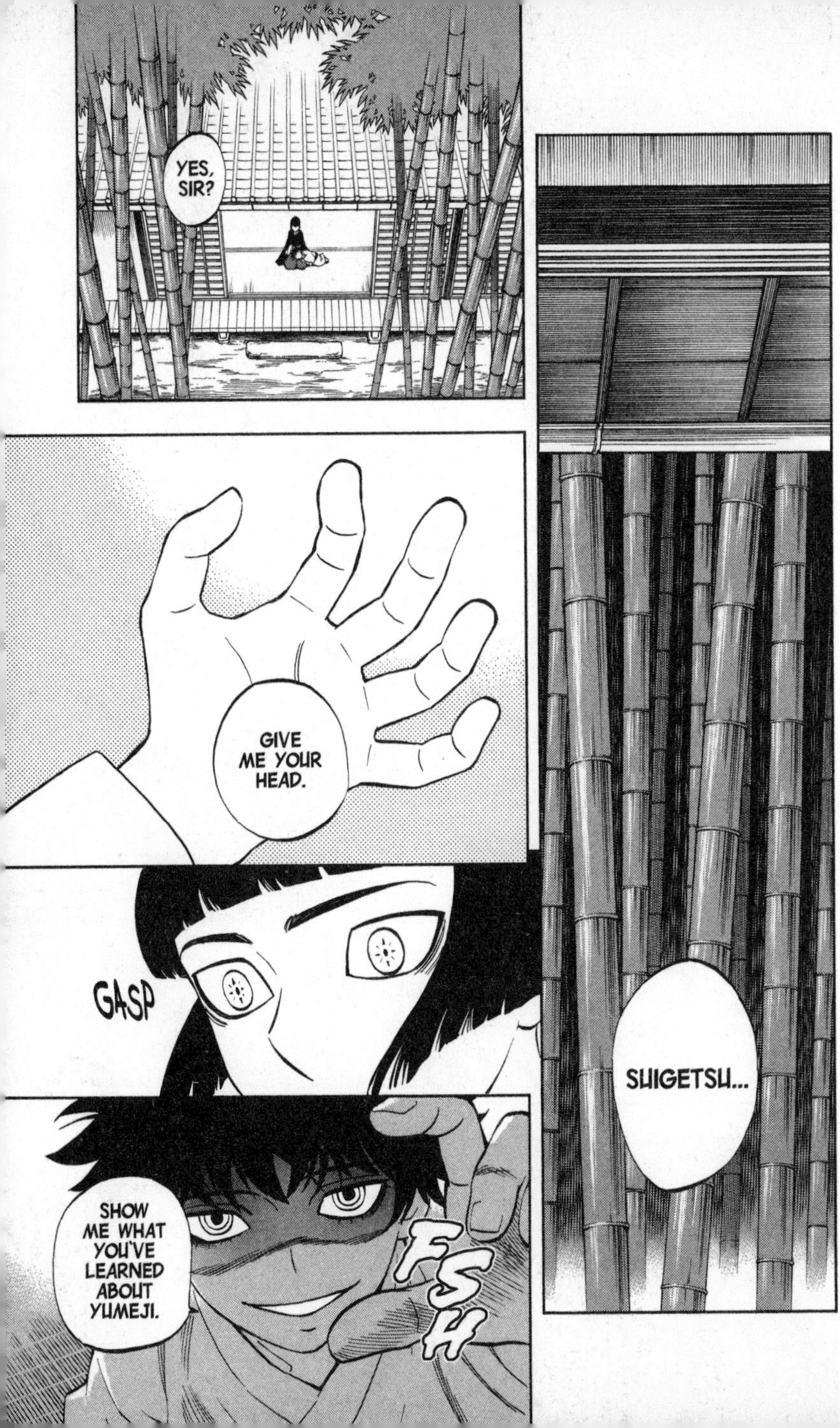
SUIGETSU...
YES, SIR?
GIVE ME YOUR HEAD.
GASP
SHOW ME WHAT YOU'VE LEARNED ABOUT YUMEJI.
FSH

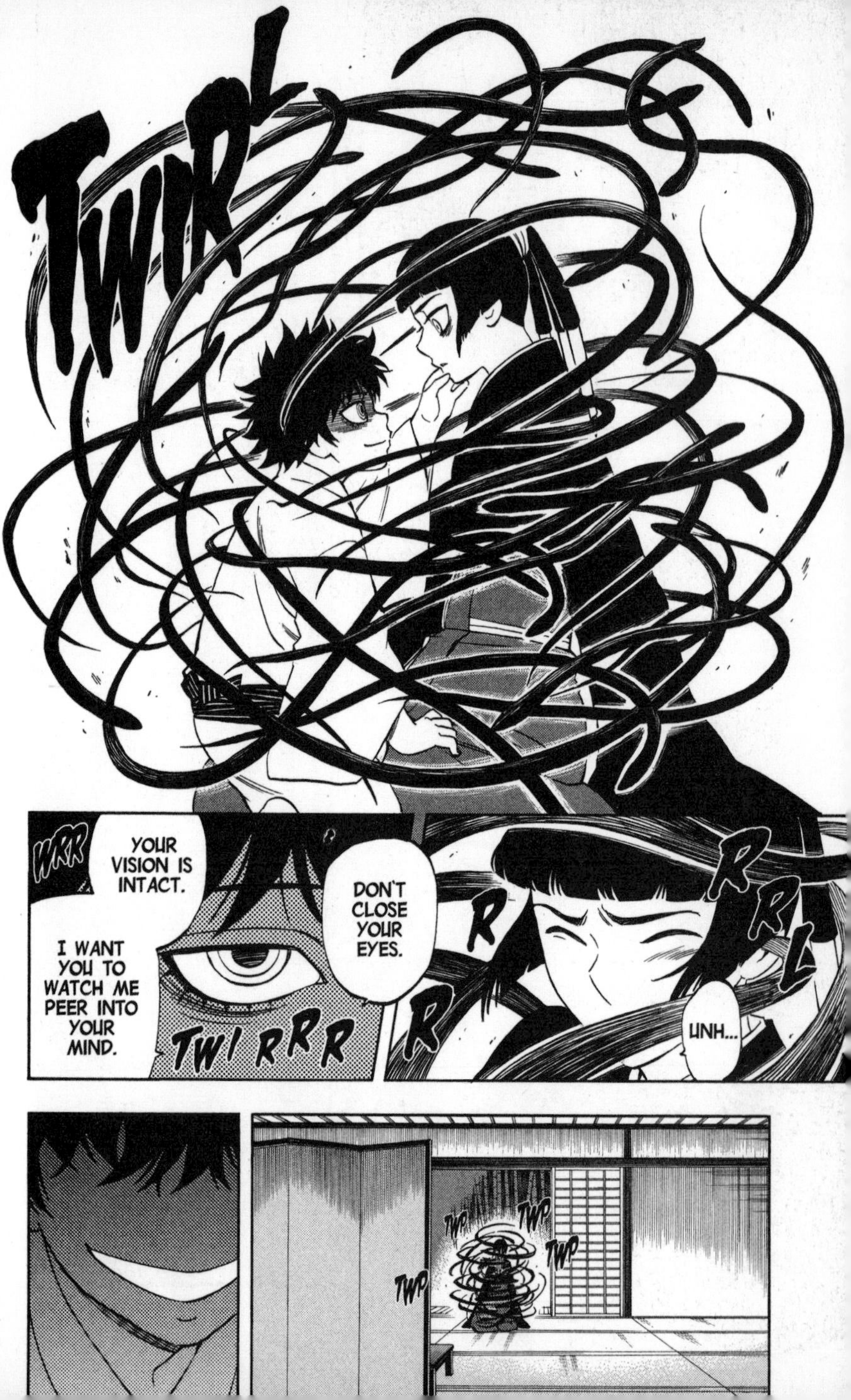
TWIRL
RRRL
R
R
UNH...
WRR
YOUR VISION IS INTACT.
DON'T CLOSE YOUR EYES.
I WANT YOU TO WATCH ME PEER INTO YOUR MIND.
TWIRRR
TWP
TWP
TWP
TWP

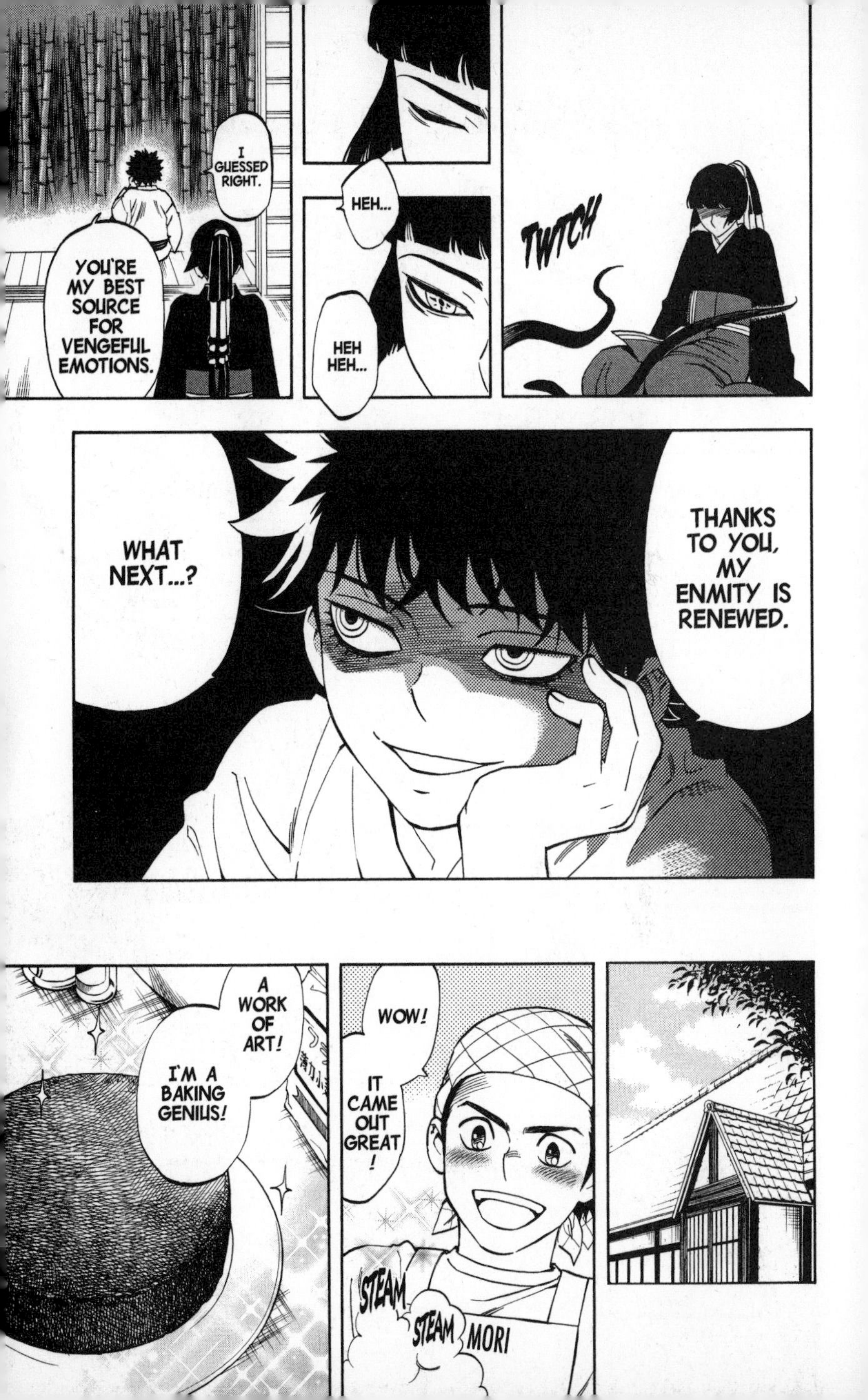
TWITCH
HEH...
HEH HEH...
I GUESSED RIGHT.
YOU'RE MY BEST SOURCE FOR VENGEFUL EMOTIONS.
THANKS TO YOU, MY ENMITY IS RENEWED.
WHAT NEXT...?
WOW!
IT CAME OUT GREAT!
STEAM
STEAM
MORI
A WORK OF ART!
I'M A BAKING GENIUS!

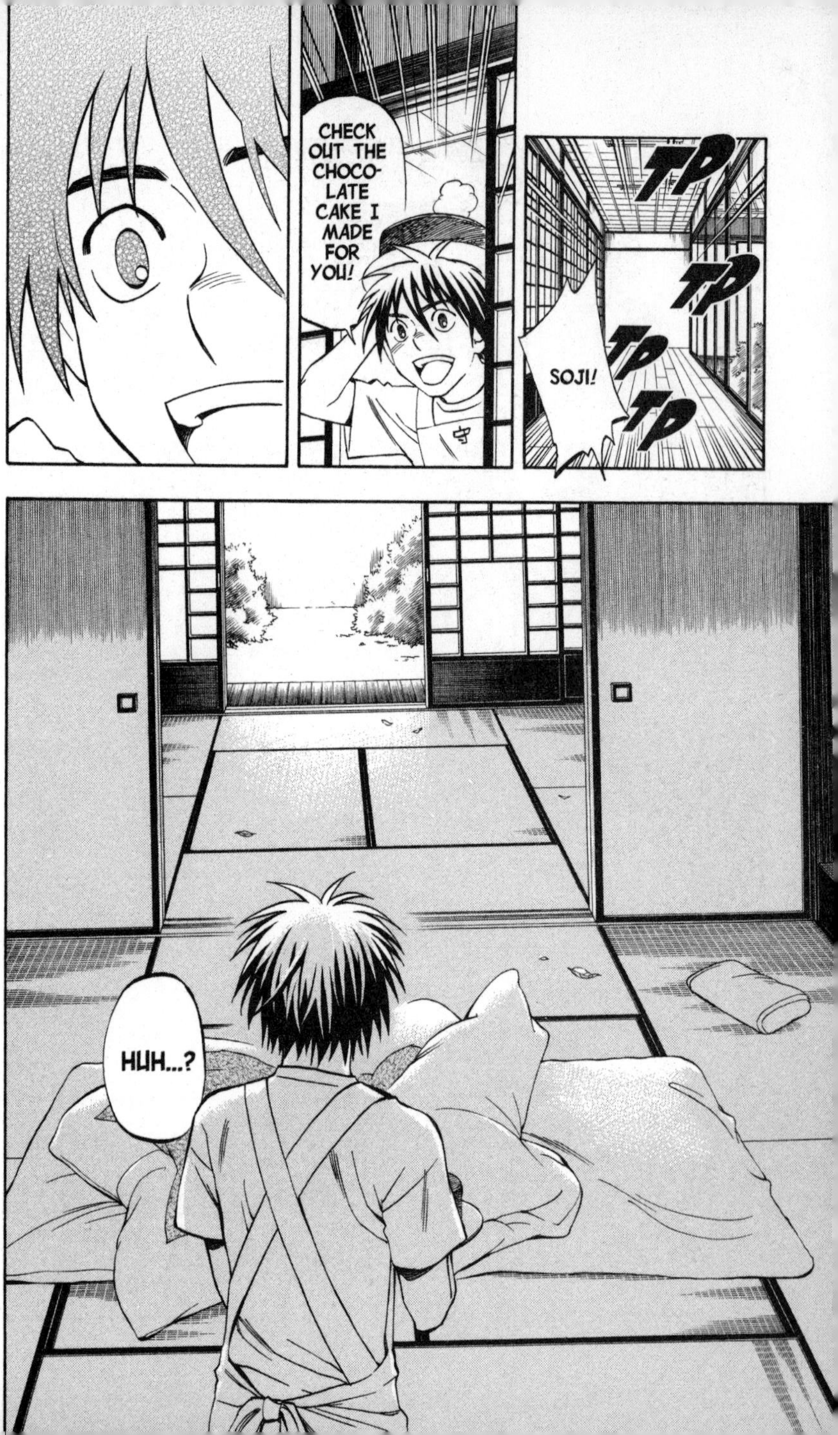
TP TP TP TP
SOJI!
CHECK OUT THE CHOCO-LATE CAKE I MADE FOR YOU!
HUH...?

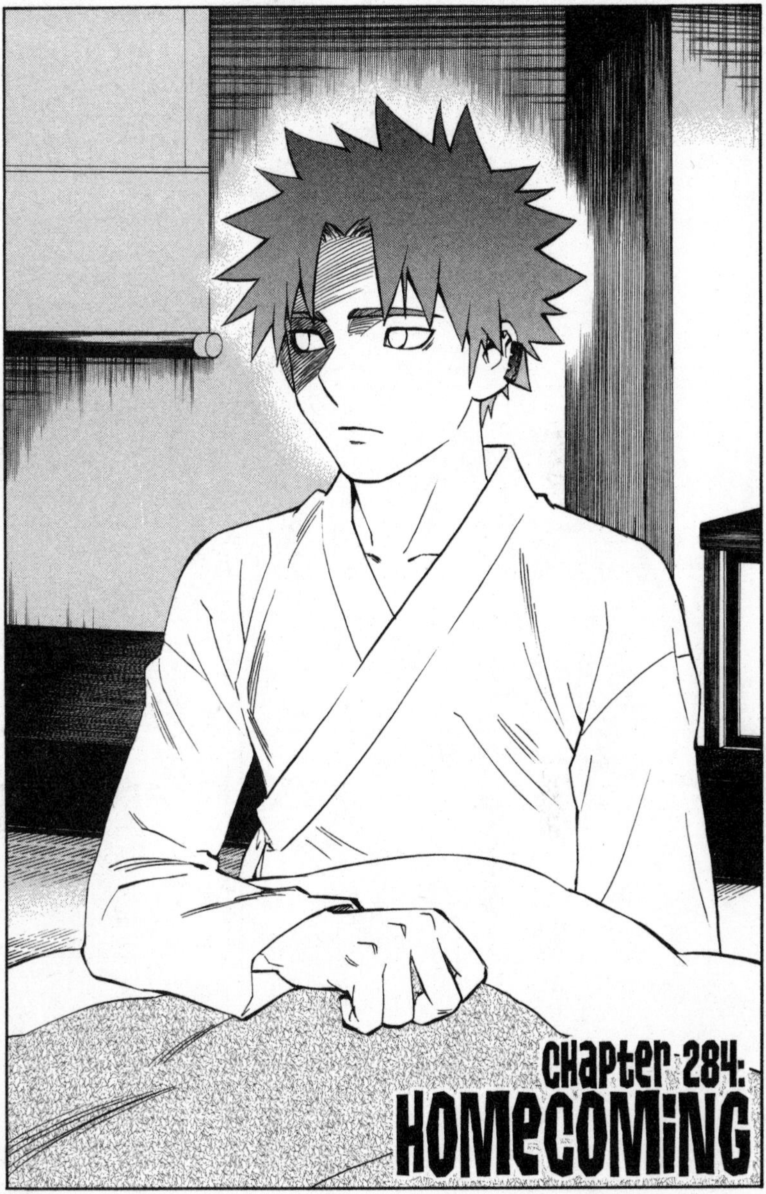
Chapter 284:
HOMECOMING

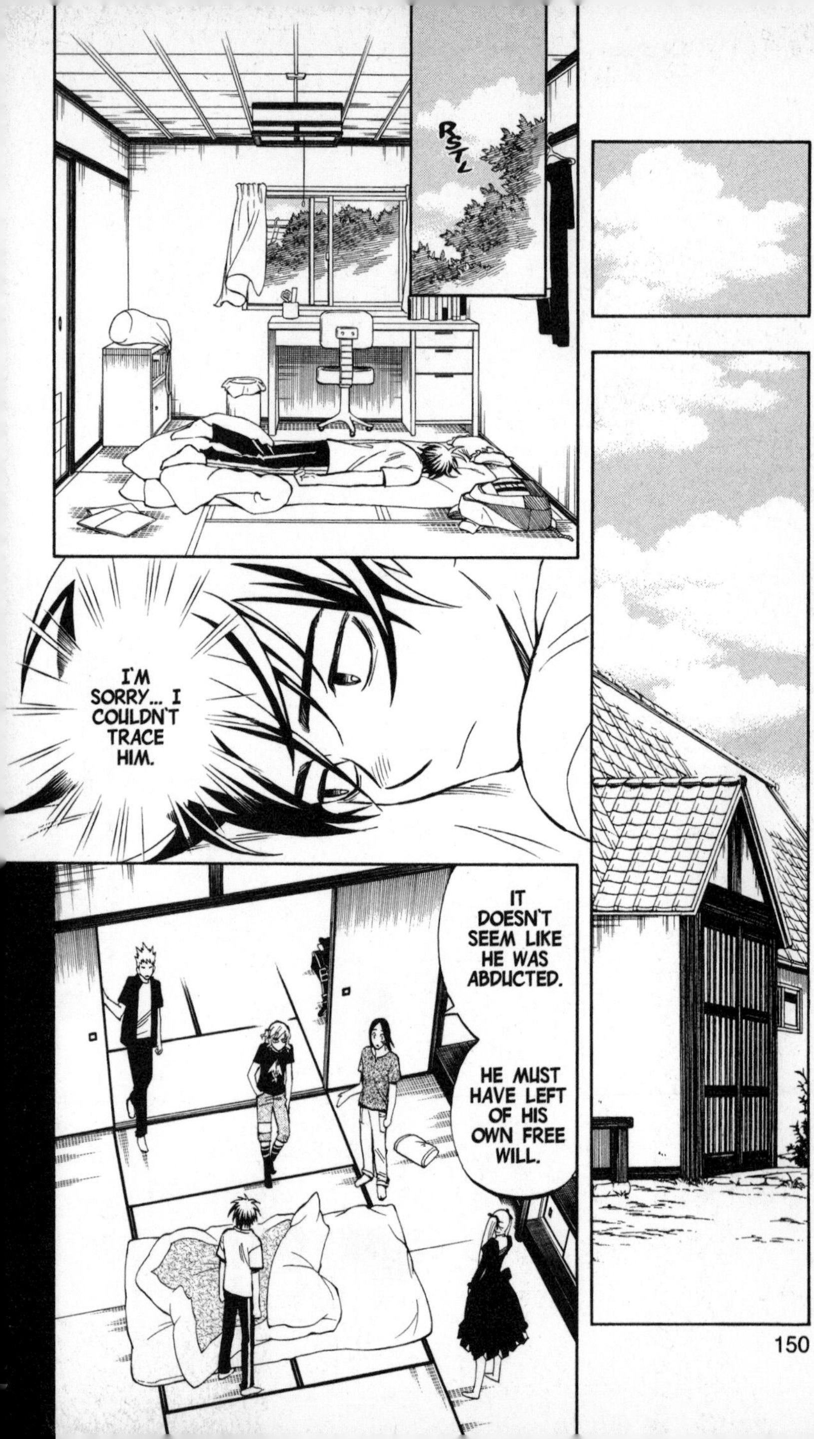
RSTL
I'M SORRY... I COULDN'T TRACE HIM.
IT DOESN'T SEEM LIKE HE WAS ABDUCTED.
HE MUST HAVE LEFT OF HIS OWN FREE WILL.

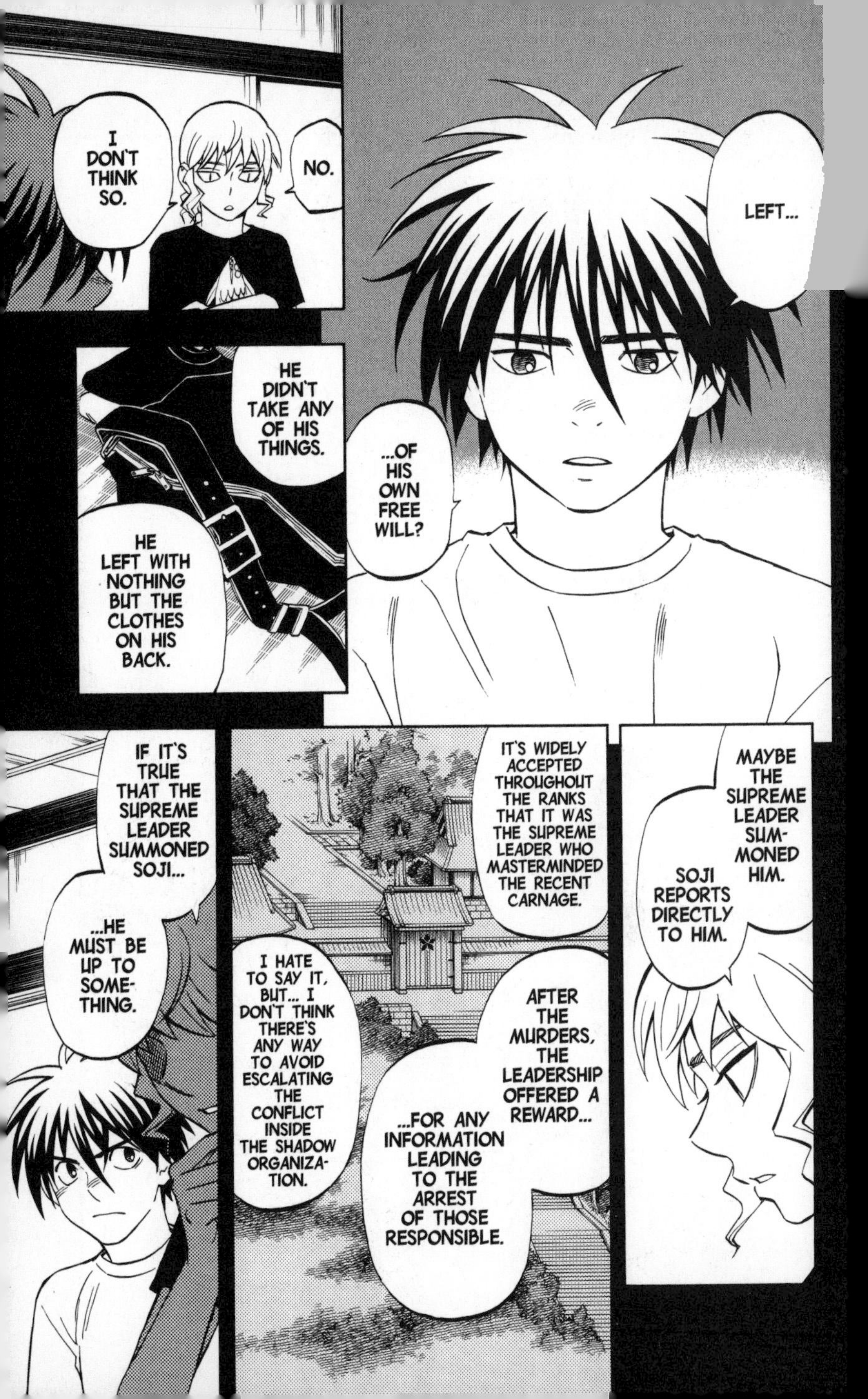
LEFT...
...OF HIS OWN FREE WILL?
NO.
I DON'T THINK SO.
HE DIDN'T TAKE ANY OF HIS THINGS.
HE LEFT WITH NOTHING BUT THE CLOTHES ON HIS BACK.
MAYBE THE SUPREME LEADER SUMMONED HIM.
SOJI REPORTS DIRECTLY TO HIM.
IT'S WIDELY ACCEPTED THROUGHOUT THE RANKS THAT IT WAS THE SUPREME LEADER WHO MASTERMINDED THE RECENT CARNAGE.
AFTER THE MURDERS, THE LEADERSHIP OFFERED A REWARD...
...FOR ANY INFORMATION LEADING TO THE ARREST OF THOSE RESPONSIBLE.
I HATE TO SAY IT, BUT... I DON'T THINK THERE'S ANY WAY TO AVOID ESCALATING THE CONFLICT INSIDE THE SHADOW ORGANIZA-TION.
IF IT'S TRUE THAT THE SUPREME LEADER SUMMONED SOJI...
...HE MUST BE UP TO SOME-THING.

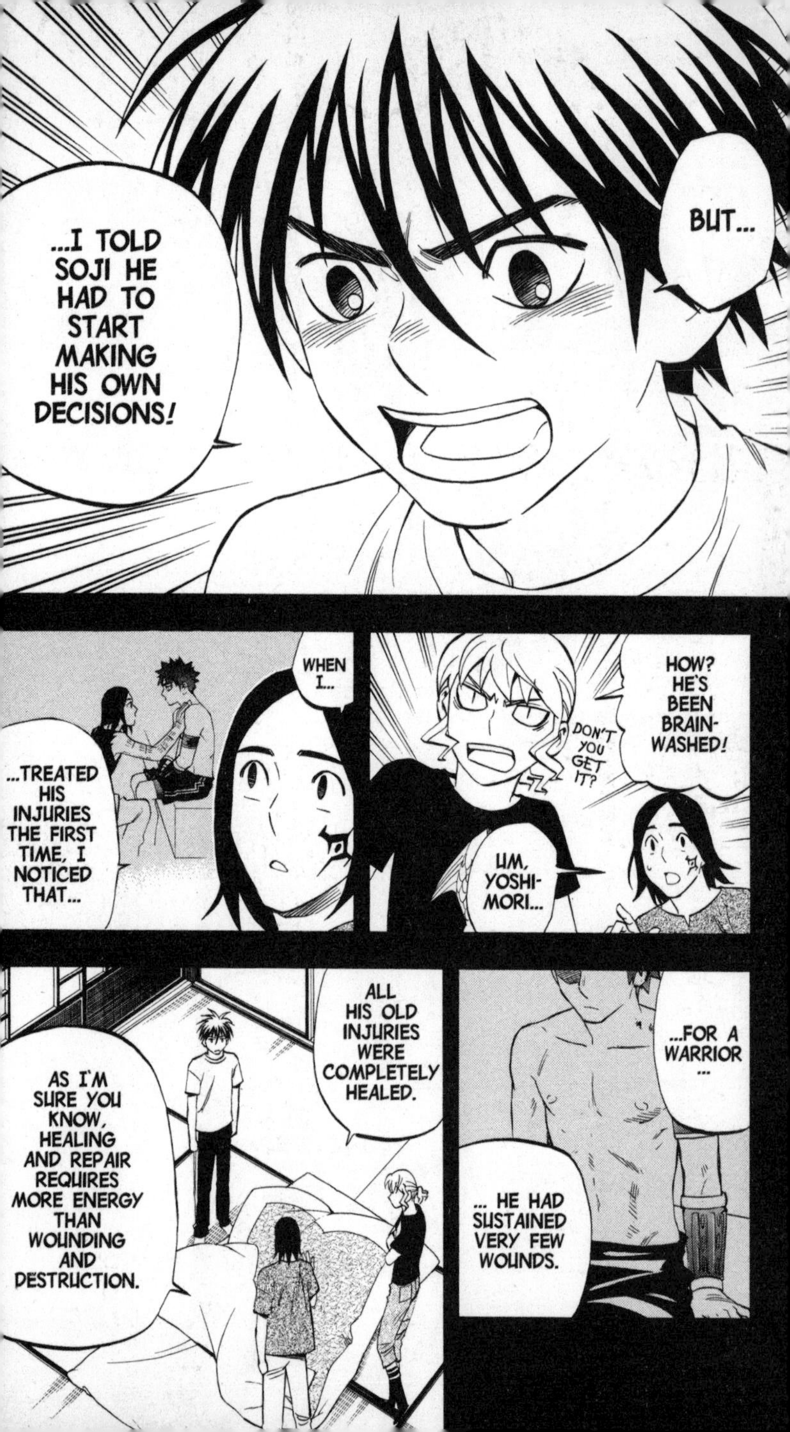
BUT...
...I TOLD SOJI HE HAD TO START MAKING HIS OWN DECISIONS!
HOW? HE'S BEEN BRAIN-WASHED!
DON'T YOU GET IT?
UM, YOSHI-MORI...
WHEN I...
...TREATED HIS INJURIES THE FIRST TIME, I NOTICED THAT...
...FOR A WARRIOR...
... HE HAD SUSTAINED VERY FEW WOUNDS.
ALL HIS OLD INJURIES WERE COMPLETELY HEALED.
AS I'M SURE YOU KNOW, HEALING AND REPAIR REQUIRES MORE ENERGY THAN WOUNDING AND DESTRUCTION.

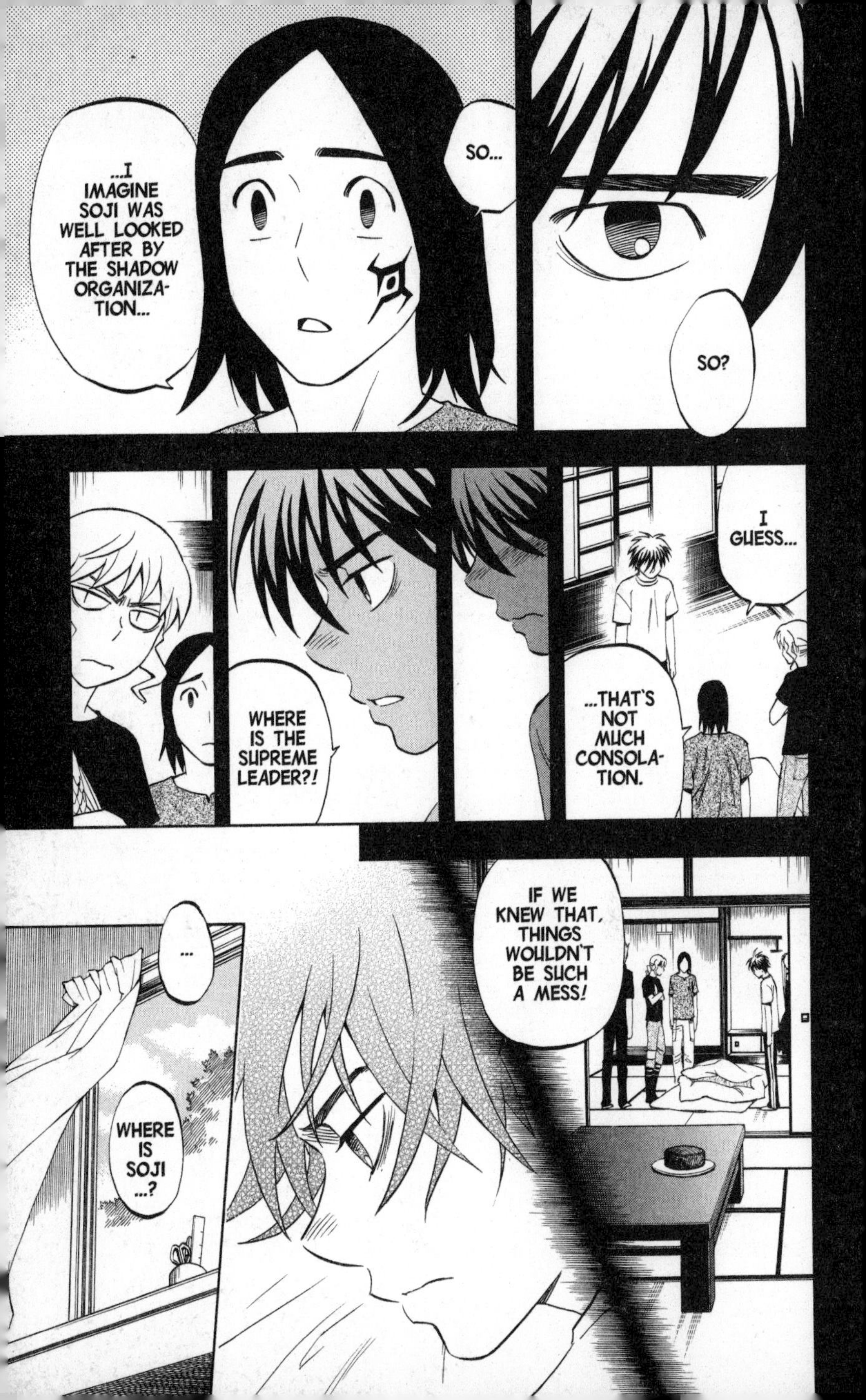
SO...
...I IMAGINE SOJI WAS WELL LOOKED AFTER BY THE SHADOW ORGANIZA-TION...
SO?
I GUESS...
...THAT'S NOT MUCH CONSOLA-TION.
WHERE IS THE SUPREME LEADER?!
IF WE KNEW THAT, THINGS WOULDN'T BE SUCH A MESS!
...
WHERE IS SOJI ...?

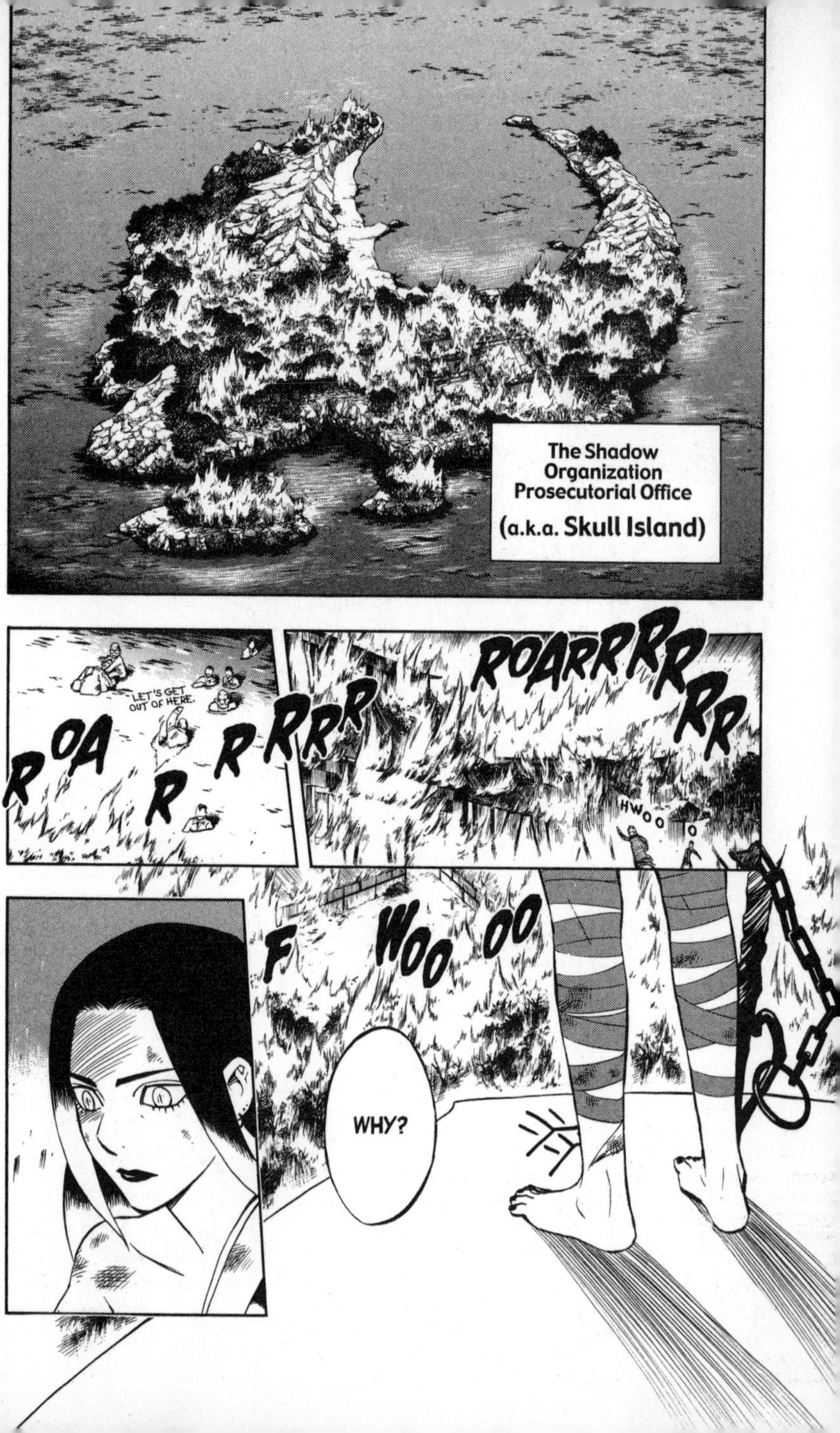

The Shadow Organization Prosecutorial Office
(a.k.a. Skull Island)
ROARRRRRR
HWOOO
LET'S GET OUT OF HERE.
ROARRRRR
FWOOOO
WHY?

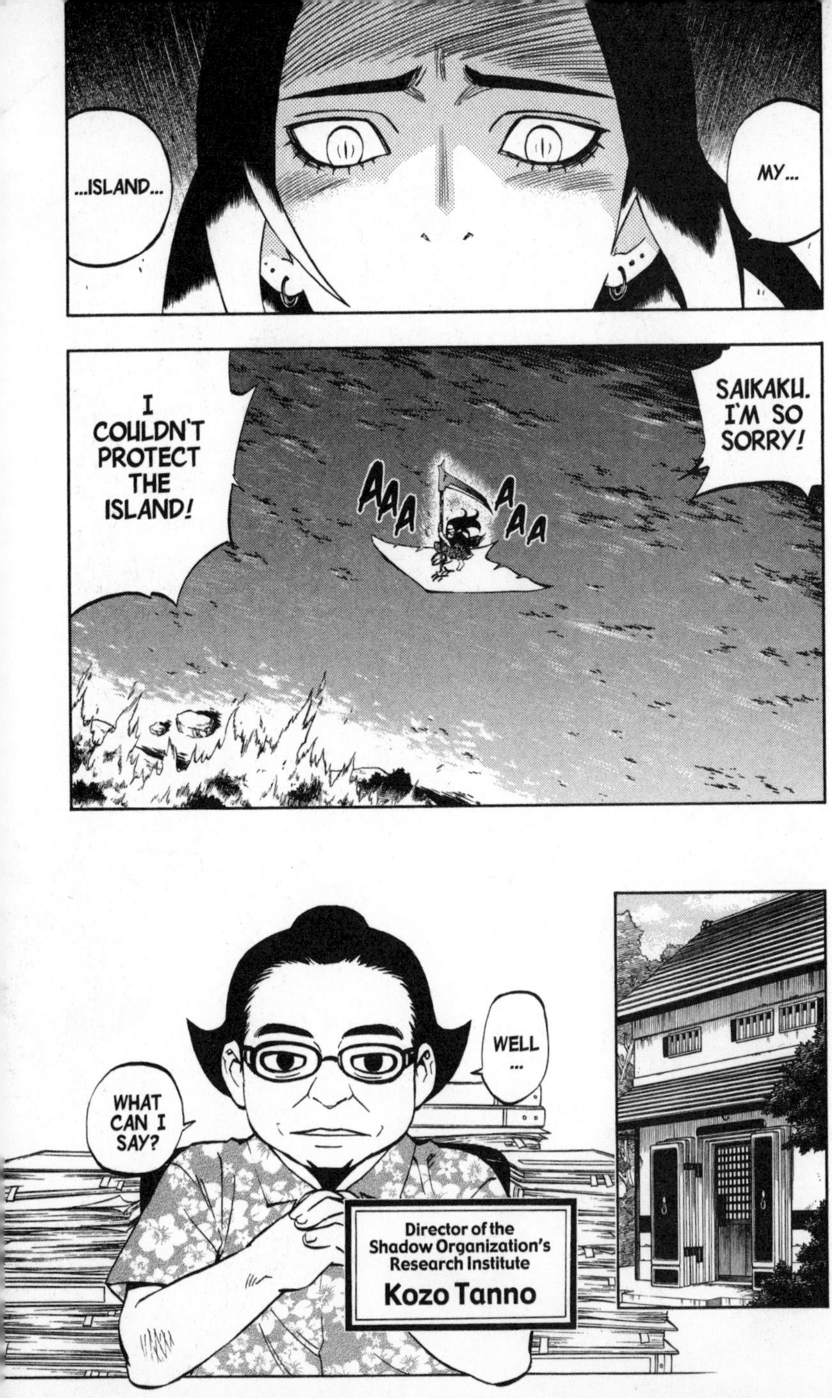
MY...
...ISLAND...
SAIKAKU. I'M SO SORRY!
AAA
AAA
I COULDN'T PROTECT THE ISLAND!
WELL ...
WHAT CAN I SAY?
Director of the Shadow Organization's Research Institute
Kozo Tanno

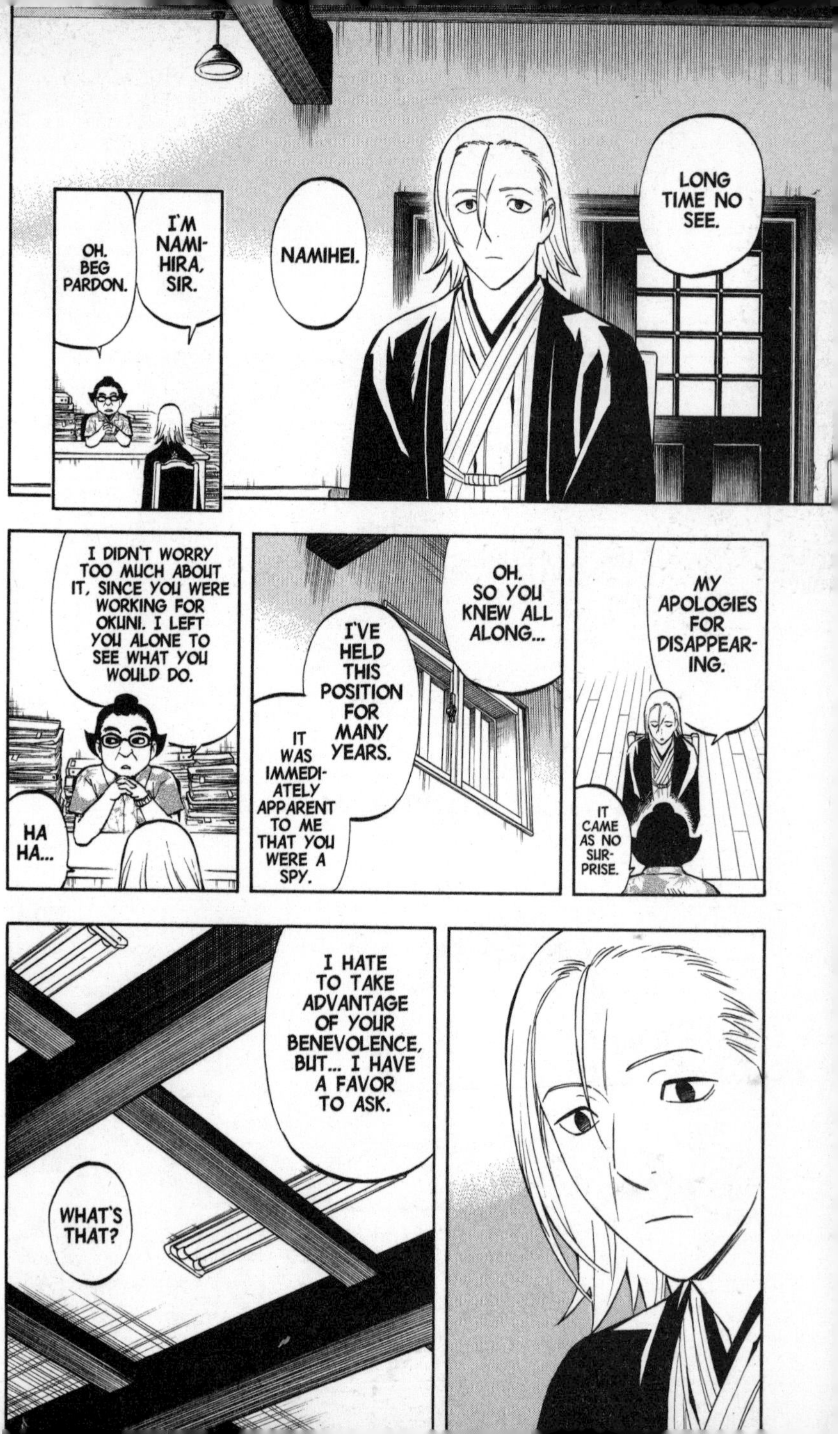
LONG TIME NO SEE.
NAMIHEI.
I'M NAMIHIRA, SIR.
OH. BEG PARDON.
MY APOLOGIES FOR DISAPPEARING.
IT CAME AS NO SURPRISE.
OH. SO YOU KNEW ALL ALONG...
I'VE HELD THIS POSITION FOR MANY YEARS.
IT WAS IMMEDIATELY APPARENT TO ME THAT YOU WERE A SPY.
I DIDN'T WORRY TOO MUCH ABOUT IT, SINCE YOU WERE WORKING FOR OKUNI. I LEFT YOU ALONE TO SEE WHAT YOU WOULD DO.
HA HA...
I HATE TO TAKE ADVANTAGE OF YOUR BENEVOLENCE, BUT... I HAVE A FAVOR TO ASK.
WHAT'S THAT?

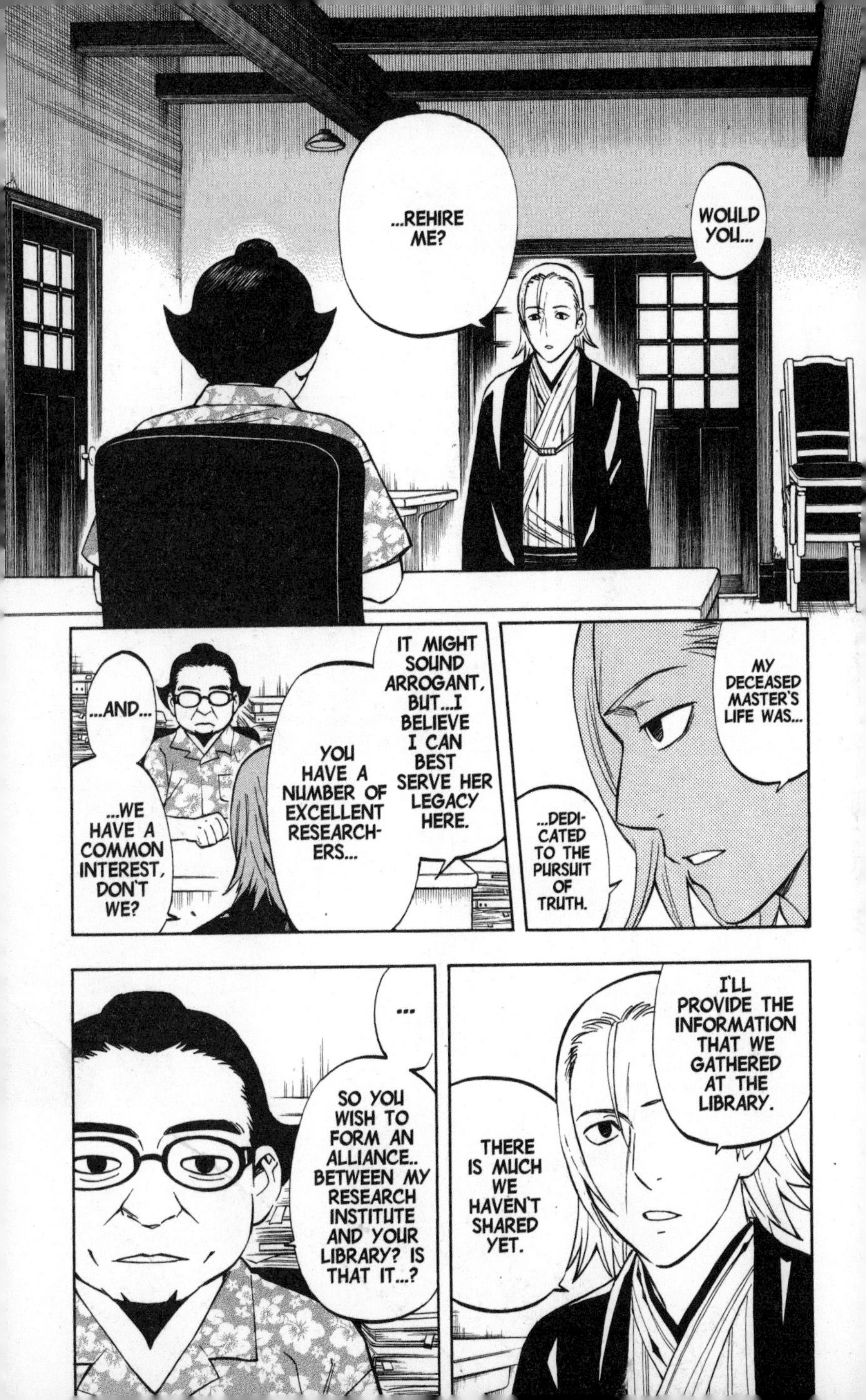
WOULD YOU...
...REHIRE ME?
MY DECEASED MASTER'S LIFE WAS...
...DEDICATED TO THE PURSUIT OF TRUTH.
IT MIGHT SOUND ARROGANT, BUT...I BELIEVE I CAN BEST SERVE HER LEGACY HERE.
YOU HAVE A NUMBER OF EXCELLENT RESEARCHERS...
...AND...
...WE HAVE A COMMON INTEREST, DON'T WE?
I'LL PROVIDE THE INFORMATION THAT WE GATHERED AT THE LIBRARY.
THERE IS MUCH WE HAVEN'T SHARED YET.
...
SO YOU WISH TO FORM AN ALLIANCE.. BETWEEN MY RESEARCH INSTITUTE AND YOUR LIBRARY? IS THAT IT...?

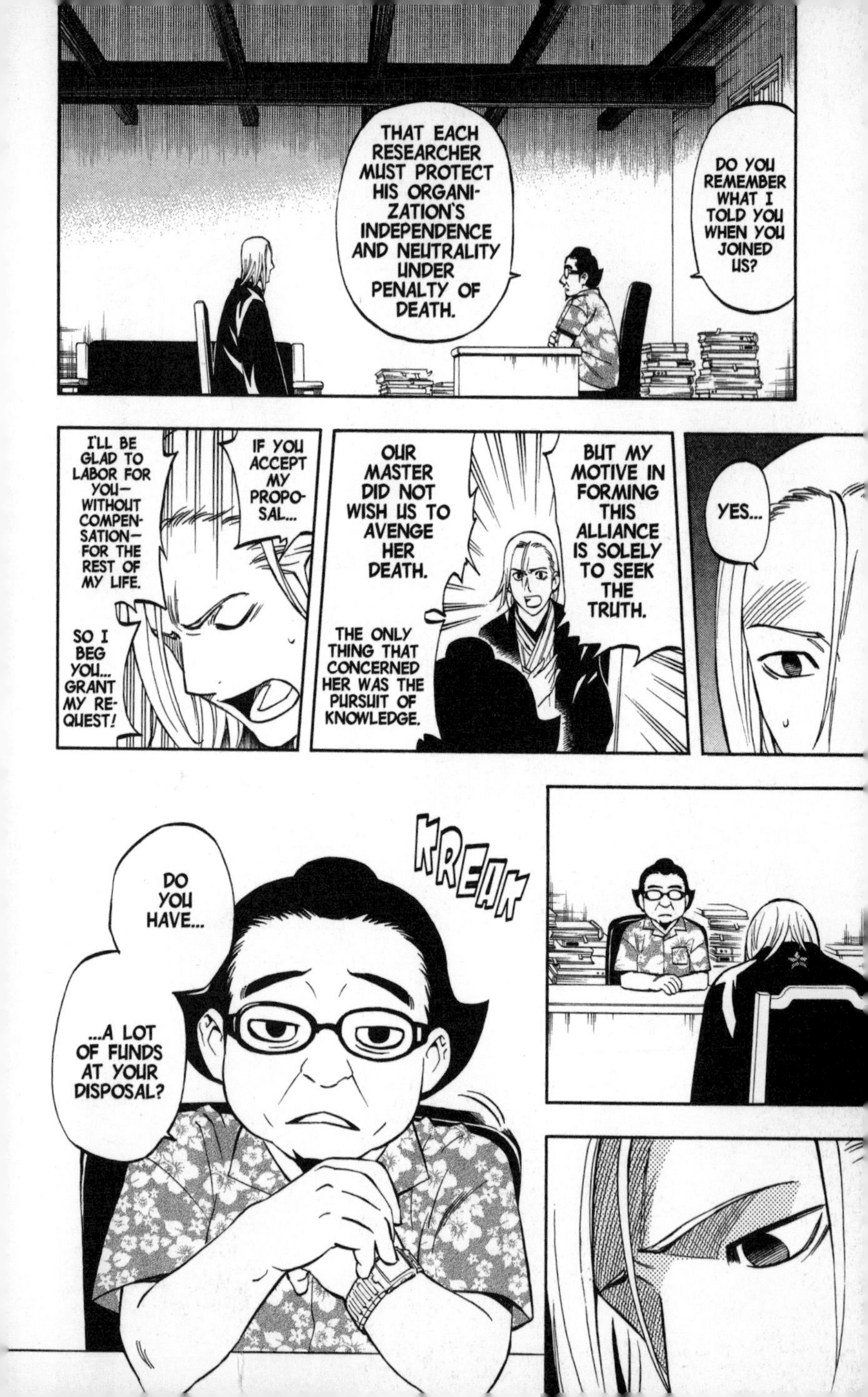
DO YOU REMEMBER WHAT I TOLD YOU WHEN YOU JOINED US?
THAT EACH RESEARCHER MUST PROTECT HIS ORGANIZATION'S INDEPENDENCE AND NEUTRALITY UNDER PENALTY OF DEATH.
YES...
BUT MY MOTIVE IN FORMING THIS ALLIANCE IS SOLELY TO SEEK THE TRUTH.
OUR MASTER DID NOT WISH US TO AVENGE HER DEATH.
THE ONLY THING THAT CONCERNED HER WAS THE PURSUIT OF KNOWLEDGE.
IF YOU ACCEPT MY PROPOSAL...
I'LL BE GLAD TO LABOR FOR YOU—WITHOUT COMPENSATION—FOR THE REST OF MY LIFE.
SO I BEG YOU... GRANT MY REQUEST!
KREAK
DO YOU HAVE...
...A LOT OF FUNDS AT YOUR DISPOSAL?

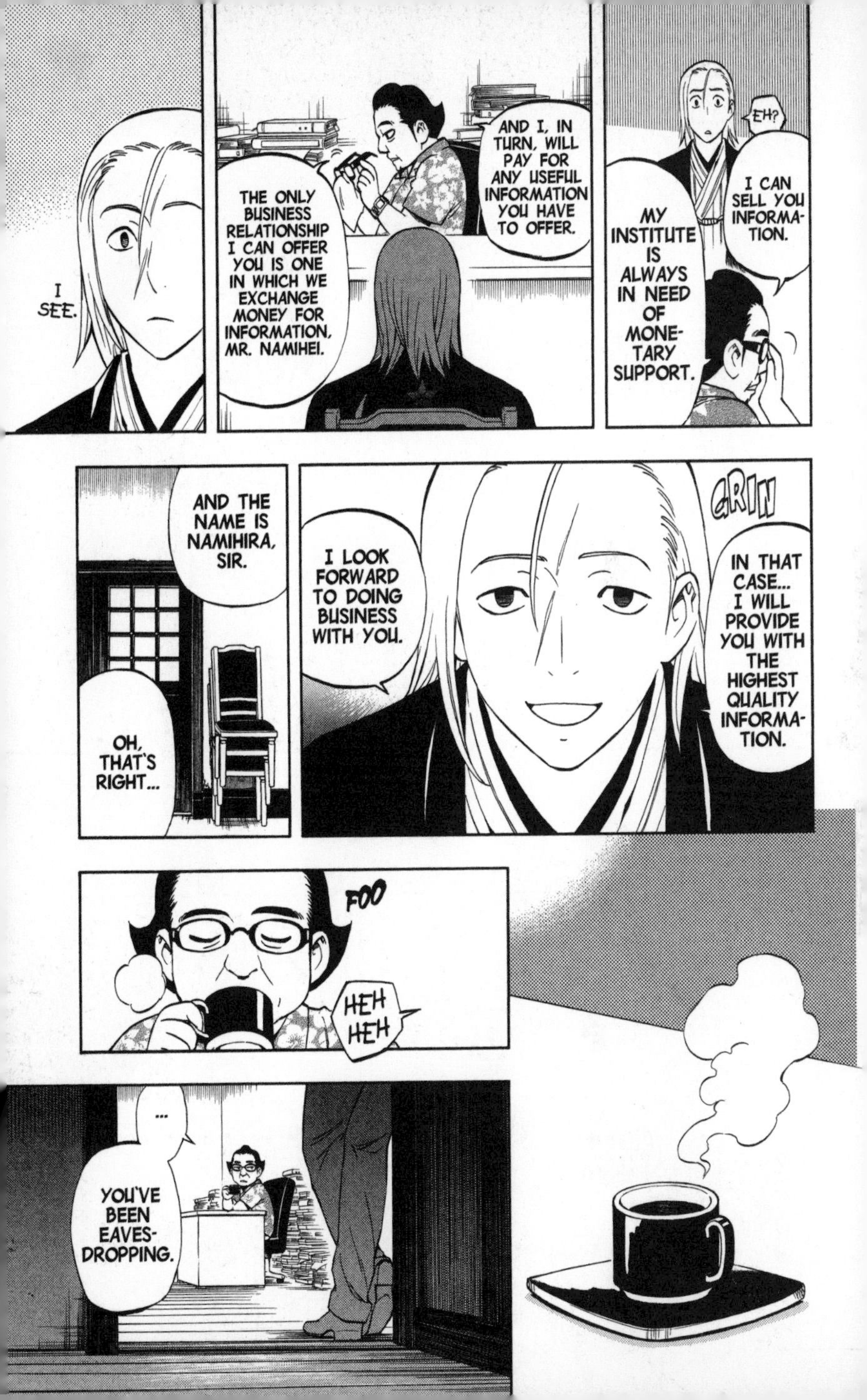
EH?
I CAN SELL YOU INFORMATION.
MY INSTITUTE IS ALWAYS IN NEED OF MONETARY SUPPORT.
AND I, IN TURN, WILL PAY FOR ANY USEFUL INFORMATION YOU HAVE TO OFFER.
THE ONLY BUSINESS RELATIONSHIP I CAN OFFER YOU IS ONE IN WHICH WE EXCHANGE MONEY FOR INFORMATION, MR. NAMIHEI.
I SEE.
GRIN
IN THAT CASE... I WILL PROVIDE YOU WITH THE HIGHEST QUALITY INFORMATION.
I LOOK FORWARD TO DOING BUSINESS WITH YOU.
AND THE NAME IS NAMIHIRA, SIR.
OH, THAT'S RIGHT...
FOO
HEH HEH
...
YOU'VE BEEN EAVESDROPPING.

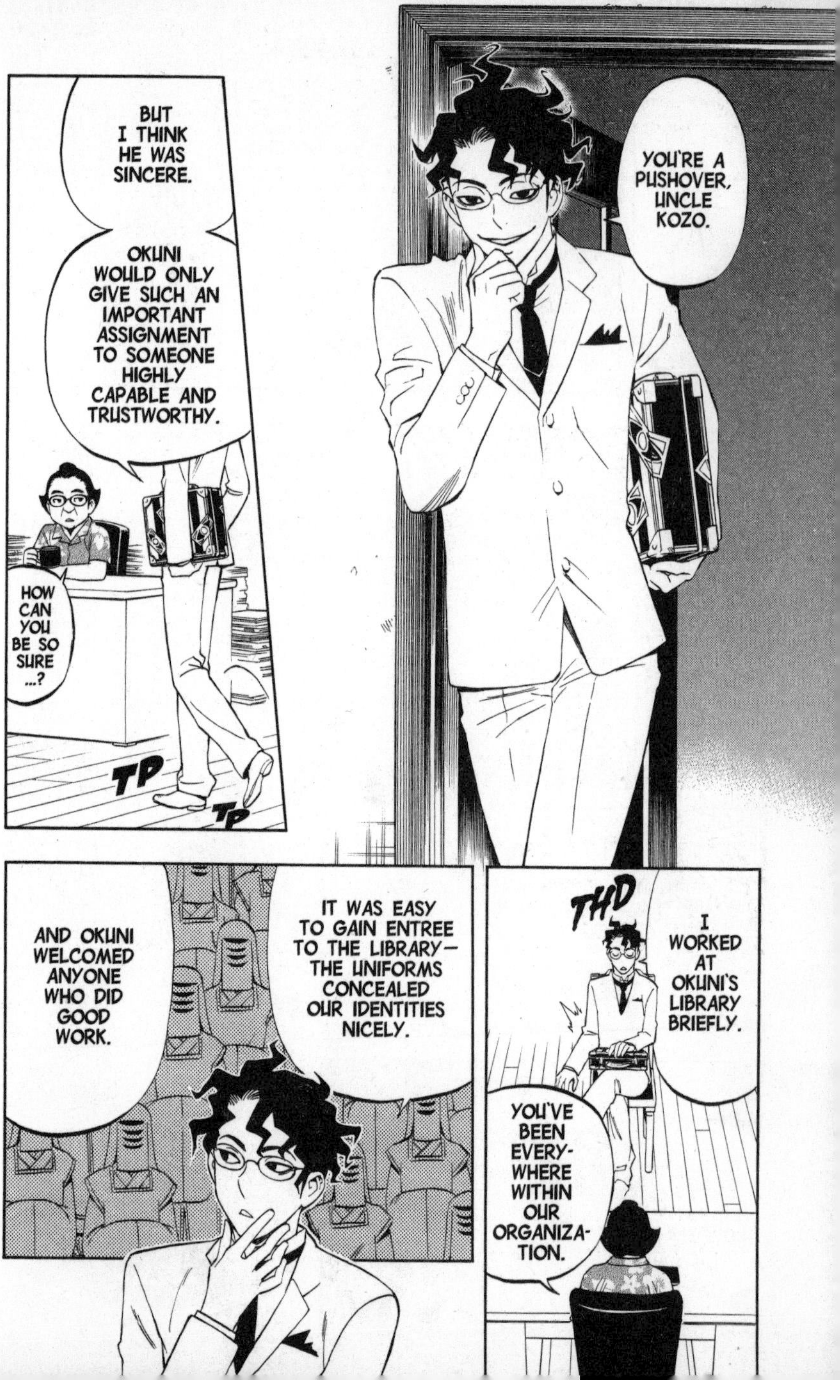
YOU'RE A PUSHOVER, UNCLE KOZO.
BUT I THINK HE WAS SINCERE.
OKUNI WOULD ONLY GIVE SUCH AN IMPORTANT ASSIGNMENT TO SOMEONE HIGHLY CAPABLE AND TRUSTWORTHY.
HOW CAN YOU BE SO SURE ...?
TP
TP
I WORKED AT OKUNI'S LIBRARY BRIEFLY.
THD
YOU'VE BEEN EVERY-WHERE WITHIN OUR ORGANIZA-TION.
IT WAS EASY TO GAIN ENTREE TO THE LIBRARY— THE UNIFORMS CONCEALED OUR IDENTITIES NICELY.
AND OKUNI WELCOMED ANYONE WHO DID GOOD WORK.

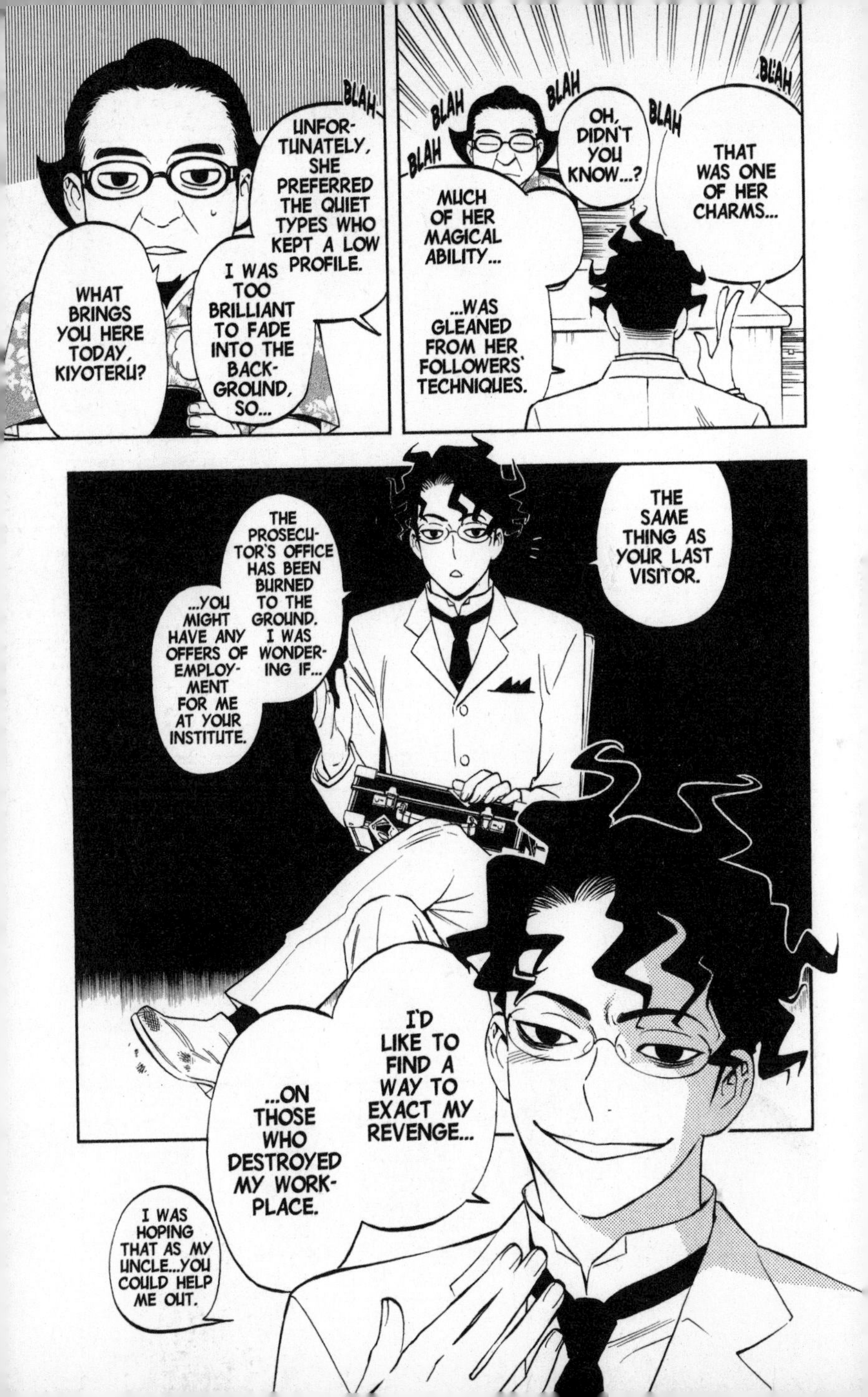
BLAH
THAT WAS ONE OF HER CHARMS...
BLAH
OH, DIDN'T YOU KNOW...?
BLAH
BLAH
BLAH
MUCH OF HER MAGICAL ABILITY...
...WAS GLEANED FROM HER FOLLOWERS' TECHNIQUES.
BLAH
UNFORTUNATELY, SHE PREFERRED THE QUIET TYPES WHO KEPT A LOW PROFILE.
I WAS TOO BRILLIANT TO FADE INTO THE BACKGROUND, SO...
WHAT BRINGS YOU HERE TODAY, KIYOTERU?
THE SAME THING AS YOUR LAST VISITOR.
THE PROSECUTOR'S OFFICE HAS BEEN BURNED TO THE GROUND. I WAS WONDERING IF...
...YOU MIGHT HAVE ANY OFFERS OF EMPLOYMENT FOR ME AT YOUR INSTITUTE.
I'D LIKE TO FIND A WAY TO EXACT MY REVENGE...
...ON THOSE WHO DESTROYED MY WORKPLACE.
I WAS HOPING THAT AS MY UNCLE...YOU COULD HELP ME OUT.

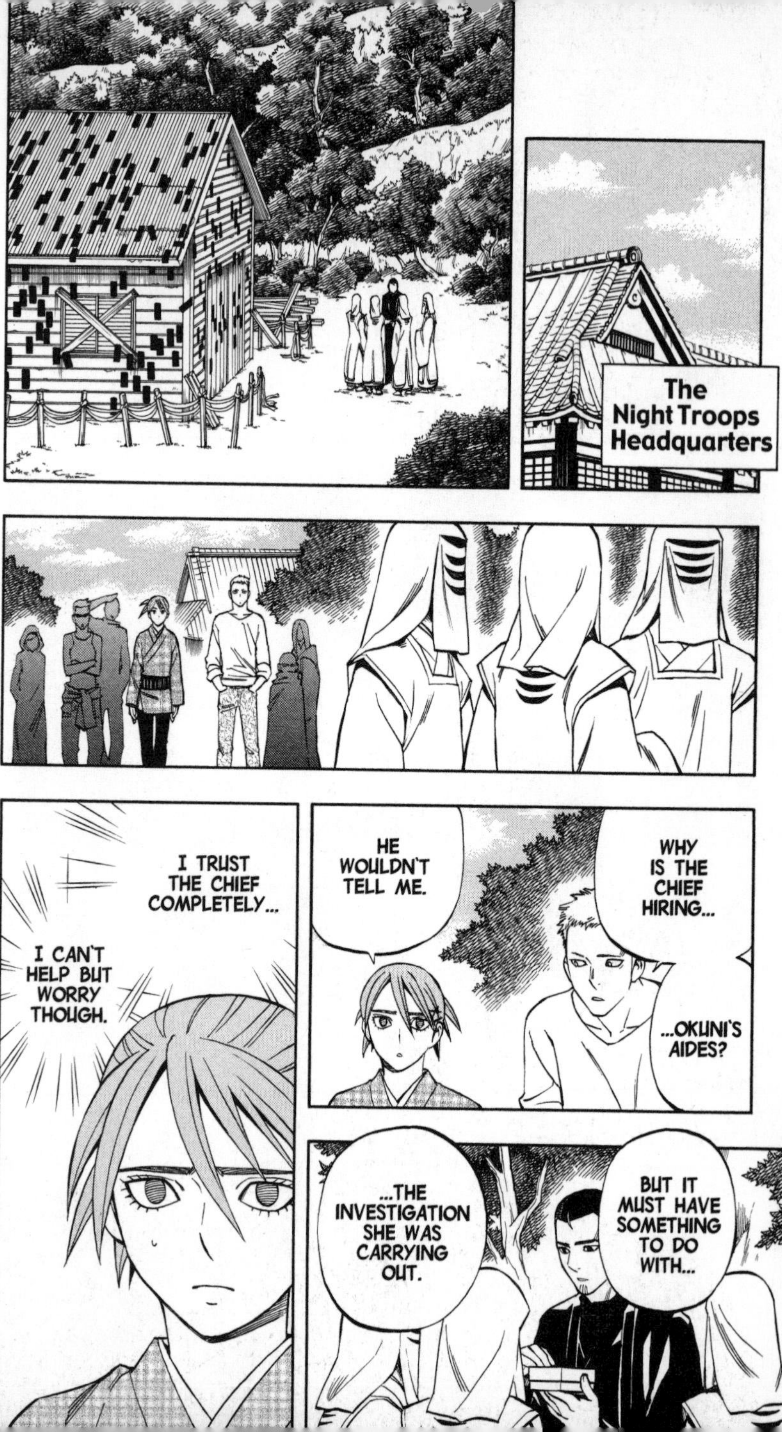
The Night Troops Headquarters
WHY IS THE CHIEF HIRING...
...OKUNI'S AIDES?
HE WOULDN'T TELL ME.
BUT IT MUST HAVE SOMETHING TO DO WITH...
...THE INVESTIGATION SHE WAS CARRYING OUT.
I TRUST THE CHIEF COMPLETELY...
I CAN'T HELP BUT WORRY THOUGH.

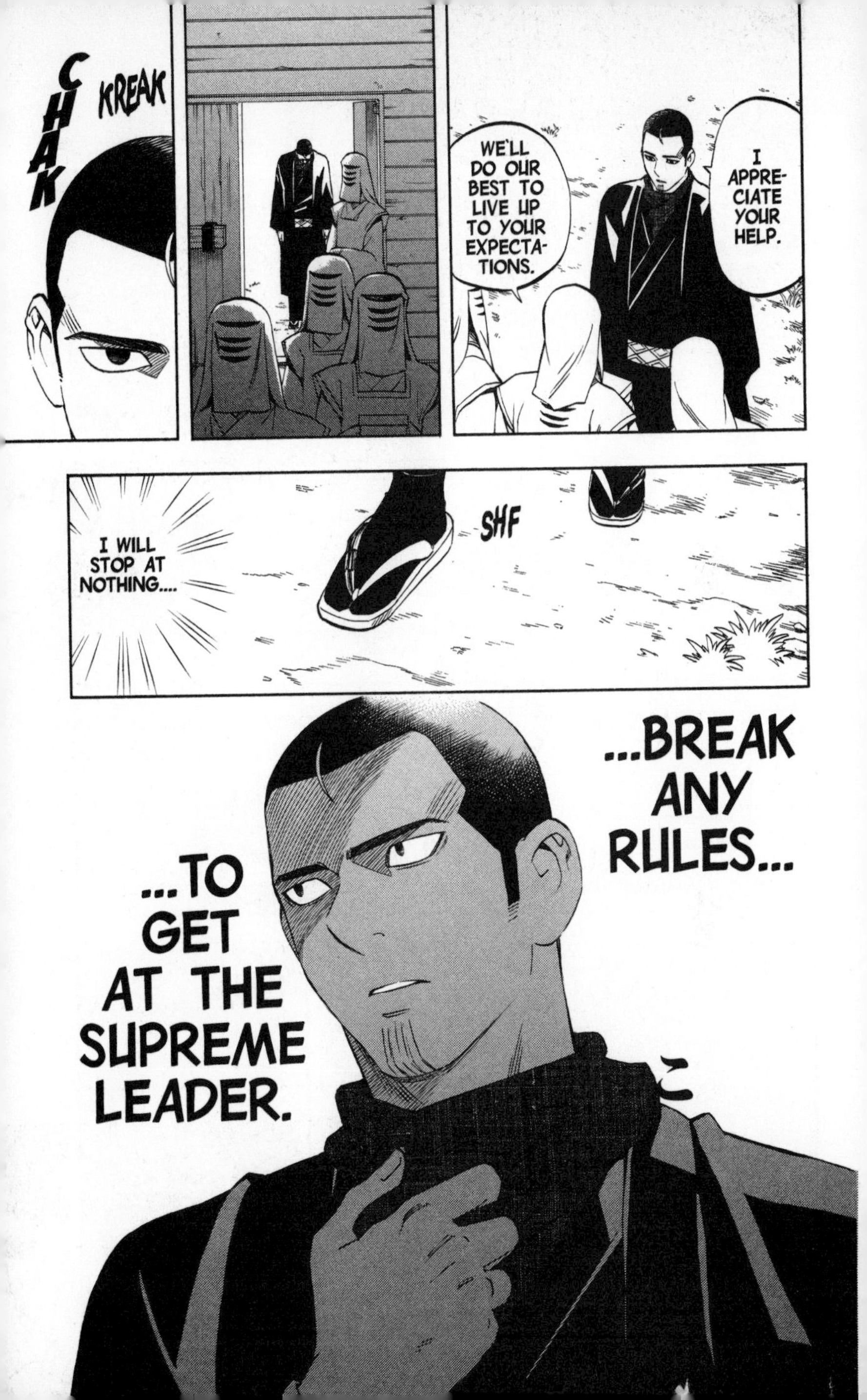

I APPRECIATE YOUR HELP.
WE'LL DO OUR BEST TO LIVE UP TO YOUR EXPECTATIONS.
KREAK
CHAK
SHF
I WILL STOP AT NOTHING....
...BREAK ANY RULES...
...TO GET AT THE SUPREME LEADER.

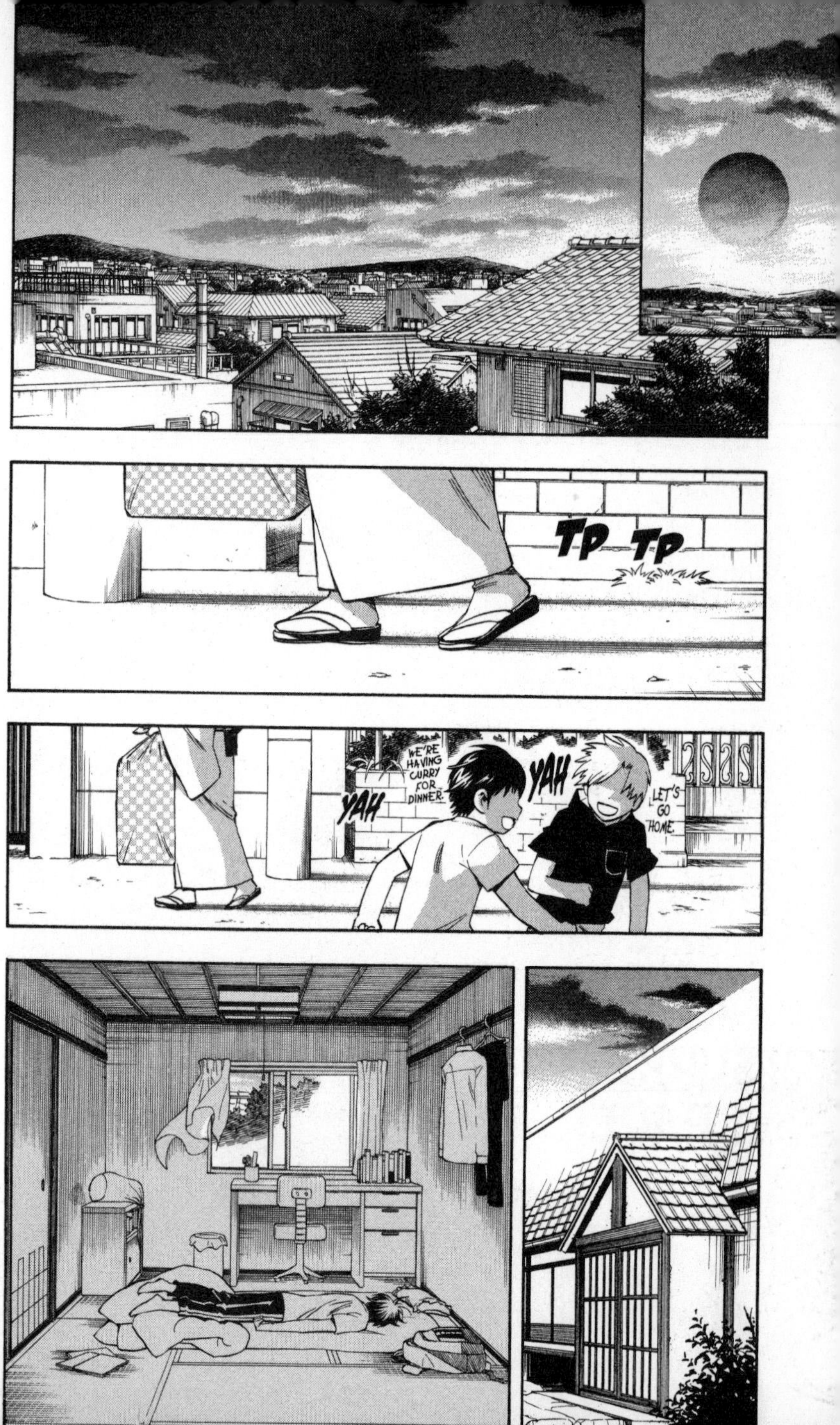
TP TP
LET'S GO HOME.
YAH
WE'RE HAVING CURRY FOR DINNER.
YAH

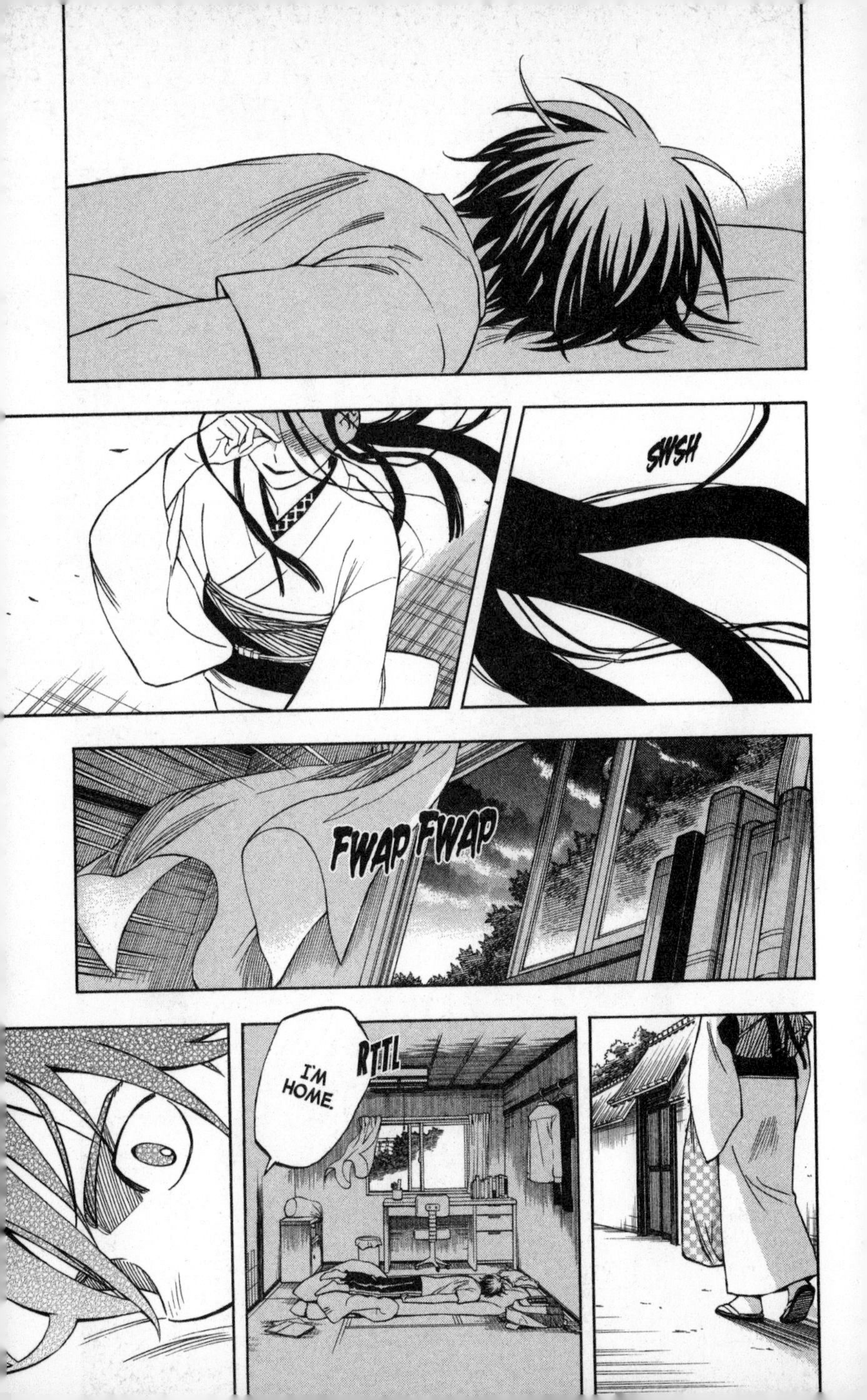
SWSH
FWAP FWAP
RTTL
I'M HOME.

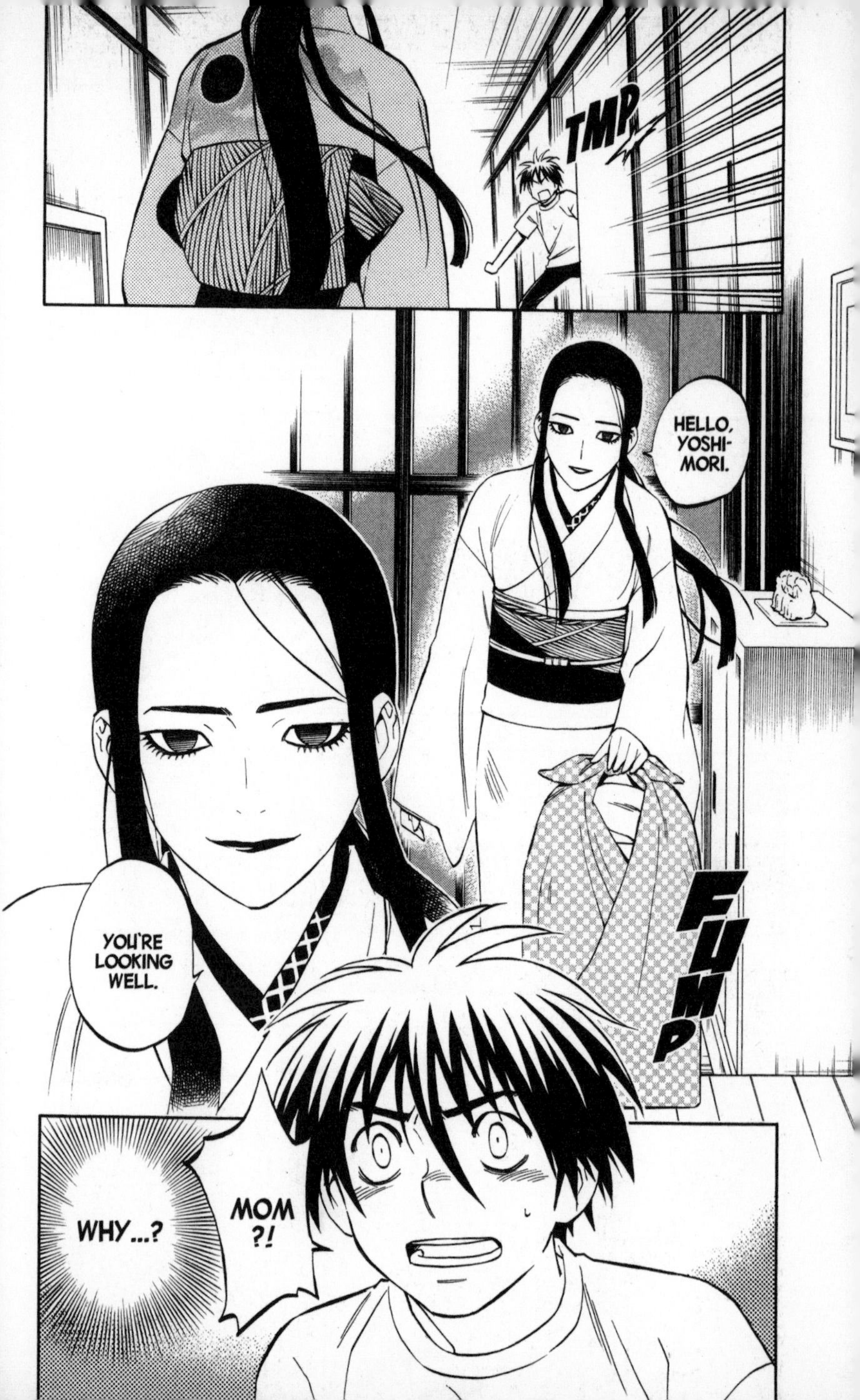
TMP
HELLO, YOSHI-MORI.
FUMP
YOU'RE LOOKING WELL.
MOM ?!
WHY...?

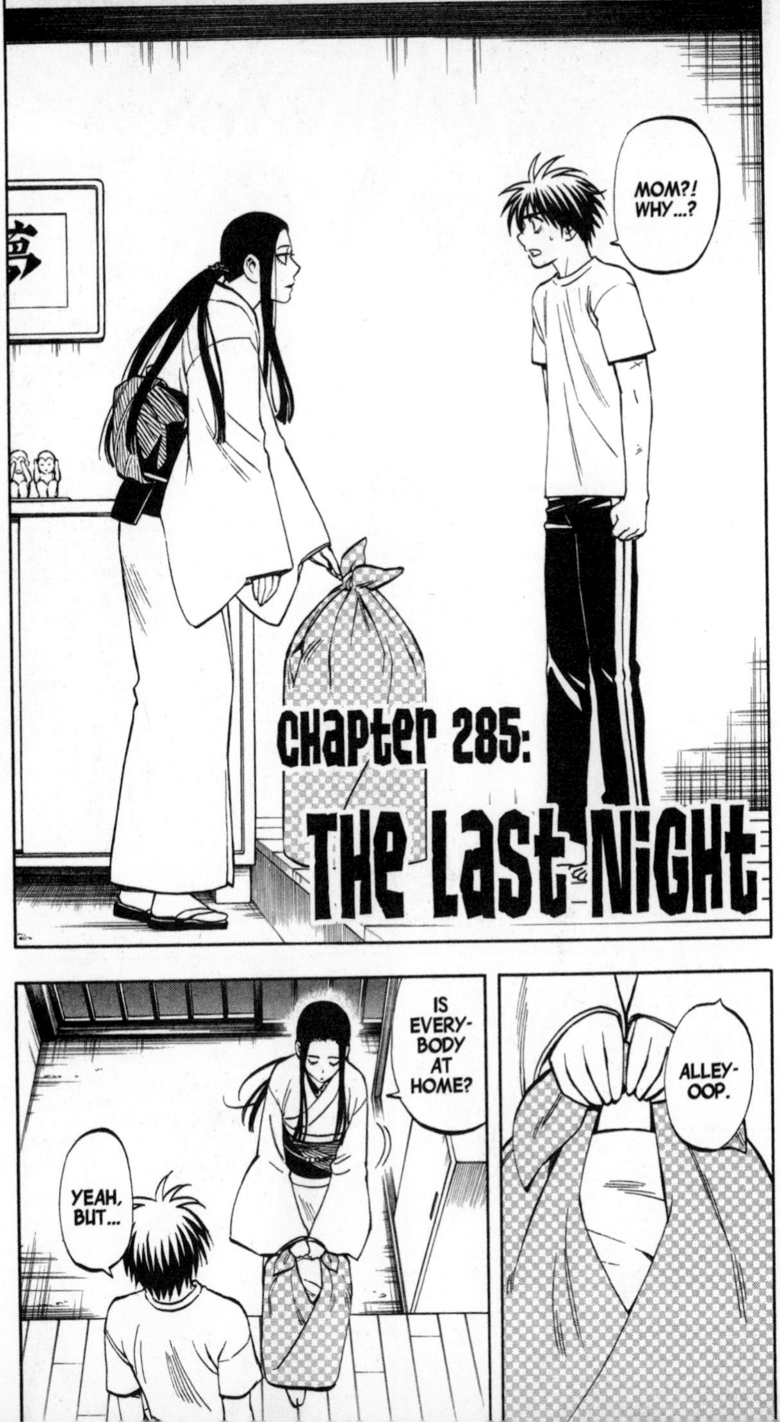
MOM?! WHY...?
Chapter 285:
The Last Night
ALLEY-OOP.
IS EVERY-BODY AT HOME?
YEAH, BUT...

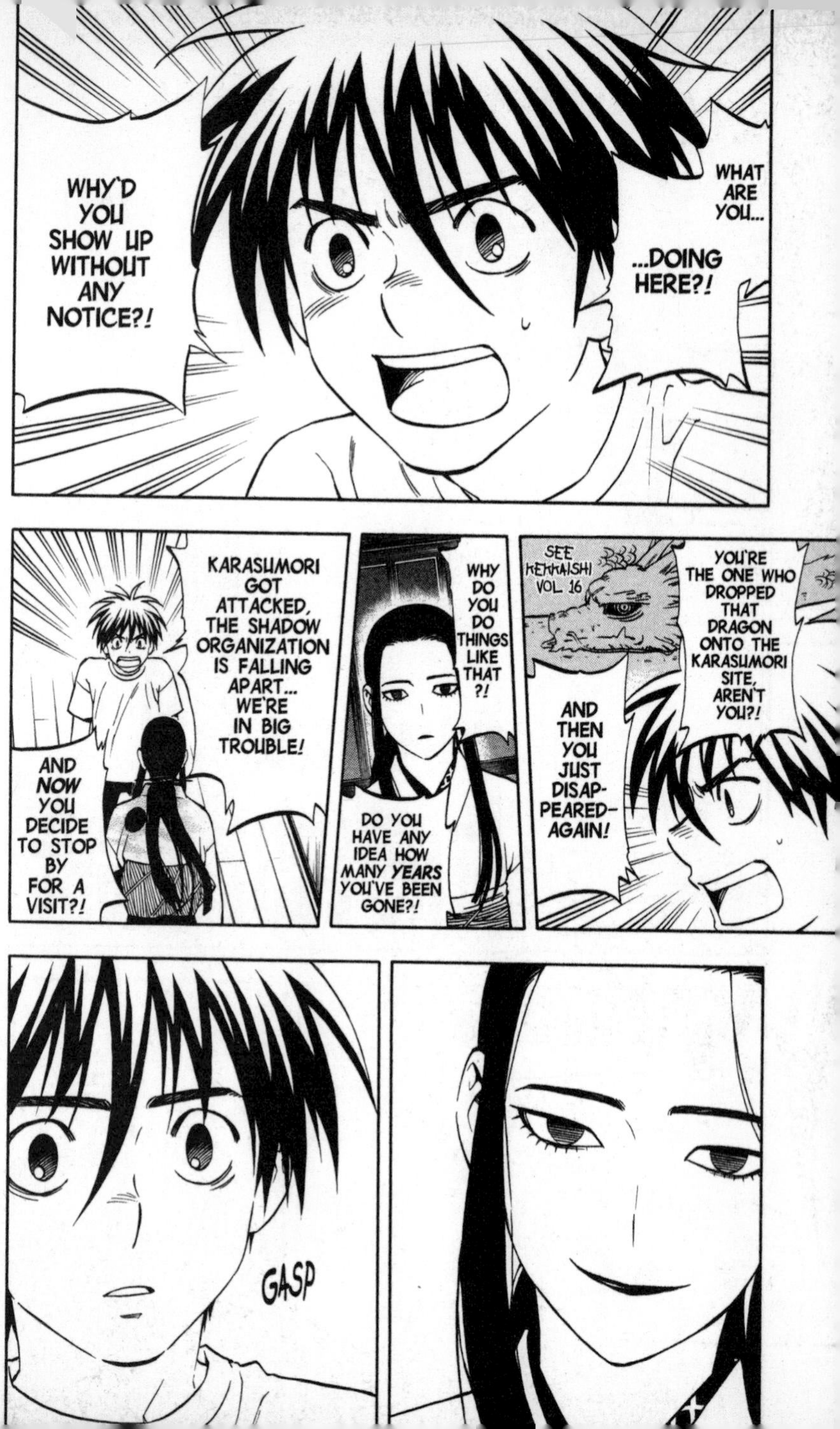
WHAT ARE YOU...
...DOING HERE?!
WHY'D YOU SHOW UP WITHOUT ANY NOTICE?!
SEE KEKKAISHI VOL. 16
YOU'RE THE ONE WHO DROPPED THAT DRAGON ONTO THE KARASUMORI SITE, AREN'T YOU?!
AND THEN YOU JUST DISAPPEARED—AGAIN!
WHY DO YOU DO THINGS LIKE THAT?!
DO YOU HAVE ANY IDEA HOW MANY YEARS YOU'VE BEEN GONE?!
KARASUMORI GOT ATTACKED, THE SHADOW ORGANIZATION IS FALLING APART... WE'RE IN BIG TROUBLE!
AND NOW YOU DECIDE TO STOP BY FOR A VISIT?!
GASP

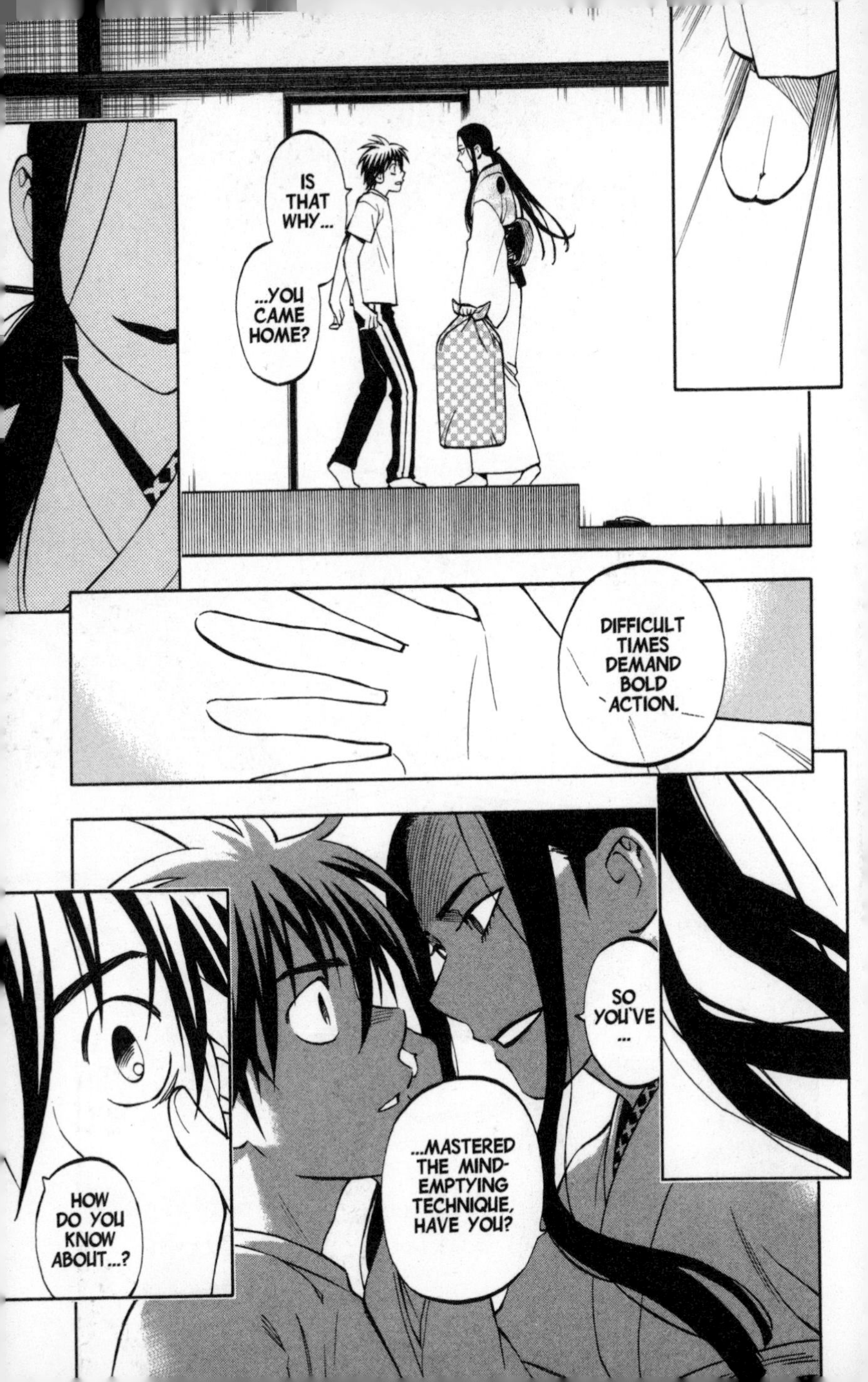
IS THAT WHY...
...YOU CAME HOME?
DIFFICULT TIMES DEMAND BOLD ACTION.
SO YOU'VE ...
...MASTERED THE MIND-EMPTYING TECHNIQUE, HAVE YOU?
HOW DO YOU KNOW ABOUT...?

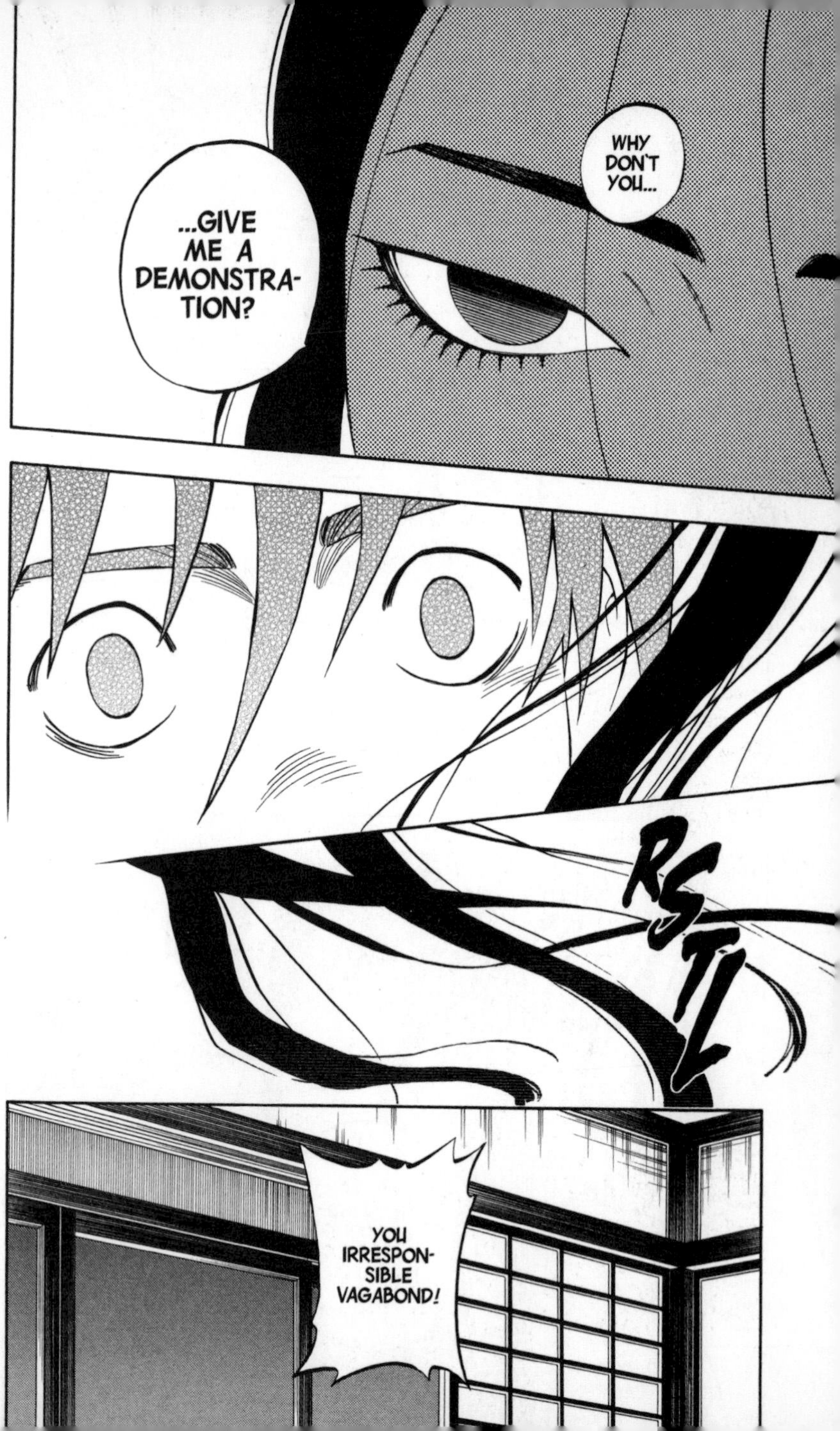
WHY DON'T YOU...
...GIVE ME A DEMONSTRATION?
RSTL
YOU IRRESPONSIBLE VAGABOND!

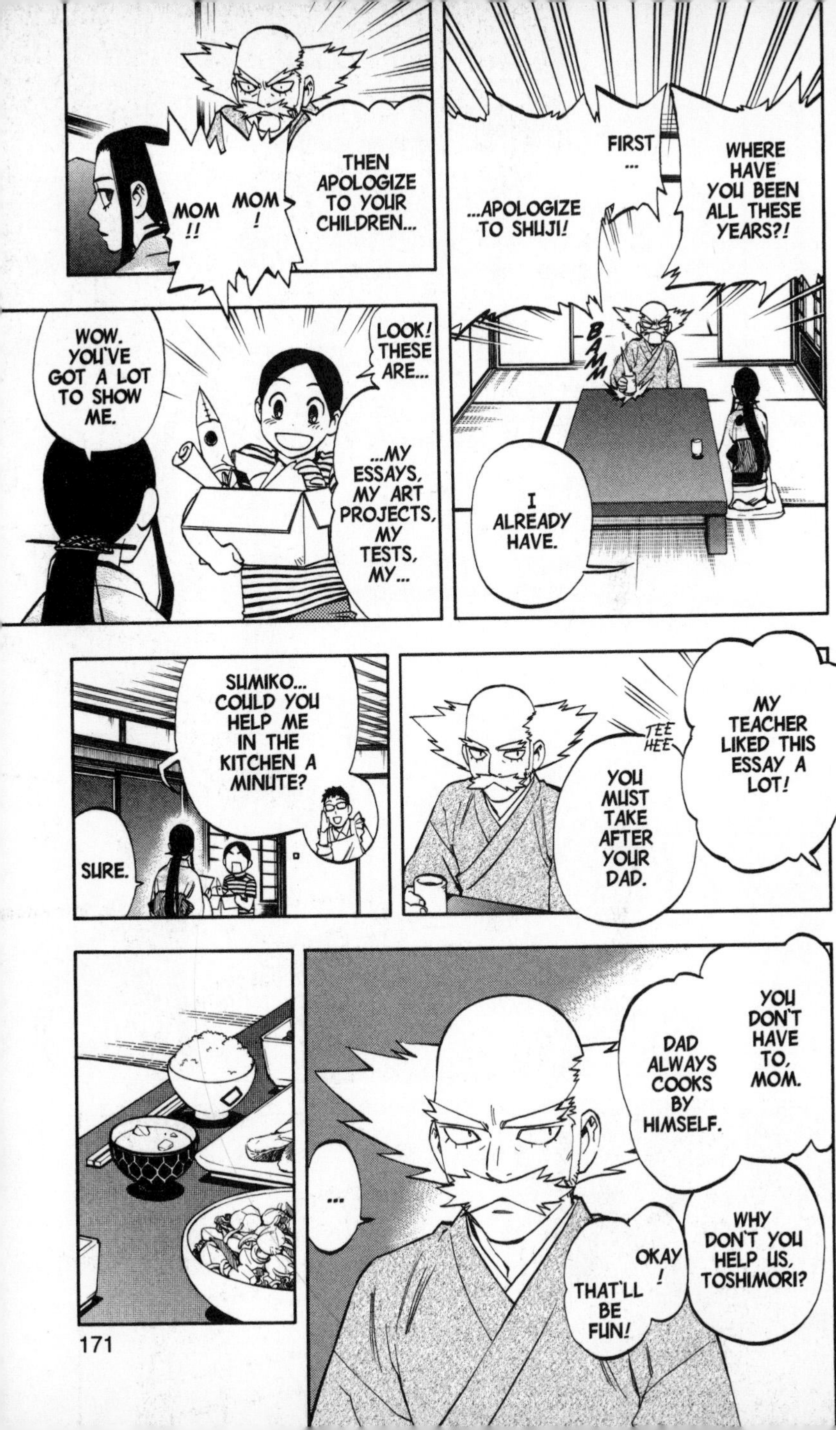
WHERE HAVE YOU BEEN ALL THESE YEARS?!
FIRST ...
...APOLOGIZE TO SHUJI!
THEN APOLOGIZE TO YOUR CHILDREN...
MOM!
MOM!!
BAMM
I ALREADY HAVE.
LOOK! THESE ARE...
...MY ESSAYS, MY ART PROJECTS, MY TESTS, MY...
WOW. YOU'VE GOT A LOT TO SHOW ME.
MY TEACHER LIKED THIS ESSAY A LOT!
TEE HEE
YOU MUST TAKE AFTER YOUR DAD.
SUMIKO... COULD YOU HELP ME IN THE KITCHEN A MINUTE?
SURE.
YOU DON'T HAVE TO, MOM.
DAD ALWAYS COOKS BY HIMSELF.
WHY DON'T YOU HELP US, TOSHIMORI?
OKAY!
THAT'LL BE FUN!
...

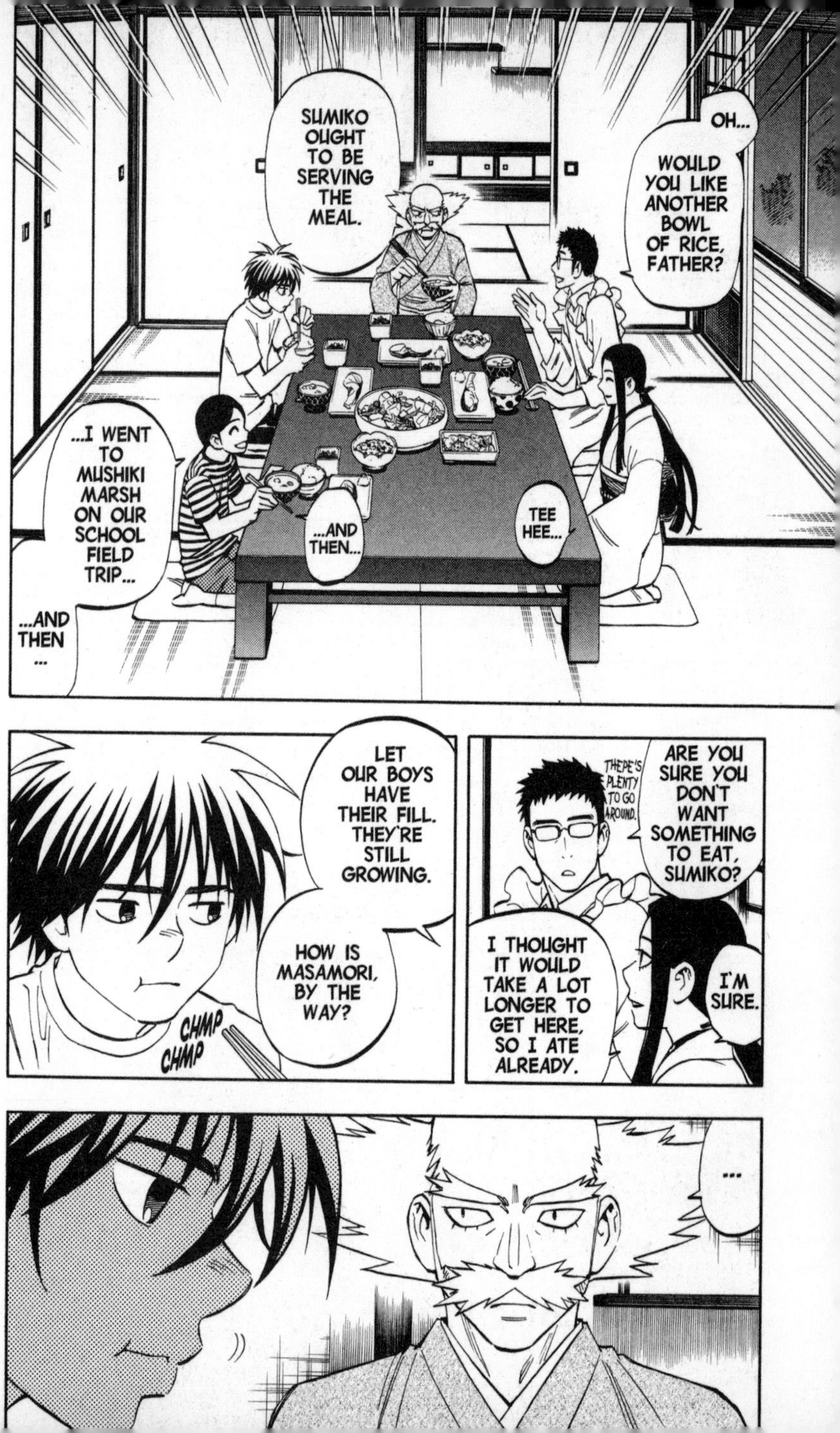
OH...
WOULD YOU LIKE ANOTHER BOWL OF RICE, FATHER?
SUMIKO OUGHT TO BE SERVING THE MEAL.
TEE HEE...
...AND THEN...
...I WENT TO MUSHIKI MARSH ON OUR SCHOOL FIELD TRIP...
...AND THEN ...
ARE YOU SURE YOU DON'T WANT SOMETHING TO EAT, SUMIKO?
THEPE'S PLENTY TO GO AROUND.
I'M SURE.
I THOUGHT IT WOULD TAKE A LOT LONGER TO GET HERE, SO I ATE ALREADY.
LET OUR BOYS HAVE THEIR FILL. THEY'RE STILL GROWING.
HOW IS MASAMORI, BY THE WAY?
CHMP CHMP
...

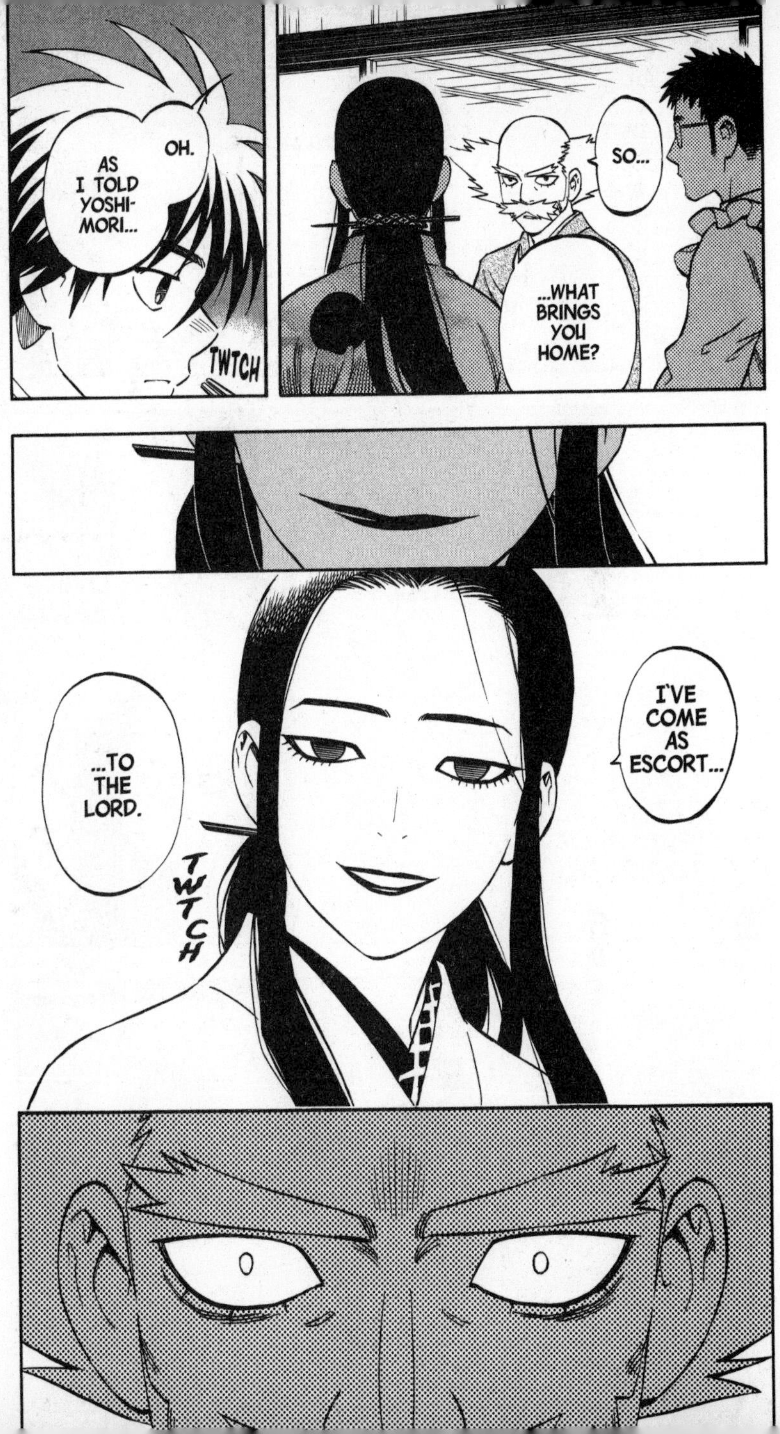
SO...
...WHAT BRINGS YOU HOME?
OH. AS I TOLD YOSHIMORI...
TWTCH
I'VE COME AS ESCORT...
...TO THE LORD.
TWTCH

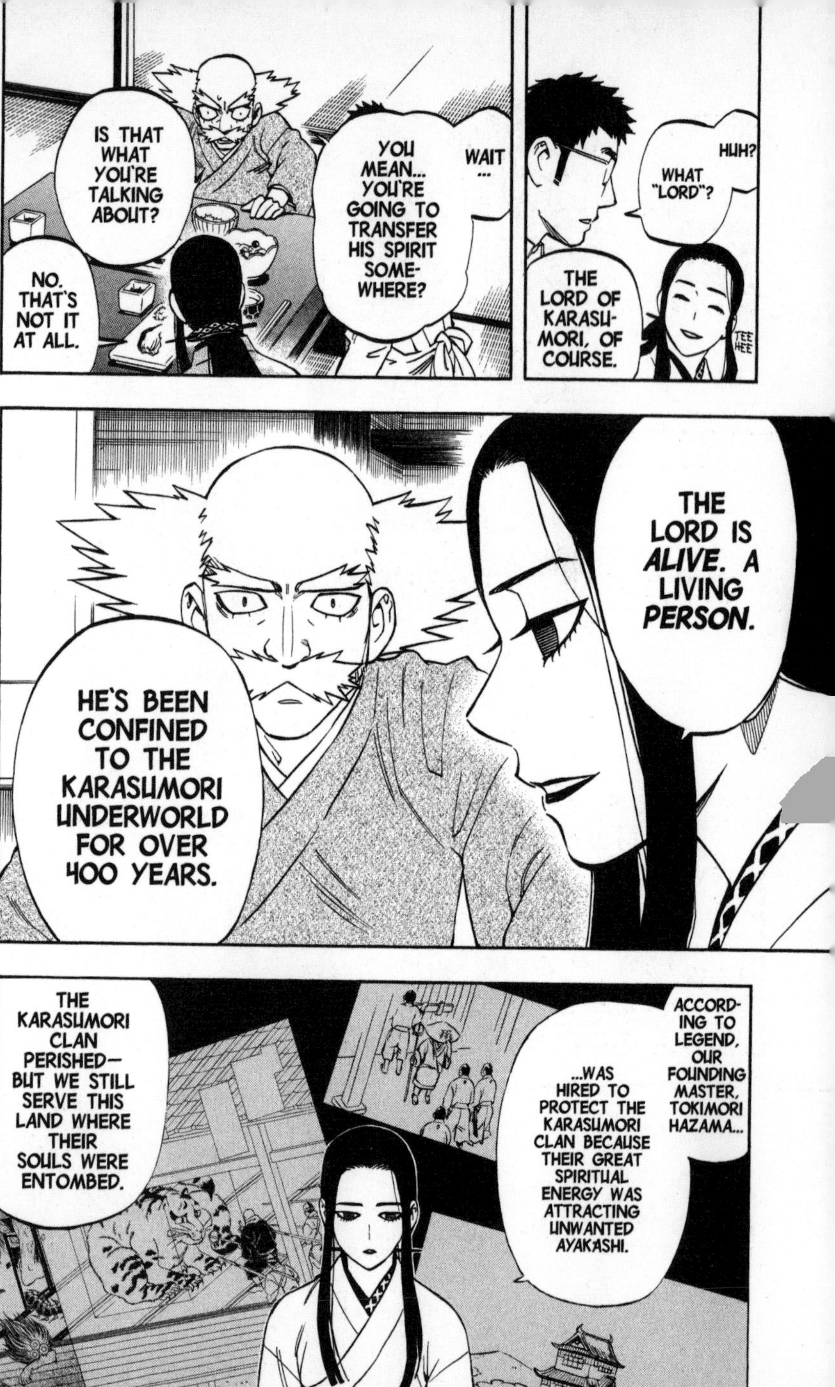
HUH?
WHAT "LORD"?
THE LORD OF KARASUMORI, OF COURSE.
TEE HEE
WAIT...
YOU MEAN... YOU'RE GOING TO TRANSFER HIS SPIRIT SOMEWHERE?
IS THAT WHAT YOU'RE TALKING ABOUT?
NO. THAT'S NOT IT AT ALL.
THE LORD IS *ALIVE*. A LIVING *PERSON*.
HE'S BEEN CONFINED TO THE KARASUMORI UNDERWORLD FOR OVER 400 YEARS.
ACCORDING TO LEGEND, OUR FOUNDING MASTER, TOKIMORI HAZAMA...
...WAS HIRED TO PROTECT THE KARASUMORI CLAN BECAUSE THEIR GREAT SPIRITUAL ENERGY WAS ATTRACTING UNWANTED AYAKASHI.
THE KARASUMORI CLAN PERISHED—BUT WE STILL SERVE THIS LAND WHERE THEIR SOULS WERE ENTOMBED.

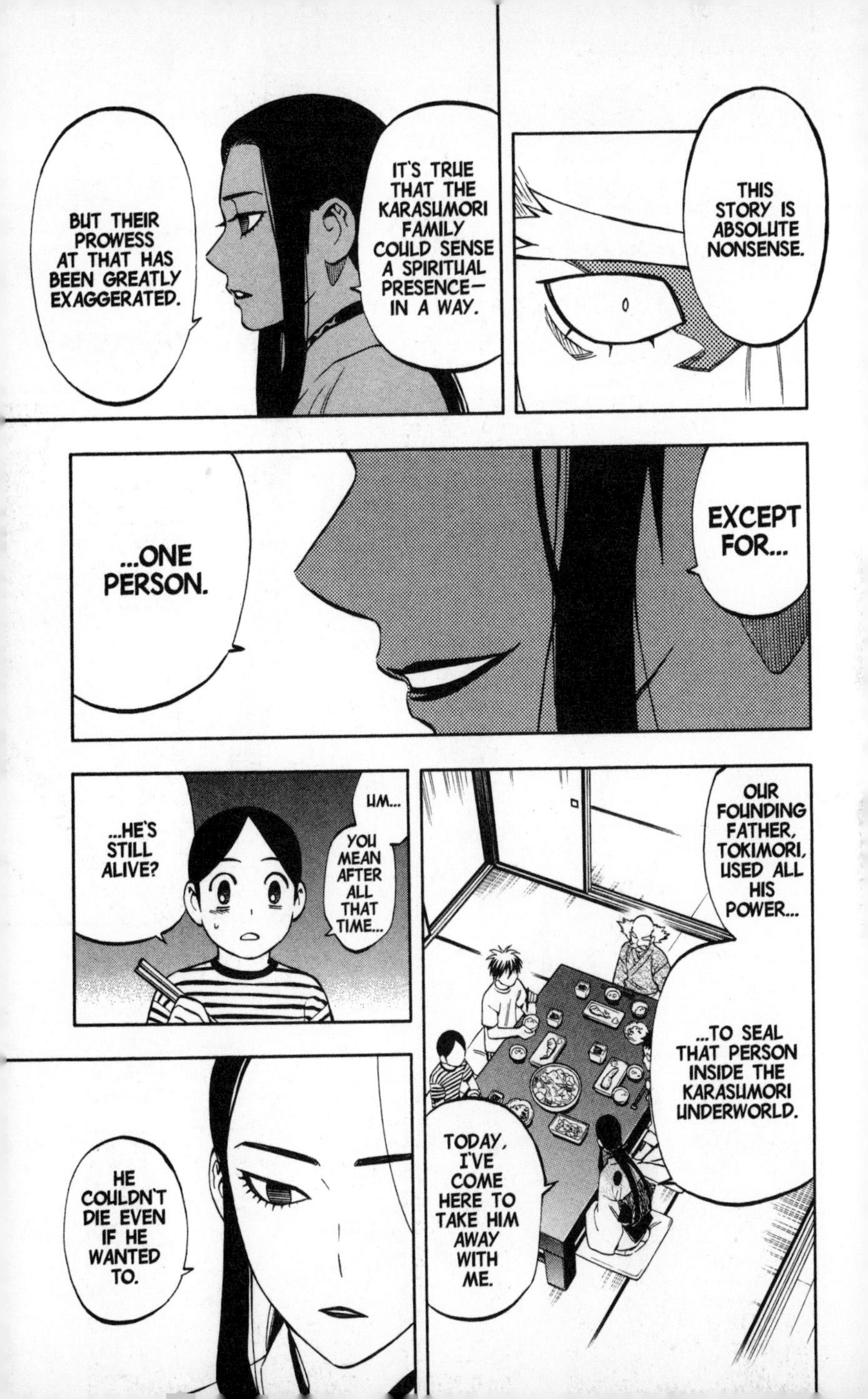
THIS STORY IS ABSOLUTE NONSENSE.
IT'S TRUE THAT THE KARASUMORI FAMILY COULD SENSE A SPIRITUAL PRESENCE—IN A WAY.
BUT THEIR PROWESS AT THAT HAS BEEN GREATLY EXAGGERATED.
EXCEPT FOR...
...ONE PERSON.
OUR FOUNDING FATHER, TOKIMORI, USED ALL HIS POWER...
...TO SEAL THAT PERSON INSIDE THE KARASUMORI UNDERWORLD.
TODAY, I'VE COME HERE TO TAKE HIM AWAY WITH ME.
UM...
YOU MEAN AFTER ALL THAT TIME...
...HE'S STILL ALIVE?
HE COULDN'T DIE EVEN IF HE WANTED TO.

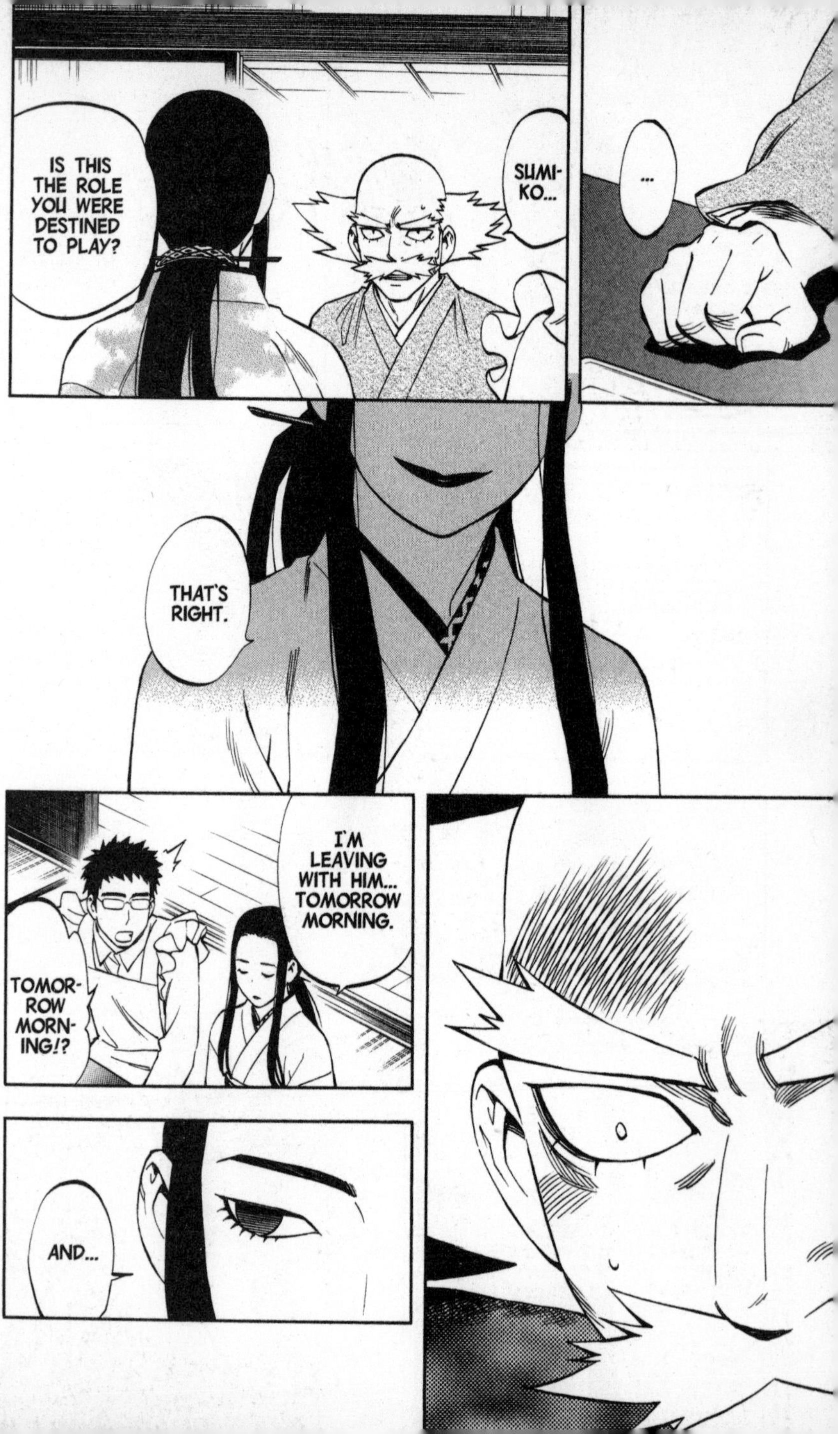
...
SUMI-KO...
IS THIS THE ROLE YOU WERE DESTINED TO PLAY?
THAT'S RIGHT.
I'M LEAVING WITH HIM... TOMORROW MORNING.
TOMOR-ROW MORN-ING!?
AND...

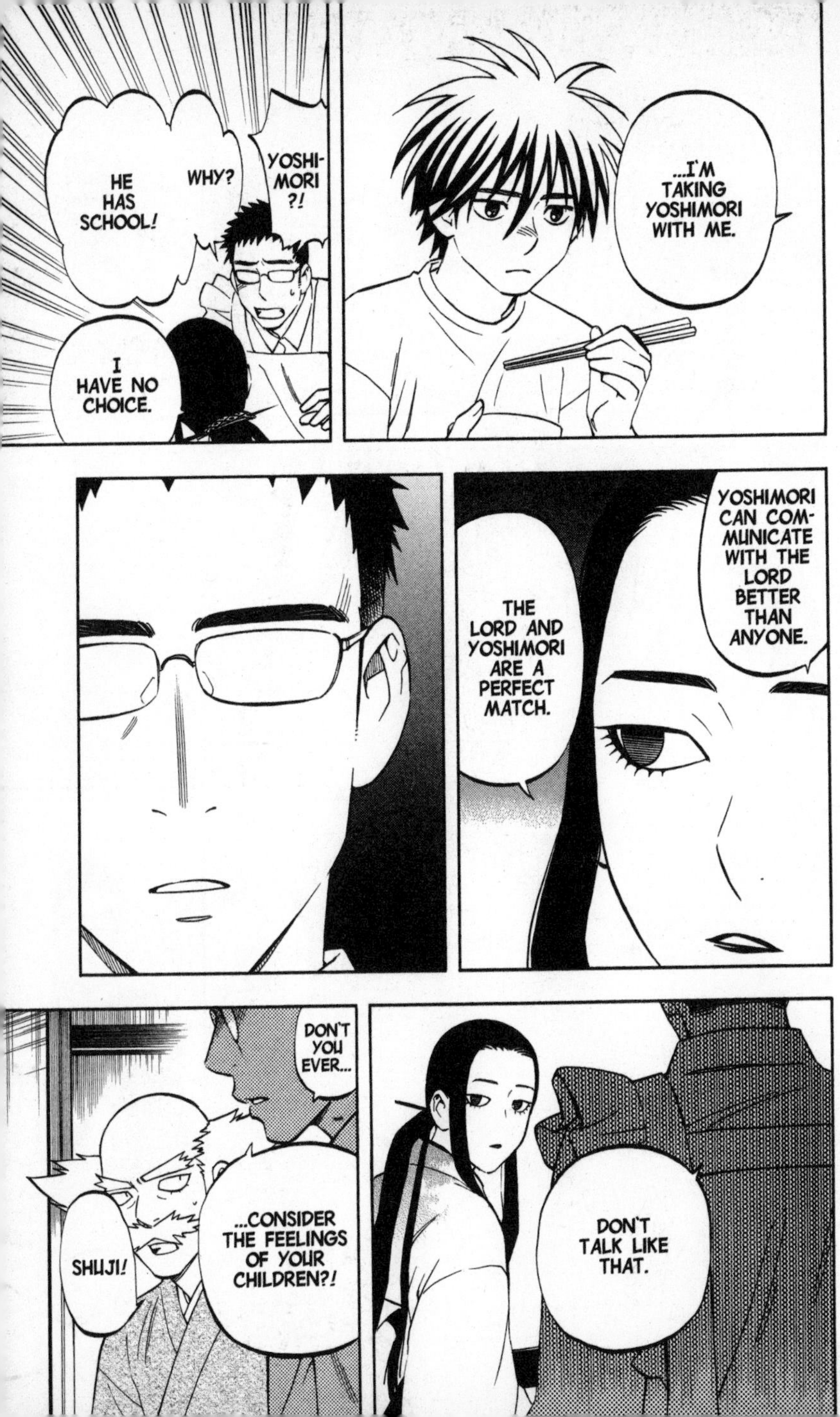
...I'M TAKING YOSHIMORI WITH ME.
YOSHI-MORI?!
WHY?
HE HAS SCHOOL!
I HAVE NO CHOICE.
YOSHIMORI CAN COM-MUNICATE WITH THE LORD BETTER THAN ANYONE.
THE LORD AND YOSHIMORI ARE A PERFECT MATCH.
DON'T TALK LIKE THAT.
DON'T YOU EVER...
...CONSIDER THE FEELINGS OF YOUR CHILDREN?!
SHUJI!

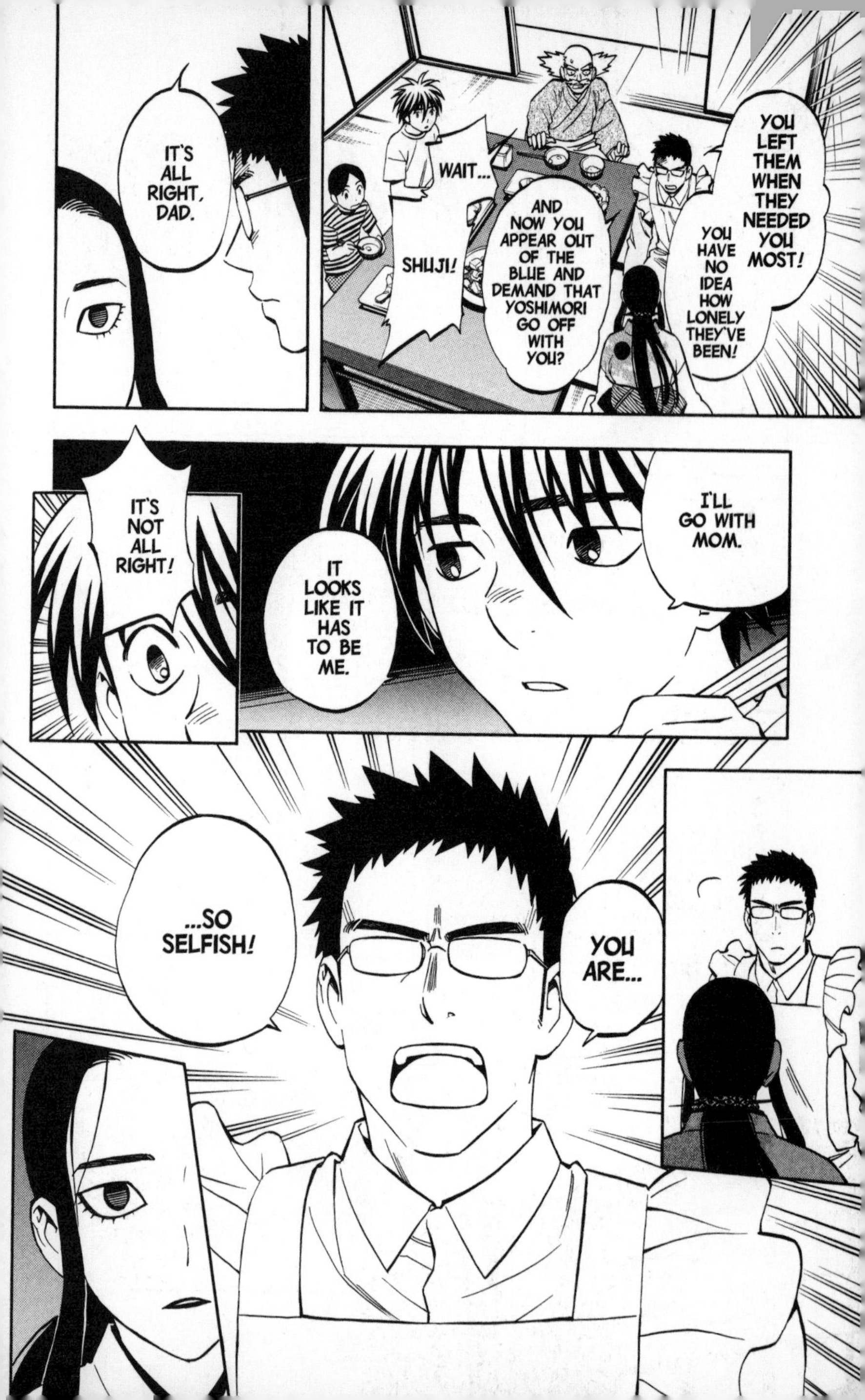
YOU LEFT THEM WHEN THEY NEEDED YOU MOST!
YOU HAVE NO IDEA HOW LONELY THEY'VE BEEN!
AND NOW YOU APPEAR OUT OF THE BLUE AND DEMAND THAT YOSHIMORI GO OFF WITH YOU?
WAIT...
SHUJI!
IT'S ALL RIGHT, DAD.
I'LL GO WITH MOM.
IT LOOKS LIKE IT HAS TO BE ME.
IT'S NOT ALL RIGHT!
YOU ARE...
...SO SELFISH!

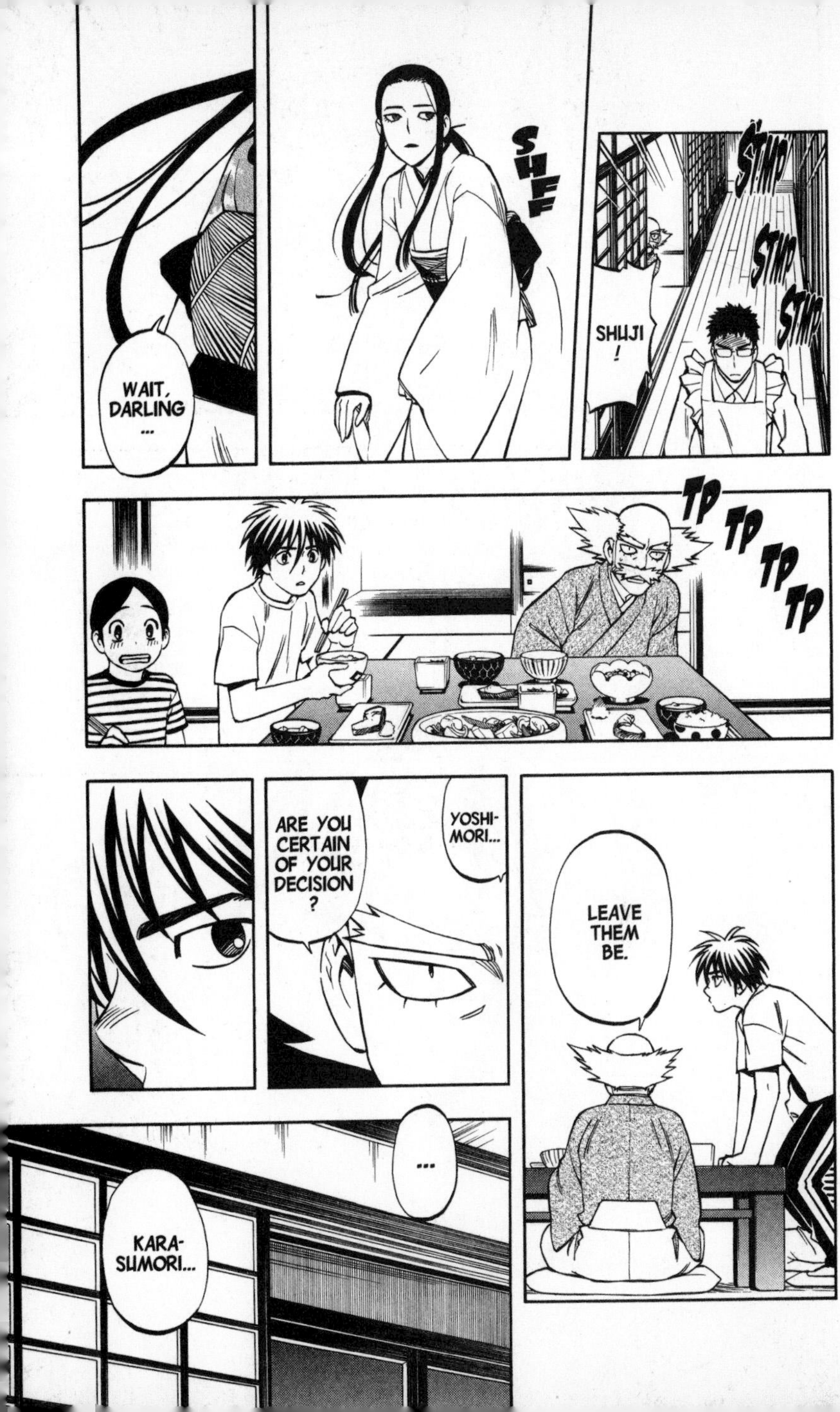
STMP STMP STMP STMP
SHUJI!
SHFF
WAIT, DARLING...
TP TP TP TP TP
LEAVE THEM BE.
YOSHI-MORI...
ARE YOU CERTAIN OF YOUR DECISION?
...
KARA-SUMORI...

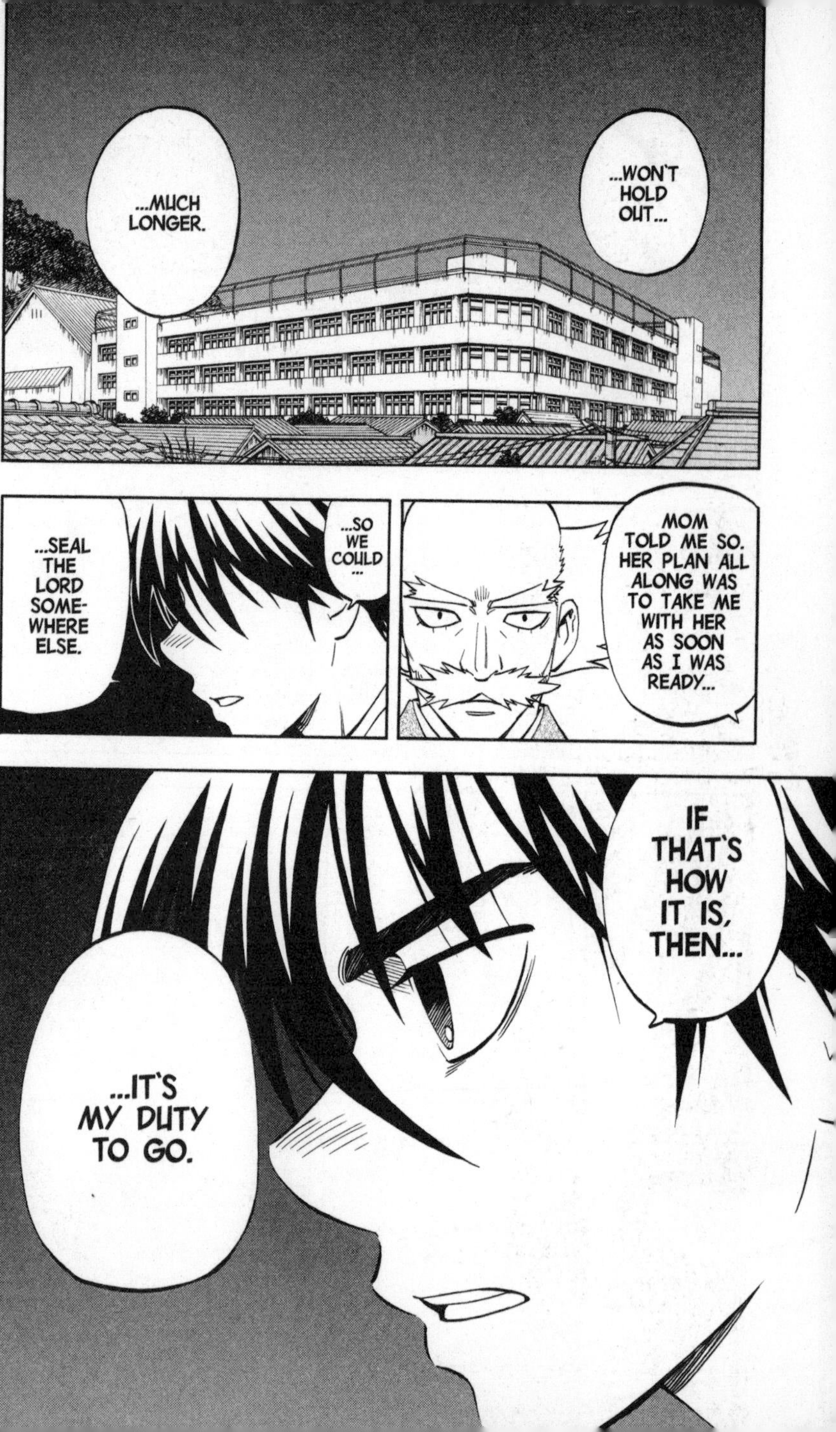
...WON'T HOLD OUT...
...MUCH LONGER.
MOM TOLD ME SO. HER PLAN ALL ALONG WAS TO TAKE ME WITH HER AS SOON AS I WAS READY...
...SO WE COULD ...
...SEAL THE LORD SOME-WHERE ELSE.
IF THAT'S HOW IT IS, THEN...
...IT'S MY DUTY TO GO.

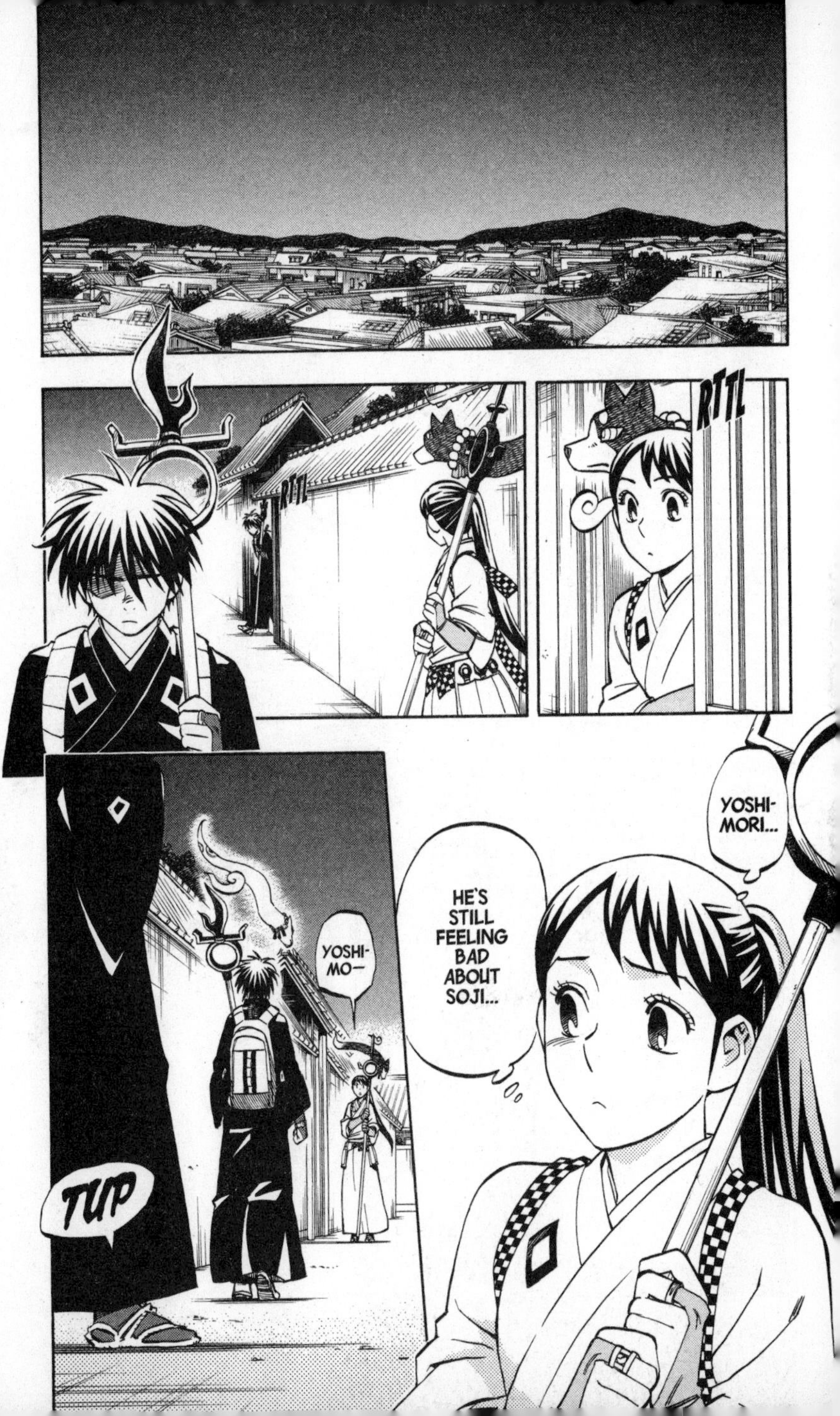
RTTL
RTTL
YOSHI-MORI...
HE'S STILL FEELING BAD ABOUT SOJI...
YOSHI-MO—
TUP

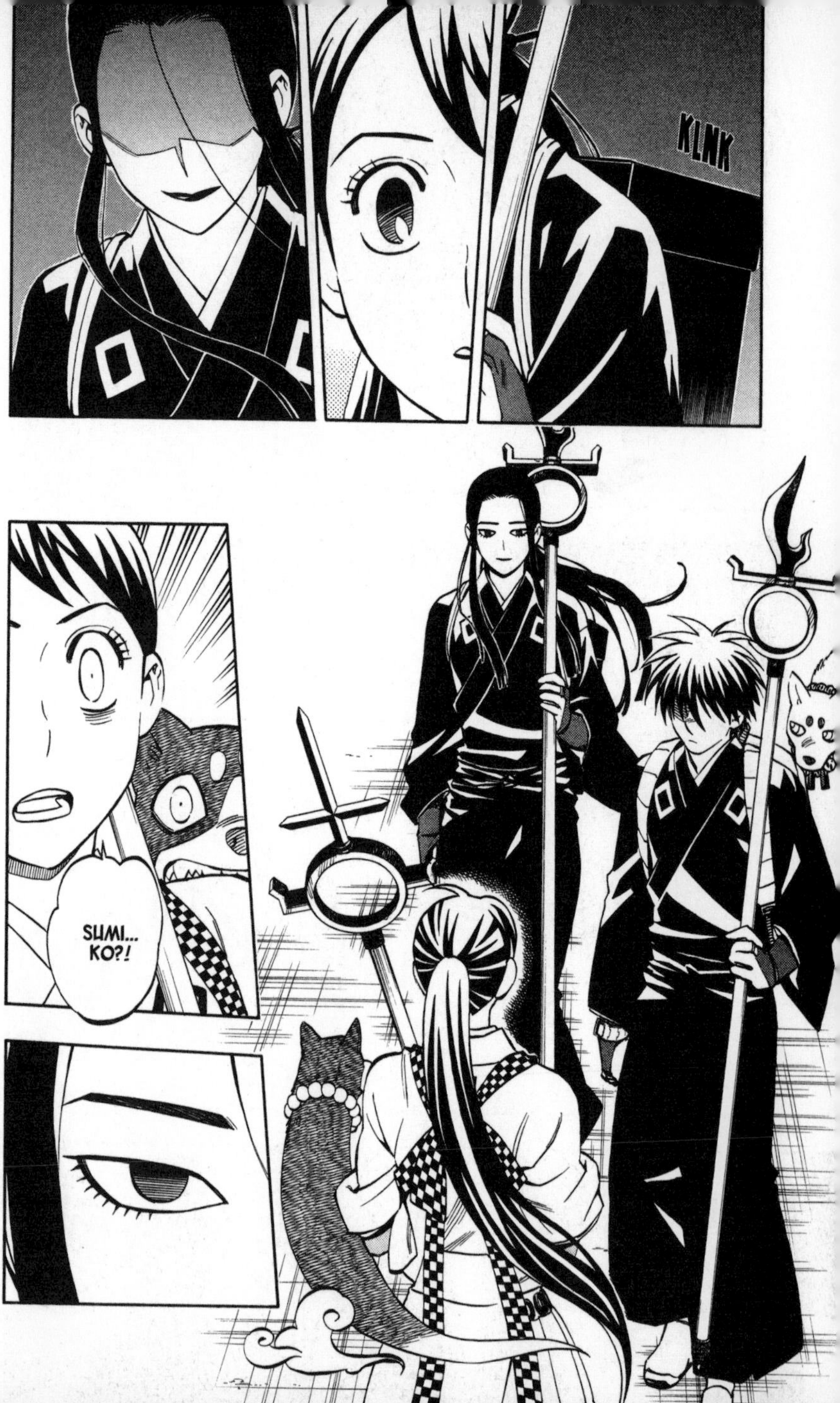
KLNK
SUMI... KO?!

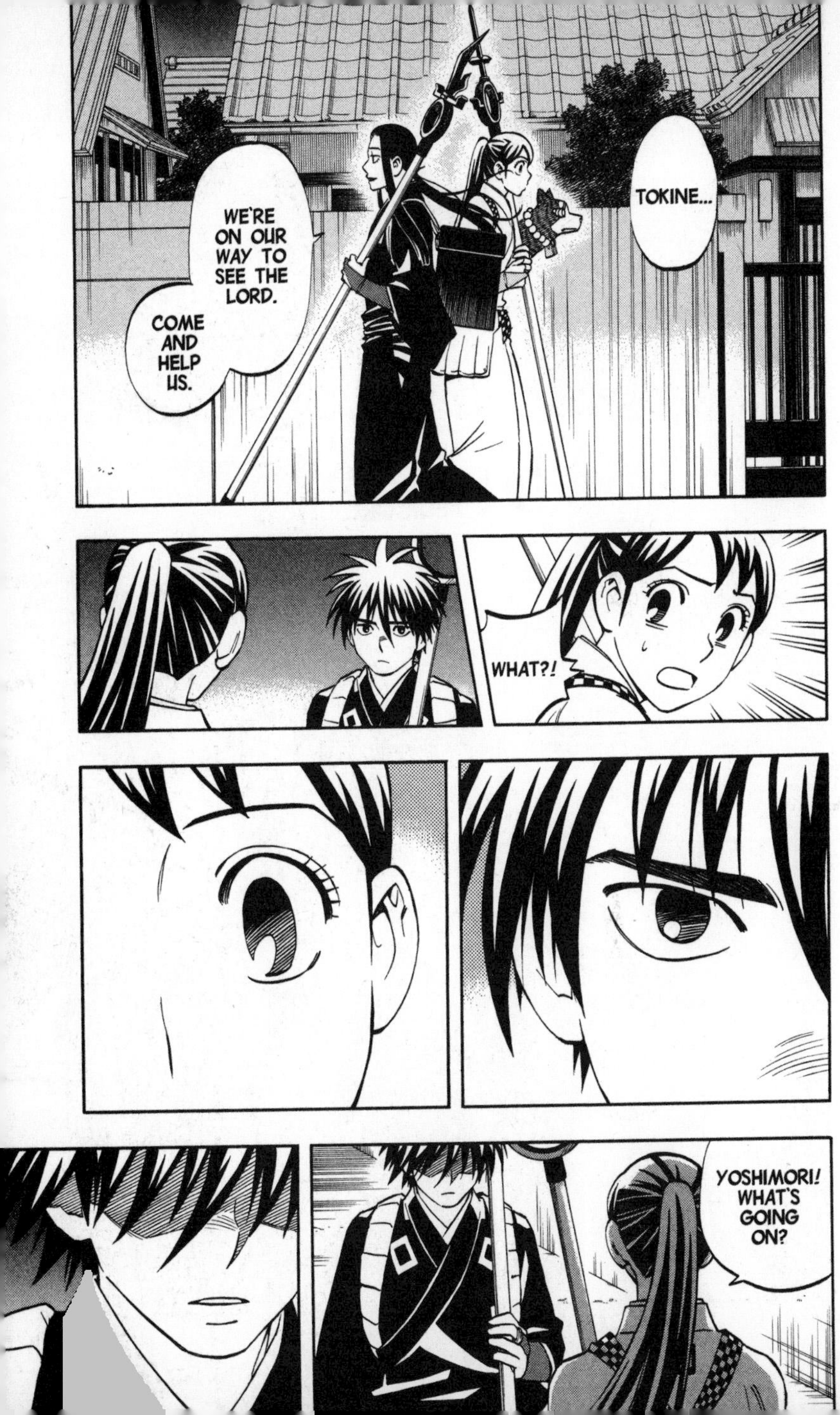
TOKINE...
WE'RE ON OUR WAY TO SEE THE LORD.
COME AND HELP US.
WHAT?!
YOSHIMORI! WHAT'S GOING ON?

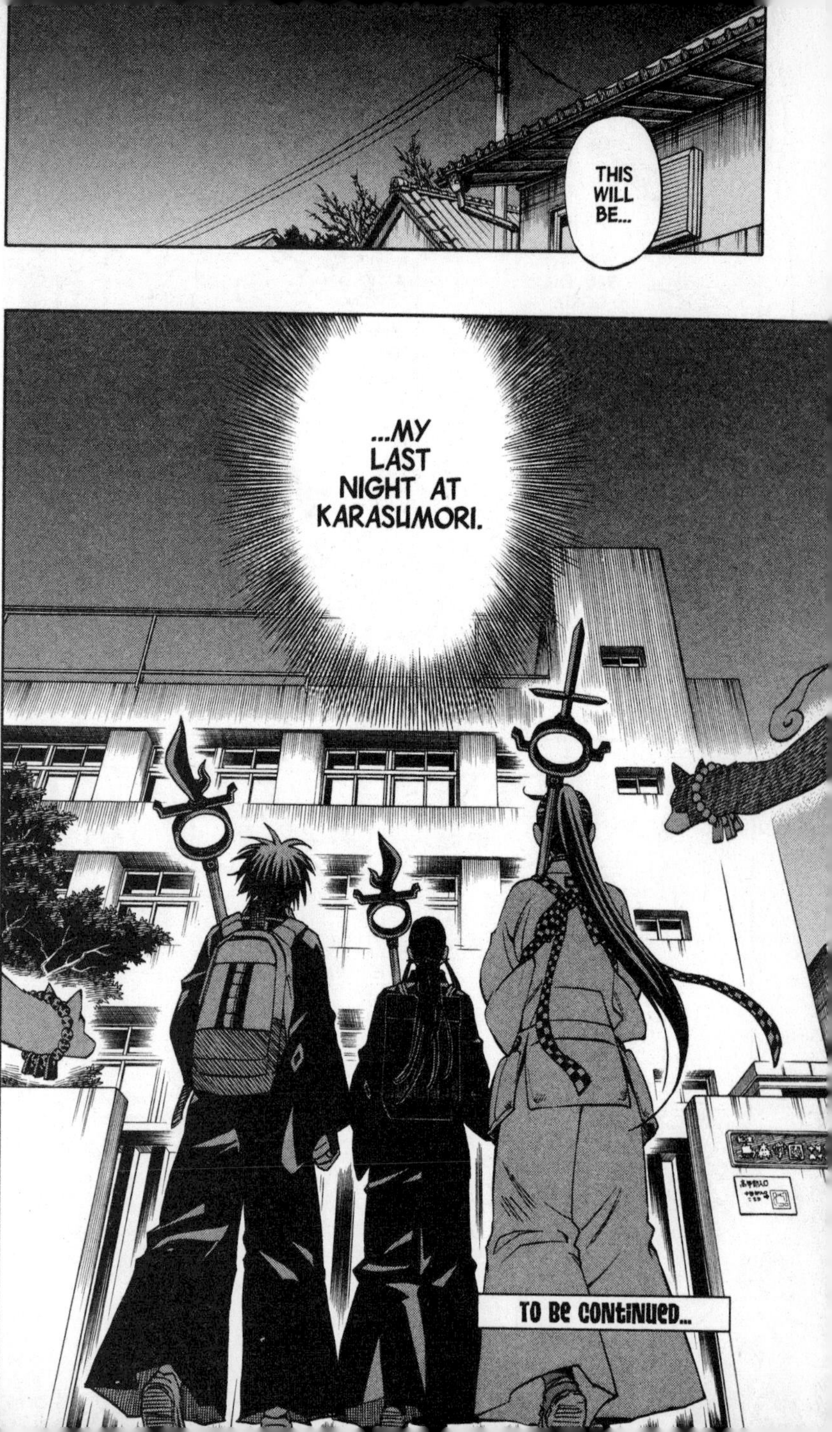
THIS WILL BE...
...MY LAST NIGHT AT KARASUMORI.
TO BE CONTINUED...

THERE'S MORE TO BADMINTON THAN HITTING A SHUTTLECOCK WITH A RACHET!

MESSAGE FROM YELLOW TANABE

Do you exercise? I don't.

I've never really gone in for sports. But I did belong to a badminton club when I was in junior high.

If I had it to do over again, I'd play using every dirty trick in the book to make up for my lack of athleticism.

KEKKAISHI

VOLUME 29
SHONEN SUNDAY EDITION

STORY AND ART BY YELLOW TANABE

© 2004 Yellow TANABE/Shogakukan
All rights reserved.
Original Japanese edition "KEKKAISHI" published by SHOGAKUKAN Inc.

Translation/Yuko Sawada
Touch-up Art & Lettering/Stephen Dutro
Cover Design & Graphic Layout/Ronnie Casson
Editor/Annette Roman

Printed in the U.S.A.

Published by VIZ Media, LLC
P.O. Box 77010
San Francisco, CA 94107

10 9 8 7 6 5 4 3 2 1
First printing, December 2011

PARENTAL ADVISORY
KEKKAISHI is rated T for Teen
and is recommended for ages
13 and up. It contains fantasy
violence.
ratings.viz.com

www.viz.com

WWW.SHONENSUNDAY.COM

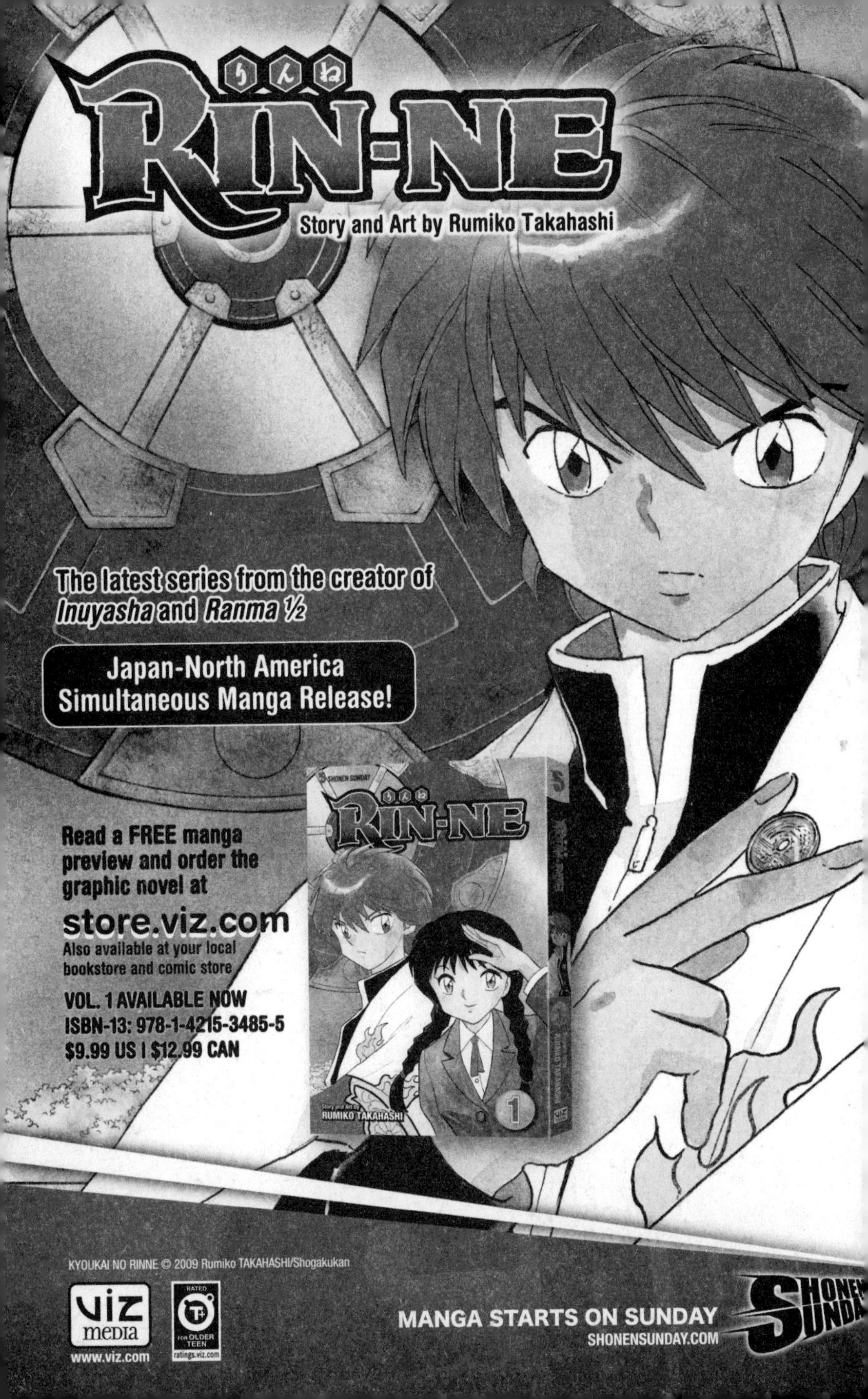
らんね
RIN-NE
Story and Art by Rumiko Takahashi
The latest series from the creator of
Inuyasha and Ranma ½
Japan-North America
Simultaneous Manga Release!
SHONEN SUNDAY
RIN-NE
Story and Art by
RUMIKO TAKAHASHI
1
Read a FREE manga
preview and order the
graphic novel at
store.viz.com
Also available at your local
bookstore and comic store
VOL. 1 AVAILABLE NOW
ISBN-13: 978-1-4215-3485-5
$9.99 US | $12.99 CAN
KYOUKAI NO RINNE © 2009 Rumiko TAKAHASHI/Shogakukan
viz media
www.viz.com
RATED T+ FOR OLDER TEEN
ratings.viz.com
MANGA STARTS ON SUNDAY
SHONENSUNDAY.COM
SHONEN SUNDAY

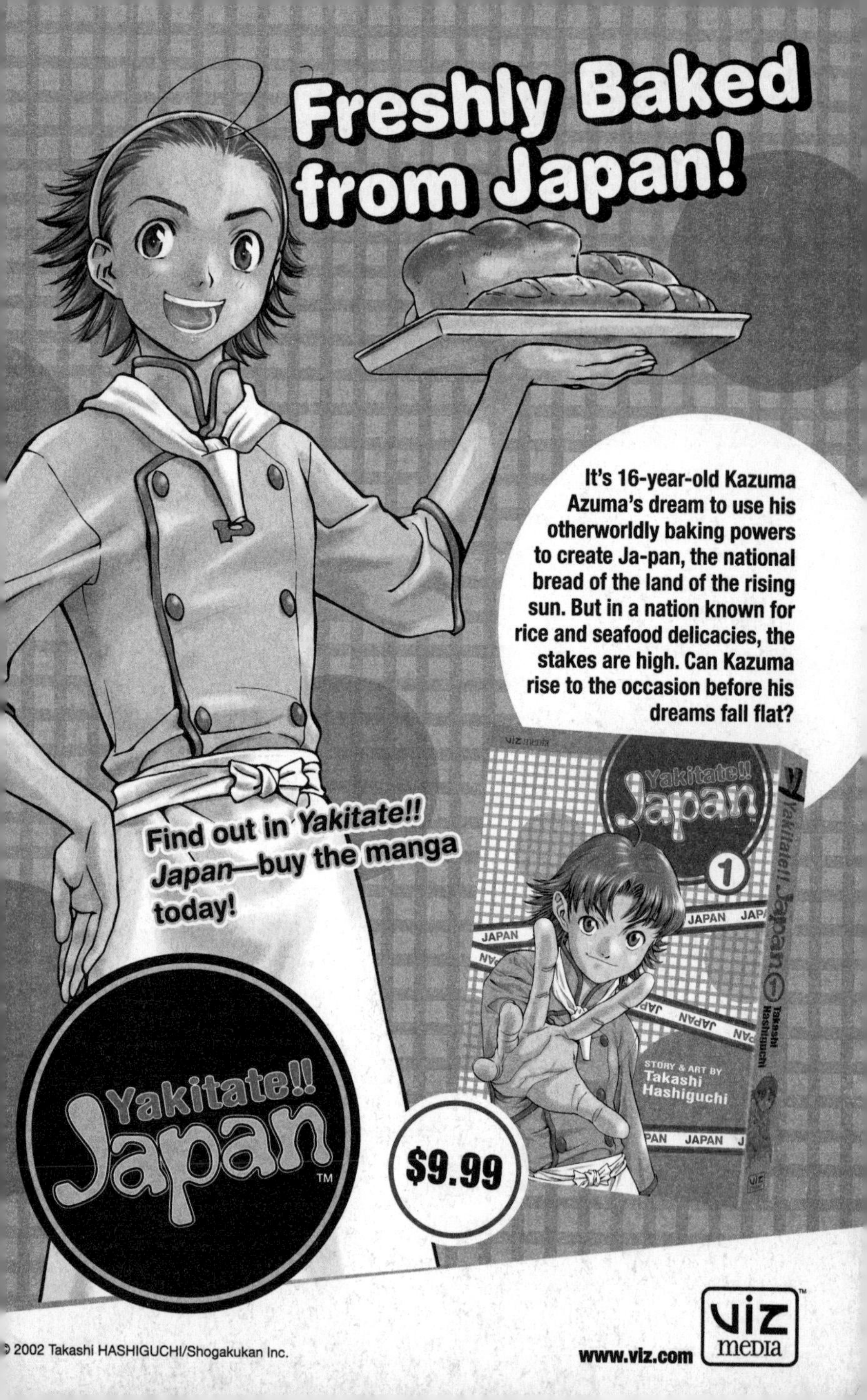
Freshly Baked from Japan!
It's 16-year-old Kazuma Azuma's dream to use his otherworldly baking powers to create Ja-pan, the national bread of the land of the rising sun. But in a nation known for rice and seafood delicacies, the stakes are high. Can Kazuma rise to the occasion before his dreams fall flat?
Find out in Yakitate!! Japan—buy the manga today!
Yakitate!! Japan™
$9.99
Yakitate!! Japan
1
STORY & ART BY Takashi Hashiguchi
© 2002 Takashi HASHIGUCHI/Shogakukan Inc.
www.viz.com
viz media

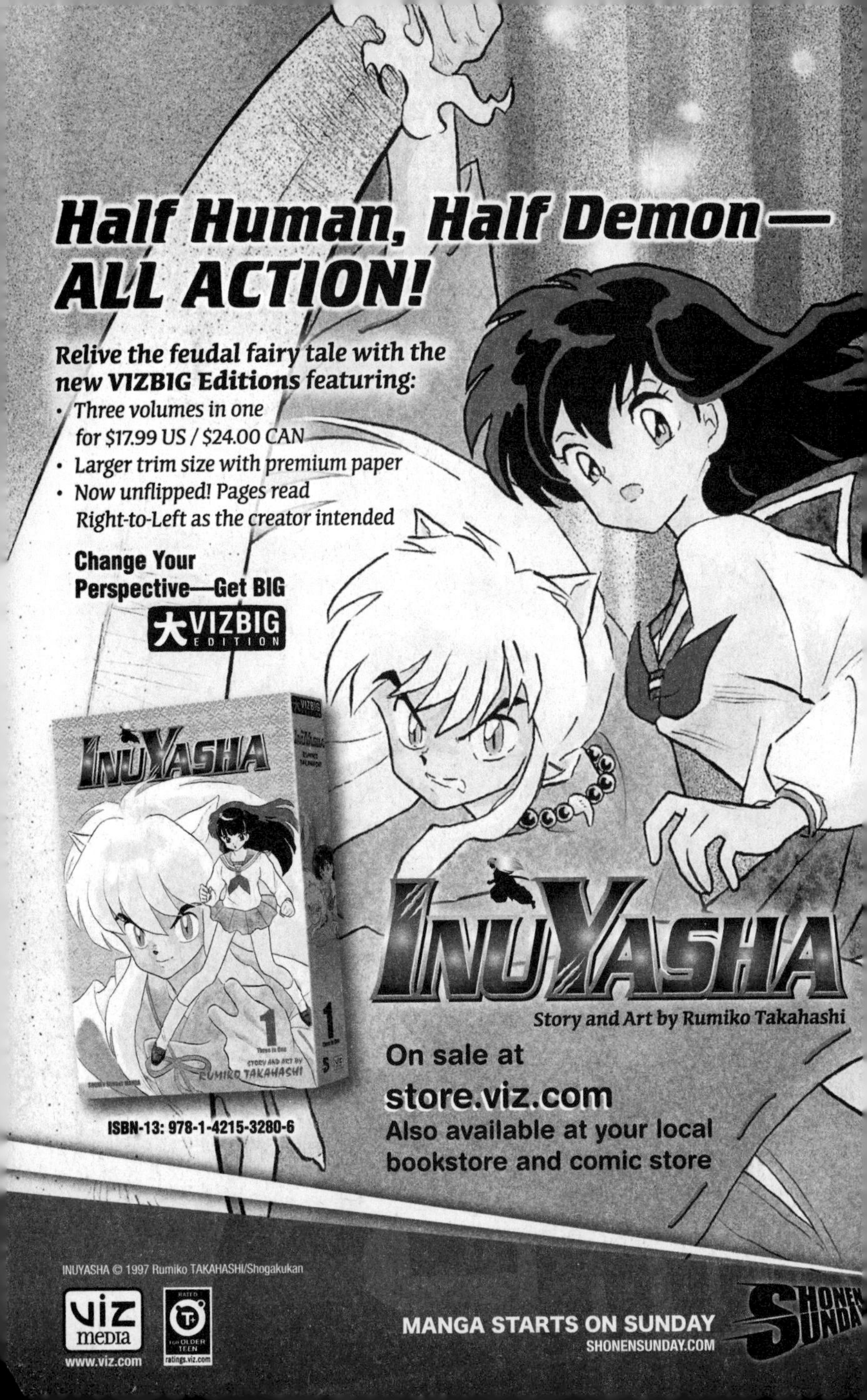
Half Human, Half Demon—
ALL ACTION!
Relive the feudal fairy tale with the new VIZBIG Editions featuring:
• Three volumes in one for $17.99 US / $24.00 CAN
• Larger trim size with premium paper
• Now unflipped! Pages read Right-to-Left as the creator intended
Change Your Perspective—Get BIG
大VIZBIG EDITION
INUYASHA
1
STORY AND ART BY RUMIKO TAKAHASHI
ISBN-13: 978-1-4215-3280-6
INUYASHA
Story and Art by Rumiko Takahashi
On sale at
store.viz.com
Also available at your local bookstore and comic store
INUYASHA © 1997 Rumiko TAKAHASHI/Shogakukan
viz media
www.viz.com
RATED T+ FOR OLDER TEEN
ratings.viz.com
MANGA STARTS ON SUNDAY
SHONENSUNDAY.COM
SHONEN SUNDAY